Childhood in
the Middle Ages

Childhood in the Middle Ages

SHULAMITH SHAHAR

Translated by Chaya Galai

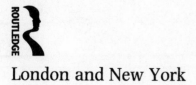

London and New York

First published 1990
First published in paperback 1992
by Routledge
11 New Fetter Lane, London EC4P 4EE

Simultaneously published in the USA and Canada
by Routledge
a division of Routledge, Chapman and Hall, Inc.
29 West 35th Street, New York, NY 10001

Printed in Great Britain by Butler & Tanner Ltd, Frome and London

British Library Cataloguing in Publication Data
Shahar, Shulamith
    Childhood in the Middle Ages.
    I. Title
    940.17083

Library of Congress Cataloging in Publication Data
Shahar, Shulamith
    Childhood in the Middle Ages/Shulamith Shahar.
        p. cm.
    Includes index.
        1. Children—Europe—History.   2. Social history—Medieval,
    500–1500.   3. Education—Europe—History—Medieval, 500–1500.
    I. Title.
    HQ792.E8S53 1989   89–6227
    305.2'3'094092—dc20   CIP

ISBN 0–415–07329–4

To my children, Meir and Dinah
with love

And who would not shrink from the alternative, and elect to die, if it were proposed to him either to suffer death or to be again an infant?

St Augustine, **De Civitate Dei**

The next day, therefore, when he recalled to his mind's eye all that he had seen, like a simple and innocent boy he believed that he had been in heaven, and that he had been fed with the bread of God, and he asserted as much to others in public.

Eadmer, **The Life of St Anselm, Archbishop of Canterbury**
(twelfth century)

Childhood is the foundation of life. On good foundations one can build great and good edifices.

Philip of Novare, **Les Quatre Ages de l'homme**
(thirteenth century)

... for it is the nature of man that his growth to adulthood is slower, and this stems from his very nobility and perfection, since the nobler man is than other creatures, the greater the toil of nature, the handmaiden of the Creator, around his maturation.

Konrad of Megenberg, **Ökonomik**
(fourteenth century)

You know what is the love of fathers and mothers for their children. Many of you experienced it in your childhood.

Jean Gerson, a sermon
(fifteenth century)

Contents

Contents

Preface

The idea of writing a study of the history of childhood in the Middle Ages occurred to me in the wake of my study of the history of women in that period.[1] In the chapter on married women in *The Fourth Estate* (Chapter 4) and in other chapters on women in the various strata of society, I discussed their maternal role and their upbringing, but the main focus was on women in adulthood and not on their childhood or their own offspring. When I started my research on medieval women, I was still enthralled by the work of Ph. Ariès[2] and I tended to accept his theories on the conception of childhood and the attitude to children in Western Europe from the Middle Ages to the present day. Doubts gradually dawned in my mind as to his assumptions, but I was unable to tackle them within the framework of a book on women. I merely expressed my reservations with regard to several points he had raised.[3] On completing my book, I turned to the subject of childhood in the Middle Ages and was able to confront Ariès's theories.

The chronological framework of the book is the Central and Late Middle Ages, namely the period stretching approximately from the beginning of the twelfth century to the beginning of the second quarter of the fifteenth century. If I have on occasions reverted back to an earlier period, this was done merely in order to delve into the sources of ideas and customs. The geographical domain is Western Europe – the countries in which Latin was the tongue of the higher culture, in which the western pattern of feudalism prevailed, in which the material culture and the socio-economic structure were similar, and in which the Christian (Catholic) faith was predominant. At the same time, within this common framework there were differences in the character of the feudal regime, in customary law, in family structure, and in popular culture between the various countries, and even between regions within the same country. Nor were the demographic and economic conditions identical in all regions (although the demographic and economic rise was universal from the eleventh century on, and the economic crises, as also the decline in population in the wake of the 1348 Black Death and the epidemics which followed, affected all the countries of Western Europe). In view of these facts, there were differences in the conditions under which children were raised and in the method of childrearing and socialization, not all of which have been dealt with. Books naturally strive to describe characteristic features and to create a general picture in which local variations are obscured. Future regional studies which will devote attention to the history of childhood will no doubt instruct us in the differences in local customs which are not detailed in my own book. The scholarly conception of childhood, the recognition of the stage of childhood, and the norms which the authors of didactic literature attempted to foster did not vary from country to country or according to region, whether written in Latin or the vernacular. Nor can one point to significant differences in approach between the secular and ecclesiastical writers. (A considerable proportion of the didactic literature was composed by the Mendicants who belonged to an international order and moved from place to place.) To the extent that there were differences in theory and approach, they derived from differences in the type of work (theoretical or didactic, for example) or in the individual outlook of the author.

I would like to thank my students who took part in seminars at the School of History of Tel Aviv University where we discussed various aspects of the annals of childhood in the Middle Ages. Their questions and comments were a great help to me. I would also like to extend thanks to my student, Mrs Yael Waldman, who called my attention to material on childhood in medieval Scandinavian sources; to my friend, Dr Miri Rubin, with whom I discussed various problems pertaining to my research, who pointed me to sources and chapters in research literature and found relevant material on the history of childhood; to the psychologist, Professor Zvi Giora, who read the manuscript and made several important comments; and to my friends and colleagues, Dr Ron Barkai and Professor Zvi Razi. Dr Barkai read the third chapter of the manuscript and called my attention to sources and research literature relating to midwifery and childhood ailments. Professor Razi read the entire manuscript, and his comments were very helpful. It is also my pleasant duty to thank Clare Hall, Cambridge, where I spent a year as an associate fellow. This sojourn enabled me to conduct research under ideal conditions, and to benefit from fruitful contact with colleagues in a congenial environment.

Abbreviations

AB	Analecta Bollandiana
Annales ESC	Annales: Économies Sociétés Civilisations
MGHS	Monumenta Germaniae Historica Scriptores
PL	Patrologia Latina

Introduction: on the history of childhood in the Middle Ages

The central thesis of this book is that a concept of childhood existed in the Central and Late Middle Ages, that scholarly acknowledgement of the existence of several stages of childhood was not merely theoretical, and that parents invested both material and emotional resources in their offspring. Conceptions of parental roles, of the image of children, and of attitudes towards them, as well as theories and methods of upbringing and education, undoubtedly differed from those prevailing in contemporary western society. Childraising practices and educational methods as well as parent–child relations are determined not solely by biological laws but are also culturally constructed. They vary with historical development and hence are mutable factors, open to historical contextualization. They must be examined in any specific society against the background of the material culture and economic conditions, levels of medical knowledge and hygienic standards, political and social structure, and prevailing beliefs and value systems. And yet, although it cannot be valid to discuss childraising and parent–child relations purely in terms of instinct and natural conduct, there are certainly immutable factors involved. A considerable part of the developmental process is biologically determined, and the continued existence of a society is impossible without the acknowledgement (and conduct attuned to this acknowledgement) that, up to a certain stage in its life, the child has need of nurturing and protection in order to survive. No society could physically survive without a tradition of child-nurturing. And no society with any awareness of its own essence and aims could endure as a society without ways of transmitting knowledge and cultural traditions during the late stages of childhood, and without an effort on the part of those entrusted with the task of socialization of the young generation.

In respect to early childhood, Ariès[1] and his disciples chose to ignore the immutable and universal elements, perceiving recognition of the special needs of children and readiness to devote effort to ensuring their survival as historical phenomena and the outcome of cultural conditioning. But, despite this appreciation of the role of cultural conditioning, they essentially ignored the wider cultural context in which children were raised in the past. The high rate of mortality of infants and children in the Middle Ages was the consequence of limited medical skills and not of the absence of emotional involvement. In San Marcos la Laguna in Guatemala Indian infants are nurtured devotedly by their mothers, who maintain almost constant bodily contact with them and nurse them on demand. Notwithstanding, the infant mortality rate is extremely high (or, at least, was still so in the 1970s) – 40 per cent die before the age of 2. The reason lies not in the lack of maternal feeling but in malnutrition and the proliferation of contagious diseases.[2] Various methods of nurturing which may appear to us ineffective, if not downright harmful, should be judged against the background of contemporary medical beliefs, whether scholarly or popular, and should not be attributed to sinister intentions on the part of parents. It is true that in the Middle Ages children were closely involved in adult society (a custom which was in no way unique to pre-industrial western society) but should one therefore infer that the concept of childhood was non-existent and that childhood was not recognized as a separate stage in human life? Ariès himself has described vividly how people lived in close and dense proximity, men and women, clients and patrons, masters and servants, without the urge for privacy which characterizes modern western culture. Does this mean that the way of life of women and men did not differ and that the former shared in all the activities of the latter? Did this proximity prevent them from distinguishing between patron and client, or master and servant? Ariès, in his study, concentrates mainly on the problems of the structure and character of the family, and the concepts of childhood and education, rather than on the raising of infants. He mentions briefly that infants and small children were neither noticed nor acknowledged, and asserts that parents did not treat the child as an individual but erected emotional barriers against any attachment to the tiny creatures whose chances of survival were very slim. Of the historians who followed his lead, some developed the view (which is only implicit in Ariès) that parents made no effort to keep their children alive and accepted their death with equanimity.

There is no place for idealization of the life of children in the Middle Ages. The society was poor in resources and, because of the hierarchical structure, assets were concentrated in the hands of the over-privileged few. It was violent, yet impotent against disease and epidemics. Religion, as interpreted by the Church, provided not only moral norms but also a sanction for extremism, with all that it entailed. Nor was the lot of most adults a happy one. And, again, the outlook of some churchmen on childhood, and on the place of parental obligations within the duties of the Christian believer, did not unequivocally stress the welfare of the child. Yet, as I shall attempt to show in the following chapters, various medical theories were expounded by authors and compilers of encyclopedias on infant- and child-development and on childcare. There were prevailing norms as to the duties of parents toward their children; there was a tradition of childcare practices, and parents invested both materially and emotionally in their children.

In discussing the conception of childhood as a distinct period in human life, one should distinguish between the question of the existence of this conception, which inevitably shapes attitudes on the nature of childhood, and on educational theories and norms – and value judgments of these attitudes. In contrast to Ariès, I believe that childhood was in fact perceived as a distinct stage in the life cycle, that there was a conception of childhood, and that educational theories and norms existed. These norms were broached and formulated by theologians, secular and ecclesiastical legislators, jurists, the authors of medical and didactic works, and preachers. Some norms were depicted as general and universal. On another level, some were presented as educational goals in the second stage of childhood in accordance with social standing and gender. Later chapters will deal with the evaluation of these educational theories and norms. In the present context, it should be noted that it is not only highly doubtful whether any 'emotional evolution' has occurred in the attitude of parents to their children, but also debatable whether the evolutionary model of constant and consistent advancement towards a more humane and enlightened theory of education is valid. The educational theories of the Middle Ages were, in several respects, closer to those accepted by modern psychologists and educators than were those evolved in the eighteenth century. Whereas the dominant view of medieval authors was that up to the age of 7 the child should be treated with tenderness and not burdened with excessive demands for discipline and self-restraint, a number of eighteenth-century authors advocated rigid discipline from the very earliest age and relentless battle even against infants to force them to obey parental commands. Diversionary tactics were frowned on as means of dissuading a child from action which parents considered impermissible; direct measures were advocated: intimidation, whipping, and humiliation, aimed at breaking the child's will and subduing him. Moral arguments were cited in support of this educational method: it taught children not only discipline and order but altruism as well. Needless to say, a child aged 2 or 3 has not yet reached the stage of development which enables him to be instructed in altruism.[3] Ariès notes that, from the seventeenth century, pressures and disciplinary demands were increasingly brought to bear on children. But he views the change in the context of the emergence of awareness of childhood as a distinct stage in life, and of the first glimmerings of educational theory. He attributes the gentler treatment of small children in the Middle Ages to the lack of educational theories and to benevolent neglect.

After an examination of medieval norms, educational theories, and stances, we should analyse the extent to which they were applied and internalized, or, in other words, how parents treated their children in the various social classes and how they educated them. One should bear in mind that internalization can be for good or bad, according to our conceptions. Parish priests were enjoined, in accordance with the resolutions of synods, to inform their flocks of their duty to take proper care of their children, but authors of didactic works and preachers exhorted parents to avoid demonstrations of affection towards children over the age of 7 lest the children become proud and stray from the path of righteousness. Some churchmen not only expressed their reservations about bringing children into the world, but failed to specify concern for offspring as a prime obligation. The extant sources undoubtedly reveal more about theories, norms, and stances than about their application and internalization and there is little documentation on childcare and educational practices. The attempt to cast light on this area belongs within the sphere which Barraclough has defined as coping with problems posed by the reality of the past rather than by the documents.[4] It is most difficult of all to ascertain the degree of internalization of norms where the lower strata of society are concerned. Here, I have utilized a wide range of sources: excerpts from chronicles, the Lives of Saints, manuals for confessors (which indicate what was considered a sin by prevailing norms but not how prevalent it was); guild registers, apprenticeship contracts, and wills; court registers (which, again, indicate deviations but not their prevalence). Sermons obviously relate to the ideal, but the method of presentation and the constant repetition of certain themes can sometimes indicate what the prevailing situation was, as also can the resolutions of synods. I have also made use of secondary literature based on these sources, even when the history of childhood was not their central theme.

Ariès has many 'pessimistic' advocates for his view on the attitude to children in medieval society; in some cases, they have adopted his theory of the absence of a conception of childhood as a separate and distinct stage in human development.[5] Yet the book has also had its share of critics.[6] Of the medieval historians who have tackled the issue, such as Holmes, Mclaughlin, Forsyth, Demaitre, Hanawalt, and Wilson, some have pointed out the weaknesses in the arguments of Ariès and his followers and the contradictions in their basic theses (*inter alia*, on the link between demographic conditions and emotional investment), criticizing their sources and methodology. They have also demonstrated, on the basis of contemporary sources, that children played a part in the various manifestations of medieval culture.[7] Their work, and other studies I have consulted, were of great assistance to me. None the less, I am aware that the picture is incomplete, even where childraising and education are concerned. As for childhood experiences, it is difficult to uncover these even in later periods which have left us a wider range of sources such as biographies, autobiographies, journals, letters, and literature in which such experiences are described. The journals of children are an important but problematic source, since, generally speaking, they were written with the knowledge that parents would read them.[8] As for the writings of adults, it is well known that they have difficulties in reliving some of their childhood experiences on the conscious level. Even the most sincere and honest of adults, convinced that he or she has recorded 'what really happened', can only describe childhood and relations with parents through the filter of selective memory. Autobiographies are often dictated unconsciously or deliberately, by the author's perception of himself and the world at the time of writing rather than in the distant past. St Augustine of Hippo perceived his entire life until his conversion through the prism of his ideological commitment. The literature describing children can reveal the way in which they are perceived, attitudes towards them, and educational methods. The courtly romance which provides a realistic description of the lifestyle of the nobility (and, with Auerbach, we must stress that it is only the external life, and of the nobility alone, which is described realistically)[9] can serve as a source on educational practices in this class. But, to the extent that we find literary descriptions of childhood experiences, even in the nineteenth-century novel, they stem from the memory or imagination of an adult. Kuhn has already noted that it is usually easy for an adult to summon up those childhood moments which are most in affinity with his adult thoughts and emotions, or to imagine situations in which the child acts, thinks, and feels in a manner closest to that of adults and understandable to them.[10] The psychological truth expressed in the work is usually that of the adult and not the child.

Stephen Wilson has pointed out that interpretation of the fragmented and oblique extant testimony on this difficult sphere of family intimacy – the mentality of people who could not express themselves in writing – requires empathy, a feeling for nuances, and objectivity, a deliberate attempt to set aside one's own cultural assumptions.[11] We should endeavour to comprehend what we find unacceptable, or consider physically or emotionally harmful or even cruel, against the background of the character of the society, its weaknesses, and its inner contradictions. In addition to empathy, or sensitivity to nuances and objectivity, a degree of humility is required. Even in contemporary western society, where people enjoy material prosperity in comparison to the past, and where the child is allotted a central place in the family, there are mothers who have difficulty in forging proper biological and emotional links with their offspring in the early days. Normal parents may unconsciously sense hostility toward their children and have problems in creating significant ties, and normal mothers may sometimes admit explicitly that they find childraising burdensome, even if the admission causes them feelings of guilt. Some children still suffer physical and psychological neglect, and as is becoming increasingly clear, a disturbing degree of abuse. These things happen, but any psychologist or anthropologist who concentrated on them alone and presented them as a dominant feature in the attitude of modern western society towards children would be drawing a distorted and flawed picture. Yet certain historians have acted in precisely this fashion in delving into court registers and reporting cases of maternal cruelty or infanticide, or searching the records of foundling homes for reports of child abandonment. These cases have been documented and are worthy subjects of research, but, although it is clear that they represent deviations from the norm which were unacceptable to society (and whose scope cannot be gauged because they are incompletely documented), they have been cited to support generalizations about parent–children relations.

As noted, medieval educational theories and childraising practices differed from those accepted today. But it should be pointed out that there are several concepts which are customarily considered to have been formulated in later periods but which actually originated in the Middle Ages or were respected in that period as the legacy of the ancient world. The concept of childhood innocence, so popular in the romantic era of the nineteenth century, was derived from medieval Christian scriptural commentary. Conversely, the belief that children were ruled solely by their drives, which anticipated Freud's theories of childhood sexuality, was based on other commentaries on the same texts. As illustrated by two of the quotations at the beginning of this book, some writers perceived the childhood years as the basis for the development of the future adult, noting that the period of dependence and education of the young is longer in human beings than in any animal. Some authors recognized that children had need not only of physical nurturing but also of affection and contact with adults in order to develop normally. The authors of medieval didactic literature divided childhood into stages (as we shall see in the following chapters) reminiscent of the classifications of Piaget or Erikson. Views and customs which were unpopular in western industrial society for lengthy periods but were rife in medieval society (and other societies) are now gradually gaining acceptance again. Some modern physicians, echoing the medical authors of the ancient world and the Middle Ages, favour a gradual transition from the environment of the womb to the outside world, and avoid exposing the newborn infant to strong light and rough handling. They even recommend delaying the cutting of the umbilical cord for several minutes. Physicians and psychologists now accept that the infant should be suckled on demand and not submitted to a rigid schedule, such as was popular in the first half of this century. The practice of carrying the infant or small child in a sling attached to the parent's chest or back is also now increasingly popular in western society.

By learning about the attitudes of a society towards the children in its midst we expand and deepen our understanding of its nature. In the case of medieval society, perusal of this attitude can contribute both to elucidating its historical singularity and to casting new and significant light on the question of continuity and change in western culture.

The first chapter in this book is devoted to attitudes toward procreation and toward the child, and the image of children. The second chapter deals with the division of childhood into stages and the definition of each by medieval scholars. The order of the chapters devoted to the stages of childhood has been dictated mainly by this division. Childbirth, infant care, and baptism are discussed in the third chapter. The nursing period in the Middle Ages usually covered most of the first sub-stage of childhood – from birth to 2 years. It has been allotted a separate chapter both because of its great relevance to the subject of infant-nurturing and because of the problems it entailed (Chapter 4). The next chapter deals with the first stage – from birth to 7 years, with a division into two sub-stages: birth to about 2 years, and 2 to 7 years. It encompasses children from all social classes in an attempt to assess differences in childraising methods. Chapter 8 is devoted to general views on education in the second stage, from 7 to 12 years for girls and 7 to 14 for boys. Separate chapters have been allotted to the education of those dedicated to the church and the monastic life, the nobility who were destined for a secular life, the town-dwellers (with distinctions between the patricians and prosperous burghers and the workers), and the peasants (Chapters 9–12). The sixth chapter focuses on a phenomenon which was marginal but none the less real: abandonment and infanticide. It also discusses the various accidents which befell small children. Chapter 7 deals with the material and emotional investment in children in cases of disease and handicap, and with reactions to bereavement and orphanhood. These chapters precede those dealing with the second stage of childhood, for several reasons: most of the cases of abandonment and murder related to small infants; the proportion of small children injured and killed in accidents was high; and, according to Ariès and his school of thought, it was infants and small children who were ignored by parents who erected emotional barriers which enabled them to accept infant death with equanimity. Some historians have even perceived accidents as the reflection of parental indifference, if not covert infanticide. These theories are examined in these chapters. Some chapters deal mainly with theories, attitudes, and manuals of guidance (Chapters 1, 2, 8); some concentrate on educational practices (Chapters 9–12); while others (4, 5, 7) are combinations of the two.

The book discusses the upbringing and education of both boys and girls. In those areas where they were treated in different fashion, whether in theory or in practice, a separate discussion is devoted to each sex. In those cases where boys and girls received equal treatment, I sometimes refer to the child as 'he' and can only apologize for this (as, indeed, does Dr Spock in the introduction to his famous manual on childcare). The usage has been adopted for simplicity's sake.

1 The attitude to procreation and the image of the child in medieval culture

Medieval Christian thought was marked by ambivalence with regard to procreation. Asceticism was considered the more Christian way of life and those who chose total dedication to the service of God – priests, monks, and nuns – renounced family life. Could there be any more burdensome subjugation than that of an individual who was no longer master of his own body? What life could be more painful than that of a man suffering the day-to-day tribulations entailed in caring for the needs of a wife and offspring? Was there any life less conducive to the worship of God than the life of a man bound to the temporal world by many loves?[1] These questions were asked by Abelard in one of his sermons after he became a monk. Bernard of Cluny, also writing in the twelfth century, regarded with concern the great demographic increase in his day. Ever growing is the horde of men who lack religious piety, whose desire to marry and whose unrestrained proliferation are the outcome of a fleshly lust which knows no bounds.[2] According to the biographer of a female saint, she was forced to struggle against the lures of Satan who tried to tempt her to bear sons and daughters. Children are depicted as a source of happiness, but this joy stems from Satan who cites the Scriptures for his purpose (Gen. 1: 22; 9: 7).[3]

Among the secular writers who composed manuals of guidance for women, some simply ignored children, and the problems of bearing and raising them. The author who enters into minute details of the way in which a woman should preserve her sexual chastity and fulfil her wifely duties makes no mention whatsoever of her maternal tasks or else dismisses them briefly and casually. The emphasis is clearly on woman's role as wife rather than mother.

The love lauded in courtly literature – whether platonic or wholly sensual – is never aimed at procreation.

Sometimes, however, secular literature cites a different argument, in serious or humorous vein, to prove that procreation is 'a huge penitence'.[4] This is so not because children are the fruit of 'carnal acts' and not because they hinder total dedication to divine worship, but because they are a source of trouble, worry, financial expenditure, and suffering and enslave a man to his wife. (The writers, almost without exception, are men.)

> It is not possible to love the small child, the middling-sized child or the older child. It is hard to raise the small infant and it does not permit people to sleep at night. The middling-sized child wanders out into the street and must be protected against horses and carts. The older child fights his father and mother for the inheritance and must be dragged out of the tavern[5]

– writes a satirist. And Eustache Dechamps, the pessimistic poet of the Late Middle Ages, writes:

> Happy is he who has no children, for babies mean nothing but crying and stench; they give only trouble and anxiety; they have to be clothed, shod, fed; they are always in danger of falling and hurting themselves; they contract some illness and die; when they grow up, they may go to the bad and be cast into prison. Nothing but cares and sorrows; no happiness compensates us for our anxiety, for the trouble and expenses of their education. Is there a greater evil than to have deformed children?[6]

According to Abelard, when Heloïse tried to dissuade him from his decision to marry her, she not only quoted the anti-marriage arguments of St Paul and the church fathers, as well as classical philosophers, but also described the realities of life in the household of a philosopher who was also a father. Could a Christian philosopher contemplate and write in a poor household, filled with the chatter of servant girls, the lullabies of wetnurses, the wailing of infants, the constant untidiness and disorder of small children?[7] asked Heloïse. The Cathar heretics were alone in the Central Middle Ages in totally and unequivocally rejecting sexual relations and procreation, but the fact that theologians and authors of moral treatises presented abstinence as a supreme value enabled the secular authors noted above (and others like them) to write as they did about the fate of those who chose to beget and raise children, without fear of being charged with heresy.

Moreover, some churchmen not only advocated abstinence but also failed to cite devotion to children as the prime task of those who rejected abstinence and became parents. Preachers and authors of moral works denounced parents who pampered their children and who, ambitious on their behalf, committed the sin of pride. In order to supply all their children's needs and to guarantee their future, such parents waste their time in arduous labour, sometimes denying themselves food, pawning their property and borrowing money. Some are unable to repay their debts and some even steal. They do not pay the tithe and do not give charity to the poor. Children are depicted not only as a source of suffering and worry but also as a hindrance, preventing parents from doing good deeds, and even at times as a factor for sin. On the other hand, 'those who have no offspring donate their money to the church and give charity to the poor' (writes one of the authors).[8] In a popular morality tale, the king asks the wise man if a man should love his children. The latter replies that a man should love God first, then himself, and afterwards his children. He who loves his children, 'the fruit of his body', more than himself invests all his energy and his money in their support and advancement, and does not act for the salvation of his own soul.[9] Inspired by the same belief that total dedication to divine worship is a supreme value and on the basis of the words of Christ in the Gospel according to St Matthew ('and he that loveth son or daughter more than me is not worthy of me', 10: 37–8), church writers sometimes lauded women and men who chose to retire from the world into a monastic order even if this entailed abandoning their children.

This justification of the abandonment of children for the sake of dedication to God appears in several Lives of female saints, and two examples will suffice. Margaret of Cortona, daughter of peasants, was the mistress of a nobleman for several years and bore him a son. After the death of her lover under tragic circumstances which she regarded as divine retribution, she repented and went to live in Cortona with her son under the guidance of the Franciscans. She spent her days in prayer, did not cook for her son, and scarcely spoke to him in order not to interrupt her prayers. All fresh food apportioned to her she gave to the poor, and she and her son fed on scraps. When she joined the Third Order of the Franciscans, the boy was sent to Arezzo to be educated there. One day, while she was absorbed in prayer in church, her son's tutor appeared to tell her how the boy was faring and to receive his pay. But she no longer remembered that she had a son. According to the author, the reason was her total detachment from the world and from any maternal emotion and her utter dedication to God. When the boy did not arrive to spend his Easter vacation with her, the rumour was spread in the village that, due to her poverty and despair, she had killed the child. In the eyes of the author, however, she was the exemplification of the Gospel injunction 'and for love of the beloved bridegroom, Jesus, she banished her only son from her sight'.[10] Michelina of Pesaro, a widow, had a friend who exerted strong influence over her and tried to persuade her to join the Franciscan Third Order. However, Michelina had an ailing small son and as long as he was alive she could not join the order. The two women decided to pray to God and to promise him that, if the child died, Michelina would become his servant to the day of her death. This indeed came to pass. While they were praying, they heard a voice saying: 'I want your son in Heaven at my side. I release you from his love. Go in peace.' When she returned home, she saw that the child was dead and angels were bearing his soul away.[11] If this was indeed the course of events, then, even in the context of medieval culture, the incidents belong in the sphere of psychopathology. But the actual facts are immaterial; even if the tale is imaginary, it reflects a certain cultural attitude. The conduct of the two women was presented by their biographers as the expression of a supreme piety, and an indication of sanctity.

The issue, however, was not unequivocal. Since it advocated the sanctity of all human life, Christianity, from the outset, emphatically opposed both infanticide, including the killing of handicapped and illegitimate children, and abortion, which was also considered a violation of the injunctions to love God and one's fellow men.[12] Even the unborn child of a woman condemned to death was accorded the right to life, and it was customary to postpone the outlawry or execution of pregnant women.[13] Although St Paul permitted marriage as a concession to the weakness of the flesh and did not consider procreation to be its objective (1 Cor. 7: 9), the begetting of children was one of the three objectives of matrimony (together with the prevention of sin, and companionship), and was the main justification for sexual relations in marriage. Barrenness was not perceived as justification for annulling marriage, but the marriage-ceremony was accompanied by a blessing for procreation[14] and by Christian versions of pre-Christian rites aimed at ensuring fertility. Preachers admonished bachelors who refrained from marrying for economic reasons (and were suspected of engaging in sexual relations outside the marital framework), as well as married men who performed 'the act of Onan' (namely coitus interruptus) or abstained from marital relations for fear of begetting additional children whom they would be unable to support for reasons of poverty.[15] In other words, a clear distinction was drawn between those who chose chastity within the framework of the church, and laymen. The latter were exhorted to wed and to beget children. Alongside the popular religious literature, from the second half of the thirteenth century, Aristotelian theories were cultivated, including his views on the natural desire to procreate and on the family as the first basic partnership. Accordingly, Thomas Aquinas and others depicted the desire to beget children as stemming from natural law originating in natural instinct.[16] An abundance of sons was considered a blessing, and preachers who exhorted their flock to honour their parents promised them reward in this world: numerous progeny, and particularly sons, equivalent to worldly riches.[17]

In secular literature, we often find that the companions of the protagonist, a feudal seigneur, insist that he take a wife and beget an heir, else they will abandon him.[18] The thirteenth-century lay author, Philip of Novare, writes that, although renunciation of this world in order to serve God and win salvation is spiritual wealth for the sake of the soul, while children are spiritual wealth for the body's sake, they are nevertheless a source of joy which their parents would not exchange for all the treasures of the world. By bearing their father's name, they perpetuate his memory and that of his forefathers.[19] The author of the early fifteenth-century work known as *Dives et Pauper* (Rich Man and Poor Man) believes that the man who leaves progeny behind him is not completely dead, since he lives on in his children, who follow in his footsteps;[20] or, as a thirteenth-century writer puts it: 'The father wishes to duplicate himself in his offspring.'[21] One of the writers who condemned women who induced abortions explained the ban on this act by saying that it hinders the proliferation of the human race.[22] It seems, therefore, that there were also cultural attitudes which supported the biological and emotional drive to reproduce, or the urge to bring children into the world for political-dynastic or economic reasons (such as the desire of noblemen to produce an heir and the peasants' need for additional working hands) which were in no way incompatible with emotion.

The children who came into the world were considered a trust from God rather than the property of their parents (this was in contrast to the situation in the Roman world where children were legally the property of their fathers, who, by force of paternal authority (*patria potestas*), could even decide whether, they were to be kept alive).[23] Theologians, preachers, and authors of didactic works enlarged on the duties of parents towards the children entrusted to them for safekeeping; it was incumbent on them to support them, protect them, raise them properly, and give them a Christian education. They were responsible for their children before God.

The twelfth century witnessed the rise of worship of the Virgin Mary, who had conceived, borne, and raised Christ. Churchmen, in praising virginity, distinguished clearly between the Holy Mother, who had given birth in violation of the laws of nature, and women who conceived and gave birth in natural fashion. But, in art and in sermons aimed at the wider strata of society, the Holy Mother was depicted as the archetypal devoted mother. She was pictured in pregnancy, suckling her son, playing with him, and caressing him – as an example to all mothers. At the opposite extreme to the extolling of women who became saints and abandoned their children in order to devote themselves to God's work, one finds in the Lives of the saints praise for the mothers of saints and even for women who married, bore children, and raised them before retiring from the world, and were beatified posthumously. In the spirit of St Paul, who said 'Notwithstanding, she shall be saved in childbearing, if they continue in faith and charity and holiness with sobriety' (1 Tim. 2: 15), the authors praise these women not only for providing their children with a Christian education but also for nursing them themselves and raising them devotedly.[24] In the customaries of several monastic orders there appears a clause permitting parents who decide to retire from the world and enter a monastery to bring their children with them. Thomas Aquinas states explicitly that it is the duty of parents who choose the monastic life to act thus if their children are still small and dependent on them.[25]

Herlihy has noted that, in the wake of the plagues which ravaged the population of Europe in the fourteenth and fifteenth centuries, fathers of families were increasingly urged to provide effective care for their wives and children, to lavish love, and to protect them. In this period, Joseph was cited as the ideal father in his role as protector of Mary and the infant Jesus. Yet it is important to emphasize that, in the period of population expansion in the twelfth and thirteenth centuries as well, the obligation of parents to raise, protect, and educate the progeny entrusted to them was stressed, and attention was devoted to the role of the husband as protector of his wife, mother of his children.[26]

Let us now examine the image of children in this period. Just as medieval culture displayed ambivalence over procreation, so it fostered two conflicting images of the child, which may be defined, simplistically, as the negative and the positive approaches. Like the different attitudes to procreation, they too reflected both conscious and unconscious emotional ambivalence. In delineating the negative image, the authors of the Central Middle Ages drew partial inspiration from Augustine of Hippo. From him they borrowed the idea that the infant was born in sin, being the fruit of his parents' sexual intercourse, which since the Original Sin and the Fall was marked by carnal lust, and the view that every child born into the world inherited the sin of Adam and Eve. Not only did Augustine perceive childhood as a period in which reason and understanding were still dormant, but, describing the infant born in sin, he emphasized its drives: importunity, jealousy, anger, and aggressiveness (on the theoretical plane, this view is highly evocative of Freud's theory of infantile sexuality), and totally rejected the good and inno-cent image of childhood. 'It is the weakness of the infant's body which is innocent, not his soul': thus Augustine interpreted Christ's words on the innocence of children.[27] Medieval authors shifted the emphasis from instincts to the helplessness, lack of reason, and pathos of the infant born in sin. This is the prevailing standpoint in the type of literature which depicts the human condition in pessimistic fashion, and the description of childhood fits in with the general view on the sadness, futility, sinfulness, and misery of human life at all stages in the earthly vale of tears. This view finds extreme expression in the work known as *De Contemptu Mundi* (On Contempt of the World), composed by Pope Innocent III. Writing of the conception, birth, and early childhood of human beings, he says that man, like the beasts, is born out of the lowest of the four elements – the dust of the earth. If you said that only the first man was created out of dust while you were born of seed, writes the author, you would be correct. He was created out of virgin soil and you from contaminated seed. Man is created out of iniquity and sins, not one sole iniquity or sin but many, his own and those of others. It is known to all that there is no sexual intercourse in marriage without carnal desire, without sexual lust, without the abominations of desire. All these corrupt, distort, and defile the seed from which man is made. And the soul which is poured into the body is defiled through the impurity and filth of the sin of the vessel in which it enters, and the good and natural forces are corrupted by the opposing forces of sin. Moreover, the foetus in its mother's womb is nurtured on the menstrual blood of the mother, which does not flow during pregnancy, and which is incomparably impure. A man emerges into the world naked and wailing. Some are born so deformed and distorted that it were better if they had never left the womb and been seen by others. But why dwell at length on these? All are born without sense, without the power of speech, and without good qualities. Pathetic, weak, and foolish, they scarcely differ from beasts. Moreover, in certain aspects they are even inferior to beasts, for the latter, immediately after birth, stand on their own feet, while we not only cannot stand alone but cannot even crawl.[28] This author, in his rhetorical fervour, appears to have exceeded even the customary style of this type of literature.

In the writings of other authors, the conception in sin of the infant is merely implied, and emphasis is placed on incompleteness: the inability to control the body, absence of reason and perception, and the lack of good deeds. These writers echoed Aristotle, who also regarded early childhood not as a period of sin but as a time of incompleteness and flaws. According to Aristotle, the child lacks the capacity to choose, which is the distinguishing feature of the reasonable creature; he is absorbed in sensual gratifications alone, and, since he is incapable of noble actions, he cannot be happy. Childhood is the lowest stage in human life.[29]

This being so, when medieval authors described an exceptional child – a future saint – they usually depicted him as having skipped this stage. Hence, the *topos* (recurrent motif of a literary genre) of 'boy–old man' (*puer senex*) is one of the most prevalent in the Lives of saints. The future saint (male or female), while still an infant, asks permission to fast on fastdays (St Nicholas, the archetype of the sainted infant, agreed to nurse on Fridays and Wednesdays only once a day!), places his arms in the form of a cross while still in the cradle, folds his hands, kneels, and raises his eyes heavenward in prayer before knowing the words of the prayer, keeps his distance from the mischief and games of his contemporaries, gives charity to the poor, and above all is as serious as an old man.

> From that hour, the little girl began to grow old. There was a wondrous maturity in her good qualities and her conduct. Her deeds were not those of a child, nor of a young woman but were entirely in the spirit of honourable old age,

one author writes about a six-year-old girl.[30] E. R. Curtius has analysed the significance of the 'boy–old man' in several literatures,[31] and it seems that, whereas in classic literature and myths of several religions, the 'boy–old man' combines the freshness and charm of youth with the maturity and wisdom of old age, the 'boy–old man' of the Lives of the saints is old in everything but years. *Topoi* are the clichés of a certain genre of literature, but they also cast light on attitudes, at least of those who introduced them into their or raised children. They did not apparently comprehend small children, and may have been intimidated by their drives. While they did not condemn them as sinners, they dissociated themselves from them and implicitly rejected them.

Stronger rejection and direct condemnation are evident in attitudes towards older children, and particularly towards adolescents. The human creature, born imperfect in body and spirit, grows and develops both physically and intellectually according to the laws of natural development, but, concomitantly, his tendency to sin grows;[32] or, in other words, he is perceived to be controlled by his drives more than by his developing reason. This predilection for sin commences at the age of 7 and reaches its peak in adolescence. Adolescents, from the age of 14 on, and young people are condemned directly as frivolous and arrogant, unwilling to accept the authority of their elders and betters; they do not respect their parents; prefer dancing, clowning, and play to the word of God delivered through His priests; they are licentious and steeped in carnal lusts. In the Lives of the saints, the exception to this rule is described as modest, pious, a diligent student, and, above all, a shining example in his sexual chastity, in his thought, speech, and deeds. And, in depicting the exceptional youth, the author condemns the reprehensible conduct of other adolescents. Many of the authors of didactic literature and the preachers wrote in the same spirit about the young.[33] The propensity to sin – or the lack of control over drives, despite the emergence of reason – is the justification cited by the authors for their demand for strict and rigorous education for young boys. Their remarks sometimes reflect actual hostility towards the young, and they appear to have projected on to their juniors their own arrogance, acquisitiveness, and carnal lusts, which often caused them feelings of guilt.

All historians who discussed the problem of the negative image of children in medieval culture have noted that it was influenced by the views of St Augustine. However, they make almost no reference to that aspect of his conception of childhood which accentuates the positive image, and which may serve as the connecting link between the two images. According to St Augustine, although the infant is born in sin and is motivated by his drives, once he is baptized he is still more innocent than his elders, as is also the older child. After dwelling on the nursing period (his own, on the basis of stories he had been told, and that of others, as a result of observation), Augustine goes on to depict the period of his schooling. He was frequently whipped. The blows caused him pain, suffering, and constant fear. He prayed to God that his teachers would spare the rod, but his parents and the other adults in his household regarded his suffering as a source of amusement and mockery. If he and his companions played, they were punished by adults who themselves engaged in play. But the adult games were known as 'business' (*negotia*) and were approved by all. Yet the child playing ball, an innocent game in comparison with the distorted and dangerous games of adults, was mercilessly punished by them. If the teacher who whipped a child for the sin of playing ball were to be vanquished by one of his colleagues in a petty academic squabble, he would respond with much greater fury and envy than a child beaten at play by a comrade.[34] The child who sins (and is justifiably whipped) is not merely no worse than the adult, he even is better than him.

Yet those who fostered a positive image of children in the Central Middle Ages did not rely on the words of St Augustine alone. They quoted Christ according to Matthew:

> Verily I say unto you, Except ye be converted, and become as little children, ye shall not enter into the kingdom of Heaven. Whosoever therefore shall humble himself as this little child, the same is greatest in the kingdom of heaven. And whoso shall receive one such little child in my name receiveth me.
>
> (Matt. 18: 3–6)

According to the literal interpretation[35] childhood was the period of purity, innocence, and faith. In discussing the second period of childhood (*puericia*), Bartholomaeus Anglicus asserts, in the wake of Isidore of Seville, that *puer*, a boy, is derived from *puritas*, and girl – *puella* – from *pupilla* – the pupil of the eye, because boys and girls are still as pure as the pupil.[36] Another author writes: 'Children are as pure as angels.' The service of the young is goodly in the eyes of God because they are more comely of soul than adults. The young offer God the best of the flour, and the old – offer bran.[37] The purity and beauty of childhood will pass away; adulthood entails loss, the loss of innocence and the joy which accompanied it.[38] Due to the wholeness of his faith, his ability to be amazed by wondrous things, and his innocence, the child is sometimes privileged to grasp a significant truth which is still hidden from adults.[39] In this conception, medieval authors were akin to the nineteenth-century Romantics who spoke of the intuition and spontaneous response of the child, thanks to which he can understand that which is hidden from the adult, who is bound by social conventions. The ardent belief of children in the sanctity of man is additional evidence of this sanctity.[40] According to the preachers and the biographers of saints, there were saints who were particularly fond of the company of children because of the children's purity and innocence which resembled their own, since in adulthood these saints preserved childlike qualities. And, because of these qualities, they were particularly beloved by children, who felt a close affinity with them.[41] The power of a child's prayer is greater than that of an adult's prayer.[42] A child lacks any wickedness and is incapable of harbouring a grudge. Even if a child has just been beaten, should the person who beat him offer him a pretty flower or a red apple, he will forget what was just done to him and run to him with open arms to kiss him and please him.[43] The child is more generous than the adult, generously distributing his bread to his companions, to his dog and cat, and, in his innocence – even to the Christ-child.[44]

Worship of the infant Jesus flourished in the twelfth century, together with worship of the Holy Mother: Christ is depicted as a human child, small, weak, laughing, weeping, eating an apple given to him by his mother, innocent, and pure, the archetypal child. Bernard of Clairvaux, in one of his sermons, and Jean Gerson some two centuries later, called on believers to give their hearts to this child, to believe in him, and to worship him so that they too could revert to being as innocent and pure as little children.[45] The child Jesus is portrayed in art and in sermons, and monks and nuns, saints and mystics claimed that he had appeared to them in visions.[46] In the thirteenth century, the 'Christmas manger' was introduced into churches, decorated with statuettes of the infant Jesus lying in the straw in the manger in Bethlehem beside the ox and the donkey. Moreover, sometimes not only the little child was depicted as the symbol of purity and innocence and as the embodiment of Christ. In one of the tales in the Lives of the saints, Jesus appears as a handsome and elegant youth, championing a future female saint against her sister who is persecuting her; he not only admonishes the sister but even beats her![47] Popular religious literature depicts Mary as a child: a small girl climbing the steps leading to the Temple without help, like an adult. Under the influence of tales about the Virgin Mary, children sometimes imagined that they saw her in visions, in childish form but with the deportment and speech of a woman.[48] One of the preachers writes that the young are easily seduced by the Devil into carnal sins, but have not yet been defiled by weightier sins, and that their as-yet-uncorrupted hearts are soft and simple. It is easy to instruct them to pray and to fast, and they are less steeped than their seniors in avarice, pride, and gluttony.[49] Aegidius Romanus lists the good and bad qualities which characterize young people and those characteristic of the old, offering physiological and psychological explanations for their origins. The rulers to whom his manual of guidance is addressed are exhorted to adopt the good qualities of the young, such as courage, hope, faith, and mercy.[50]

Since innocence and purity were attributed to small children, artists often portray the soul on its way to Heaven in the form of a little child,[51] and mystics described the relations of the soul of the believer with God as resembling those of a mother and child.[52]

One of the recurrent motifs in religious literature, in drama, and in art is the 'Slaughter of the Innocents' (namely, 'all the children that were in Bethlehem and in all the coasts thereof, from two years old and under ...' Matt. 2: 16) by order of King Herod. The children are snatched by the soldiers from the arms of their mothers, who try to protect them, and are cruelly slaughtered. This massacre is depicted as particularly horrifying because its victims are the most innocent of all creatures.[53] Under the inspiration of this description and in the same spirit, when a certain chronicler wanted to illustrate for his readers the full extent of the horrors perpetrated during the Hundred Years War in France, he wrote of children aged 2 or 3 begging for bread after the death of their parents, the infant continuing to suck at its dead mother's breast, and the mother hugging her dead babe to her bosom to warm him.[54]

Some of the authors of medical works cited not only Aristotle but also Galen, who claimed that the child was good by nature and should not be 'corrected' but only protected against evil influences: hearing and reading lewd things, witnessing sexually immodest conduct, and observing adults in their nudity.[55] In quoting Aristotle, these authors placed less emphasis on his remarks on the immaturity of children and on childhood as the lowest stage in human life, and more on his view that children tend to develop a natural affection for those who nurture them and a readiness to accept discipline.[56]

In the thirteenth-century poem *Le Roman de la Rose*, 'youth' (*joinece*) is represented by a girl not yet 12 years old. She knows nothing of the evil and falsehood rife in the world. She is innocent and lacking in any hypocrisy. Her days are passed in innocent play with a boy of her own age. Their mutual love is free of sinful lust and shame, like the love of a pair of doves.[57] In several versions of the romance of Tristan, the child, Tristan's nephew, is the ally of the lovers whose love is tainted with sin. His proximity transforms their relations into a more innocent and pure connection, and helps to atone for their sin.[58]

Ritual expression of faith in the innocence of the child and its atoning power can be found in the custom of allotting a place at the head of many religious processions to children. The statutes of the Norwich furriers' guild, for example, stipulate that 'the candle in the religious procession shall be borne by an innocent child'.[59] And the child is considered innocent primarily because he is ignorant of sexual lust on the one hand and unaware of the meaning of death, on the other. 'How great is the joy in the ignorance of little children! Being protected by absence of lust, it enjoys the security of the angels,'[60] writes Gilbert of Nogent of children who have not yet reached puberty and are not ashamed of their nudity. And the fourteenth-century English preacher, John Bromyard, describes the innocent children who do not understand the significance of death and who play merrily with the silk cloth covering the corpse of their father or mother.[61] The idea that Thanatos and Eros have no place in the cosmogony of the child can still be traced in a number of literary works in the nineteenth century. When the child becomes aware of the profound realities of death and sex, the paradise of childhood comes to an end.[62] The innocence, faith, and pure love are destined to pass with the end of childhood, as Dante wrote in the *Divine Comedy*:

> For faith and innocence are in the heart
> Of children only; both aside are cast
> Before a beard upon the cheeks may start.
> Many a stammering child observeth fast
> Who, after, when his tongue is freed, will chew
> Any food, any month, in glutton haste.
> And many a stammerer loves and hearkens to
> His mother, who, when full speech in him flows,
> Longeth to see her buried out of view.[63]

Whether the view of childhood was positive or negative, there can be no question but that, in the Middle Ages, childhood was perceived as a separate stage in human life, with its own quality and characteristics. As we know, it is easier to depict the views, educational theories, images, and stances of those who could write and express themselves in writing, than to gauge the extent of their impact on reality or the degree to which they reflected that reality – particularly since theories on the child and attitudes toward him in medieval culture were undoubtedly marked by ambivalence. In the following chapters, an attempt will be made to examine to what degree the various attitudes toward procreation and different images of the child, as well as the church ordinances aimed at parents, reflected or shaped reality: the desire to beget children, the attitude towards them, the material and emotional investment in children, and the way in which they were raised and educated in the various strata of society. One should also recall that there was indubitably a difference in the attitudes of different parents towards children within the same class, stemming from variations in personality, which, within the constraints of their environment and its values, determined their treatment of their children. The social historian endeavours to describe the accepted norm, the characteristic, and the common traits of human beings in a certain society in a certain age. But there can be no doubt that, in the selfsame period or social class, children experienced a different childhood because of those individual differences between parents, as is the case today. Hence, if we can find in the source-literature relatively detailed descriptions of an individual's childhood (and, almost without exception, such descriptions are only extant for the upper classes), it calls for cautious examination and assessment – over and above the problems entailed in depiction of childhood experiences by an adult – in order to evaluate correctly the degree to which we can learn from it something of the attitude of parents toward their children and the childhood experiences typical of that particular social class. Moreover, in gauging the impact of attitudes on reality, one should be aware that the causal connection between them and actual conduct is relatively complex and by no means direct.[64]

2 Stages in childhood

Psychologists who deal with personality development distinguish several stages in childhood. Jean Piaget, who studied the development of cognition, divided the period from birth to adolescence into four stages, in the first of which he listed several sub-stages:

(*a*) 'infancy', from birth to 18 months–2 years, the period preceding language and thought as such. (1) The reflex or hereditary stage, at which the first instinctual nutritional drives and first emotions appear; (2) the stage of the first motor habits, the first organized percepts, and the first differentiated emotions; (3) the stage of sensorimotor intelligence (prior to language), elementary affective organization, and the first external affective fixations.

(*b*) 'early childhood', from 2 to 7, the stage of intuitive intelligence, spontaneous inter-personal feelings, and of social relationships in which the child is subordinate to the adult.

(*c*) 'middle childhood', from 7 to 11 or 12, the stage of concrete intellectual operations (the beginning of logic) and of moral and social feelings of cooperation.

(*d*) 'adolescence', the stage of abstract intellectual operations, of the formation of the personality, and of affective and intellectual entry into the society of adults.[1]

Erik Erikson, who belongs to the ego-psychology trend of the psychoanalytical school, distinguished eight stages in human life, in which he perceived a universal model of personality development. The period between birth and the age of 20 covers five of these stages: (*a*) 'infancy' from birth to 15 months; (*b*) 'early childhood', from 15 months to $2\frac{1}{2}$ years; (*c*) 'the age of play', from $2\frac{1}{2}$ to 6; (*d*) 'school age', from 6 to sexual maturation; (*e*) youth, ending at the age of 20. Erikson discusses the physiological and psychological development at each stage and in parallel to the Freudian division into the oral, anal, and genital stages, emphasizing the important element which the child acquires at each stage in order to develop as a self-assured and balanced individual. Thus, the most important aspect of the first stage is the acquisition of basic trust (stemming from the infant's confidence in those who nurture him), which is the basis for the self-identity and self-confidence which will enable him to establish relations based on mutual trust in the course of his life. The essence of the relationship between the infant and his nurturer is immeasurably more important than are the technical details of the method of nurturing. The most important element of the second stage is the development of autonomy – the sense of the self as a separate personality. The objective of education at this age should be to accustom the child to adapt to the demands of society without forfeiting either his basic trust or his self-confidence. And so forth for the subsequent developmental stages, which should each contribute to promoting normal development. The pattern of development is uniform, but the educational methods vary from culture to culture. They are anchored in the values and goals of the society, which also determine which qualities and traits will be considered more desirable in that particular culture, and hence are to be fostered through education.[2]

The authors of medieval medical works, didactic literature, and moral treatises also distinguished several stages in childhood and in human life in general. Childhood was most commonly divided into three stages – (a) *infantia*, from birth to 7 years – early childhood; (2) *pueritia*, 7 to 12 (for girls), or to 14 (for boys); (3) *adolescentia*, 12 or 14 to adulthood. Most authors denote the post-adolescent period *juventus*.[3]

The conduct and achievements of a child were evaluated on the basis of normative expectations from his age-group.[4] In describing a child poised at the end of one stage and the beginning of another, the authors often use the term 'reached the border' (between one stage and another); when the child is half-way through a stage, they note that he has reached the 'middle'. The view was that, at each stage, a child requires different material and spiritual input and that the demands made of him should be adaptable to his age.[5] The conviction that certain physical movements or a certain form of conduct is characteristic of children at a given age, as well as the belief that at each stage a child attains a certain level of physical and intellectual development, and that each age has its distinguishing features, was not confined to the authors of didactic works. When one writer describes a little girl slicing bread, he comments: 'in the manner of children, she held it on her knee'. And, according to a popular proverb, a child who said or did something which was not fitting for his years (in other words, was precocious) was not destined to live long.[6]

All the authors who discuss the various stages of childhood cite the distinguishing features of each stage and the characteristic signs of development therein and dwell on the status, rights, and duties of the child and adolescent in the second and third stages. In the first stage of childhood, most authors distinguish two sub-periods, and some also divide the second and third stages into sub-periods. This acknowledgement of the existence of separate stages of childhood and adolescence is reflected, *inter alia*, in the distinction drawn in Florence in the first decades of the fifteenth century between the confraternities of children, encompassing children from the age of 10, and the confraternities of young men, membership of which commenced at 19. The latter were said to be 'too old to be among boys and too young to be among mature men'.[7]

THE FIRST STAGE OF CHILDHOOD (*INFANTIA*)

Although Bartholomaeus Anglicus does not divide the first stage of childhood into sub-periods, he emulates Isidore of Seville in listing several features of the first 7 months of life. These are the tenderness, delicacy, and 'fluidity' (*fluida*) of the infant, and the fact that he is toothless. In this period he is in need of constant, tender, and delicate attention.[8] Most authors perceive the end of the first sub-period as the age of 2, when the child has all his first teeth, has pronounced his first words, and has taken his first steps. This is considered the suitable age for weaning, and henceforth the child is believed to be less vulnerable to certain diseases which afflict many children in the first period of infancy.[9] This last statement reflects awareness of the fact that from the age of 2 onwards there was a certain decline in the risk of mortality. The twelfth-century philosopher, William of Conches, asserted that a substage ended at the age of 5, because from then on the child was capable of speaking properly, whereas at a younger age he is at first completely incapable of speech, and then his speech is flawed and incorrect.[10] The view of childhood up to the age of 7 as a period in which the human being is helpless and totally dependent on adults is reflected in the remarks of preachers and authors of confessors' manuals who exhorted parents to take good care of their children, who were under their full responsibility to the age of 7. They also cautioned them that they would be answerable to the church and before God if harm befell the children.[11] One of the six sacraments administered to the layman in the course of his life was conferred in the first stage of childhood: every infant was baptized shortly after birth. As regards confirmation, canonists were divided as to whether or not it should be administered to a child before the age of 7. Some held that it should be conferred within a year of birth. Raymond Lull, on the other hand, claimed that this sacrament should be administered only when a child attained an age when he was capable of understanding the significance of the commitment undertaken by his godparents on his behalf at his baptism. Others believed that it should not be administered to a child under the age of 12. Many only received it at this age or even later (and others not at all), but it was sometimes administered to children under 7.[12]

THE SECOND STAGE (*PUERITIA*)

Most authors specify the age of 7 as the commencement of the second stage, since from this age onwards the child can express himself properly, distinguish between good and evil, and choose between them. He has reached 'the years of choice and discretion' (*annis discretionis*). In selecting the ability to express oneself as the distinguishing feature of the second stage of childhood, the medieval scholars were following the Roman approach, according to which the inability to express oneself is one of the characteristic signs of early childhood. In this period the child is denoted *infans*, 'because he is incapable of speech', not because he is incapable of utterance, but because at this stage, he speaks in imitation of the speech of adults without true comprehension.[13] In line with the theories of the medical sages, the contemporary view was that there was a connection between the loss of milk-teeth and emergence of permanent teeth, and the acquisition of speech. A young man who still behaved childishly was sometimes denoted *infans*, and the term was also sometimes applied to an adult who, for whatsoever reason, could not express himself properly.[14] There were, of course, authors who attributed these characteristics to slightly older or younger ages. Bernard Gordon claimed that there was a sub-stage within the second stage of childhood, commencing at the age of 12. Before this age, for moral reasons, some of the classic works should not be read to a child, but from 12 on he was believed to be capable of deciding on his path in life. Philip of Novare, together with some of the canonists, asserted that a sub-stage commenced at 10 or $10\frac{1}{2}$ years. According to Philip of Novare, only from this age could the child choose between good and evil.[15] Since a child was considered capable of expressing himself properly from the age of 7, he could be betrothed at this age. But, from the second half of the twelfth century, a betrothal arranged at this age was no longer considered a binding act leading to marriage. When a boy reached 14 or a girl 12 – that is to say at the end of the second stage of childhood – they could agree or refuse to enter into a marriage with the partner to whom they had been betrothed in childhood. And the law, at least, stipulated that, even if the marriage ceremony had been held, if the groom was under 14 or the bride under 12 it was not binding and could be annulled if the young couple so wished when they reached these ages.[16] Seven was considered by most authors a suitable age for commencing schooling or vocational training, including preparation for priesthood. Since, according to those who espoused the negative view of childhood, the child who developed physically and whose reason also developed had a greater proclivity to sin from the age of 7 onward, didactic writers stress the obligation of parents, godparents, and teachers to educate the child from that age in a Christian spirit and to teach him discipline and morals. And since the child was already capable of sin, there were theologians who held that children should attend confession and do penance from that age, since even a child under 14 is capable of stealing, lying and bearing false witness, cursing, disrespectful conduct towards parents and priests and others in authority, and sexual sins. Others proposed that this sacrament be conferred only from the age of 14 (or 12 for girls). Similarly, they also differed as to whether the Eucharist and the Extreme Unction should be administered before the age of 14 (or 12 for girls).[17]

According to secular legislation, boys and girls under 14 or 12 respectively did not yet bear criminal responsibility. According to Bracton, the English jurist, the absence of intention protects the child. They could be placed on trial, but the justices, or sometimes even the town authorities, were empowered to decide whether to punish them, and they did not generally receive the same sentence meted out to adults for the same crime: the customary punishment for a child was a whipping. Only in extraordinary circumstances was the full penalty imposed on a child. As Philip of Beaumanoir wrote at the end of the thirteenth century:

> Sometimes a child of ten or twelve is so corrupt and evil ... and if such a child commits a murder of his own free will or as an agent of some other person he is to be executed. But he will not be punished by lopping of limbs or execution for the crime of theft but will rather be pardoned because of his age.[18]

Court registers reveal that children who committed murder were sometimes given the full penalty, but, on the other hand, there were cases in which they were treated leniently not only for the crime of theft but also in cases of murder.[19] This leniency towards a child who committed a crime was accepted by churchmen as well. Thomas Aquinas wrote that a child is not capable of doing all that an adult can do; for this reason the law for child and adult is not the same, and many things are permitted to children which are punished by the law, and even abhorred in adults. According to the authors of the confessors' manuals, young people from the age of 14 were made to do penance for sins of a sexual nature, but this penance was lighter than that meted out to adults for the same sin. With regard to certain sins (from the same sphere), even those over 14 were treated leniently if they were still unmarried or had not yet reached 20. It seems, therefore, that even those who favoured childhood confession and enumerated all the sins of which children were capable did not take as strict a view of the sins of children as of those committed by an adult. The legislation introduced by Pope Alexander III in the second half of the twelfth century stipulated that young people under 14 (or girls under 12) were not answerable at law. Those who followed him claimed, on the basis of tradition, that he was referring only to extraordinary cases and that children under the specified ages could do penance, though it should be less harsh than that imposed on an adult for the same sin. Moreover, an oath taken by a boy under 14 was not valid, and his father was entitled to annul it.[20]

Authors of medical and didactic works listed several additional distinguishing features of this age. The fourteenth-century scholar, Bernard Gordon, considered vigorous physical activity (running, jumping, etc.) and squabbles among boys as typical of the age-group 7–14. He therefore denoted it 'the concussion age'.[21] According to Bartholomaeus Anglicus, boys in the second stage of childhood are carefree and reject any thought of serious matters; they concentrate solely on the present without thought for the future, and prefer above all games with their peers; they are not greatly impressed with either praise or admonishment by adults, but the greatest danger they can conceive of is to be punished by a whipping. They are prone to rapid changes of mood, crying one moment and laughing the next. They cannot keep secrets and immediately reveal all they know. They are noisy and restless, and quiet only when sleeping. They covet everything they see and demand it at the top of their voices; they become dirty rapidly and kick and scream when their mothers wash them and change their clothes. They are tender of flesh, flexible, and light of movement. But their bodies are not yet strong and they cannot endure physical hardship. They like to linger in bed and are always hungry and in search of food. Sometimes they fall ill from overeating. They reveal their nakedness without shame and weep harder for an apple which falls than for their inheritance, and in general prefer apples to gold.[22] In the chapter devoted to girls, Bartholomaeus Anglicus, echoing Aristotle, describes their physical traits: hair, neck, face, bodily structure, and voice. It will be recalled that he regarded girls as still pure, but he cautions against the development of 'feminine' traits: impudence, choler, hatred, envy, impatience, lack of perseverance, a tendency to be easily tempted, bitterness, and insistence on fulfilling every foolish whim. Girls should be educated and protected against the development of these traits.[23] Bartholomaeus Anglicus seems to be confusing behavioural patterns characteristic of boys of 12–14 and of children of 7 and even younger. He believes that this age-group is still pure, but none the less advocates strict education from the age of 7, since by then children are capable of sin. The description is not complimentary, but it does indicate awareness of the attitudes and conduct characterizing children, even in a somewhat lenient manner. The view that there is 'normal' conduct typical of each age is shared by medieval sages and contemporary psychologists who deal with childhood behaviour and note, for instance, that at the age of 4 a child leaves the house, wanders off, and is lost; at 8 he demands permission to ride his bicycle in the street, etc. According to all the writers, this period ends at 12 in girls, and 14 in boys – ages which were considered to mark the beginning of puberty.[24]

THE THIRD STAGE (*ADOLESCENTIA*)

As will be recalled, the authors of moral works, the preachers, and some of the didactic writers believed that one of the striking features of this age was intensification of the predilection to sin, which commences at the age of 7 and develops concomitantly with the development of the intellect. Aegidius Romanus also claims that at this age the young tend to believe anyone, are receptive to influences, and are very fond of the company of their peers. But, since the power of judgment, the ability to distinguish between good and evil, and the intellect are all developing at this stage, it is already possible to teach them any theoretical subject and to educate them, and care should be taken to do just this.[25] At this age the sacraments of the Eucharist, Confession, and Penance were administered, as well as Extreme Unction if they died then. During the Inquisition trials in the Haute Ariège region at the end of the thirteenth century and beginning of the fourteenth, all males aged 14 and over and all females from the age of 12 were obliged to take a vow of faith and to deny on oath any affiliation to heretic sects. The Cathars, for their part, were also of the opinion that, although young people attained full understanding only at the age of 18, they could be accepted into the faith at 12 (girls) and 14 (boys).[26] From this age up they could give evidence in civil courts[27] and were supposed to bear full responsibility for certain criminal offences, at least in some regions, although at this age as well they did not always receive the full penalty.

The authors of epics and courtly literature also characterized this age, though in very different manner from the church writers. The young boy training for knighthood is depicted as distinguished by outstanding physical prowess and even more so by beauty, and the same is said of young girls.[28] And, since beauty was a distinguishing feature of young men, authors who wanted to describe outstanding beauty in a small child, like the biographers of saints, described their future hero as having skipped the phase of childhood: 'at the age of seven he was as handsome as another child is at twenty'.[29] Needless to say, beauty was a knightly rather than a religious ideal. Churchmen perceived beauty if not as a corrupting factor then at least as a source of danger.[30] Only rarely is the author unable to avoid the temptation to describe the future (male or female) saint as a particularly beautiful child, noting that he (or she) avoided the dangers inherent in physical beauty thanks to modesty and sexual chastity.[31]

Among peasants it was sometimes the commencement of independent labour and the acquisition of manual skills which marked the transition to the third stage of life. Thus, in the Haute Ariège, a boy was denoted *adolescens* once he began to work more independently and was given greater responsibility as the herder of his father's flocks or the apprentice of another shepherd.[32]

Whereas all writers agreed that the second stage of childhood ended at the age of 12 for girls and 14 for boys, they differed on the question of the conclusion of the third stage. According to Bartholomaeus Anglicus, this period lasted from 14 to 21, and some sources, he adds, extend it to 28 or 30 or 35. Most of the figures are multiples of 7. Isidore of Seville, who considered 28 to be the age of maturity, elaborated on the role of the number 7 in the universe and in the annals of mankind as in the life of man.[33] Vincent of Beauvais also states that the period of *adolescentia*, which ends at the age of 25, is followed by *juventus*.[34] George Duby's research reveals that, in north-western France in the twelfth century, young boys of 15 to about 19, who had not yet completed their military training and become knights, were known as *pueri* or *adolescentes*. Once a young man completed his military training and joined the knighthood, he was known as *juvenis*, and continued to be known thus until he acquired his own fief or took a wife, even up to the age of 30. Only as a married man did he become a *vir* (man) in the eyes of the chroniclers. The term *juventus*, therefore, denoted a certain age-group but also a specific socio-economic and familial situation: it was intended to describe the young and less young, bachelors without land-holdings whose economic and family situation determined their way of life – the search for a feudal seigneur who would accept them into his ranks, and for tournaments, adventure, drinking, and merrymaking in company.[35] These young errant knights, some of whom at least were bachelors against their will, since they had not yet acquired a fief (or taken a wife who brought a dowry with her) were enthusiastic exponents of the ideal of courtly love – the love between a married woman and a young bachelor – since it was germane to their condition and aspirations.[36] According to Dante, in *Convivio, adolescenzia* ended only at 25. Only at this age did the rational element in the human soul reach its full development, and hence only from this age on was a man's judgment complete. This being so, a young man under 25 could not carry out certain actions without a guardian. After *adolescenzia* came the period of *gioventute*, lasting until 45.[37] For Dante, the term *gioventute* (corresponding to the Latin *juventus*) denotes both a stage in the spiritual and intellectual development of an individual and the stage of full legal independence, the former providing justification for the latter. In fixing 25 as the age of full maturity, Dante was following in the wake of Roman law, according to which only at this age was a young man freed of legal guardianship in civil matters. In the Middle Ages, it was only from this age that a young man was permitted to take part in the political life of Italian towns. It is also possible that, in dating the commencement of adulthood at 25, Dante was also taking into account the fact that the sons of Italian town-dwellers, similarly to the sons of the nobility and the peasants throughout Europe, did not generally attain economic independence before this age (although it should be recalled that some of them did not achieve this condition even after 25).

Whatever term medieval authors used in order to denote full adulthood, they indubitably found it difficult to determine with precision the age at which a young man reached this stage (irrespective of whether he was known from the beginning of this stage as *juvenis* or *vir*). This is not only because young men from the same social stratum became financially independent at different ages. Age was, in fact, one of the criteria for bestowing various positions and powers, but the age at which a young man was entitled to act independently in certain spheres or to serve in various posts varied greatly. In essence, there was no uniform age of maturity in the Middle Ages. The minimum age for marriage, the ages at which a man could do as he chose with his inheritance, sue, or give evidence in civil or criminal cases, and bear full legal responsibility, take up ecclesiastical posts, become a monk, or serve in a lay public position – these ages were not the same.[38] The right to manage one's assets independently varied according to the type of asset involved. The law differed with regard to peasant land leased from an estate-owner, land under full ownership, urban property, or a fief. In England, for example, the heir to land held by socage was released from guardianship and entitled to realize his inheritance at the age of 15; urban property was released to an heir from the age when he was able to count money and to distinguish true from counterfeit coins, or to measure cloth (usually at 15), or, in the case of a fief, only from the age of 21.[39] The age at which a young man reached independence and full accountability in civil matters varied from region to region. The age of full criminal responsibility varied from region to region and according to the crime. Historians have often noted that, in the Middle Ages, childhood in the western world was a briefer period than today. This is undoubtedly true. Children in peasant society and in the urban labouring class began to work younger, and were considered to be a significant factor in the labour-force at an earlier age. The training of children who were to become knights, merchants, priests, and monks began at an early age, and girls married early. On the other hand, however, not everyone achieved financial independence at an early age; the period of apprenticeship and study in certain occupations was protracted, and, as is clearly evident from the different definitions of adulthood, the young were acknowledged by society to be adults at a relatively advanced age, by no means earlier than would happen today. Among the learned jurists who followed Roman law, some asserted that a son was not released from the authority (*potestas*) of his father until the latter granted him emancipation, until the son was appointed to some particularly elevated position, or unless the father was banished in perpetuity.[40] And authors of didactic works and theologians recognized that the period of dependence and education of a human being (the sole living creature equipped with moral perception and intellect) was longer than that of all other creatures.[41]

In discussing the first stage of childhood, *infantia*, writers refer to both boys and girls. In analyses of the *pueritia* stage, they usually devote separate sections or chapters to boys and girls, but emphasis is on education of the former. In discussions of the third stage, on the other hand, which in girls commenced at 12, the proportion devoted to girls is much smaller, and they are almost overlooked in discussions of problems of transition to full adulthood. Girls could inherit in all strata of society, but, almost without exception, boys took precedence. In secular society girls were not accorded higher education or protracted vocational training. They were also barred from serving in public office (unless they inherited a fief which involved rulership of some kind), and the secular church was also barred to them. Those who married usually did so at an early age, at least earlier than those males in the same social class who took wives, and on marriage they forfeited the full independence in civil matters which they had enjoyed since reaching adulthood. Those earmarked for the monastic life entered convents at a very early age. The transition from childhood to married life with all the responsibility and duties it entailed was very rapid, without the transitional stage undergone by young men from the nobility and urban class before they married and settled down. Even the problem of development of the rational element in the human soul which engaged the attention of Dante was of interest to him only where men were concerned. It was no accident that authors felt no need to attend at length to girls when discussing *adolescentia* and the transition to full adulthood. The criteria which determined maturity for young men did not apply to young women, and the significance of adulthood differed for men and women.

The present work is concerned with the first two stages of childhood, and does not contain a chapter on the third stage, *adolescentia*, which (according to some writers) ended only at 35. We refer only to the transition from the second to the third stage and to several of its characteristic features in various social strata. The problem of 'youth', 'youth groups' (of men alone, and in the Late Middle Ages),[42] relations between parents and adult offspring, and the generational conflict in medieval society, studies in the third stage, and theories on methods of transmitting knowledge in this stage, these deserve a separate volume. The present work does not attempt to describe childhood in the Middle Ages according to any particularly psychological model of personality development. But in order to comprehend and elucidate what is revealed by historical sources, Erikson's model has been followed. This seemed almost to be required in the light of the similarity in division into stages. In clarifying the psychological significance of certain phenomena in childrearing and education in the Middle Ages, I have also had recourse to other psychologists' interpretations of corresponding phenomena in contemporary society or other societies.

Piaget and Erikson point to additional indications to those cited by medieval sages for each stage in childhood, and the distinctions they draw are, of course, more subtle and sophisticated. (With regard to infancy, it should be noted that modern theory now tends to greater differentiation than Piaget did and recognizes the interdependence of emotional, personality, and motivational functions.)[43] However, medieval scholars did not perceive the child as differing from the adult in size alone or in composition of bodily humours.[44] They, too, acknowledged the existence of distinct features of childhood at all its stages, and also recognized a process of progressive development of the logical constructs, even if they did not formulate their convictions in these terms. And they, too, perceived termination of stages at 2 to $2\frac{1}{2}$ years, at 7, and at adolescence.

3   A child is born

From the twelfth century, with the burgeoning of the worship of the Holy Mother and Child, certain images became universally familiar: Mary heavy with child, and St Elizabeth, pregnant with John the Baptist; Mary immediately after the birth of Christ, Mary and Elizabeth holding their infants and smiling at them. Through popular literature and drama, and mainly through painting and sculpture, these sacred maternal archetypes were known to all strata of society. At the same time, it was well known that childbirth was hazardous for both mother and child. The authors of medieval medical works were aware of the difficulties and risks of childbirth and attended to them in their writings. Preachers who exhorted offspring to honour their parents referred to the sufferings and dangers to which mothers were exposed in pregnancy and delivery.[1] Those writers who advocated virginity and scrupulously warned young girls of the tribulations of marriage and raising children elaborated on the uncleanness of conception, the suffering and ugliness of pregnancy, and the agonies and mortal risk of childbirth.[2] The priests were instructed to ensure that the pregnant women in their parishes attended confession and received the Eucharist before giving birth.[3] A number of saints, like Antony of Padua, St Margaret, and St Dorothy, were regarded as the patron saints of pregnant women, and midwives encouraged women in labour to pray to them or to the Holy Mother to help them in their delivery. There were special benedictions in the Church for the 'pregnant woman' and 'the foetus in her womb'.[4] Mention is sometimes made in literature of pregnancy and the hazards of childbirth, and the actual delivery is sometimes the tragic or positive dramatic peak of the narrative. According to Wolfram of Eschenbach's epic poem in German, *Parzival*, for example, word of the death of her husband reached Parzival's mother in the eighteenth week of her pregnancy when the foetus was already moving in her womb. It is her unborn child, 'seed of his [the husband's] life, which our mutual love gave and received', who deters her from killing herself in her grief. When her time comes, she gives birth surrounded by her female companions. Because of the size of the infant, the delivery is difficult and she has a brush with death. Another heroine of the same poem, Parzival's maternal aunt, Schoysiane, dies in giving birth to her daughter.[5] The Danish ballad 'Redselille og Medelvold' ('Birth in the Grove') tells of two lovers who flee after the girl's parents learn of her pregnancy. The birth-pangs begin while they are *en route*, and the girl dies in childbirth.[6] Conversely, one finds in the sources reflections of the joy and hopes of the couple during the wife's pregnancy. In the fourteenth century Giovanni Morelli recorded in his diary that he had preserved in his memory the date, place, and way in which his son was conceived, and describes the joy he experienced in touching his wife's belly and feeling the movements of the foetus, and their anticipation and hopes as the birth approaches.[7]

BIRTH

In writing of birth and midwifery, and in discussing gynaecology and other medical issues, the authors of Latin medical treatises in the Central Middle Ages cited Greek and Roman medical scholars: Hippocrates, Galen, and Soranos of Ephesus, as well as the Moslem medical scholars of the ninth to twelfth centuries, such as Albuckasis, Hali Abbas, Rhazes, and Ibn Sina, and, in particular, the writings of Arib ibn Să id of Cordova. They discussed female diseases, conception, pregnancy, barrenness, and its causes, miscarriages, infant care, and birth itself. However, there are very few instructions aimed at guiding the midwife in her task. Although some of the encyclopedias devote relatively extensive space to gynaecology, they include no discussion of birth itself. The work called *De Passionibus Mulierum Curandarum* (On the Cure of Women's Ailments), which for a long time was attributed by scholars erroneously to a woman author, Trotula of Salerno, discusses at length irregular menstruation, cessation of menses as a cause of failure to conceive, barrenness in general, symptoms of pregnancy, difficult deliveries, physical problems arising after childbirth, pain and diseases of the vagina and the womb, and methods of infant care, and treatment of diseases unconnected with gynaecology. But, even in this work, instructions on delivery are also limited. This failure to discuss childbirth itself stems from the fact that the authors had no personal experience of the subject, and found little data in the works of Greek, Roman, and Moslem writers. According to the classical and Moslem medical tradition, physicians were not trained in obstetrics, and deliveries were carried out only by midwives. One guidance on the subject, for example, is confined to the statement that if the birth is natural – that is to say, if the infant is born head first – there is no need for manual intervention. If it is in any other presentation, however, the midwife must try to turn it by hand. Moreover, the vagina and cervix of the woman in childbirth should be rubbed with oil to expedite the delivery. Another author, who knows that in a natural delivery the infant should emerge head first and face down, confines himself to advising that the mother be made to sneeze and that an agrimony plant be tied to her thigh to expedite the delivery. The view of medical sages that childbirth was a matter for women and hence should be discussed only in very general terms is clearly reflected in the remarks of one of the Late Medieval writers. After very brief mention of the difficulties of delivering twins or triplets, he adds 'and since this matter requires attention on the part of the woman there is no point to studying it at length'. Bartholomaeus Anglicus writes 'This is the skill of women to help the mother to deliver as easily as possible.' At the same time, we learn from the sources of some scholars who discussed proper delivery methods. From the statements by Albertus Magnus (thirteenth century), who stressed the need to train midwives, we learn that he acknowledged their professional skills if not from actually being present at deliveries, then from contact with midwives and talks with them about their profession.[8] From the Late Middle Ages, there was a gradual increase in works in the vernaculars dealing with women's diseases and with obstetrics. Some were translated from Latin (or at least contained texts translated from Latin – usually one of Trotula's versions or Musico's text); others were composed in the vernacular, apparently also by women. They were aimed at midwives, healers, and literate women in general, to enable them to treat themselves and their companions without recourse to the help of a male physician. In some of these writings, which were also based on observation and experience, one finds more detailed guidance on childbirth itself than in the Latin writings. The work known as *An English Trotula*, for example, mentions sixteen possible complications and unnatural presentations such as a large head presented forward which does not pass through the birth canal, commencement of emergence before full opening of the cervix, width presentation, breech presentation, etc. Apart from instructions to shift the child or turn it over in order to return it to the proper presentation, and to oil the vagina and cervix, the authors also propose producing vapour by boiling a herb near these parts of the body, and placing on the genitals bandages soaked in liquids extracted from various plants, or preparing a bath in which various herbs have been steeped. If the head of the infant was too large to pass, the midwife was instructed to endeavour to expand the cervix. The authors also listed indications that the foetus had died *in utero*: lack of movement in the uterus, contraction of the nipples, chills, bad breath, sunken eyes, lack of sensation in the lips and the face as a whole. In order to cause expulsion of the dead foetus, the authors propose use of vapours, introduction of liquids into the uterus, baths of various herbs, and various potions. If all these efforts failed, the midwife was instructed to extract the dead foetus from the uterus with a hook with the aid of a mirror. If it could not be extracted whole she was to remove it in parts. If the mother died and the foetus was still alive, it was the obligation of the midwife, according to both the authors of medical works and the synodal decrees, to make an incision in the left side of the corpse with a razor and to extract the living infant. In one of the manuals for priests, advising them to instruct midwives to carry out this operation in order to save the life of the child, the author adds that, if the midwife lacks the courage to do this herself, she should summon a man to her aid lest the child be lost through her fault.[9]

If the delivery was spontaneous without special difficulties, so much the better, but, in the event of any complication, the midwife could do very little, even if she was a townswoman who had been well trained. Manual intervention might, at times, help to shift the child into a normal position for delivery, but, to the same degree, there was a chance that it might be twisted further out of position, creating the risk of detachment of the placenta from the wall of the uterus or pressure on the umbilical cord, which could prove fatal. There was also a strong danger of infection for the mother in cases of manual intervention, particularly when a hook was used to extract the dead child, not to mention the immediate danger of haemorrhage in these cases. Caesarean operations were apparently only carried out when the mother had died during delivery and an attempt (as outlined above) was made to save the child. Means of easing the suffering of a woman during a protracted delivery were almost non-existent.[10] Many mothers died in childbirth and many infants died in the course of delivery. Some 20 per cent of all married women who died in Florence in the years 1424, 1425, and 1430 died in childbirth. In English ducal families in 1330–1479, some 36 per cent of boys and some 29 per cent of girls died before the age of five.[11] There are no figures to indicate how many died during the delivery or immediately *post partum*, but the number was undoubtedly high. Since it is highly feasible to assume that the mortality rate among infants in the Middle Ages was no lower than in the sixteenth to eighteenth centuries, and perhaps even higher, the more accurate demographic data extant from the later period can serve as a guideline to the mortality rate among both mothers and infants in the Middle Ages. The demographers estimate that some 25 out of every 1,000 women died in childbirth in England in the sixteenth and seventeenth centuries, and some 200–300 out of every 1,000 infants died before the age of 5. According to a study by Lebrun, out of every 1,000 infants in eighteenth-century France, 280 died before the age of 1, and only 574 out of every 1,000 reached the age of 5. In periods of famine and plague, the number was even higher in all countries. From an additional study of several English parishes in the sixteenth century, we learn that some 50–60 per cent of all infants who died before their first birthday died in their first month and some 30 per cent during delivery.[12]

In view of the high mortality rate and the limited medical means in that period, it was only natural that women in childbirth, midwives, husbands, and relatives appealed to divine aid through special prayers, or vows to visit the shrines of saints and bring offerings to the churches in which they were buried, and also relied on charms and incantations. Apprehensive pregnant women often went on pilgrimages to the shrines of saints before the anticipated delivery date, or asked to be anointed with consecrated oil, and amulets were prepared for the event itself. The risks of pregnancy were particularly high in the case of women who suffered from some disease, particularly deformities of the spine, and what was known at the time as ydropsis – a general swelling of the tissues – or anaemia.[13] One of the prayers customarily recited three times at the bedside of the woman in labour was the opening of the Athanasian creed ('quicumque vult'). Also popular was the incantation 'O infant, whether living or dead, come forth because Christ calls you to the light.'[14] If the woman in labour was a member of the high nobility, the local priest sometimes recited a special prayer for her well-being.[15] Among the most popular talismans were 'birth girdles' and precious stones. The origin of the custom of using belts lay in the pre-Christian era, and in England it was known from the time of the Druids. Some of these girdles were handed down in families from generation to generation. Some were acquired as relics of saints. And many religious houses kept such girdles for use in childbirth. As for precious stones, Jews, Moslems, and Christians alike believed that the eaglestone (*aetities*), attached to the thigh of a woman in labour, would draw out the child, whether alive or lifeless.[16] The use of amulets and incantations during childbirth did not disappear from Western Europe and both Catholics and Protestants continued to use them until the nineteenth century, when significant changes occurred in standards of hygiene and in medical science, and obstetrics became one of the branches of academic medicine.[17] In the Late Middle Ages (and later as well), midwives were sometimes accused of causing the death of the child.[18] Midwives were also considered likely to engage in witchcraft, and, of the women charged with witchcraft, some were midwives who had failed in their efforts.[19]

We have mentioned the appeals to the aid of saints. Since people tended to seek their help in order to cure or banish afflictions which they were powerless to deal with alone, very many of the miraculous acts attributed to saints related to opening the womb of barren women or saving mothers and children during delivery. One can find very few saints whose recorded miracles do not include response to the appeal of childless couples and the saving of mother and infant. Just as special prayers were said for pregnant women and their unborn children, there were special incantations and masses for barren women. Childlessness was quite common. According to a study of English ducal families in the fourteenth to fifteenth centuries, some 16 per cent of the males and 17 per cent of the females in these families whose marriages lasted throughout the age of fertility of the couple had no progeny. Among the labouring classes, it seems that in many cases women suffered from temporary infertility as a result of the cessation of menses caused by a starvation trauma or due to malnutrition or strenuous work.[20] Those who appealed to saints for succour (childless couples,[21] midwives, pregnant women, and their families) made a vow to go on pilgrimages to the shrines of saints and to give offerings if the woman conceived or if the mother and child were saved. Of the childless couples, some vowed that any son or daughter born to them would be dedicated to the religious life. It would appear, therefore, that, although certain reservations were expressed with regard to procreation (mainly by churchmen, but sometimes by laymen as well), people who married wanted children of their own. Apart from the yearning for children, nobles wanted to continue their line; prosperous town-dwellers wanted an heir to their property and peasants wanted additional labour for their farms. If people had not wanted children, they would not have sought the aid of physicians and various kinds of healers, and employed amulets, incantations, and other means (including stealing the Host from the altar in order to bring it to the barren woman), nor would they have appealed to the saints to cure barrenness and to save new-born infants. Failure to procreate could disrupt the marital life of a couple, and the misery and the helplessness which childlessness caused sometimes led to the levelling of charges of witchcraft against people, particularly women, believed to have caused impotence or infertility. In literature, we often find descriptions of the desire of a childless couple for a child, their prayer, their suffering, and their eventual joy when a child is born to them.[22]

The authors of medical works acknowledged that a man too might be infertile, but, in theological writings and popular belief, infertility was considered, primarily, to be the failure of the woman. A woman who did not take the veil but never gave birth had failed in the central function assigned to her by nature according to Divine will. According to Thomas Aquinas, a woman who was spared the penalty of 'In sorrow shalt thou bring forth sons', imposed on all women because of the Original Sin, suffered from the flaw of barrenness more heavily than did other women from the pangs of childbirth.[23]

The few women who gave birth in hospitals included the most poverty-stricken, who were widowed while pregnant, and, in particular, women who conceived outside wedlock (just as with the sick in general, it was only the poorest and the homeless who were treated in these institutions, which were houses of refuge rather than hospitals in the modern sense of the word). In some hospitals in various European countries in the thirteenth to fifteenth centuries, beds were allotted for deliveries.[24] Most women, however, gave birth at home. Some did so without a midwife with the help of female relatives and neighbours, and assistance to a newly delivered mother, like despatch of food to poor mothers, was considered an act of charity.[25] Other women, particularly in towns, were assisted by midwives. In the tale of the good deeds committed by a certain saint in his lifetime, it is related how he passed by the house of a woman in labour who was alone and heard her cries. He hastened to bring her a midwife, and she was delivered safely.[26] Women of the nobility or the prosperous middle class, in all the countries of Europe from England and Germany to Italy and Spain, were often attended by several midwives.[27] One of the authors of tracts in praise of virginity considered it contemptible even to require the 'indelicate skills of old women' (namely, midwives) whose aid the woman in childbirth could not forgo.[28] During many deliveries the father was in the vicinity. It was he who made a vow to the saint when the situation was desperate, and it seemed that mother or child or both were close to death, and expressed his deep concern for the fate of the two, or pain and sorrow at their death.[29] In rural areas, in families living in isolated hovels with neither midwives nor even neighbours nearby, it was the husband who assisted his wife during the delivery.[30] Childbirth was undoubtedly considered a most important event, and, within the limitations of the means and the know-how at their disposal, people did all they could for the mother and child.

An illustration in an English fifteenth-century manuscript depicts a woman in labour pulling on a rope tied to a beam above her bed. Women also apparently gave birth while seated on a stool known as the 'birth-stool', which had been recommended by Soranos of Ephesus. The authors cautioned as to the size of the empty space at its bottom which should be neither too wide nor too narrow. In the fourteenth century, the stool apparently evolved into a chair with back and armrests.[31] What were the characteristic situations in which the aid of the saints was evoked? Many women ceased to feel the movement of the foetus *in utero* and, fearing that it was lifeless, appealed to saints.[32] Many other appeals were made when a delivery was difficult and protracted – 2, 3, 6, 7, 9, 15, and even 25 days[33] – or so, at least, the writers claim. The mother was sometimes so weakened by labour that she was unable to summon the strength required for the final effort. If she was a young girl, the authors sometimes attributed her difficulties to her age, in line with contemporary medical beliefs. The authors of medical works believed that sexual intercourse at too early an age not only caused the birth of deformed infants, but also placed the young mother at particular risk.[34] In breech deliveries, which were particularly dangerous, appeals were also made to saints. If the infants survived such a delivery or were 'restored to life' this was attributed to miracles.[35] Surgeons were summoned only when there was no alternative but to operate, when the foetus died, or when the mother had died or was dying. People greatly feared surgery, rejected it whenever possible, and preferred to seek the aid of saints. In one case in which the foetus was lying in horizontal position in the uterus, and only one of its arms had emerged while the rest of the body was unable to advance, a surgeon was summoned by the father, to be ready to extract the child by surgery (*incisio*) in the event that the mother died. In another case, the infant died *in utero* and the surgeon was called to extract it 'with an iron instrument'. The fact that it was eventually extracted without surgical intervention (after a relic of the saint was placed on the mother's body) was considered a miracle.[36] The mother of one of the saints died while giving birth to him, and he was removed from her womb by incision by the midwife alone, no surgeon being available.[37] Only very rarely were academic physicians (*medici, physici*) summoned to the aid of the women from the nobility during difficult confinements.[38] They were undoubtedly capable of doing no more than were the midwives and surgeons.

Medical supervision during pregnancy was non-existent, and, even if it had been available, it is unlikely that physicians would have been capable of diagnosing complications. Many women miscarried. In the labouring classes, the miscarriage was often caused by strenuous work in general and the carrying of heavy loads in particular. It was not only the authors of medical works who discussed the precautions the pregnant woman should adopt to prevent a miscarriage. The priests were also instructed to inform the women in their flock of the risk of miscarriage through over-strenuous work during pregnancy, and the men of the hazards of sexual intercourse during pregnancy. It is to be doubted whether women of the labouring class could, in fact, abstain from hard work during pregnancy (and one of the authors of didactic works comments on how poor women continued to work hard during pregnancy), but they wanted their children and feared miscarrying. The records of the Inquisition tribunal at Pamiers refer to two women, one a noblewoman and the other a peasant, who expressed concern as to the fate of the infants in their wombs: the noblewoman when she was urged to leave her home and join the Cathars; the peasant woman when she crossed the river by boat. According to the latter, everyone feared drowning, 'and I particularly, since at the time I was with child'.[39] Among the women who miscarried, some appealed to saints during the next pregnancy to forestall another miscarriage. In one case, a woman appealed to a saint in his lifetime. He did not perform a miracle but gave her spiritual support. This woman miscarried or gave birth to dead infants five times and considered this a punishment for some sin she had committed. The saint heard her story, offered her some of his food and drink, and ordered her to go to the priest and confess her sin. When her time came, she was delivered of a healthy son.[40] In cases where the survival of the child is attributed to a miracle or its 'restoration to life' is described, the descriptions are sometimes realistic and touching. Thus, for example, one tale relates how a certain woman, for six years, gave birth to dead infants. When she again experienced a difficult confinement, the midwives feared that this time as well the new-born child would die, but, after prayers were recited and vows made, he was seen to move, his tiny chest rose, his tiny mouth opened, and he began to breathe, and after half an hour or so began to cry like all new-born babies.[41]

PRIMARY CARE

The authors of medieval medical works, like those of the classical world, recommended creating for the new-born infant conditions as similar as possible to those prevailing in the womb. An early fourteenth-century work, known as *De Regimine Sanitatis*, attributed to Arnold of Villanova, surveys various methods of infant care, and praises those who ensure a gradual transition from the conditions of the womb. He writes of the practice in Gaul of placing the new-born child on straw and rubbing him gently with straw, and adds that this custom is praiseworthy if carried out with lukewarm rather than cold straw.[42] Another practice praised by the author is placing the infant in its mother's arms after it has been swaddled in warm cotton or wool fabric. The writer stresses that the temperature of the fabric should be as close as possible to that of the womb, since any sudden change is harmful to the new-born child.[43] He recommends bathing the child immediately after birth in lukewarm water so as to alleviate the shock of the encounter with the cold air and to cleanse him. Under no circumstances, he adds, should the child be washed in cold water, as was the custom of the barbarians, a condemnation which may also be found in Galen. This belief (shared by Hippocrates) that the transition should be as gradual as possible, in order to protect the infant against the abundant stimuli he encounters upon emerging from the womb, was advocated by most medieval authors. The infant's first cry, which they interpreted as a cry of pain, was attributed to the transition from the dampness and warmth of the womb to the dry, cold outside world.[44] An interesting point is the similarity between the outlook of the authors of medieval medical works and the theories of Dr Leboyer as expounded in his book *Birth without Violence*.[45] Leboyer recommends a series of measures aimed at protecting the new-born child against the intensity of the sensual experiences to which he is exposed immediately after birth; in other words, he suggests a gradual change from the conditions to which the infant has become accustomed in the womb to those of the outside world. Accordingly, he recommends refraining from exposing the infant to strong and dazzling light, noise, and the touch of cold and hard materials (such as metal scales). In order to alleviate the pain caused by rapid entry of air into the lungs, he proposes gradual change-over from aspiration through the umbilical cord to inhaling through the lungs. If the severing of the cord is delayed for several minutes, the infant will receive oxygen in the interim from two separate sources, and the transition from one state to another will be gentle.[46] An illustration from the Late Middle Ages shows a midwife placing an infant, whose umbilical cord has not yet been severed, on his mother's stomach.[47]

Bartholomaeus Anglicus and Aldebrandin of Sienna not only state, like Leboyer, that the infant should be delivered in a semi-dark room, but also assert that up to the age of 7 months, it should not be exposed to strong light which could harm its delicate eyes. The fourteenth-century translator of Bartholomaeus's book adds: 'At this age he requires particularly tender and delicate care.' The authors explain how to sever and tie the umbilical cord with a not-too-coarse woollen thread, note that about four-fingers' breadth should be left, and describe what should be placed on the cut surface. Among other substances, the following can be applied: saliva, the ash of a snail, powdered dragon blood, and more innocuous powders such as cumin or cicely. The umbilicus should be bandaged with cotton cloth soaked in olive oil. Bartholomaeus Anglicus suggests rubbing the infant's body with rose-water and salt, in order to both cleanse the skin and create a pleasant sensation in the limbs. According to Francesco of Barbarino, care should be taken to avoid rubbing the nose and mouth with salt. The work attributed to Arnold of Villanova establishes that the salt should be ultra-fine. He claims that the salt strengthens the limbs against both cold and heat and protects the skin against infection. But since the salt may be painful ('it bites') some sources recommend using oil for the selfsame purpose. The hot and thin infants – those of sanguine or choleric humour (*sanguineus vel cholericus*) should be anointed with oil; for others, salt is more effective. Bartholomaeus Anglicus proposes rubbing the gums of the infant with a finger dipped in honey in order to pacify him and arouse his appetite. After the first bath in tepid water, the child should be bathed regularly and rubbed with oil. Bathing in tepid water is aimed at cleansing the infant and preventing his body from 'changing', i.e. being harmed by too hot or too cold air. The nostrils and ears should be cleaned by introducing the little finger dipped in oil (after the nails have been clipped!).[48]

If the barbarians did in fact practise the custom of dipping the new-born baby in the cold river-water in order to gauge his nature and strengthen his body, it became extinct in the Middle Ages. In the Lives of the saints, one case is mentioned in which the infant was placed in cold water on a cold winter's day, and another case in which water and wine were poured on a new-born child's face. But in both cases this was done in order to ascertain that the child was indeed dead, as it appeared.[49] This was clearly not a prevalent custom. If we consider the means of illumination at the time, the European climate, at least in the northern countries, and the few windows with panes in dwellings, it may be assumed that most women gave birth in shadowy rooms, as the authors recommended, and it is also possible that the room was darkened as was customary in seventeenth-century England. Metal scales were not present in the delivery room. The midwife apparently cared for the infant in the first few days of life and sometimes even participated in the baptism ceremony (the mother could not attend this ceremony, which was held one week after the confinement). Gilbert of Nogent, who was probably born in 1064, relates in his autobiography how his mother underwent a difficult confinement and how both were close to death. After his father had made a vow near the altar of the Virgin Mary that, if the child were born alive and lived to maturity, it would be dedicated to the religious life, the child was born safely. He was a scrawny, pathetic, and weak infant, and nobody believed that he would survive. He was baptized on the same day, and the midwife appears to have attended the baptism.[50] There is no description, however, of the way in which he was nurtured. In any event, anointing with oil and bathing were accepted practices. One learns of the anointing from a rare description of the care of an infant several days old in the biography of Peter Damian, who was later to become one of the important eleventh-century reformers and was canonized. The author tells of the circumstances of his birth and nursing. His parents were poor and had numerous children. The mother, weary of her interminable maternal duties and fearful of the delivery of yet another child, appears to have suffered from pathogenic regression during pregnancy. After the delivery, one of her adult sons came to her and said that it was a disgrace to add another mouth to the many in the little home who would one day fight among themselves over the inheritance. When she heard these words, she cried out in pain that her end had come, sank into a deep depression, and ceased handling the infant. The depression does not seem to have generated infanticidal tendencies, but she totally refused to care for the child. The wife of a priest[51] saved the baby's life when he was almost dead from hunger and cold. She rubbed his body with oil and anointed him with various unguents, spread a fur by the fire, and laid him on it. His circulation was gradually restored to normal, and his body regained its heat and natural colour. She then admonished the mother, condemning her conduct as unnatural and unchristian, swaddled the infant, and left him in his mother's arms. The mother responded and began to nurse him. The neglect of the child was apparently a displacement of her suicidal impulses. It is known that mothers who suffer from depression *post partum* sometimes develop long-term symptoms of pathological anxiety and anger in their conduct towards the child. However, Peter Damian was orphaned of both parents in childhood, and there commenced a period of suffering and new isolation, to which we will return below. According to his biographer, at least, from the moment when the priest's wife placed him in his mother's arms to the day of her death, she cared for him devotedly and lovingly.[52] We learn, from a description of an accident, of the custom of bathing infants in warm water immediately after birth, at least in towns (a practice also recommended by Leboyer). A woman was bathing the new-born child in water which was too hot, and, according to the author, the child died from the bath, and only the intercession of a saint restored him to life.[53] In illustrations and paintings from Italy, France, and Flanders in the fourteenth and fifteenth centuries depicting the birth of Christ, there appear scenes of the bathing of the new-born child in a round basin.[54]

Expressions of anxiety about the survival of the new-born child, even after a safe delivery, can be found in the manual of guidance which the Chevalier de La Tour Landry wrote for his daughters. He wrote that one should not rejoice excessively at the birth of an infant, and certainly should not celebrate the birth with pomp and circumstance. This could appear evil in the eyes of the Lord and cause the death of the child.[55] Is this attitude perhaps a manifestation of the guilt-feelings of parents conscious that their progeny were conceived in sin? Is it prompted by the desire to prepare people to receive with the same equanimity the birth of a child and its death, or is it inspired by some other emotion? It is impossible to answer these questions with certainty.

SONS AND DAUGHTERS

Did men and women express the wish for the birth of a son rather than a daughter? Did parents respond with disappointment to the birth of a girl? Like the writers of ancient Greece and Rome, the authors of medieval medical and didactic works listed signs which, they claimed, made it possible to establish whether a woman was carrying a male or a female foetus. And, together with general advice as to the ideal conditions (such as the alignment of the celestial bodies) for the conception of healthy children with noble qualities,[56] we find words of instruction on how to act in order to ensure the birth of a son or a daughter. Clear and fresh complexion in the pregnant woman, for example, was regarded as a sign that she was carrying a boy – the implication being that the male was superior to the female. A clearer indication of belief in the superiority of the male is reflected in the superstition that the male child lay on the right side of the womb and the female on the left. Thus greater swelling of the left breast or stronger movement of the foetus on the right side of the uterus were also considered signs that the child was male. Some authors believed that over-ardent intercourse between husband and wife could cause the birth of deformed and weak males or of females. This was a direct return to the Aristotelian and medieval theory that a female was an incomplete male.[57] Aegidius Romanus held that the most suitable season for conceiving males was the winter. The midwives suggested to women who wanted sons that they pray mainly to Saint Felicitas. There were, of course, also various potions which allegedly guaranteed the conception of a male. The authors of manuals of guidance apparently conceded that it was possible to desire a daughter. But, since the advice on how to ensure the conception of a girl is directed solely at women, it was evidently assumed that only women could want daughters. The woman who wanted a daughter was instructed to dry the testicles of a hare, and, at the end of her monthly cycle, to ground them into a powder and prepare a potion, which she was to drink before retiring to her bed 'and then go to play with her mate'.[58] Preachers like Bernardino of Siena, who exhorted children to honour their parents as commanded in the Scriptures, promised them many offspring, mainly sons who would some day resemble their fathers. At the same time Bernardino reprimanded fathers who did not welcome the birth of daughters. Giovanni Morelli writes in his memoirs that he was particularly happy when his first child was born, since it was a son.[59] And one of the interlocutors in *I Libri della Famiglia* (The Books of the Family) by Alberti describes how, immediately after their marriage, he and his wife prayed for sons.[60] In the event of the birth of a daughter in urban Late Medieval Italy, relatives and friends would endeavour to console the parents by saying that the girl would certainly be a beauty so that they would not be obliged to give her a large dowry which would be a burden to them.[61] As for royalty, it was not only necessary to comfort and encourage Louis IX of France on the birth of a daughter, but his courtiers were afraid to give him the news; some members of his Capetian dynasty even divorced their wives for bearing only daughters.[62] Wolfram of Eschenbach describes how, when Parzival's mother regained consciousness after the delivery, she and her female companions carefully scrutinized 'the tiny pizzle' between the legs of the infant. And, the author adds, 'He could not be other than fondled and cherished, for he was possessed of the organ of a man.'[63] The saints also sympathized with those women who wanted male children. One woman poured out her heart to a living saint and told him that her husband had begun to hate her. The saint promised her that she would be delivered of a handsome and good son and that then her husband would like her again, and this indeed happened.[64] A woman in Spain, who adored St Dominic and his order, prayed to him for a son, who would some day join the order. When she heard from the midwives that she had borne a daughter, she continued to pray, to complain, and to weep, and a miracle occurred – the female became a male![65] However, a woman who had been delivered of dead infants several times prayed to a female saint and took a vow to go on a pilgrimage to her shrine and to make an offering, irrespective of whether the living child born to her would be a son or a daughter.[66] A noblewoman who underwent a difficult confinement, and bore a healthy daughter after fifteen days of labour, thanked the saint with all her heart.[67] When a girl-child was in mortal danger immediately after birth, or when her parents thought her dead, both often expressed their sorrow and grief and appealed to the saints, as in the case of a male infant.[68] In the Late Middle Ages in Italy, some heads of families proclaimed that daughters brought them no less joy than sons, despite the problem of the dowry, and even though it was customarily said that daughters, unlike sons, did not set up families but disbanded them.

In prosperous merchant families in Florence and in London at the beginning of the fifteenth century, it was usual to record in the family registers the place and exact date of birth of each of the children. One of the interlocutors in Alberti's *Libri della Famiglia* states that these records should be placed in safekeeping together with the most precious family belongings. The day might come when someone might have need of the information contained in them.[69]

BAPTISM

The custom of baptizing an infant several days after birth was inspired by the negative image of childhood. The human infant, having been born in sin as the fruit of the sexual intercourse of his parents, which since the Original Sin have been marked by carnal lust, and as the heir of the sin of Adam and Eve, must be cleansed of the sin of his conception and heritage immediately after his birth. This liberation from sin is achieved by baptism. Through this 'rite of passage' grace and mercy are bestowed on the child and it is accepted into the covenant of the believers. According to St Paul, baptism was intended for the spiritual élite, and underlying it was the belief that man, born in the image of God, is destined and able to rise above Sin and Death. The baptized adult was like one who was dead and is reborn. He was repeating the death and rebirth of Christ, a fact which was symbolized by the descent to the place of baptism, where the body was totally immersed, followed by ascent. He thereby achieved mystic salvation. But from the fourth century on, although the concept of spiritual rebirth was preserved, the emphasis was shifted to the act of absolution of the Original Sin. From the fourth century on, this absolution was bestowed immediately after birth – in other words there was a changeover from adult baptism to infant baptism.[70] St Augustine played a decisive part in the formulation of the concept of the Original Sin as the inherited sin which required baptism of infants. Additional elements in baptism were exorcism – driving out Satan – and leaving a 'character' that marked the soul of the baptized infant for ever through the gift of the Holy Spirit. Baptism also replaced the Jewish circumcision ritual. From the moment the child received the sacrament of baptism, its will was restored, and the path to doing good was open before him. He was not immune to the possibility of sinning after baptism, and still required the grace of the other sacraments, but the baptismal font represented the borderline between the impossibility and possibility of salvation. St Augustine believed that an infant that died without being baptized was condemned to hell-fire.[71] This stand, however, was not adopted, and, from the twelfth century on, it was believed that, although the unbaptized infant would not enter Paradise and would not enjoy eternal bliss and dwell in the Divine presence, neither would it suffer the tortures of hell as would adult sinners. Since its sins were not personal but inherited, it was believed to be consigned to Limbo. Churchmen who were obsessed by a sense of sin, like Gilbert of Nogent, still believed, at the beginning of the twelfth century, that an infant who died unbaptized would suffer the tortures of hell.[72] However, such views were, by then, unusual. Dante described Limbo and its inhabitants in the *Divine Comedy*:

> Here was no sound that the ear could catch of rue,
> Save only of sighs, that still as they complain
> Make the eternal air tremble anew.
> And this rose from the sorrow, unracked by pain,
> That was in the great multitude below
> Of children and of women and of men ...
> These sinned not: but the merit that they achieve
> Helps not, since baptism was not theirs ...[73]

Such churchmen as Innocent III wrote about the human condition, and man's fate from conception to old age. It is doubtful whether they actually envisaged a flesh-and-blood infant. The authors of medical works (including churchmen) discussed infants in different contexts and usually perceived them with different eyes. Parents certainly did not consider the children born to them to be miserable sinners. Moreover, few laymen were closely acquainted with the theology of sin, grace, and baptism. But they too believed that an infant who died unbaptized would not be saved, and the fact that a child died before baptism was regarded as an additional catastrophe to the death itself. Only various heretic sects objected to the baptism of infants in the Middle Ages. Citing the words of Jesus in the Gospels on the innocence of children, they rejected the need for infant baptism, since the children whom Jesus regarded as the symbol of purity had not been baptized. They had not brought sin with them into the world but were born into a world of sinners, and it was incumbent on them to preserve their innocence. Others argued that the infant knew nothing of his need for salvation and hence did not request grace and rebirth, nor did he comprehend what was pledged in his name during the ceremony.[74] The Catholic theologians conceded that the infant had neither intention nor will nor faith, but believed none the less that its baptism was essential. Since his birth had led to his perdition through Adam, it was only through baptism, which was like rebirth, that he could achieve salvation through Christ.[75]

The proper baptism was carried out one week after birth. In the tenth century, there was apparently a gradual transition from immersion of the body in the font to affusion of water over the baptized infant, although in the thirteenth century there were still churchmen who favoured immersing the entire body for fear that when affused, the infant would not be fully baptized; hence this form of baptism did not disappear.[76] In all representations of baptism, the infant is depicted as naked, and this exposure to cold (even though it was recognized that infants required heat) indubitably endangered the health of infants. Nor was the baptism water necessarily clean.[77] Some Cathars, in addition to citing theological arguments against baptism, also claimed that baptism was harmful to the infant, since it cried in the course of the ceremony. According to one of the Cathars, it was baptism in cold water which caused the death of an infant immediately afterwards.[78] A pinch of salt was placed in the infant's mouth and his chest and back were rubbed with oil. The godparents (*compatres, commatres*) could be either strangers or relatives, but neither the father nor the mother of the child. It was the godparents who lifted the child from the font after his baptism by the priest; they answered on behalf of the infant, reciting the Credo in his name, recited the Paternoster, repelled Satan, and vowed to teach the child the basic tenets of the Christian faith and to educate him or her in their spirit when the time came. The exorcism of Satan provided ritual testimony to the faith that the unbaptized infant was in the clutches of Satan. The church prohibited priests from requesting payment for baptism,[79] but this was an accepted practice which was not easily abolished. The confessors' manuals also state that, if the parent could not receive what was due to him in any other way, he should give the priest what he demanded, 'like one throwing a bone to a dog in order to choke him'.[80] In a description of the good deeds of a certain saint who had been an archbishop, it is related that in Cologne he baptized the son of a poor man who had been unable to find a priest to carry out the baptism gratis. The archbishop even provided the white robe in which it was customary to wrap the infant for the ceremony.[81] In prosperous circles it was customary for godparents and relatives to send the mother presents: cakes and sweetmeats, candles and torches for the celebration, rich fabrics and lavishly ornamented trays known as the 'birth tray'.[82] (The satirical literature describes the obligation to entertain the female relatives and friends of the new mother, who came to visit her bringing gifts, as a financial burden and inconvenience for the husband.) From the fact that the Cathar *Perfectus* in Montaillou in the early fourteenth century reprimanded those peasants who, despite their leaning to Catharism, refused to forgo infant baptism and spent most of their money on holding baptism celebrations we learn not only about the religious syncretism among the peasants of the region but also that they considered the birth and baptism of a child as a highly important event, which called for celebration.[83] Despite the cautions of the Chevalier de La Tour Landry, there can be no doubt that in all social strata birth was an important event, the source of joy, and a cause of celebration. (Had this not been so, he probably would not have felt the need to caution his daughters.)

It is also clear that people believed that baptized infants had a better prospect for survival than unbaptized children, and that, after baptism, they would be cured of illness or even of handicaps and would be healthy and handsome, even though these beliefs did not form part of church teachings. Just as they were convinced that a child who had not yet been baptized was more vulnerable to disease and death, they also believed that it could be stolen away by fairies. According to popular beliefs, fairies sometimes stole the newborn child and set their own child in its place, and this was easier to do before the human child had been baptized and named.[84] In addition to baptism, people had recourse to amulets and incantations in order to protect the newborn child. Anxiety as to the fate of the infant in its early days is not confined to the Middle Ages or to other societies where hygienic standards or medical knowledge are undeveloped. Even in the last quarter of the twentieth century in the western world, many suffer similar anxiety. Needless to say, the anxiety and the adoption of all the measures at their disposal to protect the infant indicate the desire of parents to keep their child alive.

When a child was found abandoned, and it was not clear whether it had been baptized, the priest was expected to conduct a 'conditional baptism', adding to the text the words 'If thou hast been baptized, I do not baptize thee.'[85] In the foundlings' homes in Florence, a foundling was baptized if nothing was known about its background and if it was younger than two weeks (it being customary to baptize at several days after birth). It was also customary to tie around the neck of an abandoned infant a bag of salt as a sign that it had not yet been baptized.[86] In the poem known as *Galeran* it is related how a bag containing salt was placed in the cradle of the abandoned girl-child as a sign that she had not yet been baptized.[87] According to the decrees of the synods, it was incumbent on the priest to clarify before the baptism whether the infant was the fruit of legal wedlock, but even if it was revealed to be a bastard whose parents deserved punishment it was obligatory to baptize the child.[88]

A proper ritual of baptism also is sometimes described in literature. In the epic poem, named after its protagonist *Raoul de Cambrai*, mention is made of three baptisms: of Raoul, of Bernier, the illegitimate son, and of Julien, son of Bernier. Raoul is born several months after the death of his father, and hence, despite the joy of his mother and all his father's knights, they act with restraint. However, the baptism occasion is ceremonial. Two barons bear the infant to the baptism in the church, after his mother has wrapped him in a white christening robe (made of precious cloth), with a scarlet wrap above it. He is baptized by the Bishop of Beauvais, his mother's cousin. His paternal uncle is also present, and the child is given his father's name. The baptism of Bernier is mentioned only in brief, since he was illegitimate, and he is not named after his father. Bernier's son, on the other hand, has a distinguished godfather – the seigneur of St Gilles, after whom he is named. But the emphasis in the tale of Julien's christening is on the 'character' marking the soul. Immediately after the baptism, he is taken prisoner by the Saracens and adopted by one of the warriors, who raises him with love and devotion. He himself grows up to be a brave warrior fighting the Christians, and falls prisoner as a result. His father, who is in the Christian camp, recognizes him and releases him, and his godfather declares him his heir. But Julien, who is one of the most positive characters in the poem, feels no gratitude towards the man who adopted him, and it is his father, Bernier, who arranges for the release of the older warrior from captivity. Julien even declares that he could never love his adoptive father and that, when he lived among the Saracens, they were resentful of him for having been born among Christians. The 'character' set on him at his baptism has caused him to feel a stranger among the infidels and has estranged him from his adoptive father, even though he was not raised as a Christian.[89]

The child was also named at the baptism ceremony. Some were named after their fathers or paternal or maternal grandparents, some after a brother or sister, uncle or aunt who had died shortly before their birth; others were given the names of popular saints or of their godparents.[90]

So far, we have discussed the baptism of infants who, at least up to the time of the baptism, were not perceived to be at immediate risk of death. But in light of the high rate of mortality among infants during or immediately after birth, churchmen were well aware of the possibility that the child might not survive until baptized. Explaining the ban on postponement of the baptism of infants, Thomas Aquinas wrote, amongst other reasons, 'that there is danger to their lives, and baptism is the sole succour we can extend to them'.[91] In so saying, he was justifying the custom of conducting the baptism ceremony several days after the infant's death. However, since the danger existed that the child might not live to be baptized, special regulations were formulated in the event that a newborn child seemed unlikely to survive. Such baptism (*in articulo mortis*) could be conducted by any person – laypeople as well, both men and women. Moreover, any person near the dying infant was not only permitted to baptize it, but was obliged to do so as a Christian duty.[92] If the child was born alive, but seemed unlikely to survive, it could be baptized by its father or any other male relative present. On the other hand, if during delivery it appeared that the child would be stillborn, the midwife was permitted to baptize any limb which emerged. In the manuals of guidance for priests based on synodal decrees, the priest was instructed to order the midwives in his parish to carry out this obligation and to keep clean water at hand for emergency baptisms. The midwife should sprinkle water on any limb which emerged from the birth canal and pronounce the following sentence: 'God's creature, I hereby baptize thee in the name of the Father, the Son, and the Holy Ghost.' This could be said in any language and even if the order of the words was not observed, as long as they were uttered with the proper intention, the baptism was binding. According to Thomas Aquinas, it was permissible to baptize an infant even if the head alone was protruding, since the head is the seat of the consciousness. None the less, he also permitted baptism even if only an arm or leg was protruding.[93] If the child survived, its parents brought it to church as soon as it was sturdy enough in order to complete the baptism; the priest anointed it with consecrated oil and exorcised Satan; and the godparents answered on behalf of the child, rejected Satan, and vowed to raise him as a Christian.[94]

Baptism was no less important than was saving the child's life. It will be recalled that, when the mother died in labour, the midwife was instructed to make an incision in her body with a knife: this was in order not only to try and save the child but also so as to baptize him 'For that ys a dede of charyte'.[95] Parents also attributed prime importance to the baptism of their son or daughter. Particularly anxious were those parents who had already suffered the death of an infant before baptism, like a certain father whose previous children had all died at birth before being baptized.[96] In the Lives of the saints we find numerous cases in which parents despaired of the life of the infant, and prayed to a saint that the child be born alive and that they be given respite time to baptize it – 'and let it but be baptized'.[97] If the child lived a few days or even only a few hours and they were able to bring it to church for baptism by the priest, they regarded this as a miracle, and gave thanks to the saint. Even if they did not manage to bring it to church and it was baptized in the delivery room by one of the men or women present, this was still seen as a miracle, since the child 'then ended its life in happiness'.[98] Even if it were not clear that the child was alive, it sufficed for one of the women present to declare that it was breathing for it to be baptized hastily.[99] It was believed that children who were baptized and had had no chance to sin were guaranteed a place in Heaven. Dante allotted them a special place in Paradise and described their singing:

> For these are spirits that were all released
> Ere they had made a true choice, unperplext.
> And by their faces this is manifest
> And also by their voices' childish note,
> If looking heedfully thou listenest.[100]

Medieval preachers, desirous of consoling parents, or reproaching them for excessive mourning for the children they had lost, reiterated the notion that God had acted mercifully toward the children by removing them from this world in childhood.[101] This idea survived in different forms in European Christian culture. The description of the innocent child which had experienced orphanhood and tribulations and was released by death from its suffering and taken to Heaven to enjoy eternal bliss was a recurrent motif in nineteenth-century European literature. Often, as in Gerhard Hauptmann's play *Hanneles Himmelfahrt* (The Ascension of Hannele), we find a realistic description of the child's agonies and an excess of sentiment in the description of its death and path to Paradise.[102]

Perhaps most horrific of all for the modern-day reader is the fact that some of the women who murdered their infants immediately after birth first baptized them. They did so because this was expected of them. The baptism or non-baptism of a child was a weighty factor in the decision whether to punish the infanticidal mother or to pardon her,[103] and it may be assumed that, by internalizing the belief that the baptized infant would go to Heaven, these mothers convinced themselves that they were ensuring the salvation of its soul. The infant who died unbaptized could not be saved; but, according to church teachings, it was to be considered unclean rather than an object of pity. A woman who died in childbirth could not be buried in church, but only in the churchyard. And even there, if her child had died *in utero*, the foetus – conceived in sin, nurtured on menstrual blood, and unbaptized – contaminated the mother, and she could be buried only after it had been extracted from her womb and buried outside the churchyard.[104] Of course, the custom of quarantining a woman after the confinement for fear of defilement was accepted in various cultures. It was prevalent in several primitive societies, in China,[105] in biblical Israel (Deut. 12: 2–5), and endures among Ethiopian Jews to the present day. In medieval Catholic society, the new mother was not isolated after delivery, but was obliged to be 'churched'. At her churching she gave thanks and received a blessing (and Catholic historians emphasize these elements of the ceremony), but was also cleansed of her impurity and received back into the bosom of the church.[106] Ecclesiastical injunctions, intended to draw distinctions between the pure and the impure, as well as church beliefs on the fate of the child who died unbaptized, in contrast to the baptized infant, filtered down to the common people and were internalized. Parents made every effort to ensure that their progeny were baptized, and the fact that they succeeded in baptizing a child before it died was of solace to them. The death of an unbaptized infant not only caused grief but also raised fear, inspired by a combination of the Christian conception as to the infant's fate and archaic customs and beliefs originating in pre-Christian times.

Among the synodal decrees aimed at rectifying flaws in the functioning of parish priests, the clause dealing with the priest's obligation to ensure that deceased members of his flock were given Christian burial makes particular mention of women who died during pregnancy or childbirth.[107] This suggests that parish priests sometimes displayed zeal beyond the official stand of the church, which merely prohibited burial of these women in church, and refused to grant them Christian burial of any kind. Perusal of one of the questions which the priest was supposed to ask confessants (according to Burchard of Worms's eleventh-century *Decretorum Libri Viginti*) indicates that, in his period or at least in earlier times (Burchard used earlier texts), an unbaptized infant was sometimes buried with a stake in its heart. A child who was baptized before death was buried with a chalice of wine in one hand and a chalice containing the Host in the other. The church condemned both practices, but, whereas two years of penance were imposed for the act of driving a stake into the heart of an unbaptized infant (if mother and child died together, they were sometimes both buried with stakes in their hearts), the burial of a baptized infant with chalices in its hands required only ten days of penance.[108] There was good reason for this discrepancy. The significance of the two burial customs differed. The baptized infant was not considered a fearful object. Due to a combination of an ancient pagan custom with ritual artefacts of Christian significance, it was buried with those items which were thought to be of spiritual benefit to him in the next world. The unbaptized infant cast fear into the hearts of the living, and the stake driven into its heart was intended to prevent it from returning to harm them. Dread of the return of the dead and, in particular, of the return of that dead individual who had never belonged to the community of the living is both ancient and universal, but the specific dread inspired by the unbaptized who had no part in the world of the living in the Christian sense was implanted by the church itself. Augustine's inflexible stand was somewhat mitigated in the course of the Central Middle Ages. The unbaptized infant was now consigned to Limbo, but the attitude toward those who died unbaptized still appears to have been dominated by negative images.[109]

4 Nursing

Present-day physicians and psychologists recommend maternal breast-feeding. The composition of the amino acids in mother's milk is more suited to the metabolism of the infant than is that of cow's milk: although the latter contains the same amount of iron as mother's milk, its absorption ratio is lower. Moreover, unlike prepared milk, mother's milk immunizes the infant against a number of diseases. The intimacy of the act of nursing strengthens the bond between mother and child. Conversely, both physicians and psychologists can be heard to state that exertion of social pressure to breast-feed on an unwilling mother can rouse anxiety and guilt-feelings which transform the act of nursing into an unpleasant experience for both mother and child, and disrupt it. In such cases, it is preferable for the infant to take milk from a bottle. The positive reciprocal contact between mother and child, which creates the child's first attachment to another person, and which greatly promotes the development of the child's self-confidence and trust in others, can also be fostered through bottle-feeding.[1] In so far as we know, the institution of wetnurse is now extinct, at least in western society. In the Middle Ages, and in the modern era until the invention of pasteurization, matters were different. The prospects for survival of an infant nurtured on the milk of cows, goats, or sheep were slim. Since this fact was well known, we rarely encounter in the medical literature of the period discussions of infant nutrition based on the milk of she-animals. Only the authors of didactic literature cautioned both mothers and wetnurses against feeding infants on animal milk. Since, like some of the ancient philosophers, medieval authors believed that milk had similar qualities to sperm and influenced the moulding of the personality, they cautioned women against the dangers to both the physical and the spiritual development of the infant inherent in a diet based on the milk of cows, sheep, or goats. Thomas Chobham, in his confessors' manual, writes that pagans used to feed their infants on the milk of wild animals in order to instil in them something of their savagery.[2] Other authors stress that the milk of beasts could not only cause disease, but could also render the child bestial.[3] But despite the fact that this view was accepted, and that the infant which did not receive mother's milk had a slim chance of survival,[4] animal-milk was fed to infants, at least when there was no alternative. The very fact that the warning had to be issued indicates that the authors had encountered the practice. Innocent III accused Jewish women of selling milk to Christian women which they themselves were unwilling to feed to their own children.[5] Irrespective of whether Jewish women did in fact sell milk to Christians, the reference to the selling of animal-milk for infant consumption indicates that it was used for that purpose. In the foundlings' homes, infants of only a few days old were apparently fed on pap diluted with the milk of she-animals.[6] The Life of Saint Gilbert relates how he gave his blessing to a barren woman. After the blessing bore fruit and she was delivered safely of a child, the saint rejoiced in her happiness and sent her a cow to enable her to feed her child.[7] Giorgio Vasari tells of a two-month-old baby whose mother died in the plague and who was fed solely on goat's milk.[8] A diet of pap based on animal-milk or water was apparently more prevalent in some regions than in others. In fifteenth-century southern Bavaria it was habitually fed even to infants of several months old, while in adjacent regions maternal breast-feeding was the norm.[9] The risk of stomach upsets and disease was undoubtedly greater in towns than in rural areas where it was easier to obtain fresh milk. We know of the existence of a special utensil for feeding animal milk to infants – a small cow's horn was planed smooth, a small hole was pierced at the end, and a kind of two-fingered glove of parchment attached, through which the infant drank.[10] In the epics of the period, one of the recurrent motifs is the miraculous appearance of a goat, she-deer, or unicorn whose milk is used to feed an infant when no woman is available to breast-feed it.[11] On the other hand, one finds evidence of total dependence on mother's milk in one of the Icelandic sagas: the tale of Thorgisl. The infant's mother is murdered with her child in her arms. Although she is lifeless, the child continues to nurse at her breast. After burying the mother, the father spends the long night hours gazing at the baby, and eventually decides to act in order 'to prove his manhood'. He cuts his nipple with a knife until blood gushes forth. When the infant begins to suck, water gushes forth and then milk, and it drinks its fill.[12] The story reflects not only total dependence on mother's milk in a geographical region where people lived by hunting and fishing in isolated huts, without domestic animals, but also paternal love and readiness to make a sacrifice for his child. We also discern therein an echo of the contemporary medical belief on the connection between milk and blood. According to this belief, menstrual blood, which during pregnancy served to nurture the foetus, was transformed after the birth into milk to feed the new-born infant. It reached the breasts through the arteries and veins, and was transformed there into milk. Purification of the blood was the function of the breasts.[13] However, although the writers claim that God gave women breasts only in order to feed their children,[14] not all infants nursed at their mother's breast. Some were fed on animal-milk and others, at least in the upper classes, were fed by wetnurses.

WETNURSES

Wetnurses are mentioned in many types of medieval sources: in medical and didactic works, in the writings of preachers and authors of confessors' manuals, in chronicles, in the Lives of saints, in memoirs, in ordinances fixing the maximum wage for workers, in population records drawn up for tax-collection purposes, in ecclesiastical legislation aimed at restricting the contacts between Jews and Christians, in epic poems, courtly romances, and satirical literature. However, the problem arises that these sources do not supply statistical data, and one cannot determine, on this basis, the number of wetnurses or the number of infants handed over for wetnursing within the total population in a certain place at a given time in the Middle Ages, as one can with regard to the eighteenth century. It is known, for example, that in eighteenth-century Hamburg there were 4,000–5,000 wetnurses in a population of 90,000. The data for Paris in the last quarter of the eighteenth century are even more accurate. The population of Paris was then 800,000–900,000. The number of infants born annually was some 21,000. Of these, 1,000 were breast-fed by their mothers, and some 1,000 had live-in wetnurses. All the remainder (namely 19,000) were handed over to wetnurses who nursed them in their own homes. Some 2,000–3,000 were given into the care of wetnurses who lived in the suburbs of Paris, while the remainder were despatched to remote villages.[15] There is no possibility of obtaining similar statistics for the Middle Ages, with the possible exception of Late Medieval Florence, but one can learn from the sources the class-origin of the women who made use of the services of wetnurses, the conditions under which the children were handed over to the wetnurses, and the causes of this phenomenon.[16]

Authors of medical works, preachers, authors of confessors' manuals, and, almost without exception, authors of secular didactic works favoured maternal nursing. Like modern physicians and psychologists they recommended maternal breast-feeding for both physical and emotional reasons: 'The most suitable milk for an infant is that of his own mother.'[17] Mother's milk is considered the best for the physical development of the child, and nursing by the mother is the most desirable form of nutrition, because of the special relationship established between mother and child. As Bartholomaeus Anglicus writes, 'She conceived him in lust, she bore him in suffering, she loves him and kisses him.' Because of her love, her nursing is the best of all, and helps to reinforce maternal emotion.[18] This view finds expression in various forms in the writings of most of the authors. The art of the fourteenth to fifteenth centuries, particularly in Italy, repeatedly depicts the Holy Mother nursing her child – the ideal image for all mothers in this world. The authors caution against the milk of wetnurses who are sick in body and corrupt in spirit. Their milk endangers the physical and emotional well-being of the child, since both their sickness and their negative traits will be passed on to it through the milk. But, despite these convictions, all the writers dwell at length on the ideal wetnurse and aim most of their advice at her. Vincent of Beauvais, in quoting the Moslem medical sages, discusses the ideal age for wetnurses; perusal of all the opinions he cites suggests that she could be of any age between 15 and 40. However, according to most of the western writers, she should not be younger than 25 and not older than 35. She should not begin nursing immediately after her own confinement, since the milk was not yet at its best at that time, or too long after the birth: about two months *post partum* was considered the ideal time. Before hiring a wetnurse, parents should clarify that she had had a healthy delivery and did not have a tendency to miscarry. She should be healthy and clean, with fresh complexion and large breasts. During the nursing period, she should refrain from eating spicy and sour foods such as onions, colworth, or leeks. If her milk-supply dwindled, she should be given a drink consisting of a blend of pulses, of rice-flour, milk, and sugar, with the addition of several fennel seeds. Her normal diet should be determined by the consistency of her milk, whether fat or lean. Since sexual relations during the breast-feeding period caused the milk to spoil and dwindle, due to the resumption of the menses, she should abstain totally from intercourse while nursing. Conception during nursing was considered highly dangerous to the nursing infant, since during pregnancy the woman's good blood served as food for the foetus, and only the bad blood remained for milk. The wetnurse should also avoid any anxiety which could cause the recommencement of menstruation.[19] Thus Vincent of Beauvais. Similar instructions, as well as a description of the ideal wetnurse, are given by most authors. Many of them also state that the wetnurse should be a woman of congenial temperament, since her traits will be transmitted to the infant through her milk. Some writers also preferred a wetnurse who had given birth to a son to one who had been delivered of a daughter.[20] In an attempt to reconcile the preference for maternal nursing with the sanctioning of wetnurses, some writers suggested that parents seek a wetnurse as similar as possible in temperament and appearance to the mother, and with similar milk.[21]

The ambivalent attitude to maternal nursing is more striking in the didactic works, and in the writings of preachers and authors of confessors' manuals, than in medical works. The latter, borrowing from the medical sages of the ancient world and the Moslems, reiterated their advice to wetnurses immediately after having lauded maternal nursing. Were it not for the fact that ambivalence towards maternal nursing is evident in other types of writings as well, we might have explained the anomaly as stemming from the authors' simultaneous acceptance of the Christian standpoint, which advocated maternal nursing, and of the views of the Greek, Roman, and Moslem writers who justified the employment of wetnurses. But it transpires that a similar ambivalence marks the works of the preachers and authors of confessors' manuals, who did not cite those medical works. They censure women who refuse to nurse their own infants, but at the same time sanction the hiring of wetnurses. Thomas Chobham not only reproved these women but even defined the refusal to breast-feed as murder. None the less, he concluded by adding 'If the mother cannot carry the whole burden alone, she should nurse and bathe her infant at least when she is able, and thus will not be like one who acts unnaturally and never goes near her child.'[22] In other words, a wetnurse will be present together with the mother. It is necessary to attempt to explain this ambivalence.

In literature nursing is the symbol of maternity, and, in human memory, the suckling breast is the first symbol of childhood and of contact with the mother. None the less, the wetnurse also makes an appearance in literature, sometimes in the same work which presents breast-feeding as the symbol of the bond between mother and child. Thus spoke and acted Parzival's mother in pregnancy:

> She tore the garments away from her bosom, clasped her soft, white breasts, and pressed them to her red mouth with the wisdom of mother-wit: 'You are the holders of an infant's nourishment. The infant has been filling you in advance ever since I felt him alive within my body.'

And the author adds:

> The lady found satisfaction in seeing that nourishment lying above her heart, that milk in her breasts, and pressing some of it out, the queen said: 'You come from faithful love . . .'

After giving birth,

> The queen took those little brownish-pink buds of hers – I mean the tips of her little breasts – and pressed them into his tiny mouth, for she who had borne him in her womb was also his nurse, like the most elevated of queens, who gave the breast to Jesus.[23]

In these excerpts breast-feeding is undoubtedly the most perfect expression of maternity, the Holy Mother serving as the ideal and the source of inspiration. In the religious literature of the Central Middle Ages, writers often borrow images from the sphere of nursing to describe religious experience and ecclesiastical institutions. In their visions nuns and female mystics saw themselves nursing the infant Jesus, and monks and male mystics described Christ as nursing them. Suger of St Denis described the monastery to which he was sent in childhood as a nursing mother.[24] But the remarks of the author of *Parzival* clearly indicate that, in the upper strata of society, maternal breast-feeding was not taken for granted.

One of the symbols of Christ, who saved mankind through the sacrifice of his blood, was the female pelican who nourishes her chicks on her own blood.[25] This symbol recalls the medical theory that milk was purified blood. The nursing mother was somehow associated with Christ and his sacrifice. However, in Raymond Lull's literary work, *Blanquerna*, the eponymous hero is an only son, born after many years of prayer and hope. None the less, immediately after his birth, his parents, prosperous townspeople, bring him a wetnurse, 'healthy in body and of moral conduct'.[26] In the literary works in which the future hero is an illegitimate son,[27] or motherless,[28] a wetnurse is naturally brought to suckle him and raise him. And lastly, in the satirical literature, which is coloured by mockery of and hostility toward women, the wetnurse appears alongside other women. She is the accomplice of the wife in her intrigues against her husband, and complains that she has too much work, and that the lives of wetnurses in other homes are pleasanter and easier. She claims that the wetnurse must sleep, rest, eat, and drink to her heart's content so as to have sufficient milk, and should even receive gifts.[29]

Some sources provide direct evidence for wetnursing as an occupation. Some Christian women were ready to hire themselves out as wetnurses (and some Jews in the Middle Ages were ready to utilize the services of such wetnurses) as we see from the compilation of ordinances issued by bishops from various European countries and by popes, aimed at curtailing the contacts between Jews and Christians, which reiterate the ban on employing Christian wetnurses.[30] Likewise, a decree issued in France in 1350, fixing the maximum wage for workers in the various occupations, includes wetnurses.[31]

From chronicles, journals, Lives of the saints, and tax-collection records in Late Medieval Tuscany we can learn something of the social status of women who had recourse to the services of wetnurses, and the conditions under which infants were handed over to wetnurses – whether the nurse lived in the home of the infant's parents, or cared for the child in her own home. It is clear that wetnurses in medieval society, as in all other societies which utilized this service, were employed by the nobility and the upper echelons of the urban population, and there is no dearth of evidence of this. It is less clear whether the phenomenon was also widespread in the urban middle classes, as was the case in France and Germany in the eighteenth century and even in the first half of the nineteenth. In this period the families of (in the main) bakers, butchers, and silkweavers, where the women worked by the side of their husbands, also entrusted their infants to wetnurses. Nor can one know with certainty whether the practice was particularly prevalent in the Late Middle Ages in general and in Tuscany in particular, or whether it is just the case that more data extant from this region at this period than from earlier periods and other parts of Western Europe.

Generally speaking, the women in the peasantry, which constituted the great majority of the population of Europe, suckled their own children, with the exception of those peasant women who were employed as wetnurses in the homes of the well-to-do, even if their own children were living. The lowest of the low among the women of the village of Montaillou in the Pyrenees, an illegitimate girl named Brune Pourcel, agreed only with great reluctance to the urgings of her neighbour to bring her infant to be nursed by a woman who was visiting the neighbour and had a surplus of milk. The practice of handing over an infant to another woman for nursing was so alien to the villagers that Brune feared that the milk of a strange woman would harm her child. Even in the prosperous sheep-breeding families, like the Pierre family, the mother herself suckled her children. Only the very poorest of the village women, who gave birth outside wedlock, sometimes entrusted their babies to wetnurses, like Raymonde Arsen, who transferred her illegitimate daughter from one wetnurse to another when she changed her place of employment. And, naturally, if the mother fell sick or died, a wetnurse was found for the child.[32] In Saxo Grammaticus's *Gesta Danorum* (History of the Danes), written in the twelfth century, when a peasant woman tries to bind up the wounds of one of the warriors, he dismisses her with contempt, and tells her to go and nurse her daughter, since she knows better how to give suck to her flesh and blood than how to bind the wounds of a stranger.[33] In England in the first half of the seventeenth century, maternal breast-feeding was considered natural in peasant society. Of the girls who gave birth to bastards and who were brought to trial, those who had evaded nursing their illegitimate infants were sentenced to particularly harsh and humiliating whippings (like those who had sinned before, or those who lied as to the father's identity). The justification for the sentence was that she 'hath unmotherly and most unnaturally stopped and dried up her milk by means whereof she cannot nourish and breed up her said child, but must be suckled and brought by another woman'. In another case, it was stated by the judges that the mother had, in unmotherly and unnatural fashion, fled the spot and left the infant unprovided.[34] The judges meted out harsh sentences since, in cases where the mother abandoned her infant, the burden of raising it rested on the parish, but the reasons they gave also indicate that it was customary in peasant society for mothers to suckle their own children. There is no reason to assume that a different practice prevailed in the Middle Ages. A rare illustration to a fourteenth-century manuscript shows a woman sitting at the entrance to her home and suckling an infant. Close by stands her husband, apparently a peasant, holding the infant's twin brother or sister.[35]

Women in the urban labouring class also nursed their own children, again with the exception of those of them who worked as wetnurses in the households of others. According to the statutes of several guilds in Denmark in the Late Middle Ages, nursing mothers were permitted to bring their infants to the social gatherings of the guild, but were banned from bringing older children.[36] In the *Acta Sanctorum* (Lives of the Saints), both in the section of the biography devoted to the childhood of the saint, and in the tales of the miracles attributed to him, numerous wetnurses figure, all of them in the context of employment by noble and prosperous middle-class families. The only case I have found of a lower-class family requiring the services of a wetnurse is that of the family of Catherine of Siena. The father was a cloth-dyer whose wife bore him twenty-five children.[37] Other women from the same social class – the wife of a *magister* (artisan in a guild or clerk of any kind), the wife of a monastery clerk in Naples, or an Englishwoman who had a servantwoman in her house – suckled their infants themselves.[38] In fifteenth-century Florence the practice of putting infants out to nurse was well established – whereas in the fourteenth century it was customary only in the upper class, by the fifteenth century it had spread and reached the middle classes (families where the father was a notary, an established artisan, a reasonably prosperous merchant, or a small landowner)[39] – but the practice did not filter down to the lower classes. Lower-class mothers of future saints are described in the Lives of the saints as having breast-fed their children.[40] It should be recalled that the mother of Peter Damian nursed him herself. Many women from the labouring classes appealed to saints not only when their infants fell sick or were injured in accidents, but also when their milk dried up or when the infant had difficulty in nursing.[41] A poverty-stricken woman whose milk-supply ran out could not find a wetnurse for her child. A man from Bologna, who apparently belonged (together with his wife) to the Franciscan Third Order, found an abandoned girl child in the gateway of a hospital. The child needed mother's milk (the author writes) but his wife was elderly and had long since ceased to give birth. Because of their poverty, the couple could not find a wetnurse for the child they had taken into their home, nor could they find a woman who would agree to nurse it as an act of Christian charity. In the end, he made a vow to the saint, and a miracle occurred. The woman's breasts filled with milk, and she was able to nurse the child ... In another Life a very young girl, who (according to the author) had no milk because of her youth, was unable to hire a wetnurse because of her poverty, and appealed for the aid of the saint.[42]

That noblewoman did not generally nurse their own children can be gauged from the fact that writers see fit to make special mention of those women who chose to nurse, and praise them for their action.[43] However, as noted, there is no lack of direct testimony on wetnurses in the homes of nobles from the twelfth century onward in all of Western Europe, from Sweden to Italy.[44] As in the eighteenth and nineteenth centuries in France, so in Late Medieval Italy the wages of live-in wetnurses were higher than those of wetnurses who took children into their own homes. The children of royalty were sometimes nursed by women from the minor nobility, who (apparently), in contrast to other wetnurses, brought their own infants to the royal residence and suckled both their own and the royal children together. It is related of Alexander Neckham that his mother bore him on the same night in which the future king of England – Richard I – was born. Alexander's mother suckled the prince at her right breast, and her own son at her left breast. In literature as well, the wetnurses of princes are the wives of knights.[45] From the case of the wife of Robert Curthose, Duke of Normandy and son of William the Conqueror, we learn about the way in which women who did not want to nurse their children stopped their milk-supply. The historian, William of Malmesbury, writes that, after the delivery, the midwife bound up the mother's breasts because of the abundance of milk, and she fell sick some time later and died.[46] This method of stopping the milk-flow is still sometimes used today.[47] Prosperous town-dwellers sometimes employed wetnurses in their homes, as did a thirteenth-century goldsmith from Toulouse. Thomas Becket, son of a twelfth-century merchant from Rouen who settled in London, apparently also had a live-in wetnurse.[48] In Italian towns in the Late Middle Ages – Florence and Genoa – as well as in Catalonia, both rural and urban women as well as female slaves were employed as live-in wetnurses. The slave could be hired from her owner if his wife had no need of a wetnurse at the time. The authorities of foundlings' homes and orphanages in Italy usually also hired slaves. If the children of these women did not die shortly after birth, then, almost without exception, their mothers handed them over to foundlings' homes on the orders of their masters.[49]

Other parents put their infants out to nurse. The closer the wetnurse's home to the parental home, the higher her wages. Wetnurses from rural areas who took children into their homes received the lowest wage, sometimes only half as much as the live-in wetnurse. Many of the infants put out to nurse were sent immediately after birth. The fifteen children of the Florentine merchant, Antonio Rustici, in the early fifteenth century, were all sent away immediately after birth. Others, like the children of the notary from Siena, Christophano Guidini, enjoyed a brief period of maternal nursing (two weeks to one month) and were only then sent away.[50] Those women who took in children for wetnursing apparently nursed two children simultaneously – their own and the strange child. Women suckling two children feature in literature as well. In Marie de France's poem *Le Fresne* (The Ash Tree) the monastery keeper finds the abandoned girl-child in the branches of the ash tree, brings her to his daughter who has an infant of her own, and the daughter suckles both babes.[51] The demand for wetnurses in north and central Italy in the early fifteenth century was greater than the supply, and fathers tried to obtain a wetnurse and to sign an agreement with her husband or with an agent even before their infants were born. One of the interlocutors in *I Libri della Famiglia* (The Books of the Family) by Alberti, a husband and father, describing to a young bachelor the responsibility and tribulations of childrearing, speaks *inter alia* of the need to find a wetnurse in good time, and adds 'You know too how rare is a good nurse and how much in demand.' It is characteristic that the bachelor, who has not faced the problem and is free to develop theories, elaborates on the advantages of maternal nursing. He declares that, when he weds, he will not hire a wetnurse unless his wife falls sick or her milk dries up, and he will not do it simply in order to release her from her obligation toward her children and to allow her more leisure time. It is clear, says he, that the mother will rear her child with more devotion, diligence, perseverance, and love than a strange woman who does it for money. Through caring for her child, her love for him will grow.[52] Like writers who praised noblewomen who suckled their own children, Christine de Pisan, daughter of a middle-class Italian family, writes in her *Livre des trois vertus* (Book of the Three Virtues) that her mother loved her so much that she herself nursed her.[53] This suggests that in the urban middle strata of northern Italy in the second half of the fourteen century, where Christine de Pisan spent her early childhood (or perhaps in the noble circles in early fifteenth-century Paris, where she wrote her book), maternal nursing was considered a sign of special love.

As noted, there is less information extant on wetnurses in other European countries, but unquestionably their services were not confined to Tuscany alone. The fact that one of the most vehement opponents of the farming out of children to wetnurses was the thirteenth-century Englishman, Thomas Chobham, indicates that the phenomenon existed in the England of his day. And evidence exists on the presence of wetnurses not only in the homes of the English nobility[54] but also in the households of the prosperous middle class. Margery Kempe, who was to become a mystic, and who was married to a prosperous merchant in fourteenth-century Bishop's Lynn, had fourteen children. Notwithstanding, she opened a brewery and even purchased a mill in order to grind wheat. She wrote that she did so because she had leisure time and could not bear the thought of any other woman in the town being as elegantly dressed as she. Had she nursed her own children, she would surely not have had the time to engage in this economic activity.[55] According to Gerald of Wales, the wives and concubines of English parish priests at the end of the twelfth century also called on the services of wetnurses: denouncing these priests, he writes *inter alia* that they did not observe the rule of celibacy as should all the clergy, and that their miserable homes were 'cluttered up with small infants, cradles, midwives, and nurses'.[56] Since the book in which this description appears has the flavour of satire, it may be assumed that the author was exaggerating somewhat. But, had he not been acquainted with the phenomenon of wetnurses in contemporary households, he would not have described how the wives of priests also used them. The lay legislation of the twelfth century already contains references to the death of a child under the weight of the body of an adult (male or female) with whom it shared a bed, and to whom it had been entrusted for nursing or for education.[57] The thirteenth-century synods by mothers and wetnurses, caution against sharing a bed with an infant for danger of smothering.[58] There is no way of telling whether these cautions related only to live-in wetnurses or also to those who took the infants into their own homes. The rolls of the manorial court of Havering in the year 1401 record the claim of a tanner against a burgher of Romford, the small town adjacent to the manor. The tanner demanded payment of 22 pence for the cost of burial of the burgher's son, who had been wetnursed by the tanner's wife. It is not clear whether the infant was put out to nurse because its mother had died or had no milk, or because the custom of putting infants out to nurse was already common. Perusal of parish records starting from the second half of the sixteenth century shows clearly that in this period there were women in that community who took infants into their homes for nursing, mainly from London residents.[59]

In fourteenth-century Paris there were go-betweens who mediated between the servantwomen and wetnurses and the employers, and received payment from both parties for their efforts. In the ordinance of 1350 aimed at fixing the maximum wage for French labourers, the wage of a chambermaid was fixed at 30 shillings per year, of a wetnurse at 50 shillings, and of a wetnurse who cared for the child in her own home at 100 shillings per annum.[60] This may constitute indirect evidence that the custom of sending children away to the homes of wetnurses was not yet well established in mid-fourteenth-century France. It will be recalled that both in seventeenth- and eighteenth-century France and in Tuscany in the Late Middle Ages live-in wetnurses received the higher wage. The question, therefore, is why, according to the 1350 ordinance, they received only half the wage of a wetnurse who took the child into her own home. This ordinance was issued in a transitional period, after the 1348 Black Death, when the economic conditions of both rural and urban workers improved as a result of the vacating of lands and of the increased demand for labour due to the decimation of the population. It is possible that since the custom of putting infants out to nurse was not yet well established, in cases where labouring families had no urgent need for additional income, the supply decreased and the price rose. However, the practice existed (the very fact that the wages were mentioned in the ordinance attests to this), and there is also evidence extant for notable urban families which gave their infants to wetnurses from nearby villages. The testimony of Konrad of Megenberg, writing in Germany in the mid-fourteenth century about live-in wetnurses and the despatch of infants to be nursed by wetnurses in their own homes, attests the existence of the practice in the Germany of his day.[61]

In attempting to assess the consequences of wetnursing, one should distinguish between two categories and their corollaries: first, entrusting of infants to live-in wetnurses and the lot of the neglected children of these wetnurses; second, putting infants out to wetnurses and the fate of the wetnurses' children in their own home. It is clear that the child whose nurse lived in was the more fortunate. She was nursing only one child and was under the supervision of her employer as regards proper nutrition and the carrying out of instructions. The author of the work in praise of virginity, who pointed out the risks of childbirth and the problems of childrearing, writes 'Even if you are rich and have a wetnurse, you must, as a mother, supervise everything that is done by her.'[62] (It should be noted that his text was in general intended to be descriptive rather than prescriptive.) The wetnurse in the parental household lived apart from her husband and hence did not usually conceive while nursing, and there was a reasonable prospect that she would suckle the infant for the entire nursing period – about two years. The bond between the mother and the wetnursed infant probably varied from household to household. The sources contain examples of maternal involvement in the care and rearing of the infant. The biography of Catherine of Vadstena cites a motif which is reiterated in the Lives of many saints: she refused to suck at the breast of the wetnurse, since the woman was a sinner. The truth probably was that she had difficulty in nursing at the woman's breasts. (There was contemporary awareness of the phenomenon: 'The temperament of the wetnurse is sometimes unsuited to that of the infant,'[63] writes one of the authors. He was apparently referring not only to difficulties of biological origin, but also to emotional incompatibility between the two.) The wetnurse was sent away, and Catherine's own mother nursed her until another wetnurse could be found.[64] There seem to have been cases where both the mother and a wetnurse nursed the infant (and this was certainly true in the case of twins). A woodcut from Strasburg in 1483 shows a mother nursing one infant while his twin lies in his cradle, and in a nearby bed are two wetnurses.[65] On occasion both the mother and the wetnurse gave evidence to committees discussing the possibility of canonizing a future saint, and told of the child's illnesses, the prayers they had offered up together, and the vow one of them had made.[66] When lightning struck the family castle of Thomas Aquinas, his mother hastened to the room where he was sleeping with his wetnurse to see if harm had befallen him. A chronicle from the second half of the twelfth century tells of an infant from the nobility who had a wetnurse, but whose cradle stood at night by his mother's bed.[67] According to Erikson and others, in the first stage of infancy, up to about fifteen months, the most important thing is to create basic trust in the infant, which is the foundation of self-identity and self-confidence, which enable him to establish relations based on trust in the future. At the same time, it is usually agreed that an infant can establish ties with more than one person, and that there are no indications of any biological need for an exclusive primary tie. The maternal role can be shared by several people without emotional damage to the child, on condition that the tie is good and stable. Thus, the task could be divided up between the mother and the wetnurse. The degree of success in creating the tie was dependent on the goodwill and personality of both the mother and the wetnurse, and on that of the infant. On the other hand, just as some of the wetnurses undoubtedly became attached to the infants they nursed, others were probably indifferent or even resentful, whether they had lost their own infants or because they had weaned them prematurely. If the child was particularly attached to the wetnurse and contact with the mother was restricted, then it undoubtedly underwent a crisis when the wetnurse left, since there were certainly cases where the child was reared exclusively by the wetnurse. In the Lives of the saints, we read of a wetnurse who succeeded for some time in concealing from the mother the congenital defect in the arm of the infant, so as not to distress her.[68] Had the mother sometimes nurtured the infant, she would have noticed the handicap for herself. The extent to which the child overcame the emotional damage caused by the departure of the wetnurse doubtless depended on the conditions of its rearing, the treatment it received in the year which followed, and its sensitivity. Some wetnurses apparently stayed on in the household in the role of nurses. The sources often mention wetnurses (nutrix) of children of 3 and 5 and even of adults.[69] But since this word was used to denote both wetnurses and nurses there is no way of ascertaining whether these women had once been the wetnurses of the children they reared.[70]

It will be recalled that authors of medical and didactic literature recommended hiring the wetnurse several months after her own confinement. If she began to suckle her charge several months after giving birth, what then was the fate of her own child? As far as we know, the practice of nursing of the child by the mother's neighbours and female relatives, which was rife in several non-European societies, was unknown in Europe. From Margaret Mead's observations, we learn that among the Manus in New Guinea and the Samoans, it was customary for a nursing mother who came to visit another woman who had just given birth to suckle the hostess's child during the visit. If the mother's milk dried up, one of her female relatives suckled the child; or, if she went on a visit to her family and her husband did not permit her to take the child with her, it was nursed by a paternal female relative in her absence.[71] In some societies it was the custom for two mothers who gave birth at around the same time to suckle one another's infants in order to create a special bond between the two families, and, when the children grew to adulthood, they regarded themselves as adopted brothers.[72] This does not appear to have been the case in medieval Europe. One need only recall the couple who took in an abandoned girl child and found it difficult to find any woman ready to nurse her, and the revulsion of Brune of Montaillou at the possibility that a strange woman might suckle her child. If an infant abandoned by its mother was fortunate enough to get human milk, it was that of a woman who suckled it for payment lower than the wage its mother received in her employer's home, and the child certainly would not have received good care. If it was placed in a foundlings' home, its fate was even more pitiful. There is no need to dwell on the impact of maternal abandonment at the age of several months on the emotional development of the child, since its prospects for survival were very slim. The question of the fate of the progeny of live-in wetnurses did not concern the authors of medical and didactic works. Their mothers were expected to refrain from worrying about these children, since, as Vincent of Beauvais writes, the wetnurses should avoid any anxiety which could induce the renewal of menstruation. The paterfamilias in Alberti's book also requests that the wetnurse be a 'happy' woman.

As for children put out to nurse, they were abandoned almost entirely to the mercies of the wetnurse. The very fact that the authors of didactic works advise parents to visit their children regularly, and to check the health of the wetnurse frequently, indicates that not all parents troubled to do this.[73] We know of parents who maintained more or less regular contact with the wetnurse and the child, of others who visited only rarely[74] and supervised the wetnurse from afar, through emissaries, and of some who did not see the child even once throughout the nursing period. The most neglected were the illegitimate children, those orphaned of their mothers, and those whose fathers had died and whose mothers returned to their parental homes. Giovanni Morelli writes in his journal of the fate of his father, Pagolo. He was born in 1355 and sent to a wetnurse immediately after birth. His mother died shortly afterwards and his father, who already had grown children, took no interest in him and left him at the wetnurse's home till the age of 10 or 12 without ever visiting him. The wetnurse–nurse was a harsh woman who beat him mercilessly. Even as a grown man, he would go into a rage whenever he recalled this wetnurse, whom he described as the most bestial woman he had ever encountered.[75] Since these wetnurses were not separated from their husbands, many conceived, and the infant charge was transferred to another wetnurse. Thus, children sometimes moved from nurse to nurse. In 1385 twins were born to the Guidini family in Siena. The mother nursed one of them for two weeks, and he was then sent to a wetnurse with whom he stayed for two months, until she conceived. He was then brought back home, and eleven days later was sent to a second wetnurse, who kept him for sixteen months until she too became pregnant. His twin brother was nursed by their mother for five weeks, and then sent to three wetnurses consecutively, who kept him for periods of six, nine, and three months. Two of them conceived while nursing him.[76] Needless to say, under these conditions it was highly difficult to foster basic trust and inner confidence in a child through positive and continuous contact with one individual.[77] Even if the child remained with one wetnurse, there was no way of telling how she would treat him, how much empathy she felt for him, and how she divided her milk and her attention between her charge and her own child. It is well known that maternal sentiment is not limited to biological mothers: it can be felt by nurses and adoptive mothers as well, and there are isolated examples of dedicated and loving care on the part of a medieval wetnurse. Ambrose of Siena, who was later canonized, was born with a handicap and was sent to a wetnurse on the outskirts of the town immediately after birth; she cared for him devotedly and lovingly.[78] Yet it is hard to believe that this example was typical, since it was certainly not their motherliness which impelled wetnurses to take in children for nursing, but their desire and that of their husbands to earn extra money. Nor can one ascertain how the older children in the family treated the infant charges or how the wetnurse's husband treated them. He was interested in the additional income (since the infant was taken in with his approval if not at his insistence). On the other hand, in order to guarantee his wife's income, he was forced to abstain from sexual relations with her, lest she conceive and be forced to stop nursing. He too might be resentful of the strange infant.[79] According to several psychologists, such as John Bowlby, if a child in its first years – up to $2\frac{1}{2}$ – experiences total deprivation of close and warm relationships, it will suffer irreparable harm. If, in those first years, it does not develop the ability to establish contact with others and does not receive any affection, its own capacity for establishing normal personal relations in the future will atrophy.[80] Other psychologists refute these conclusions on the basis of observation of children who spent the first years of their lives in institutions, where they lacked stable ties and warmth, and were later adopted and enjoyed affection and stability; they claim that no grave anomalies were revealed in the social conduct of these children. In other words, the treatment they received after the age of $2\frac{1}{2}$, and after leaving the institution, was the determinant factor.[81] It is clear, on the other hand, that, if in the years that followed these children had suffered deprivation, they would have been irreparably harmed – becoming loveless people incapable of loving. If we adopt this last approach, we can say that the degree to which the child succeeded in overcoming the deprivation it suffered while living in the wetnurse's home depended on the treatment it received upon returning to its own home, as well as on its own personality. At best, mother and child underwent a period of difficult adaptation, since they were not acquainted with one another. But, beyond the impact on infant emotional development of the wetnursing period, it is clear that the prospects for the survival of these infants were slimmer than those for children who remained at home. From Garden's study of the putting of infants out to nurse in Lyon at the end of the eighteenth century[82] and other studies on eighteenth-century Paris and Rouen we know that the mortality rate among infant charges in the homes of wetnurses was very high.[83] In Tuscany in the Late Middle Ages, the mortality rate was particularly high among infants put out to nurse by the foundlings' home in Florence and among illegitimate children given out to wetnurses by private individuals.[84] We cannot gauge the number of acts of infanticide and criminal neglect as against natural deaths. The foundlings' home did not always respect its obligation to pay the wetnurse, and a considerable number of these infants apparently died of unnatural causes. The legitimate offspring of prosperous families, whose wetnurses received higher wages and were more strictly supervised, and whose parents visited them, were better treated.[85] If the wetnurse became pregnant or fell sick, the child was taken away from her. The Guidini family mentioned above acted so, as did other families. Wetnurses were also apprehensive about facing the parents of an infant which died. One wetnurse summoned the mother when a three-month-old infant refused to nurse at her breast or to touch any other liquid, and burned with fever for five days. The mother came at once.[86] Another wetnurse in early fifteenth-century Venice sent a message to the mother that there was an outbreak of plague in her household. The mother came at once, took away the infant, and found another wetnurse who came to live with the family.[87] In another case, when the girl-child fell sick and appeared to be dying, the wetnurse brought her to her parents' home, placed her in her mother's arms, and fled.[88] But despite the supervision and the contacts with the wetnurse the mortality rate was undoubtedly higher among children sent away to wetnurses than among those kept at home, and some authors of didactic works made explicit note of this fact.[89] None the less, many parents in late medieval Tuscany and in other regions sent their infants to wetnurses; their wages were low, and the mother who put out her infant was free of the burden and the responsibility of rearing it.

The prospects for survival of the infant children of wetnurses who took charges into their own homes for nursing were better than those of infants abandoned by their mothers who were live-in wetnurses. However, if the mother persisted in nursing her infant charge, she was unable to nurse her own child for two years. Margareta Datini, who was active in finding wetnurses for her female relatives, writes in one of her letters that one cannot trust a wetnurse who has a small infant of her own: 'I shall never believe that, if they have a one-year-old infant of their own, they do not give it a little of their milk.' One would be hard put to find a more crude expression of the price which the wetnurse was forced to pay within this system.[90] Fathers in Florence did not conceal the fact that they preferred a wetnurse whose own child had died or been sent to a foundlings' home; and the slavewomen were forced to send their infants there.

Why did mothers hand over their children for nursing to strange women, whether under their own roofs or in the wetnurse's own home? None of the preachers and authors of didactic works who advocated maternal nursing charged women with refusing to nurse their children because they found nursing repellent, boring, or even bestial, as some women claimed in the eighteenth century.[91] Nor did they accuse them of refusing to breast-feed because they preferred to spend their time in other occupations or diversions, or because they feared spoiling the shape of their bodies. If, among the few women in the Middle Ages, some expressed revulsion at nursing, they (at least, those who express these views in literature) were unmarried, and their revulsion was part and parcel of their reservations with regard to marriage and procreation in general.[92] One writer lists the objective reasons why certain women are unable to nurse their own children, such as disease, sores on the breasts, or blunt nipples. Generally speaking, however, the accusations centred on the actual refusal to nurse, the significance of which was non-fulfilment of their maternal obligations, and unnatural conduct. If the writers went into detail, they claimed that women believed themselves to be too delicate and were too proud to endure the effort involved in breast-feeding.[93] The implication is that hiring a wetnurse was a feature of class. Certainly, some women could not nurse because they had no milk, since they suffered from various sicknesses after the confinement, and because of inflammations, sores, and growths in the breasts.[94] In the case of the birth of twins, the mother would undoubtedly have difficulty in nursing both. It is known that the commencement of lactation can sometimes induce postnatal depression, and, consequently, refusal to continue nursing. From the story of Peter Damian's mother, we can learn that in the Middle Ages there were women who suffered from such depression. When the mother died in childbirth, it was, of course, necessary to find a wetnurse. But all these factors together do not explain the scope of the phenomenon of hiring wetnurses in the upper classes. And, since, in so far as we know, the custom was prevalent in the Middle Ages only in the upper echelons of society (with the exception of unmarried mothers from the labouring classes who, because of the shame and economic distress involved, did not raise their own children), the economic consideration – unwillingness to forgo the wife's labour – which played an important part in the decision of tradesmen and artisans in the eighteenth century, was non-existent. This was an additional expense which was not counterbalanced by the wife's labour, and there were heads of households (at least, so they claimed) who found the expenditure burdensome. When people in late Medieval Tuscany requested tax concessions, they argued, among other things, that they were faced with constant expenditure on wetnurses.[95]

One of the main reasons for hiring wetnurses was apparently the frequency of pregnancies. People did not abstain from marital relations during the nursing period, and most of them did not use contraception. Among women who nursed the intervals between pregnancies were longer than among those who did not (which could explain why some women nursed for about eighteen months), but breast-feeding by no means protected all of them against the possibility of an additional pregnancy during the nursing period.[96] As noted above, sexual intercourse during the nursing period was regarded as harmful to the nursing since it induced the renewal of the menses, and hence the spoiling, dwindling, and sometimes drying up of the milk-supply. Pregnancy during nursing was considered even more harmful since it was thought that the good blood of the woman served as food for the foetus, and only the bad blood was left as milk for the infant. The contemporary medical explanation was, of course, erroneous; but the medical experts were correct in their belief that a woman who conceived could not usually continue nursing for long. A nursing woman, even when not pregnant, requires additional calories if she did not receive sufficient fats during pregnancy, and additional proteins, vitamins, and minerals. Even the rich did not have access to an abundance of foodstuffs containing all these elements.[97] Nursing women who were not pregnant also often suffered from lack of these elements; and, when a woman conceived, her milk certainly dwindled and she was unable to continue nursing throughout her pregnancy. Since the medical view that the spoiling and dwindling of milk was a result of sexual relations was well known in the upper classes, and since it was also known that a woman could conceive during lactation and be forced to stop nursing, some of the women who could afford to do so waived the idea of nursing in advance or shortly after the delivery, and entrusted their infants to wetnurses. Since they did not breast-feed, they lacked the (temporary and unreliable) means of birth-control at the disposal of women who nursed their own children and who conceived less frequently. As a consequence, among the women in the prosperous urban class and the nobility who entrusted their children to wetnurses, some gave birth to their fullest biological capacity: 10, 17, and even 19 children. In the homes of the nobility, there were sometimes several wetnurses at the same time, apparently also because the age differences between the children were so small that two required wetnurses at the same time.[98] The handing over of infants for nursing freed women of their second biological obligation and allowed them respite between deliveries. Some women gave out their infants for nursing only after conceiving their next child. The mother of Catherine of Siena told her daughter's biographer that Catherine was the first of her children (she bore 25) whom she nursed herself until the child was weaned, and that hence she loved her in particular. She said that, because of her frequent pregnancies, she had been unable to nurse her previous children, but was able to nurse Catherine for more than a year because that time the interval between pregnancies was longer.[99] (Catherine had a twin sister, who was put out to nurse and died shortly afterwards, and, after she was weaned, another sister was born.) In the Guidini family (mentioned above), not only the twins born in 1385 were sent to a wetnurse, but also the other four offspring. Only the seventh and last child, a daughter, was nursed by the mother for a whole year until it died, because the mother did not conceive during this period.[100] In the *Acta Sanctorum* we find the tale of a woman who bore thirteen children, none of whom she was able to nurse herself. In anger at his wife, the husband reluctantly hired a wetnurse. (He was not apparently one of the moneyed people for whom the hiring of a wetnurse was a status symbol.) After an appeal to a saint, a 'miracle' occurred, and the mother succeeded in nursing her fourteenth child. It is not difficult to understand this miracle – since she did not conceive during the nursing period, she was able to continue nursing her last child.[101] It is well known that, in the past few centuries in western society, the oldest son enjoyed special privileges and that parents invested considerable resources in him, and that girls were less privileged than boys. Hence, the fact that in the Middle Ages it was often the youngest boy or girl who was nursed by the mother and not the oldest reinforces the view that in the period under discussion, at least, frequent pregnancies were the main reason for the hiring of wetnurses. Had totally free choice been available, it is reasonable to assume that the oldest child would have enjoyed maternal nursing as long as he needed it. Those men who asked for tax concessions because of the cost of wetnurses explained the need for their services by claiming that the mother was ailing, had no milk, or had conceived.[102]

The church was the arbiter of all matrimonial matters in the Middle Ages. In order to prevent the frequent pregnancies which precluded women from nursing their children, one of two methods could be employed: a strict ban on marital relations during nursing, or granting permission to employ contraceptive methods (mainly *coitus interruptus*). The church refused to contemplate either method. Marriage was monogamous, and the mutual obligation of the marriage partners (*debitum*) was supposed to serve as a deterrent against adulterous or licentious conduct.[103] Hence the church did not demand the cessation of sexual intercourse during nursing as was customary in several other societies.[104] The use of contraceptive measures was regarded as a grave sin and was unconditionally prohibited.[105] Jean Flandrin, who dealt with problems of nursing in later periods, pointed out that ecclesiastical writers were aware of the contradiction between marital duties and the infant's right to maternal nursing (or, in other words, of the incompatibility between wifely and maternal functions). This awareness was at the root of their inconsistency: advocacy of maternal nursing, on the one hand, and acknowledgement of the function of the wetnurse, on the other. Since they did not insist unequivocally on abstinence from marital relations during nursing, they knew that the wife was liable to conceive again and hence, though sometimes only half-heartedly, they sanctioned the function of the wetnurse. This inherent contradiction is particularly striking in the statements of Thomas Chobham, one of the fiercest opponents of wetnursing. He was far removed from any sense of empathy with those women who claimed that the burden of childrearing was too great for them: 'If the woman is weak and says that she cannot shoulder the burden, was she not equally weak when she endured coitus and childbirth?' he asks. But several lines further on, as noted, he confirms the need for wetnurses: 'If she cannot carry the whole burden alone, she should nurse and bathe her infant at least, when she is able, and thus will not be like one who acts unnaturally and never goes near her child.'[106] And 'when she is able' means before she conceives again. The second possibility – of employing contraception – was never broached. Judaism anticipated Christianity in advocating the sanctity of life; the Talmudic sages permitted the nursing mother to use contraception.

> Three classes of woman may use an absorbent [flax or hackled wool] in their marital intercourse: a minor, and an expectant and a nursing mother. The minor, because otherwise she might become pregnant and die. An expectant mother, because otherwise she might cause her foetus to degenerate into a sandal [a fish-shaped abortion]. A nursing mother, because otherwise she might have to wean her child prematurely and this would result in his death.

> (Niddah 45*a*)

They also permitted men to practise *coitus interruptus* as long as their wives were nursing ('During all the twenty-four months one may thresh within and winnow without: these are the words of R. Eliezer' (Yebamoth 34*b*)[107]). Whereas none of the ecclesiastical writers permitted contraception during nursing, some authors advised parents to abstain from marital relations during nursing, from Pope Gregory the Great at the end of the sixth century,[108] through Ivo of Chartres in the early twelfth century[109] to both Catholic and Protestant writers in the sixteenth and seventeenth centuries.[110] These, however, were merely suggestions, emanating from only a few sources, and undoubtedly were also impractical. An unequivocal demand to refrain from intercourse while nursing was addressed in the Central and Late Middle Ages only to wetnurses, as if they and their husbands belonged to a different breed from other men and women.[111] When a wetnurse in Florence conceived and continued to nurse for several months while concealing her pregnancy, the parents reacted with great anger to the fact that their child had been fed on the milk of a pregnant woman, which was disgusting and unhealthy.

The practice of hiring wetnurses was not, of course, the invention of medieval Christian Europe. The scope of the practice in other societies is unknown, but it is known to have existed in Pharaonic Egypt (Exod. 2: 7); in biblical Israel (Gen. 35: 8; 2 Kgs. 11: 2; 2 Chr. 22: 11); in Greece and Rome; among the Anglo-Saxons and Vikings; and in the Arabian Peninsula in Mohammed's day. Nor is there certainty that, in the period before the invasions, all the Germanic women suckled their own children, as Tacitus reports.[112] In all these societies, there were women who handed over their children to wetnurses, because they had no milk, because they were ill or had conceived, or – mainly – because such was the custom in their social class, and they accepted it without protest. Needless to say, in all the societies where wetnurses were employed, the hiring was done, at the least, according to the father's wish, even if the medieval opponents of the practice castigated women alone (I have encountered only one text in which the father too is reproached).[113] According to Klapisch's study, which is based on family journals, in Tuscany it was the father who negotiated with the husband of the wetnurse (and not, as was usual, with the woman directly), and it was he who signed the contract with the husband. The task of visiting the child and supervising the wetnurse was carried out by the father, who also decided when the child should be weaned and brought back home. Medieval societies had to face, in addition, difficulties caused by the attitude of the church. The church did not originate the practice of wetnursing, but neither did it make effective attempts to uproot it. What is more, the church's abolition of polygamy and official concubinage (it is easier for a man to abstain from marital relations with his wife when he has another wife or official concubine), and the total ban on contraception, particularly within the marital framework, led, in retrospect, to the spread of the practice. Sermons in praise of maternal nursing did not suffice to prevent the handing over of infants to wetnurses. The church did in fact succeed in its efforts to introduce change in the matrimonial law and familial norms of conduct which had prevailed in Israel, in Rome, and among the Celts and Germans. In addition to abolishing polygamy and official concubinage, it succeeded in extirpating the custom of adoption practised in Rome and in introducing, in its stead, spiritual parentage as represented by the godparents, and with it a new system of spiritual affinity. The church banned divorce and extended the prohibition on marriage between kin to more distant blood-ties than had been accepted in the other societies mentioned above, with the aim of fostering extreme exogamy and changing the entire patterns of family structure. There is no room, within the context of our present study, to deal with the factor or factors which induced the church to introduce these changes.[114] For our purposes, the important fact is that the church anchored in canon law all the changes it effected, and that transgressions against matrimonial law were considered a sin. Needless to say, the church did not succeed in preventing deviations from the norms it established (there were always cases of extramarital sexual relations, which sometimes produced bastard children; *coitus interruptus* was apparently practised; and the ban on incest was also not observed strictly). It did, however, attempt to enforce them, and often brought into play all the means at its disposal in order to do so.[115] Yet, where maternal nursing was concerned, it did not act in this fashion. While advocating it, the Church disregarded the central factor which rendered the services of the wetnurse essential – the fact that people engaged in marital relations with the sanction (somewhat reserved at times) of the church, and were forbidden to use contraception (which though inefficient, could still help delay the next pregnancy). In this manner, the church placed the lives of infants at risk, and contradicted its own principle of the sanctity of life. This was a vicious circle in which someone always paid the price, and which created a social problem of the highest order to which the church turned a blind eye.

The women who entrusted their infants to wetnurses came from the upper echelons of society. We cannot guess how peasant women would have behaved if the rural economic and social system had permitted them to conduct themselves like noblewomen and prosperous townswomen. It may be that peasant women extended the period of nursing because they were aware that breast-feeding was a provisional contraception measure, which extended the intervals between pregnancies.[116] The fact is that maternal nursing was withheld from infants in those social classes which did gradually internalize ecclesiastical law about matrimony, while in peasant society, which in the main did not internalize this law and ecclesiastical norms of sexual conduct, mothers suckled their own children (and continued to do so after conceiving again, as long as the milk flowed).

Ariès, and others in his wake,[117] have asserted that medieval people constructed an emotional defence mechanism against bonding with an infant whose prospects for survival were slim. They did not take the infant into their homes or into their hearts. One can agree that those mothers who sent their infants away to wetnurses immediately after the delivery did not become attached to them. This, however, was not because of emotional defences but because they did not nurture them and were not acquainted with them. Motherliness is not a fixed and imprinted pattern of conduct which is automatically manifested in the same form irrespective of circumstances. It is a system of skills and emotions based on the maternal instinct, but is by no means expressed in the same manner under all conditions. This is not to say that maternal instinct is non-existent, as Badinter has claimed. Nobody has ever questioned the existence of the sexual instinct, the instinct of eating and drinking, and the instinct of life. None the less, there have always been societies in which some men and women chose to live a life of abstinence and to forgo sexual experience; there are societies in which people fast at fixed intervals, and others in which, in specific circumstances, the individual is expected to commit suicide. These instincts exist to the same extent as the maternal instinct, which finds expression in different forms and with varying intensity not only because of individual differences between women, but also because of differences in the social structure, the norms of conduct, and the values of various societies.

In the Middle Ages, people were aware of the importance of the primary tie of the infant to another human being, and knew that it was through nurturing that the contact was established and the love reinforced. We have only to recall the words of Bartholomaeus Anglicus and of one of the interlocutors in Alberti's book. This awareness was even more clearly expressed by Philip of Novare. However, while he disregards the range of problems entailed in hiring a wetnurse (and primarily the question of the fate of the wetnurse's own child), his remarks indicate that it is immaterial whether the first bond is created with the wetnurse or with the mother. He writes that God has bestowed on infants three types of knowledge and love. The source of the first two is within the infant itself, while the third stems from those who nurture it. The first knowledge and love are the infant's recognition of the woman who nurses him – whether his mother or the wetnurse – and his love for her. He may often refuse to suckle at the breast of another woman. The second knowledge and love are his recognition of those who caress him, play with him, and carry him in their arms from place to place, his love for them and joy in them. The knowledge and love of those who nurtured infants came from nature, from compassion, and from the act of rearing them. And it is essential that this should be so (the author writes), since in infancy children are so dirty and troublesome, and become so bad and capricious when they are a little older, that, were it not for this, no person would agree to rear them. With nurturing comes love.[118]

Despite the praise lavished on maternal nursing, it seems that a mother from the upper classes who handed over her child to a wetnurse, even outside the home, was not considered to be a bad mother. The same is true, in so far as we know, of a woman who abandoned her child in order to take up employment as a wetnurse. This was customary and, as we know, people (with few exceptions) tend to accept the prevailing customs of their time and place as self-evident. Most women who entrusted their children to wetnurses did so not because they did not value their children or because they lacked maternal feeling, but because this was the done thing. It should also be recalled that the daughters of the upper class married young and bore their first children at a very early age (and were also younger than their husbands). It would undoubtedly have been difficult for them to rebel against prevailing practice. Since they were not regarded as bad mothers, it may be assumed that they experienced neither guilt nor shame. We have no way of knowing whether some of them felt anguish at parting from their new-born infants since there may be a discrepancy between accepted social conduct and emotion.

Progress, as we know, does not take a straight and consecutive path, and the same is true of the change for the better in society's attitude towards the child. In the centuries which divided the Middle Ages from the nineteenth century, the custom of handing children to wetnurses spread to the middle classes in all European countries and in some of them (France and Germany) also to the urban labouring class. Since in the Middle Ages the urban population was generally smaller, and apparently more women in the middle class, and certainly within the labouring class, nursed their own children, not only did a larger proportion of urban children benefit from maternal nursing, but a smaller number of children in rural areas were abandoned in foundling homes, weaned prematurely, or condemned to sharing their mothers' milk with strange children.

5 The first stage of childhood

The term 'paediatrics' came into existence only in 1872. However, books devoted to paediatric medicine and including guidance on methods of child-raising were composed from the sixteenth century onward. Some of these works were based on the writings of medieval medical scholars who did not usually devote separate works to the medical problems of children, but discussed them within the framework of general treatises (such as manuals on obstetrics). In composing those chapters devoted to paediatrics and to the rearing of infants and children in general, the medieval experts had recourse to Greek, Roman, and Moslem medical sources.[1] The authors of didactic works and of encyclopedias also discussed proper methods of infant-care and childrearing (and they too cite the works of the classical authors, particularly Aristotle). Hence, they provide a picture of contemporary – or, to be more exact, expert – views on proper rearing and education. It is, of course, harder to know to what extent the manuals of guidance were known in wider circles and to what degree people followed their advice. We shall return to this issue below.

BREAST-FEEDING AND SOLID FOOD, WEANING, AND TEETHING

In order to facilitate nursing in the first few days and to stimulate the sucking reflex, the authors recommended that the mother or wetnurse squeeze a little milk from her breast to the infant's mouth or insert a little honey, before the child began to suck. They also instructed them on how to overcome difficulties in breast-feeding in the first few days by patiently adjusting the angle of the nipple.[2] They continually caution against poor-quality milk which is liable to cause stomach-aches, fever, spasms, and sores in the mouth, whether it is the milk of a wetnurse or an animal.[3] At the same time, the authors state that medication should not be administered to a small infant; if a child fell ill, medication should be given to the wetnurse.[4] Physicians acted in accordance with this advice. In the Lives of the Saints it is sometimes related how parents summoned a physician who told them that he had a stock of medicines but that it would be dangerous to dose the infant.[5] As regards nursing schedules, it is universally agreed that the infant should be fed on demand and not according to a rigid schedule. None of the authors expressed fear that response to the infant's cry and nursing on demand might cause stomach upsets or over-pampering. Moreover, giving the breast was considered the most accepted method of pacifying the crying infant.[6] 'Good' mothers and 'good' wetnurses apparently followed this advice. In Marie de France's poem *Milun*, the protagonist is an illegitimate child who, immediately after his birth, is sent by his mother with companions and a chosen wetnurse to his aunt in Northumberland. During the day, the entourage halts seven times *en route* in order to enable the wetnurse to nurse the child.[7] This may have been considered the desirable number of feedings for a newborn infant, and it is also possible that the poetess chose the number 7 because of its magic power. Outside courtly literature, mothers adapted themselves to their babies' rhythm. In the *Acta Sanctorum* (Lives of the Saints) we read of a child who, in his jealousy, strangled his infant brother as he lay sleeping in his cradle. When the mother wondered at the fact that the infant was sleeping so long, she went over to its cradle and discovered what had happened.[8] This suggests that the infant had evolved its own feeding pattern to which its mother had grown accustomed: when the interval between feeding-demands was longer than usual, the mother's concern was aroused even though the child was not crying. Undoubtedly, overfeeding was often a health hazard when infants were given the breast every time they cried. On the other hand, psychologists generally agree that the infant fed on demand has a better prospect of developing into an unneurotic and self-confident adult than the infant fed according to a strict schedule. Needless to say, the nursing period of infants fed on demand was likely to be more tranquil than that of infants fed according to a rigid timetable.

It will be recalled that Bartholomaeus Anglicus considered the first months of life – up to about 6–8 months – to be of vital importance. Modern psychologists also consider this age to be a landmark in the development of the child. The view is that from this age the infant begins to develop a sense of separate identity and is capable of establishing significant and continuous emotional bonds with certain people whose company he seeks, and is suspicious of strangers and their attentions. He no longer merely responds to the physical presence of his mother, but misses her and seeks her incessantly when she is not within his field of vision. He is a social creature who invites his mother to play and creates interaction between them.[9] Bartholomaeus Anglicus, who concentrated on mainly physical characteristics – the tenderness, delicacy, and fluidity of the infant in the first six months of its life – did not write about these traits. But it is interesting to note that he too distinguished a turning-point in the infant's development at this age.

In literature, we often read of a future hero who was weaned at the age of 3.[10] However, it will be recalled that most authors of medical and didactic works recommend weaning at the age of 2 when all the milk-teeth have appeared and the child is capable of eating everything.[11] According to Konrad of Megenberg, the normal period of breast-feeding in Germany was one year, sometimes eighteen months, and rarely two years among the poor.[12] In Tuscany in the Late Middle Ages, we know of children who were nursed for two years by wetnurses. If the wetnurse conceived before the child reached the age of 2, the parents often sought a replacement to avoid weaning the child prematurely.[13] In fifteenth-century Montpellier the average period of nursing for orphans and foundlings put out to nurse was 1 year and $9\frac{1}{2}$ months.[14] In the *Acta Sanctorum*, there is mention of mothers from various regions who nursed their infants for $1\frac{1}{2}$–2 years.[15] Already during the nursing period, they gave the infants water, honey-water, and, in northern countries, beer as well.[16] The authors of medical works caution against offering wine to infants and small children, since it may cause various illnesses.[17] Solids were also given to infants some time before they were weaned, in accordance with the advice of those authors who recommend introducing solids into the diet after the appearance of the first two front teeth.[18] They write that the mother or wetnurse should mash or pre-masticate the food before giving it to the infant, and that at first soft food should be offered, such as bread soaked in honey-water, clear wine, or meat or chicken soup, and gruel of flour and milk with added honey. This dietary supplement of solids during nursing served as gradual preparation for weaning. At the same time, the experts warn that offering solids prematurely could be dangerous for the infant's health.[19] As regards the final weaning, some writers advocated rigid methods and others more flexible ones. In the work attributed to Arnold of Villanova, the author writes that at the age of 2, after the child has all its milk-teeth and is capable of eating, it should be weaned. If the infant cries and asks for the breast, the mother or wetnurse should smear her breasts with a bitter and repellent liquid like mustard or bitter aloes. Francesco of Barbaro is gentler. He too proposes smearing the breasts with a bitter (and innocuous) substance, but, if the child cries and refuses to eat the solid food, it should be given the breast again and then offered other food. Aldebrandin of Siena also says that, if the child spits out or vomits the solid food, it should be offered the breast again.[20] We do not know by what method most mothers chose to wean their infants. As for children put out to nurse, most of them were left in the wetnurse's home for two years to be weaned gradually. There were, however, some who were returned home suddenly and were weaned without a transition period. It is also impossible to assess how much time and patience mothers devoted to nursing. Most medieval women lived under hard conditions and worked strenuously, which would have made it difficult for them to find time for patient and protracted attention to their infants. On the other hand, since concepts of efficiency and order were much laxer than in modern western society (and in agriculture there were also dead seasons in which there was little work), it is also possible that nursing was carried out without haste and even with patience in a relaxed atmosphere. We learn from con-temporary illuminations that it was customary for mothers to nurse in public, which made it easier for them to respond to the infant without having to make special arrangements and without pressure.[21] As regards solid food, it seems that both parents and nurses believed that a child should be fed frequently and given large quantities, even when reluctant to eat. Manuals for preachers exhort them to reiterate admonitions against sin, like a nurse repeatedly offering food to a child who refuses to eat, until he finally agrees to put it in his mouth. The Franciscan, Berthold of Regensburg, who preached throughout Germany in the thirteenth century, writes that the rich overfeed their children, thereby overloading their stomachs, hampering digestion, and eventually bringing them to an earlier grave than the children of the poor. This, he writes, stems from the fact that food is abundant in the household, and from love and concern for the child. No sooner has the child's sister prepared gruel and fed him than his aunt appears and does the same, and then comes the nurse and cries 'My child has eaten nothing all day long' and feeds him against his will, even if he cries and shouts and thrashes out in protest.[22] Since these remarks are part of the preacher's denunciation of the sin of gluttony, we may assume that he was exaggerating somewhat. Another author, who also denounces gluttony and says that two meals per day should suffice, hastens to add that small children may be given three meals.[23] It was not only the preachers, however, who disapproved of children being overfed. The authors of didactic literature believed that prosperous parents tended to spoil their offspring, and even permitted them to gorge on sweetmeats, fruit, and other delicacies between meals.[24] Children of different temperament should be given different diets and should not be forced to eat food which is not suited to them, writes another author.[25] In a society which lived in constant fear of famine and in which full granaries instilled a sense of confidence and were a sign of prosperity, and where the infant mortality rate was very high, it was only natural for people to believe that overfeeding (according to our conception and also that of the didactic writers) would make children healthy and strong, and would increase their chances of survival.

It will be recalled that some writers favoured maternal nursing, not only because the mother's milk is the best source of nutrition for the infant, but also because of her special attitude toward him. Francesco of Barbaro writes at the beginning of the fifteenth century that the breasts of a woman are higher than the teats of she-animals to enable her to caress her infant while suckling it.[26] A description of the close bond between a nursing mother and her child, which is based on closer observation than were the statements of didactic writers in favour of maternal nursing, can be found in the writing of the German mystic, Henry Suso. He compares the relations of the soul and 'the eternal wisdom' (*ewige Weisheit*) to the relations of mother and infant. She not only nurses him, but also stands him on her knee. And he, through the movements of his head and little body, clambers up towards his loving mother and expresses his joy through his movements and his smile.[27] This description, marked by tenderness and affection, is unquestionably the outcome of observation of mother–child relations. That infants and small children received affection, which was expressed through physical contact, can be clearly seen from the repeated descriptions in the Lives of the saints of the future saint as an infant wiping away the kisses of his mother, nurse, and aunt, and bathing his mouth with water.[28] Had infants not been treated in this fashion, authors would not have used this description in order to illustrate the saint's unique traits from childhood.

Did parents feed their male infants better than their girl children? Some medical treatises and manuals of guidance assert that the female, being biologically inferior to the male, requires less food. The author of the work attributed to Arnold of Villanova writes that, since the male is hotter and drier than the female, he has more strength, courage, and reason. The female is smaller in body, colder and moister, and less perfect. Therefore, the author goes on, some people believe that the male should be weaned later than the female.[29] Konrad of Megenberg and Paolo of Certaldo write explicitly that the female, who is less active physically than the male because of her biological inferiority, requires less food. Paolo of Certaldo points out that this does not imply discrimination against girls, since parents are instructed to love all their progeny equally, but rather indicates the need for a different mode of nurturing deriving from the biological difference. 'Hence', the author writes, 'nourish the sons well. How you nourish the daughter does not matter as long as you keep her alive. Do not allow her to wax too fat.'[30] These authors were referring to older children rather than nursing infants, but some writers believed that, even when nursing, the boy required better nutrition and should be weaned later than the girl.[31] I have encountered no testimony of a nursing mother favouring her son over her daughter, nor is there any way of ascertaining whether mothers in general tended to favour their male children where nursing was concerned. It is known, however, that slightly more female infants than males were handed over to wetnurses. There is also evidence that the boys who were wetnursed were better fed than the girls in the same situation. Records drawn up in early fifteenth-century Florence for tax-collecting purposes show a quite unrealistically higher number of male infants than females. This numerical discrepancy doubtless stems from the fact that less care was taken to register girls. This was not only because girls were held in less esteem, but also because more girls than boys were sent away to wetnurses, and thus disappeared from the records. Since children sent away to wetnurses received inferior nutrition and suffered a higher mortality rate than those who were nursed by their own mothers, it may be assumed that the numerical discrepancy did, indeed, exist, even if smaller than indicated by the records.[32] There are several examples of the putting of girls out to cheaper wetnurses than those to whom infant boys of the same family were sent, as well as examples of earlier weaning of girls. In one case, the wetnurse conceived when the girl infant was 1 year and 4 months old, and the parents did not seek a new nurse but left the child with the pregnant wetnurse for gradual weaning. In contrast, infant boys of the same age whose wetnurses became pregnant were sent to a new wetnurse so as to postpone weaning. The accepted rule in Florence of the Late Middle Ages was for female babies to be brought home from the wetnurse about a month and a half earlier than boys. This meant that the transitional weaning period, in which they both nursed at the breast and were given solids, was shorter.[33] In addition, more girls than boys were placed in foundlings' homes, both among children born in wedlock and among the illegitimate, which also explains the numerical difference between the sexes in the records. But, again, we are speaking not only of the discrepancy in recording. Since more female infants were placed in foundlings' homes, more girls died in infancy. Moreover, according to Trexler's study, since more fathers of boys than of girls guaranteed to return some day to redeem their infants, the authorities of foundlings' homes kept most of the boys there, and put out most of the girls to wetnurses in the country. The prospects for survival of boys raised in foundlings' homes were, needless to say, better than those of infant girls sent away to cheap wetnurses in remote villages.[34]

Although we find no indication in the sources that boys received preferential treatment over nutrition in the parental home, there are examples of greater affection and concern being manifested for one of the offspring than for others. In this context, we are not referring to the privileges extended to the oldest son but to displays of particular affection toward one of the children, not necessarily the oldest and not always a boy. As noted above, when lightning struck the castle of Thomas Aquinas's parents, his mother hastened in panic to the room where he slept with his wetnurse, in order to make sure that no harm had befallen him. And, the author adds, 'She was more concerned for her son than for her daughter.' In the Lives of the saints it is also often related that their parents favoured them over their brothers and sisters because they were particularly easy and lovable infants, who did not cause their mothers trouble, or because it was clear that they were destined for greatness. Since the reference is to future saints, the authors do not rebuke the parents for not having loved all their children in equal measure. On the other hand, when Salimbene wrote of how his mother favoured his sisters more than him, he was less forgiving. He declared that, throughout his childhood and youth, he was unable to love his mother because of an occurrence in his infancy, of which he learned only later. When an earthquake struck Parma and his mother feared that her home would be damaged, she seized his two sisters and ran out to seek shelter in her parents' house, leaving him at home. She claimed to have done it because they were lighter than he and she could carry them in her arms. Salimbene does not express disapproval of the fact that one child was preferred to another, and says only that she should have been more concerned for him, the boy, than for her daughters.[35] Since at that time he was still an infant in his cradle, it is difficult to accept his mother's excuse that his sisters were lighter to carry. She apparently favoured them.

Medical works all take note of the appearance of the first teeth. Bartholomaeus Anglicus considered toothlessness to be one of the characteristics of the first years of life. Others considered the appearance of all the milk-teeth to be one of the signs of the end of the sub-period of the first stage of childhood – *infantia*, and denoted the second period *dentium plantativa*. They were aware that this process was accompanied by pain and sometimes even various ailments, and suggested ways of helping the child: the gums should be rubbed with honey mixed with a little salt and liquids extracted from various roots. The child should be bathed in this period only infrequently and should often be held. While the canine teeth were coming through, he should not be given solid food. According to the author of the work attributed to Arnold of Villanova, since children tend to suck a finger while teething, thus causing irritation of the neck, the neck should be rubbed with rose-oil diluted in water, and the child should be given a root of liquorice (*ireus*) which was not yet dry as a replacement for his finger.[36] It should be noted that the author does not suggest that the child should be forcibly prevented from sucking his finger, but rather that his attention should be diverted by a substitute. This advocacy of tenderness and of avoidance of head-on clashes with the infant or small child is echoed in additional manuals. Bartholomaeus Anglicus's description of the ideal wetnurse, who loves the child, rejoices in his pleasure, shares his sorrows, consoles him, gives him rides on her shoulder, and rocks him on her knee also implies that the small child should be treated tenderly and lovingly.

BATHING, HEATING, AND SWADDLING

All writers recommend washing the infant in a bath, once or even twice or three times a day. He should be bathed before nursing, since bathing after food hampers digestion and could cause vomiting. The bathwater should be clean and lukewarm in the hot season, and hot in the cold season. Care should be taken to prevent water from entering the child's ears, and after the bath he should be rubbed with oil.[37] The advice on bathing also reflects the authors' view that infants and small children should be treated tenderly and that hardening should begin only at a later age, and then only gradually. Hence it is emphasized that the infant should be bathed in lukewarm or hot and not cold water – in contrast to the view of several eighteenth-century physicians that infants and small children should be bathed in cold water irrespective of the weather.[38] Francesco of Barbaro even adds that the infant should be allowed to splash in the water if he wishes. Bathing and oiling of the newborn infant (in this case the infant Peter Damian) have been mentioned in the previous chapter. Bathing of older infants is sometimes mentioned in literature and sometimes even in the visions of female saints, who saw the infant Jesus in his bath. In Marie de France's poem *Milun*, the wetnurse not only suckles the infant seven times a day but also bathes him with the same frequency! In the poem *Le Fresne* (The Ash Tree) the gatekeeper of the monastery brings the infant he finds to his daughter for nursing, and even orders her to heat water and bathe the infant in a bath before suckling it.[39] Marie de France attributes to these simple people – the gatekeeper and his daughter – a custom with which she was apparently acquainted from the nobility, although we do not know how prevalent the custom was in that class (there were no bathing arrangements for adults in castles). On the other hand, in towns with bathhouses, for example in Tuscany and southern Italy or in Paris, the women who went to bathhouses took their small children (and not infants) with them, and some of the prosperous townspeople had their own private bathhouses. When Thomas Aquinas's mother went to the bathhouse in Naples, the wetnurse went with her, carrying the infant Thomas in her arms. The biographer writes of this because of an event which occurred on the same occasion, which reflects the extreme piety of the future saint from his infancy. The wetnurse had difficulty in undressing him because his fist was clenched. She tried to open it, but the child began to cry and she desisted. She bathed, dried, and dressed him while his fist was still clenched. Eventually, when they reached home, despite his cries, his mother forced him to open his fist and discovered that he had been holding a slip of paper on which was written a prayer to the Holy Mother.[40] Thomas Aquinas's mother supervised his rearing and education, but the wetnurse was apparently more tender and loving than she was. The author's description of the baby refusing to open his clenched fist, in any event, indicates his close observation of infants. To return to bathing, it is unlikely that children in the urban labouring class were bathed as frequently, and even less likely that peasant children were given baths. The origin of some of the sores and carbuncles from which infants suffered was undoubtedly the dirt which accumulated on their bodies, since not only were they not bathed regularly but often their swaddling clothes were not changed with sufficient frequency, although medical writers recommended changing them whenever the infant soiled them. If the infant did not fall asleep after nursing and continued to cry, the mother or wetnurse was advised to examine whether he had wet or soiled his nappy, and whether discomfort was the cause of his distress.[41]

What undoubtedly reduced the number of times per day that the infant's swaddling clothes were changed was the fact that it was not usually dressed only in a small nappy (known in Latin as *panniculus* and in Italian as *pezze*) but was wholly swaddled in swaddling bands (*fasciae*) with only its head protruding. The infant resembled a small mummy or larva as can be learned from contemporary illuminations.[42] The authors of medical works write that the swaddling bands should be neither too loose nor too tight, and that the genitals should be free to enable the infant to urinate without difficulty, and also that the swaddling bands should be lukewarm and not cold.[43] In an Italian carnival song, the wetnurse says, in the course of proclaiming her skills, that she can swaddle an infant in swaddling bands in a jiffy, and in fact, it appears, from the study conducted by Alexandre-Bidon and Closson, and in contrast to the view which prevailed among historians of childhood, that some forms of swaddling did not take long to carry out.[44] None the less, in the lower classes, mothers and wetnurses who took in nurslings did not apparently change swaddling clothes frequently either because they were unaware of the importance of this practice or because they had no time. One of the tales of miracles attributed to a saint describes a mother who saw spots of blood on her son's swaddling clothes. When she undressed him, she discovered that he was suffering from abscesses and from a severe handicap and that his legs were completely deformed.[45] This suggests that she rarely removed the swaddling bands and undressed him. The girl infant taken in by an elderly couple at the gate of the Bologna hospital was afflicted with abscesses and sores all over her body[46] as a result of infrequent changing of soiled swaddling and possibly also because the swaddling bands were too tight. A midwife who gave evidence before the Barcelona tribunal in the early fourteenth century told of an infant which died (of infection) because of soiled swaddling clothes.[47] Konrad of Megenberg writes with fatalism that poor women who lack cloth for swaddling bands do not keep their children clean. And he adds that this is not harmful to the children of the poor ... (In the same spirit, Bernard Gordon proposes that the first milk, which is not of the best, should be given by the mother to a man of base origin or to a foundling infant.)[48] The children of the well-to-do were undressed and changed more frequently. The author of the life of St Agnes of Bohemia writes that every time her mother or wetnurse laid her in the cradle after 'having released her hands and untied her feet' the little future saint would 'arrange her limbs in the shape of a cross'.[49]

It is well known that in the sixteenth and seventeenth centuries not only was little importance attributed to cleanliness, but that it was generally believed that bathing could be harmful, and that the layer of filth accumulating on the body (particularly the skull) protected the infant or small child, dirt serving also as a shield against the evil eye. Not only infants from the lower classes were almost never bathed; the same was true of the children of royalty (as can be learned from the journal of Louis XIII's physician).[50] I have found no evidence of similar beliefs in the Middle Ages. It is possible, however, that this view was prevalent then as well, and was at least one of the reasons for the neglect of bathing and the failure to change soiled swaddling clothes in the lower classes of society. Be that as it may, it is clear that in the Middle Ages, in contrast to the following centuries, physicians were not of this opinion, as can be learned from the advice on bathing. The number of urban bathhouses was also greater in the Middle Ages than in the sixteenth–eighteenth centuries. (They were closed because of over-zealous concern for sexual morality in the wake of the Reformation, the Counter-Reformation, and fear of venereal disease.) It seems feasible to assume that infants and small children in the more prosperous urban classes which were acquainted with the medieval physicians' recommendations were bathed more frequently than children in later centuries.

The custom of using swaddling bands was certainly widespread. (It is even mentioned in the vision of one of the female saints. She saw the infant Jesus all swaddled 'as is customary for new-born infants'.[51]) Apparently, however, the body was not always completely swaddled: sometimes the hands were left free, sometimes the entire upper torso, and sometimes the lower body. Illustrations occasionally show an infant which is not swaddled at all. One medical writer advocates using exercises to stimulate the infant to move its limbs: the wetnurse should hold an attractive object such as a pebble or small bone and move it to and fro in front of the child so as to persuade it to move its eyes and neck and shoulders from side to side. She should also gently pull and move the infant's hands and arms, tickle him to make him laugh, and lift his legs cautiously one at a time. In this way he will move his entire body.[52] This writer, at least, was not referring to infants whose limbs were completely swaddled. It is most probable that the method of swaddling varied from region to region and with season. Medical scholars do not stipulate the length of the period of swaddling, and other sources do not indicate to what age the child was kept swaddled. Ambrose of Siena, who, it will be recalled, was born with a handicap, was sent immediately after birth to a wetnurse on the outskirts of the town. One day, when he was a year and several months old, a miracle occurred while the wetnurse was attending church with the child. The infant forcibly freed his arms from the swaddling bands which had confined them, and the Dominican brothers in the church then hastened to release his lower limbs. Ambrose stretched his limbs and it then became evident that he was as healthy and whole as any other child of his age.[53] However, since he was a handicapped infant (or, at least, had been considered to be such), one cannot deduce from this story that it was established practice to swaddle a child in this fashion up to the age of 1 year and several months. In seventeenth-century England, the outer layer of swaddling, at least, was sometimes removed from most parts of the body about 1–3 months after birth. The child was then dressed in a 'coat' which was actually a gown such as was also worn by children in the Middle Ages.[54] It is possible that in the Middle Ages also at least part of the body was freed at that age.

Several researchers have interpreted this custom of swaddling the entire body as a means of restraining the infant and an expression of apprehension: if an infant is not restrained it might cause harm to itself.[55] The truth is, however, that in the works of the contemporary writers there is no hint at such motivation, and it is clear that the swaddling bands were not symbols of moral restraint. The swaddling was intended to maintain the stability of the body and to preserve warmth. As noted, it was then believed that the infant's body was soft and 'fluid' and the swaddling was intended to prevent distortion or dislocation of one of the limbs and to guarantee proper and harmonious development.[56] Swaddling immediately after birth was employed also as a means of alleviating the trauma of transition from the womb to the cold outside air. It was also thought (rightly) by medical experts and people as a whole, that the infant continued to require warmth after birth, and the swaddling constituted one of the means of protecting against the cold. One of the biographers of Thomas Becket relates that his mother had a dream in which she saw the infant Thomas naked and trembling with cold. When she awoke, she ran to rebuke the wetnurse for not attending properly to the child. The nurse replied that she had swaddled the child carefully in the swaddling bands – in other words had protected him against the cold.[57] When an Italian mother learned that her infant son, whom she had entrusted for a certain period to childless friends, had wet his bed twice, she was very angry. She claimed that he had never done so at home, and that this had happened because he was not properly covered, or because a length of cloth had not been wrapped around his belly to warm it, as she had always done.[58] It is possible that the woman who tended the child wrapped the bands around his belly and also covered him well, and that he none the less wet the bed because of the shock of the separation from his parents and the move to strange surroundings. His mother, in any event, was convinced that exposure to cold had caused it. In the *Historia Comitum Ghisnensium* (History of the Counts of Guines), the author describes the interior of the count's castle at the beginning of the thirteenth century. He describes a small room in which the infants lived, to which access was gained through the bedroom of the master and mistress of the castle, and which was specially heated by a stove which burned all the time.[59] In the labouring class, both in towns and in the country, an entire family usually crowded into one room and the baby's cradle was placed close to the hearth. The infant was thus kept warm, but the proximity to the flames was risky, particularly when a cauldron of water was suspended by a chain above him for boiling, and one of the typical household accidents to infants was scalding with boiling water.[60] It is not surprising that, in colder countries in Western Europe, in periods such as the Middle Ages, when heating devices were inadequate, the mother protecting her child against the cold was part of the image of the good mother in literature and in sermons.[61] She warms him and holds him close to her heart and rubs his cold hands with straw.[62] In the Late Middle Ages, increasing numbers of houses had glazed windows, which helped to preserve the heat. In the fourteenth century, buttons appeared on clothing and woollen underwear was introduced, both helping to preserve the infant's body-heat.[63]

As regards swaddling, there can be no doubt that since it hampered the easy removal of urine and faeces, and since it was not changed frequently, it caused irritations and sores. Swaddling which was too tight could cause dislocations of the hip. But psychologists contend that there is no harm in the infant's inability to move its limbs freely during the first stage of life, and that not only the increased warmth and stability but also the restraint itself pacifies the infant.[64] Be that as it may, medieval people believed that they were doing what was best for the infant. One of the authors notes an additional item in the infant's equipment, namely a napkin placed under its chin, since it tended to dribble.[65]

THE INFANT AS WAX

Belief in the softness of infant limbs engendered speculation on the proper way of treating them. The paterfamilias in Alberti's book speaks disapprovingly of the habit of certain fathers of throwing the infant into the air and catching it in their arms. How foolish are those who do not understand what injury can be caused to the child by the father's hard arms, he says. The child should be touched and handled with great gentleness, since otherwise one of its limbs could be dislocated or bent.[66] Some modern fathers continue this practice, and psychologists and paediatricians still disapprove. (Abrupt movements of the head can cause mild concussion, brain haemorrhage, and various pressures. Some infants develop fears as a result of this game.) Because of its softness and 'fluidity', some writers perceived the infant's body literally as molten wax. According to the author of the work attributed to Arnold of Villanova, the suitable time for correcting any flaw or distortion in the infant's body or appearance is after his bath. If one of his thighbones is shorter than the other, for example, it should be stretched frequently.[67] Bartholomaeus Anglicus also says that the infant can be moulded like wax, and that it is the wetnurse's task to 'correct' his limbs lest he grow up to be distorted and ugly. The most extreme view of the infant as molten wax is adopted by Francesco of Barbaro: too flat a nose should be raised; too high a nose should be lowered; a short face should be lengthened; and too wide a face 'arranged'. The eyelashes and lips can also be moulded. If the infant squints in both eyes, he should be placed so that the light comes from the opposite direction, and when he gazes in that direction his eyes will gradually straighten. If one eye is straight and the other squints, the straight eye should be covered. Teeth, as well, when crooked or not in the proper order, should be gently pressed into place. The author warns that all this should be done cautiously and gently, without use of force.[68] This advice is, of course, totally spurious, and the comparison of an infant to wax seems repellent to us, but it is known today that certain flaws should be treated at as early an age as possible before the condition is irreversible. Dislocation is now treated several weeks after birth, and various defects of vision, including squinting, are treated as early as possible.

THE CRADLE AND SLEEPING IN THE PARENTAL BED

Use of the cradle was common in all sectors of society. It appears in illuminations from the eleventh century onward[69] and is often mentioned in chronicles, in the *Acta Sanctorum*, and in literature. The expression 'while still an infant in his cradle' is used frequently to denote early childhood.[70] Among the items listed in the 'dowry' of infants sent to wetnurses in Late Medieval Italy, the cradle often appears.[71] In the homes of the rich, cradles were sometimes quite sophisticated: a rope, attached to it, was pulled to rock it.[72] (Cradles were also used in the ancient world, but in so far as is known there were no means of rocking them and the infant was rocked only in someone's arms.)[73] In a story in one of the versions of the collection of legends known as *Gesta Romanorum* (History of the Romans) there is a description of a cradle with four legs which, when overturned, did not permit the infant's face to touch the ground. The child was apparently attached by some kind of strap. Illustrations also show cradles with straps meant to prevent the child from falling out.[74] In poor families, various containers such as baskets or tubs served as cradles.[75] Although accidents also occurred to infants in cradles, a child in a cradle was certainly better protected than in the parental bed where it could be smothered under the weight of one of the parents. Some mothers and wetnurses took the infant into their bed, despite the repeated warnings of all the medical writers, which were not widely read, and of the preachers and confessors, who were heard by all. According to deMause, this custom of taking the infant into bed is an expression of the yearning of the adult woman to be mothered; reversing the situation, she perceives her infant as her own 'security blanket'.[76] It is difficult to accept this psychological explanation, which totally ignores the living conditions of the period and the very real everyday difficulties. The weary wetnurse or mother who took the child into her bed could give him the breast without rising from bed in a cold room when both she and the infant were only half-awake. The poor also undoubtedly took their infants into their beds in order to warm them. Abelard, distinguishing between the deed and the intent in his book *Ethics*, writes of the poor woman who has insufficient covers with which to warm her child and takes him into her bed in order to warm him with the rags and tatters which cover her. Then the catastrophe occurs. She smothers the infant which she is hugging with great love.[77] The infant was certainly calmer and cried less because of the warmth and because of the maternal proximity. Bernard Gordon, in the fourteenth century, cautions wetnurses not to take children into their beds, not only because of the danger to the infant's life but also because the infant will find this pleasant, and it will be difficult to bar him from the bed when she wishes to do so.[78] (A similar caution can be found in Dr Spock's manual.) Warmth and proximity were obtained, but some infants paid with their lives for sleeping with their wetnurses or parents.[79]

CRYING

Parents took infants into their beds in order to pacify them, in contravention of the instructions of the medical writers. The latter, for their part, believing that an infant should not be permitted to cry at length[80] (a little crying was regarded as healthy since it developed the lungs), also proposed various methods of pacifying the baby. If, after the bath and feeding, the child would not fall asleep and continued to cry, the mother or wetnurse should examine whether its swaddling was soiled and whether the outer swaddling bands were too tight. Tender lullabies should be sung to it, its cradle should be rocked gently, or else it should be held.[81] They also warn that protracted crying can cause a hernia, particularly in boys (and we know of infants who suffered from hernias).[82] Francesco of Barbaro also proposes changing the infant's position from time to time and shifting it from stomach to back and vice versa.[83] It is well known today that changing the child's position can help to stop it crying. Preachers also exhorted mothers not to ignore the infant's wails: If your little child cries, lift it in your arms! See if it is necessary to loosen its swaddling, or to cleanse it, or to nurse it, and, if it cries because it wishes to sleep, lull it with lullabies.[84] In one of the miraculous tales attributed to a saint, in order to illustrate the degree of deafness of the woman who appealed to him for aid, the author writes that she could no longer hear even the crying of her son, that is to say the first sound to which a mother was expected to respond.[85] The various authors probably elaborated on the need to pacify a crying infant because they were aware that protracted crying, particularly at night, was one of the phenomena which some parents found it particularly difficult to endure. They all wanted to calm the crying infant, but the inability to diagnose the reason for its crying and thus to put an end to it could cause frustration, fatigue, and tension, and sometimes even generate violent response. The writers who disapprove of procreation in general and list the tribulations of childrearing, mention crying at night as a particular trial.[86] In the Lives of the saints, the future saint is sometimes described as an easy child, smiling constantly and never crying – a description which implies that he differs from other children who weary their mothers by incessant wailing.[87] The healers proposed various kinds of amulets and sleeping potions and incantations (just as they did for protection of the woman in labour and the new-born child), the aim of which was to pacify the child and put it to sleep.[88] It is also possible that the reason why the medical sages, following Aristotle, cautioned against administering wine to infants which could injure their health, was that this was sometimes done in order to put them to sleep. When all else failed, mothers sometimes took infants who cried at length to the shrine of a saint to ask his intercession, just as they did in the case of disease or handicap.[89] From the questions to confessors composed by Burchard of Worms at the beginning of the eleventh century, we learn that in that period, or at least earlier (Burchard was relying on earlier texts), a hole was sometimes dug and the crying infant placed within it to make it stop crying. Parents who did this were made to do five days' penance.[90] The fact that this was a light penance suggests that the author did not regard this practice as a veiled attempt at infanticide but as superstitious conduct which could cause harm to the child. An expression of hostility towards the fractious and troublesome infant is evident in the belief that its crying came from the Devil and his demons who had possessed the child. The mother of Gilbert of Nogent took in an orphan child. According to Gilbert, the child was of pleasant disposition during the day, sleeping and playing alternately, but at night cried incessantly. His discordant cries caused the foster mother severe headaches and sleeplessness, and drove the wetnurses and servantwomen to distraction, when all their efforts to pacify him (including shaking a rattle) proved fruitless. 'He was evil, but through no fault of his own, but because of the act of the Devil ... the child's madness was directed from within and the presence of the "enemy" caused constant disturbance.'[91] Gilbert of Nogent was among those who saw the Devil frequently. He also appears to have envied the orphaned child with whom he was forced to share his mother's attention. And, since his mother had taken in the child in order to do penance for the sin of her deceased husband, who had fathered a bastard child, which died unbaptized (and whom Gilbert envisioned in Hell and not in Limbo),[92] he was able to believe, on the basis of the accepted religious convictions, that the Devil was doing his best to foil her efforts to atone for her husband's sin and to alleviate his sufferings in the next world. Other mothers also, so it seems, attributed the crying of their children to the acts of the Devil and his demonic emissaries.[93] The main sin of one infant described as having been 'born evil, and very difficult to raise' lay in his incessant crying which prevented his mother from sleeping at night. She became so hostile towards him that she could not refrain from cursing him.[94] Those who were convinced that the incessantly crying infant was a 'changeling' (brought by fairies to replace the child they had stolen away) regarded it not only as possessed by a demon, but as the child of demons.[95] Some of these crying infants were probably the most likely victims of parental violence.

SITTING, WALKING, AND SPEECH

The authors of medical works acknowledged that children developed at different paces. Their explanations of this phenomenon were erroneous, but their awareness that the infant should not be forced to sit, stand, or walk before it was ready, but should be allowed to develop at its own pace,[96] was in itself valid. As regards sitting, parents were exhorted to take care to ensure that the child's seat was not too hard and had no protrusions. From a will written in the first half of the fifteenth century, we learn that there were small seats for children. A man bequeathed to his godchild 'a joint stool for a child and another joint stool large for to sit on when he comes to man's state'.[97] The paterfamilias in Alberti's book says that the infant who still finds it hard to sit or stand at length requires rest and long intervals without activity. If he is over-tired, this can only weaken him.[98] A detailed description of ways of encouraging a toddler can be found in a work by the mid-fifteenth-century Paduan, Michele Savonarola, directed at wetnurses. When the child begins to walk, he should be stood near a bench. He should always stand in front of the wetnurse so that they can see one another. (Therefore, it should be a round bench.) The sight of the wetnurse enhances the child's self-confidence, and she will be able to encourage him from time to time. He should not be led by the hand since an incautious movement could cause dislocation. After having acquired confidence, the child should be placed in a walker – 'a chair with wheels on the legs'. When his steps become more certain, he should be placed beside a wall, and the wetnurse should stand at a certain distance and throw him a box or purse or apple, thus luring him to walk while fixing his gaze on the object. When he feels confident when walking this distance, the wetnurse can increase it gradually.[99] The walker, as contemporary illustrations show, was known from the thirteenth century. Its infrequent appearance in illuminations indicates that it was only used in prosperous families. We also learn from this source that, as is customary today, the infant was not put into shoes until he began to walk.[100] Authors warn the wetnurse to take particular care of the child from the moment he begins to walk, and to make sure that his first steps are taken on a straight, flat surface.[101] Since toddlers fall constantly, they should be dressed in padded bonnets. Contemporary illustrations show such bonnets.

Most authors saw a connection between emergence of teeth and the commencement of speech, and believed that toothlessness hampered speech. Accordingly, they held that at the age of 2 approximately, after all the teeth had appeared, the child should be able to speak. Discussing the different pace of development in different children, they specify the beginning of walking and the beginning of speech as distinct indications of the child's pace of development. They did not consider speech to be the outcome of systematic instruction, but rather the realization of human potential through imitation. At the same time, they declared that a child should be assisted in this process of social acquisition. He should be encouraged to utter various words and praised when he succeeded; he should be shown an object he covets and told 'You can have it if you repeat what I say', and encouraged first to utter 'words which do not require the tongue to move much, such as "father" and "mother"'. According to Francesco of Barbaro, if a child had difficulty in talking, the wetnurse should take a large mirror, and place behind it a child who could speak already, and whose voice resembled that of her charge. The child behind the mirror should repeat various words on the instruction of the wetnurse, and her charge, believing it to be his own voice, would undoubtedly repeat them, and begin to speak like the child behind the mirror. This advice is probably based on Francesco of Barbaro's awareness that older children tend to talk to themselves. (The general view is that this habit of talking to himself fosters both the child's ability to control his external actions and helps him in the process of learning to integrate language and thought.) As was also the case with regard to advice on treatment of various ailments, expert views on the commencement of speech include both sound advice and groundless nonsense. Thus some writers proposed treating the mouth in order to induce the child to speak: his tongue should be rubbed with honey, salt, frankincense, and a touch of liquorice. Those who advocate assisting the child at this stage direct their advice at the wetnurse, or state in general that women have the most experience in this sphere.[102]

RECIPROCAL RELATIONS BETWEEN CHILDREN AND ADULTS

Acknowledgement of the fact that a child could not live by bread alone, and that physical nurturing, however good, without a bond with the child and without speech, warmth, and love would be ineffective underlies an ancient tale which the Franciscan Salimbene attributes to Emperor Frederick II. According to the author, the Emperor ordered that a group of children be collected, and instructed the foster mothers and the wetnurses who reared them to nurse them, bathe them, and treat them well, but not to talk to them or to make the sounds which it was customary to make to infants. He was curious to know in what language these children would begin to speak: Hebrew, Greek, Latin, Arabic, or possibly the language of their natural parents. The experiment failed, and the children not only failed to speak but died. They could not live without handclapping, friendly and joyful facial expressions, praise, and lullabies. The author's comments clearly suggest that children have need of reciprocal relations with adults through voice, smile, and movement not only for the sake of their emotional and intellectual development, but also for their very survival.[103] Descriptions of the bond between mother and child through smiles can be found not only in literature, but also in an incident reported in testimony before the Inquisition tribunal at Pamiers, headed by Bishop Jacques Fournier. One of the witnesses, telling of a noblewoman from Chateauverdun who was about to leave her home and join the Cathars, said

> She had an infant in his cradle and she wanted to see him before leaving home. On seeing him, she kissed him and the infant began to smile. She began to move away from the cradle in order to leave the room, but retraced her footsteps and again approached the infant. He again smiled and the same happened several times. He held her by his smile, and she could not leave him. In the end, she said to the maidservant 'take him out of the room'.

The young woman was eventually burned at the stake by the Inquisition.[104]

As regards lullabies, Adelard of Bath describes, in the twelfth century, the particular sensitivity of small children to sounds and attributes great importance to the first sounds they hear. A pleasant and harmonious voice soothes them and, vice versa, a discordant and harsh voice harms them. The lullaby acts as intimate consolation to the young soul and causes it to forget pain. He describes a small child still unable to talk who stands and listens to the guitar-playing of a music teacher and his pupils. The excited child begins to wave his hands and fingers to the rhythm of the music, and everyone laughs affectionately.[105] One of the interlocutors in Alberti's book also refers to infant reaction to sounds and to lullabies: if an infant responds to the snap of a finger with alert interest and pleasure, this means that his temperament is suited to masculine activity and to the art of war. If he prefers verses and lullabies he was born to a life of study and science.[106] Another speaker in the same book describes reactions to a child's first speech: the child begins to express his wishes in understandable fashion to those around him and to utter his first words. The entire family listens. The entire neighbourhood repeats his words joyfully, and everyone interprets and praises what he has said and done.[107]

There were also failures. In the tale of the miracles performed by one of the saints, it is related that parents from a lower class 'often tried to teach their little three-year-old boy to speak but could not succeed in persuading him to reply even by one word'.[108] This suggests that the parents were troubled by the problem and tried to do their best. When they concluded that there was nothing further they could do, they turned to a saint for aid. It is well known that not only can lack of attention and neglect hamper a child's development but also that frequent replacements in the nurturing figure can cause trauma and lead to psychomotor and verbal backwardness. It may be that some of the (many) children brought to the shrines of the saints because they were not yet speaking[109] were not dumb from birth because of congenital defects but had failed to develop the ability to speak because of parental neglect or because of constant replacement of wetnurses. Even a child who had been reared by only one wetnurse could experience a severe trauma which delayed the onset of speech upon being returned home at the highly sensitive age of 2. Some contemporaries were cognizant of the trauma experienced by the small child brought back to the parental home. Bernardino of Siena, reproaching mothers who sent their infants to wetnurses, adds: 'and when he comes home to you you say "I don't know whom you are like, certainly none of us!" '[110] In any event, the time came when parents ceased to be indifferent to the presence of a non-speaking child. Had this not been so, they would not have taken the trouble to make pilgrimages to the shrines of the saints.

PERCEPTION AND RECOGNITION OF THE INFANT AND TODDLER

According to Ariès, medieval society did not value the small child. And, this being so, it did not notice him or know him. To prove this last point, Ariès cites, *inter alia*, the fact that, in art up to the thirteenth century, there are no depictions of living children. The child, when it makes its infrequent appearances in painting and sculpture of the period, is depicted as a miniature adult. It was only gradually, from the thirteenth century onward, that several images of small children, approximating to our present-day conception of the child, began to appear in art (mainly in portrayals of the infant Jesus). The question is whether this necessarily proves that adults did not observe children and did not recognize them, or whether the reason for this absence of 'living' children should not be sought in the context of the history of art – in contemporary style, in artistic traditions, and in the functions of art. The appearance of children in art until the thirteenth century is perhaps much less rare than Ariès claims. Children appear mostly in illuminations, and are not entirely absent from sculpture. Children appear in Carolingian, Ottonian, and Romanesque art, and the way in which they are portrayed indicates awareness of the distinct nature of the childhood phase in life and of the special qualities of the child.[111] They appear more frequently in Gothic art. We also find descriptions of infants and small children in literary depictions of childrearing methods: bathing, dressing and undressing, nursing by the mother and wetnurse, or feeding with animal-milk which appears in miraculous fashion. In descriptions of the child himself, always described as especially beautiful, the authors often employ adjectives and images which were usually applied to women: clear, white skin, pink cheeks like the rose or lily. 'He was the rose among the children,' says the queen in *Lancelot del Lac* of the son she lost.[112] Love and pampering are lavished on the child by all those who rear him,[113] and his smile wins their hearts. The beautiful, smiling infant even softens the heart of the person who is about to kill him because he has been ordered to do so or because this is the child of his enemy.[114] It is more rarely that we find in literature a description of the infant and small child and his behaviour and responses which rises above stereotypes. These appear, however, in other sources. Henry Suso's portrayal of the infant climbing on its mother's knee, or Adelard of Bath's description of the child bouncing to music are not isolated examples. I should like to cite two other descriptions from the *Lives of the Saints* – one of a toddler and the other of an infant, both reflecting the keen observation of which contemporary writers were capable and their conception of the conduct of infants and small children. The first description was apparently written in the fourteenth century. According to the author, it was a vision dictated by St Ida of Louvain to her confessor. In her vision, she was permitted by St Elizabeth to assist in bathing the infant Jesus:

> Elizabeth brought the bath in order to bathe the infant and the other utensils required for this and bent with all courtesy in order to bathe the child in the warm water together with Ida. When the Holy Infant was seated in the bath, he began to play as is the way of infants. He made noise in the water by clapping hands, and as children do, splashed in the water until it spilled out and wet all those around. He continued to splash while moving all of his tiny body. On seeing the water splashing all around, he began to shout with joy in a loud voice ... and when the bathing was completed, she lifted the child from the bath, dried him, and wrapped him in his swaddling bands. She seated him on her lap and as mothers do, began to play with him.[115]

This vivid description purports to depict the nurturing of the infant Jesus. But, had Ida of Louvain not recalled a similar picture from her own childhood, or witnessed it somewhere, could it have appeared in her vision?

The following excerpt is taken from the biography of St Hugh of Lincoln (1140–1200), written several years after his death by the man who was his chaplain in the last three years of his life. The author describes a meeting between the bishop (Hugh) and an infant.

> I saw a child of about six months, who, when he made the sign of the cross on its forehead with the holy oil, expressed such great delight by the movement of its limbs that it reminded one of the joy of the Baptist, leaping up in the womb. The tiny mouth and face relaxed in continuous chuckles, and it seemed incredible that, at an age when babies generally yell, it could laugh in this way. It then bent and stretched out its little arms, as if it were trying to fly, and moved its head to and fro, as if to show that its joy was almost too great to bear. Next, it took his hand in both its tiny ones, and exerting all its strength, raised it to its face. It then proceeded to lick

it instead of kissing it. This it did for a long time. Those present were amazed at the unusual spectacle of the bishop and the infant absolutely happy in each other's company ... The bishop gave the boy an apple and several other things which children usually like, but he refused to be amused by any of them. He rejected them all and seemed completely absorbed and fascinated by the bishop. Disdainfully pushing away the hands of the nurse who was holding him, he gazed hard at the bishop, and clapped his hands smiling all the time.[116]

If, in fact, little children had had no place in medieval culture, could such a description have been written?

Ritual expression of the importance which parents attributed to their infant and their pride in him is evinced in the custom which prevailed in the Sens region in France in the fourteenth century. On the eve of the Feast of the Nativity of St John, which took place in the summer (24 June), parents would take their children out into the street in their cradles and set them among green branches, and, to all those who came to inspect the infants, they distributed sweetmeats.[117] It seems that, in general, mothers carried their small children with them in their arms or on their backs when they went to watch processions or celebrations, as reported by a peasant woman from Montaillou: 'It was a feast day and I was standing in the square with my daughter in my arms ...'[118] Late medieval illustrations show many mothers carrying their infants in their arms or on their backs in rucksacks of leather or cloth tied to the neck by a wide band. Peasant women are depicted carrying their infants with them to their labours in the field in small cradles tied to their backs.[119] One of the biographies of Bernard of Clairvaux relates how he came to the home of one of the young noblemen who joined his order. A large crowd flocked there to hear him speak, and the mother of the young nobleman also came. She sat at his feet with her three-month-old infant in her arms.[120] In prosperous families it was, of course, often the wetnurses or maidservants who carried the infants on feastdays or at family gatherings. This custom of going out of doors with infants or small children, thereby enabling them to see the world, is considered desirable today as well. Many mothers (and fathers) carry their small children in special slings: in the first weeks of life in a sling over the chest, and when they are slightly older in a backpack.

FROM 2 TO 7

In some cases, it is difficult to establish to which age the advice of medical manuals refers: 2, 3, or 4. Generally speaking, however, it can be said that they go into greater detail about the infant from birth to 2 years of age than about ages 2–7. This was because the risk of mortality gradually dropped from this age on, and because physical care from the age of 2 onward is simpler. The authors recommend continuing to bathe the child daily, or at least several times a week, and activating him through gymnastic exercises. These are conducive to health since they assist the digestive process and make him light-footed. However, up to the age of 7 care should be taken to avoid overstraining the child, since his limbs are still weak, and the exercises should be simple and pleasant. Heavy food and wine are not suited for small children.[121]

I have found no reference to toilet training. This may be due to the conviction that there was no need for special instruction since the child would learn habits of cleanliness gradually and of his own free will through imitating adults. It will be recalled that, according to Erikson, the most important achievement at the age of 15 months to $2\frac{1}{2}$ years is the development of a sense of the self as a separate personality, so that education must aspire to maintain suitable equilibrium between freedom and supervision. In contemporary western society one of the tests is toilet training; it is part of society's indispensable demand for adaptation, but, in the course of the process of habituating the child, it must be ensured that he does not forfeit his trust and his self-respect. We have no way of ascertaining how parents and wetnurses acted in the Middle Ages. We can only deduce from the fact that the medical writers do not relate to this issue that they did not consider it a problem requiring instruction such as was given in other spheres. The fact that, from the age of about 1 year, the infant was dressed in a shirt without underpants, enabling the escape of the bodily secretions without soiling the garment or the body, undoubtedly made life easier for the mother or nurse until the child was toilet trained. It is also known that contemporary adults were not over-modest about biological functions and were not bound by the restrictions on bodily movements and activities which govern modern western conduct in public. It is, therefore, highly feasible that children learned gradually and at their own pace through imitating adults, without specific 'toilet training'.

Some of the authors of medical works deliberately confine their discussion to physical nurturing, stating, in the wake of the Greek and Moslem authorities, that education is a matter for moral philosophers and not for physicians. The author of the work attributed to Arnold of Villanova following Aristotle's conception of the body–mind unity, adds only that there is a connection between the physical and the spiritual: distortions of the soul affect the state of the humours, and hence the temperament and the body as a whole. A corrupt soul corrupts the body. Since fear and dread cause melancholy, one should refrain, when rearing a child, from angering or saddening him. Nor should one act with excessive merriment. Everything should be done with moderation and in the proper proportion. Other authors devote slightly more space to education at this age, and all, like most didactic writers, favour essentially lenient education and granting the child freedom to act in accordance with his natural tendencies.[122]

Francesco of Barbaro, in his advice to wetnurses or nurses, prescribes diversion instead of head-on clashes with the child. A small child should not be shown something which cannot be given to him; and, if he happens to glimpse it, his attention should be diverted through offering him some other object. If he asks for something which is permissible and is not harmful, it should be given to him. If he receives an injury, the wetnurse, when binding his wound, should pretend to be taking revenge against the object which hurt him and should console him with small gifts. When the child is a little older, he should be allowed to go out to play with his peers.[123] Konrad of Megenberg counsels parents to employ a young nursemaid in addition to the nurse. (It is not clear if he is referring to a relative or a young servantgirl.) Her conversation will enrich the child's vocabulary; she will entertain him with various games and carry him in her arms when the adult nurse is occupied with other matters.[124] Raymond Lull writes that up to the age of 7 or 8 the child should be allowed to behave in accordance with his nature, permitted to play with his peers, and not forced to begin studying. The mother of the eponymous hero of Lull's book *Blanquerna* acted in this fashion. When he was old enough to go out to play with children of his own age she allowed him to do so, and he began to study only at the age of 8.[125] Konrad of Megenberg, who also emphasizes the importance of play for the physical and spiritual development of the child, also prescribes play in the open air, and notes that a child who is still capable of marvelling at small things will rejoice even in the simplest objects while at play. However, a wise nurse should know when the child is fatigued and ready for bed. When a child cries without knowing why and refuses to accept food and drink or anything else offered him, this is a sign that he is tired and should be taken to his bed.[126] These remarks are undoubtedly the fruit of observation of small children. Even the writers who asserted that everything should be done in moderation, and that a child should not be allowed to play too much, considered play to be a natural need: 'Children should be allowed to play since nature demands it,'[127] writes Philip of Novare. According to Aegidius Romanus, games arouse a positive competitive instinct. He also recommends telling children stories with an educational message, conversing with them about great events of the past, and even singing them songs. Like the author of the work attributed to Arnold of Villanova, Aegidius and Aldebrandin of Siena also stress that the child should not be saddened.[128] It was generally accepted that a child, like a tender shoot, needed suitable conditions for growth, differing from those required by an adult, and that a child could not endure certain things which an adult could suffer. A light blow to a tender branch causes it more damage than a deep cut to a mighty tree-trunk,[129] says one of the interlocutors in Alberti's book. In view of the conviction that strict instruction in Christian morals and in obedience to parents and those in authority should commence only at a later age, parents were essentially exhorted by parish priests only to guard their children against various accidents, and to ensure that they were baptized and that they learned the three most important prayers (Paternoster, Ave Maria, and Credo) and how to cross themselves morning and evening. Some authors of didactic works added that small children should also be taught the two first commandments (love of God and love of one's neighbour).[130] Those preachers who reprimanded parents for not giving their children a Christian education and for pampering them were referring, almost without exception, to children over the age of 7.

This lenient and freedom-oriented educational outlook was inspired by the prevailing theory on the pattern of child development and by both the positive and the negative images of childhood. The small child was considered weak, tender, and vulnerable. He was perceived as innocent and incapable of committing an unpardonable sin on the one hand, and as lacking the understanding and capacity for choice between good and evil, on the other. According to Konrad of Megenberg, children under 7 are blessed with only a sliver of reason, and Aegidius Romanus writes that, up to the age of 7, the child is almost totally incapable of using his reason. He can be taught neither science nor morals. He can be taught only the vernacular language (*ydeomata vulgaria*), and, apart from baptism and the sacraments of the church (he was apparently referring to confirmation), attention should be focused primarily on good physical condition or, in other words, on keeping him alive. These comments confirm Levine's view that, in societies in which infant and child mortality are high, parents concentrate in the first years of childhood primarily on ensuring the survival and physical well-being of their child. The stimuli for social and cognitive development are postponed to a later stage, when the child's survival appears more or less certain. In the second stage of childhood, Aegidius writes, in addition to concern for physical health, the educator should strive to ensure that the child's urges are balanced and co-ordinated (*ordinatio appetitus*) and he can already receive instruction. But only from the age of 14 onward, when the intellect is mature, can he engage in all types of academic study.[131] The same belief that small children should not yet be educated and that not everything can be taught even in the second stage of childhood is also reflected in the response of Anselm of Canterbury to the question why he devoted most of his time and efforts to teaching and educating the young (*adolescentes, juvenes*). He cited the image of wax, this time in the context not of the tender body but of spiritual and intellectual development. Tender children are like too-soft wax, which is almost liquid and cannot take the shape of the mould. Their understanding is slight, they find it difficult to distinguish between good and evil, and, when one discusses a moral issue with them, they do not understand. The old are like overhard wax, and also cannot be moulded. Between the two stages lie the young, who are like wax which is neither soft nor hard, and hence can be instructed and educated.[132]

The author of a manual for priests clearly expresses the view that a child under 7 is innocent and free of sinful lust. He writes that priests should inform their flock that boys and girls who have reached the age of 7 should no longer sleep in the same bed, lest they develop desires for the 'fouwle dede'. In other words, children under 7 can sleep together without being tempted to sin. At the same time, priests should also caution godparents against sleeping in the same bed as their godchildren while the latter are small, lest they smother them under the weight of their bodies.[133] From this, as well, it is clear that no objections were voiced to the accepted custom of sleeping in the same bed with small children if they had reached an age at which this no longer posed a risk.

Conflicting opinions were also expressed. The opposite extreme was represented in the early fifteenth century by Giovanni Dominici, who appears not only to have thought that a child's innocence should be protected from a very early age, but also to have questioned the very essence of this innocence. He writes that the sexual modesty of the child should be protected from the age of 5, and preferably even from the age of 3. From 3 on, it is not desirable for him to see naked people, and care should be taken to ensure that he distinguish between the sexes only according to clothing and hairstyle. From 3 to 25, neither the mother nor any other person should hug or kiss him. Although no 'natural' thought or movement will be roused in a child under 5, none the less from 3 on he should be dressed modestly (as should girls) by day and night. From this age on, brothers and sisters should not sleep in the same bed. In the same spirit, and counter to the accepted view that only older children should be whipped for purposes of education and moral instruction, Dominici asserted that three-year-olds could be whipped, albeit not severely and in proper proportion to the scope of the sin. If the child repents and confesses his sin, he should be treated leniently.[134] Like Dominici, Jean Gerson warns, in one of his sermons, against the corruption of innocent children by men- and maidservants, and he was apparently also referring to small children.[135] Unlike Dominici, Gerson does not deny the existence of infantile innocence, but he fears that it may be corrupted. Konrad of Megenberg also believed that children under the age of 7 should be whipped for mendacity. He rebukes parents who are amused by childish profanity, and admonishes those who teach girls to stimulate their genitalia, thereby rousing the sexual instinct. But he too observes that, since the child does not know what it is doing, it is the adults who are committing the sin.[136]

There were doubtless conflicting theories, just as there were two conflicting images of childhood. However, not only did the 'positive' image of the small child predominate, but in everyday life, with the exception of those who were placed in monasteries at a very early age, children up to the age of 7 generally enjoyed freedom. Few restrictions were imposed on them, nor were they kept at a distance from adults, for better or worse, according to our conceptions. Throughout society, boys and girls were not separated up to the age of 7, even in the prosperous urban households and the castles of the nobility.[137] They were a part of a society in which people of all classes were crowded densely together. Everything was more open, and western man had not yet begun to seek privacy. Even masters and servants, whose class differences were emphasized by different clothing and forms of address, lived in close proximity. The problem of the harm liable to be done to children from nearness to servants concerned educators in the next few centuries as well. Ariès has described these issues vividly, and he was, of course, correct in claiming that children were involved in adult society. Clothing was not particularly modest, since both boys and girls wore shirts with very little under them. (After the period in which infants wore nothing under their shirts, they were dressed in drawers held closed with a string. These 'peeped out' when the shirt was short or when it was long and was rolled up for comfort during play or other activities.[138]) It was customary for several members of a family to sleep in the same bed: brothers and sisters, parents and their child or an uncle and his nephew. There is a tale of a boy of 8 who at night 'was carefully laid by his mother by her side'.[139] Even a preacher such as Stephen of Bourbon describes as natural the fact that three young boys shared a bed. To quote Jean Flandrin: in the labouring classes the shared bed was one of the expressions of 'the spirit of communality in family life'.[140] Often adults and children slept naked. Not only was adult nudity no secret to children but, as a result of their nocturnal propinquity, sexual relations were also no mystery to them, for those either in towns or in villages. Nor, apparently, were manifestations of sexuality in children suppressed, as can be seen from the reprimands of the authors of didactic books. In short, adult sensuality was overt, and infantile sexuality was considered innocent and perhaps even amusing. Parents appear not to have taken a strict view of the use of profanity, but were rather diverted by the 'wit' of the child. Not only Konrad of Megenberg reprimanded them for this. According to a certain preacher, once a child has learned to walk and talk, the Devil takes the trouble to teach him coarse words and profanity. And parents, instead of fighting this phenomenon, consider it amusing and a sign of 'cleverness' in the child.[141] It seems abundantly clear that people did not internalize the exhortations of the preachers and didactic writers. But neither this fact nor the failure to keep children at a distance from adult society should be regarded as indications that childhood was not recognized as a separate phase of life, with its own characteristics and privileges. The proximity to servants did not obliterate awareness of the differences between servants and masters, and did not bestow on the former similar rights. It is typical that in fourteenth-century Venice, where sexual morals were remote from the norms which the church wished to sustain, the legal authorities of the town imposed penalties severalfold harsher for the rape of a female minor (*puella*) than for the rape of an adult woman. The authors of confessors' manuals imposed heavy penances on churchmen or monks who seduced minors. They also proclaim that a man who has committed this sin should never again be permitted to speak to a child.[142]

There is no question but that children were allowed the opportunity of playing, as writers recommended. From the sources we learn of outdoor group-games, of games played with natural objects and materials both indoors and out, and even of toys. In the tales of the miracles attributed to saints or in descriptions of boys or girls cured of ailments or injuries after accidents the expression 'went out to play with the children of his [or 'her'] age' is often reiterated; or, after the saint has performed the miracle, the father finds his daughter 'completely healthy, laughing and playing'.[143] It is only the future (male or female) saint, who differs from all other children, being as serious as an old man and shunning the company of his peers, who does not play. And, from the description of his conduct, we can ascertain what was considered typical childish behaviour.[144] Some of the accidents mentioned occurred in the course of play, while a small child was playing outdoors without supervision or when his older siblings, who were supposed to watch him, neglected their task.[145] Jean Froissart, in his work *L'Espinette amoureuse* (The Cage of Love), lists fifty-one children's games, individual games and, in particular, group-games. Most of the games he describes, particularly the group-games, are for older boys from 7 on who are already attending town-schools, and he distinguishes between the games of the under-twelves and those of children over that age. But some of the games are also suitable for small boys and girls, who were in the habit of imitating the older children. Out of earth, water, strips of wood and of cloth they build a dam, a boat, a mill, and an oven. From a shell they make a sieve, two sticks become a harrow; one stick is a hobby-horse, and a duel can be conducted with two blocks of wood. The child is unwilling to give up his treasures at any price and, however tired, will not cease his play.[146] One of the English preachers also describes a child at play at home with everyday objects and materials, transforming them into whatever he chooses with his hands and with the aid of his imagination. A stick becomes a white horse, crumbs of bread are kneaded into a boat, chips of wood become a castle, and a stick a sword.[147] In these games, as in some of the outdoor games which Froissart describes, there was a mimetic element, as in many children's games throughout the ages, and the writers who depicted these games were aware of this. Hence, when they write of a future saint who, unlike most of his kind, plays with damp sand, they attribute to him the desire to build churches and monasteries, altars and crucifixes, while they attribute to ordinary children the desire to construct houses, fortresses, and horses and riders. Another future saint loved only one game – to imitate the mass ceremony with which he was acquainted from church.[148] Giovanni Dominici, who was opposed to giving expensive toys to children, also acknowledged children's predilection for imitation and the importance of play for the child, and proposed methods of exploiting it as an educational tool. He suggests that parents playing with children deliberately lose the game and then hasten to the household chapel to pray. In this way, the child would learn to appeal to God when in distress, and would also realize that God also loves the losers. He also proposed that a kind of psychodrama be conducted: the child should deliver a sermon to the household (to which all would listen attentively without laughing), and on the next occasion the parent would preach. Instructors of the children in the 'children's confraternities' in Florence in the first decades of the fifteenth century, recognizing the predilection of children for imitation and their fondness for dramatic play, instructed them not only to observe the precepts of Christian morality and to ensure that their parents did the same, to pray, and to attend religious processions, but also to act in plays with an educational-religious message. And smaller children, who were not yet members of the confraternity, also took part in these performances.[149] (These confraternities were established in a spirit of ambivalence: apprehension with regard to children and recognition of the need to restrain them and to guide them into paths of action desirable to adults, and a kind of worship of childhood – an extreme expression of belief in its redeeming power, stemming from its innocence.)

There were some medieval games of which modern western mothers would not have approved. For example, a chick fell into a pit and drowned. The mother took it out and gave it to her child as a plaything. (The child then summoned the aid of a saint who revived the chick.)[150] Toys also existed. The generosity of a future saint, the child of noble parents, was manifested when he was only 5. He not only invited the poor children of the neighbourhood to meals, but also divided up his toys among them.[151] Medieval children are known to have played with rattles, hobby-horses, rocking-horses, blocks, bones, balls, hoops, dolls, spinning tops, see-saws, small windmills, little wooden boats, whistles, clay birds, miniature cooking utensils, marionettes, with which adults played as well, glass rings, which were also worn as jewellery by little girls, and drums and cymbals. A wood carving from the fifteenth century shows a mother teaching her son to ride a bicycle-like toy. Her expression is concentrated, and her hand rests gently on his head.[152] As is the habit of children everywhere, medieval children tried to play with the possessions of adults and were sometimes granted permission to do so. In a domestic scene described by a preacher, a child asks to play with his mother's jewellery. She tells him that he must first wash his hands and then she will give them to him.[153] The writers clearly distinguished between the form of play of older and younger children. In the German literary work, *King of Tyrol*, a child is depicted imitating older children playing peek-a-boo, and understanding the game in his own way: he covers his eyes with his hands and believes that nobody can see him.[154]

Psychologists have noted the importance of play for the intellectual and social development of the child.　According to Erikson, in the third stage of life (from $2\frac{1}{2}$ to 6) language is enriched, motor skills improve, inquisitiveness increases, and the development of the self as a separate entity continues. The most important aim at this stage is the development of initiative, which is made possible through the ability to move about freely and to try out new experiences with great energy. According to medieval sources, children appear to have been allowed the opportunity of achieving this aim. Socialization proceeded at a gradual pace and without too much pressure. Norbert Elias has noted the differences in the code of conduct in medieval western society as compared to later periods. It seems that, in the Middle Ages, people were not expected to restrain themselves or, as has been noted above, to keep their physical distance from one another or to act discreetly with regard to biological functions (defecation and urination, nose-wiping, spitting, etc.). The threshold of embarrassment was much higher than in later periods. The manuals of etiquette for adults (in the nobility) deal with the most basic matters, which in modern times are taught to small children: one should not belch during meals, should not cram large hunks of food into one's mouth, a hunk of food which has been chewed should not be put back on the communal plate, the eyes and nose should not be wiped with a table-napkin, etc. This suggests that these issues were not stressed in early education, and that only limited pressure was brought to bear on small children to learn elementary manners.[155]

Children who received an education did not usually attend school before the age of 7. Some, however, were taught at home from the age of 5 or 6, by their father or a private tutor.[156] The authors who recommended beginning to teach reading at this age stressed that study should be gradual, that the child should not be forced to study long hours each day, and that the instruction should be gentle and pleasant. Peter Damian lists several 'literary games', known by various names, which were intended to teach proper speech and apparently reading as well. Others advocated giving small prizes with the aim of encouraging the pupil. For example, letters could be formed from fruit and sweets. If the child succeeded in deciphering the letters, he should be given the fruit or sweet. Giovanni Dominici also recommends giving the child who has done well at reading a small gift, such as new shoes, an inkwell, or a slate.[157] Greater pressure was sometimes brought to bear on five- or six-year-olds who studied at home, when they were earmarked for service in the secular church or for the monastic life. Gilbert of Nogent began his studies with a private tutor in his mother's home before he was 5. Describing this period in his autobiography, he writes that the tutor was very pious and well-intentioned. However, his education was limited and he lacked any talent for teaching. Although he loved the child, 'his love was cruel'. He restricted Gilbert stringently: he did not permit him to play with his peers, forced him to study long hours, did not allow him to take a step without permission, and beat him severely.[158] Of those designated for ecclesiastical service or the monastic life, some began studying at 5 or 6 in small local schools. There were isolated cases of children who were not earmarked for the church, like Giovanni Morelli and his son, who began studying at this age.[159] In one case, the writer, who was aware that the five-year-old boy had begun his studies at an earlier age than usual, and that the other children were older than him, described him as 'short in stature and delicate'.[160] Other boys and girls, designated for the monastic life, were placed in monasteries and convents at the age of 5, and, in exceptional cases, even younger. Their lives undoubtedly differed drastically from those of most other children, and we shall discuss them in a separate chapter. Generally speaking, it should be recalled that only a small minority of children learned to read. An even smaller proportion learned to read and write, and even fewer received a proper education.

In the written sources, we encounter displays of affection for small children, expressions of understanding of their conduct and the workings of their imagination, and even tolerance, approaching permissiveness, towards mischief. In feudal literature, the mischievous conduct of the small heroes sometimes bordered on wildness, without being punished.[161] The biographer of Catherine of Siena, who learned of the saint's childhood from her mother, wrote that 'When she was weaned, she began to eat bread dishes and to walk by herself. She then began to please all those who saw her.' He relates that relatives and neighbours loved to listen to her childish and charming speech and enjoyed her cheerfulness. Her mother had difficulty in keeping her at home since neighbours and relatives continuously came to beg to take the child to their homes. When she was 5 or so, after having learned the Ave Maria, she would halt at every step, when going up or down stairs, kneel, and recite a sentence from the prayer.[162] This description is not a *topos*; it is based on observation of the conduct of a small girl engaged in ritual repetition, as is often the case with children. Understanding of the ways in which a child's perception differs from that of an adult, and of the workings of the childish imagination, is revealed in the tale of the English Franciscan Thomas of Eccleston. He relates that the minister of the order in England often visited the home of the noble, Geoffrey Despenser, and that, each time he came, the host's small son, John, would greet him with great friendliness. One day the child saw him conducting mass in the chapel. The next time he visited the house, the child ran away from him, and all his mother's persuasion could not bring him to approach the visitor as in the past. When she eventually asked him why he had run away and what had frightened him, he replied that he had seen the Franciscan friar eating a child on the altar of the chapel, and he was afraid that he too would be eaten.[163] The story sounds authentic, but even if it did not occur, and was only the projection of the author's own remembered childhood fears of the host, it still reflects acknowledgement of the fact that a child thinks and sees differently from an adult. It is not the fact that the child is described as having imagined that he saw an infant in the host which reveals the author's understanding of the childish mind, since there was a lengthy literary and artistic tradition of the revelation of Christ in the form of a little child in the host. The author's perception of the child's view is unique in that the child is said to fear that he too will be eaten by the priest.

The biographer of Anselm of Canterbury writes of a childhood memory which Anselm related to him. Having been bred in the mountains, and having lent a ready ear to his mother's conversation,

> he imagined that heaven rested on the mountains, that the court of God was there, and that the approach to it was through the mountains ... One night he saw a vision, in which he was bidden to climb to the top of the mountain, and hasten to the court of the great king, God ... He saw in the plain through which he was approaching the foot of the mountain, women – serfs of the king ... who were reaping the corn, but doing so carelessly and idly. The boy was grieved and indignant at their laziness, and resolved to accuse them before their lord the king. Then he climbed the mountain and came to the royal court, where he found God alone with his steward. For, as he imagined, since it was autumn he had sent his household to collect the harvest ... The Lord asked him in a pleasant and friendly way who he was, where he came from, and what he wanted ... Then at God's command the whitest of bread was brought him by the steward and he refreshed himself with it in God's presence. The next day, therefore, when he recalled to his mind's eye all that he had seen, like a simple and innocent boy he believed that he had been in heaven and that he had been fed with the bread of God, and he asserted as much to others in public.[164]

This story, like the preceding ones, was certainly anchored in medieval culture, with its values and images, but also reveals awareness of the unique perceptions of childhood.

The child who senses both the beauty and the pain of being, but cannot express his sensations, has been described by Wolfram of Eschenbach.

> Of sorrow he knew nothing, unless it was the birdsong above him, for the sweetness of it pierced his heart and made his little bosom swell. Weeping, he ran to the queen, and she said 'Who has hurt you? You were out on the meadow.' He could tell her nothing, as is still the way with children.[165]

The written sources teach us about children in the towns and the nobility as well as about those who were destined for the secular church or the monastic life. There is almost no direct evidence on small children from the peasantry. It is hard to believe that in the first phase of childhood they were more restricted and enjoyed less freedom than children in higher social strata. They certainly did not receive either the gymnastic exercises recommended by medical scholars (it is doubtful that these were practised in the upper classes either) or the delicate food they prescribed, nor did they suffer the overfeeding criticized by didactic writers. They ate the same food as their parents. (A study of the nutrition of peasants in the Late Middle Ages reveals that prosperous peasants ate wheat-bread, soups, gruel, pork, and (in certain areas) fish. They ate more vegetables and dairy products than the nobility, in whose diet meat played a more important part. The middling peasants enjoyed meat, cheese, and beer more rarely than the more prosperous peasants, and soup and gruels from pulses and oats played a more major part in their diet. Poor peasants and hired labourers did not always have enough grain, so that they did not always receive sufficient calories, and only rarely did they consume animal protein and beer.[166]) It is known that the average number of offspring in prosperous families was greater than in middle-income families, and in the latter was higher than in poor families in the same time and place. There were several reasons for this. The well-to-do married younger than the poor, and the fertility span of the couple was exploited more fully than in the case of poor couples. The fact that women of the labouring class nursed their own infants increased the interval between pregnancies. At the same time, it is highly likely that more of the children of the rich survived because of better nutrition and environmental conditions.[167] One should not deduce from this that the children of peasants received less affection or were less valued than those of the rich. Contemporary authors who wrote about the peasants did not assert that in this social stratum there was no material and emotional investment in children. According to a thirteenth-century preacher, peasants praised their children when small, and dressed them in many-coloured shirts, and, when they grew up, set them behind the plough. Noblemen, on the other hand, 'set their children under their feet' and force them to eat with the servants, and laud and glorify them when they grow to adulthood.[168] It is not clear whom the preacher is admonishing and whom he is praising in this statement. Nor should one take the statement literally. It seems reasonable to assume that he identifies with the spartan education he attributes to the nobility, but we also learn something of the contemporary view of the way in which peasants reared their children. A carving in the Church of the Magdalen in Vézelay shows a barefoot peasant woman affectionately combing the hair of her small son.[169] In a ballad in which the peasant and his wife exchange roles for one day the husband is given the task – amongst others – of wiping away the tears of his small children and consoling them.[170] The author apparently considered this to be part of the day-to-day activities of the peasant woman.

RECEIVING THE SACRAMENTS

As noted above, there was no consensus among the canonists and theologians nor was there uniform practice on the age at which the sacrament of confirmation was administered. Since people attributed to this sacrament, as to baptism, healing powers,[171] they tried to ensure that their children received it as early as possible. But since it could be administered only by the bishop, and people found it hard to reach his place of residence, while he himself did not always travel regularly to each place in his diocese, the sacrament was often postponed. The biographer of Anselm of Canterbury relates that, for many years, children in the St Omer area had no opportunity to receive this sacrament. Hence, when Anselm arrived, both old and young flocked to receive the sacrament. At the last moment, when he was about to depart, a little girl (or young girl – *puella?*) came and asked him to administer it to her. His companions dissuaded him, since this would bring additional supplicants. He hearkened to his companions, but his conscience troubled him for days afterwards.[172] A touching description of the administering of this sacrament appears in the biography of Bishop Hugh of Lincoln. According to the author, in the course of Hugh's travels throughout the diocese, people flocked to him to receive the sacrament and brought their small children (*parvuli*) with them to receive it as well. Although he was already of advanced years and weary, he dismounted from his steed in all types of weather and gently called the little children and their godparents to him to receive the sacrament. If any of his lay companions dared to touch them roughly, he was filled with anger and sometimes even struck them. This was in contrast to the conduct of another bishop, who was young and strong yet never dismounted even when the weather was clement. Mounted, he would sprinkle the holy oil on the children. They cried and screamed in fear, and were in real danger from the horse's hooves.[173] Children who died before the age of 7 did not receive the sacraments of the church. In the coroner's inquest rolls mention is made of a five-year-old boy who perished in an accident when a wall collapsed on him. The recorder added: 'He did not confess nor receive the communion for he was only five years old.'[174]

VIOLENCE, BEATING, AND INTIMIDATION

Was it customary to beat small children, notwithstanding the counsel of the authors of medical and didactic works, who advocated a gentle approach to infants and small children? In speaking of beating, one should distinguish between 'controlled beating' and savage ill-treatment and flogging. The phenomenon of violence towards small children undoubtedly existed in the Middle Ages, as it did in later periods (and, indeed, does today as well). In the Lives of the saints, we read of a father who, upon learning that his wife had left him, snatched his three-year-old son from the arms of the child's aunt and strangled him in his rage.[175] There were also cases of murder which reached the courts, as we shall see in the next chapter. Medieval society undoubtedly regarded as unacceptable violence which caused grievous bodily harm or death which, if not attributed to insanity on the part of the perpetrator, was considered to warrant punishment. The aunt from whose arms the father snatched his child greatly feared that she would be charged with having committed an act of violence towards the child which had caused his death. Even those who draw extremely gloomy pictures of childhood in the Middle Ages cannot but regard such cases as anomalous. We cannot, of course, assess the scope of the phenomenon. In modern society, it is easier to pinpoint such cases thanks to sophisticated methods of medical examination and particularly X-rays. The number of cases registered annually in the United States and in western Europe is shockingly high. In 1983, 851,000 cases of grievous bodily harm and mistreatment of children were recorded in the United States, and psychologists, psychiatrists, sociologists, and social workers connected with institutions dealing with the 'battered child syndrome' believe that the true figure is much higher. Study of battering parents shows that, almost without exception, they are psychoneurotic or suffer from severe personality disturbances. Some, but by no means all, of them come from disadvantaged backgrounds. Some belong to the upper middle class or are academics. If even nowadays, when it is possible to uncover the cause of the injuries and fractures of a hospitalized child, when society is highly aware of the existence of the phenomenon of child-battering, when neighbours report on it, and when battering parents sometimes come voluntarily to request psychiatric help, there is none the less no way of gauging the true extent of child-abuse,[176] it will be abundantly clear that the scope of the phenomenon in the Middle Ages is unfathomable. The mistreatment of helpless children is perhaps the most horrifying and despicable act which can be conceived, but, in the attempt to describe the attitude of a society as a whole towards the child, it is more significant to examine the question of 'controlled beating' by parents and teachers who can be described as normal and who were considered to be respectable, according to the yardsticks of their day, even though the distance between beating as an educational measure and abuse is sometimes quite narrow. There are societies, including some considered to be 'primitive', where the beating of children is not accepted, although there also parents are often exasperated by their children and experience frustrations. In medieval Christian society, on the other hand, the view that 'he who spares the rod spoils the child' was part and parcel of educational theory in the second stage of childhood. Society as a whole was violent. Some husbands beat their wives (this was permissible, if they did not do so to excess), and in doing so they sometimes injured a child, inadvertently or deliberately.[177] The man who strangled his son had previously beaten his wife so cruelly that she had fled to her parents' home. The number of impulsive, emotionally immature, and ineffectual people was undoubtedly not small, and it is such people, as modern studies show, who are liable to beat children. Many suffered the effects of poverty and distress which can often activate the latent potential for child-battering. There were also both drunkards[178] and moral zealots – two categories predisposed to mistreating children – as well as men and women who had themselves been battered children in the past. At the same time, it is difficult to locate direct testimony on the beating of small children, since, as long as it did not cause death or severe bodily injury, it was considered a private matter, like wife-beating. In light of all we know about medieval society, on the one hand, and about child-battering in later time on the other, it is highly implausible to assume that small children were never beaten, despite their 'positive' image and the fact that the dominant educational theories prescribed the commencement of strict education only at the age of 7. The abundant advice and numerous references to the crying of children at night indicate that some parents acted violently toward their crying children. Modern studies show that often some character trait in the battered child singles it out as the intended victim – sickly or handicapped children who require special care, nervous children, and those who are particularly vulnerable emotionally, who make almost intolerable demands, and whose crying (which is a symptom of their condition) creates additional emotional pressure on the parent.

If parents and nurses told children about heaven and hell, and about the Devil, who was ever lurking in wait for human beings, they did not do so as a disciplinary measure, but as truths which formed part of their own beliefs, and the same is true of various folk-beliefs. However, although authors claimed that children should be neither saddened nor frightened, it is known that intimidation was used as a disciplinary measure. William of Auvergne, discussing ways of implanting the fear of hell into the hearts of Christian believers, compares his didactic method with that of mothers and nurses who intimidate small children by means of fearsome masked creatures or drawings, known as *Maluesin* and *Barbualdos*. They show them to children and threaten that, if they do not behave properly, these creatures will come and consume them.[179] If William of Auvergne cited this practice, it must have existed, but we have no way of knowing how widespread it was and how many children suffered nightmares as a result. Spine-tingling folk-tales were also told, about the child-eating monster or the Devil who seized bad children. On the other hand, empathy for childish fears was sometimes expressed in literature. In *Parzival*, little Lohengrin's pagan uncle wants to kiss the child, but, since 'he was black-and-white speckled', the child shrank away from him. The author adds: 'Noble children feel fear even today.'[180]

PRESENCE AT AND PARTICIPATION IN ADULT ACTIVITIES

Little children, even the under-sevens, spent a great deal of time in adult company. The interlocutor in Alberti's book, who says that the infant who is just beginning to sit and stand should not be overtired, writes that the older child should be habituated from an early age to spending time in adult company lest he behave like a shy and embarrassed country bumpkin. (The writer, it will be recalled, was a member of the prosperous merchant class in Florence.) Therefore, he writes, one should abhor the custom of those mothers who seclude themselves in a room with their children and cuddle them in their arms all day long.[181] The authors of didactic literature and the preachers who urged parents to teach their children prayers also demanded that they take them to church with them.[182] From the complaints of churchmen about the commotion which children caused in church during the service and the sermon, which mingled with the noise from the street, we can deduce that parents did indeed bring small children to church. From the regulations issued by French synods banning the giving of unconsecrated hosts to children, we can also learn that small children attended church and that the ministrants sometimes failed to observe the rules and offered them the wafer.[183] It will be recalled that children also took part in religious processions, and illustrations show children marching with adults.[184] When children did not take part in the various celebrations, they watched them, together with adults, from the windows. In towns they probably also watched the theatrical performances which were considered suitable didactic means for children as well. Socialization appears to have been carried out directly in the first stage of childhood, mainly within the family milieu and mostly by women, but the child also came into contact with the outside world and with a wider circle of people than the family and household alone. These contacts also played a part in childhood socialization.

PATERNAL AND MATERNAL ROLES

As noted above, children were regarded as a trust from God, bestowed on both father and mother. Responsibility for rearing and educating them was supposed to be divided between the two, and love and concern for offspring, like the desire to procreate, were thought to stem from the natural instinct common to men and animals. We encounter in popular literature and, in its wake, sometimes in didactic works the figure of the male loving his children so dearly that he deprives himself of food to feed them,[185] like the she-animal, risking her life to defend her cubs.[186] Thomas Aquinas emphasizes the special role of the father in the human race: 'It is clear that for the raising of a human creature the nurturing mother does not suffice, but there is even greater need for the educating and protecting father.'[187] The father's obligation to care for his children, based on natural law originating in natural instinct, also included the obligation to support his illegitimate offspring. According to some of the Canonists, in the event of the birth of a bastard, both parents shared the duty of supporting it, but they too believed that it was primarily the father's task. Mothers who bore children outside wedlock could claim support in the ecclesiastical courts, which compelled the fathers to pay, in accordance with their means.[188] As for educating children, the accepted view was that up to the age of 7 this was the task of the mother, and from 7 onwards, once the child had attained the age of understanding and capacity for study, it was the father's function to educate sons while the education of girls remained the domain of the mother. Bernardino of Siena, urging men to be kind and display empathy towards their wives, described not only the woman carrying her child in her womb and bearing him in suffering, but also the hard-working and weary mother caring for her child and rearing him, while the father was as free as a bird. Support for the role of the father as educator can be found in St Paul: 'And ye, fathers, provoke not your children to wrath: but bring them up in the nurture and admonition of the Lord' (Eph. 6: 4). At the same time neither in theory nor in images is the division of tasks clearcut and definitive. Raymond Lull, for example, discussing children over 7, admonishes ladies who leave their children in the care of servantwomen, when rearing and instructing them should be their own task. According to Vincent of Beauvais, mothers should educate both their sons and their daughters in the Christian way of life.[189] Conversely, in religious literature, St Paul and Christ were often compared to a loving nursing mother. The division of functions did exist, however. All the interlocutors in Alberti's book emphasize the father's task as the educator and the person responsible for supporting his children, and also speak of his love for them. When one of them describes the infant beginning to speak and the excitement this arouses, he lists the father and the family elders among those who express their delight (in prosperous families in Italian towns the extended family maintained close ties), and argues that he does not believe that there is a father who is so harassed and loaded and bound by his obligations that the presence of his children does not cause him joy. But, at a tender age, it is not the task of the father to nurture the child. The mother will do this better, and it is best that the father does not hold him in his hard arms.[190] Canonists were of the view that, even if the father agreed to take in his bastard child in order to raise him, it was better for the mother to keep the child to the age of 3, since it had greater need of her.[191] In reality, the intensity of the bond with the father in the first years of life apparently varied from class to class. In noble and in prosperous urban families, fathers were often absent from home for lengthy periods. In Late Medieval Italian towns, men married and fathered children at an advanced age (sometimes in their late thirties). This mature age, together with their economic and political activities, usually

limited their involvement in the raising of their children. In the urban labouring class and among peasants, fathers were more rarely away from home
and the possibility of establishing a bond with the small child existed, at least
theoretically. But, as has been the case in all societies known to us, so also
in the Middle Ages in all strata of society it was the mother who nurtured
the small child – or, in the upper classes, the wetnurse and nurse. The women
who taught children to speak also transmitted the oral traditions through
songs and tales, and taught them their first prayers. It was they who created
the child's first world-picture. By means of the songs and tales of wetnurses,
the popular culture was also transmitted to the children of the nobility.
Notwithstanding, one finds in literature mention of paternal love, devotion,
and readiness for sacrifice on behalf of his children under extraordinary
circumstances,[192] and also descriptions in other sources of interest and
involvement in the raising and education of the small child, even in Italian
towns. Giovanni Morelli, eulogizing his deceased ten-year-old son, describes
how he followed his raising and development, what satisfaction he felt on
hearing his first words, and how much happiness the child's love brought
him. In the life of St Aibert, it is related that the child wanted to observe all
the fastdays, but that his father feared for his health and prevented him from
so doing. In order to fast without lying to his father, the child would take a
bite from an apple or taste several crumbs of some other food so that, if his
father asked him if he had eaten, he could reply in the affirmative.[193] After
the miracle in the church, Ambrose of Siena was sent back to his parents'
home. According to his biographer, as a small child, before learning to read,
he had been in the habit of leafing through his mother's missal. His father,
who noticed this, ordered two books especially for him. One contained illustrations of laypeople from various classes and occupations and the other had
pictures of churchmen (the future saint naturally preferred the second).[194]
Even if these anecdotes are only the fruit of the authors' imagination, they
indicate that paternal interest and participation in the raising of children was
acceptable to readers, and hence was not extraordinary. As noted, there were
fathers who first taught their sons to read. There are illuminations showing
a father playing with his son – Joseph playing at spinning top with the infant
Christ. A wood-carving in the Chapel of St Gregory at Windsor shows three
men: one is crawling with a small child tied on his back, and the second is
feeding a little child who is tied to the back of the third.[195] These artistic
depictions of fathers nurturing their children or playing with them, whether
they reflect reality, or are an expression of the wishful yearnings of the artists
for what they had never experienced, or are offered as examples to fathers,
did not cohere with the stand of the didactic writers, who regarded the father,
in the first stage of childhood, as a supporter but not as a rearer and nurturer.
In actual fact, in cases of sickness, accident, or handicap of a small child (as
we shall see in the following chapters), it was sometimes the father who took

the vow and carried the child to the shrine of the saint.

The dominant stance of medieval authors on the role of the father did not differ essentially from the opinions expressed by later thinkers. The view that the tasks of the father were limited in the first few years of life was prevalent in the nineteenth century as well. In the final analysis, Freud and his disciples allotted a limited role to the true father (as opposed to the symbolic father personifying authority, law, and the outside world). But, whereas Freud's disciples (Helen Deutsch, Winnicot, and others), who transferred the debate from the theoretical to the normative plane, made the mother responsible for any emotional disturbance in the child (originating in the first years of childhood), medieval churchmen, and to a large extent fathers as well, regarded her as being exclusively responsible for the child's welfare and physical safety.

Medieval authors, as noted, stressed the need to treat small children under 7 gently and lovingly. They did not, however, stress the importance of the mother's role as the inculcator of speech or the influence of early education on emotional development. Erasmus's statement at the beginning of the sixteenth century: 'We cannot stress enough that the first few years of life are of utmost importance for the future life of the child' could not have been written by a medieval writer. Only rarely do biographies, which go into great detail on the first years of life (such as that of Anselm of Canterbury), present the mother clearly as the creator of the child's first world-picture, and clearly indicate the impact of her methods of education and the nature of her ties with her child on the shaping of his personality.[196] In didactic literature, on the other hand, her role is presented as essentially biological. This conception accorded with the view that, for children under 7, the basic function of the nurturer was to guard their health and ensure their survival. Many considered fulfilment of these functions to be the main task of the mother, whereas in modern western culture the focus has shifted from concern for life and physical welfare to emotional wellbeing.

In his chapter on fatherhood, Bartholomaeus Anglicus, in addition to discussing a father's love for his progeny and his role as bread-winner and supporter, writes at length on the paternal role as educator. In his chapter on mothers, in contrast, the author focuses on their biological functions: nurturing the foetus during pregnancy, delivery, and nursing.[197] A similar evaluation of the paternal and maternal roles can also be found in the writings of Thomas Aquinas, and is part and parcel of the conception that woman was created primarily as a helpmate to man in procreation. The father, in whom the rational element is more developed than in woman, and who possesses the authority and power, is assigned the task of educating his sons. He will also know how to punish them.[198] In normative literature, the mother is charged with full responsibility for the health and safety of the small child. According to the authors of manuals for confessors, if the mother placed her infant beside a burning hearth, even if another person passed by (reference is perhaps to the father) and overturned the cauldron of boiling water, and the infant died of its scalds, it was the mother who did penance, since she was responsible for the child in its first 7 years.[199] According to the rulings of synods in Denmark, the mother bore sole responsibility even in cases where infants suffocated under the weight of an adult, and in cases of drowning.[200] If (as has been mentioned) the infant was placed in a pit in the ground in order to put a stop to his crying, or in an oven or on the roof in order to lower his fever, it was the woman alone who did penance.[201] Sometimes, when a child was dangerously ill, the father's sorrow was mingled with rage at his wife whom he accused of not having cared properly for the child. When children were injured in accidents in the absence of the father, mothers often expressed their apprehension about his angry reaction to their failure to guard the child properly.[202] The authors who condemned the practice of hiring wetnurses, as will be recalled, levelled their remarks almost without exception solely at women, but in this context also noted the emotional damage. Neither legislators nor authors of didactic works recommended allocating less food to women than to men; none the less, poorer families, particularly at times of famine, appear to have apportioned the meagre food supplies in their possession to the husband and children. Many more women than men in the lower classes were afflicted with blindness and various bone malformations as a result of malnutrition. Temporary infertility in women in the labouring classes was apparently sometimes caused by the cessation of menses due to starvation (famine amenorrhoea). This phenomenon of self-deprivation on the part of the mother which is accepted by the family is familiar today also in some countries in the Third World.[203]

Only towards the end of the Middle Ages did several writers dwell on the influence of early childhood instruction on human development. Early education should be carried out by visual means, writes Giovanni Dominici. During the nursing period, the mother should already make sure that there were pictures and statues in the household of the Holy Mother, Christ, John the Baptist, and John the Evangelist in childhood, as well as of Christian saints. Depictions of Christ as a child holding an apple or bird and playing with them, and the young John the Baptist wearing a hairshirt, eating drops of honey, and sleeping on the ground would appeal to children. By means of these pictures and statues, children from an early age would develop great love of God and of good qualities and hatred of sin. In the wake of this acknowledgement of the importance of early education, the role of the mother took on increasing importance since she was the first inculcator of religious and cultural values, and emphasis was placed on the bond between her and the child in the first years of life, and her influence on the formation of his personality.[204]

According to the ideal pattern, when a boy reached the age of 7, his father undertook the task of educating him and of fulfilling not only an economic function but an economic-cultural and social role in his life. In reality, as the following chapters will show, this did not always happen, and certainly not among the nobility. In all strata of society, the role was often assigned to the mother because of the death or absence of the father, while in the nobility and partly also in the urban class, in contrast to the ideal situation, the social custom prevailed of handing over children into the care of others.

GODPARENTS

The infant's godparents undertook to teach him the basic tenets of the Christian faith when the time came. In the sources (including *belles-lettres*) one can find examples of a father requesting his friend to act as godparent to his son or daughter,[205] of fathers reporting on the development of a boy or girl to the godfather (generally when the godfather was of more distinguished lineage and was the father's patron),[206] and of parish priests instructing godparents in their tasks of teaching the children the tenets of the Christian faith and ensuring that they were educated in its spirit. Failure to fulfil this role was considered a sin, and the confessor was enjoined to ask those confessants who were godparents whether they had neglected their duties.[207] Authors and preachers stressed that the precondition for fulfilling their duties was their own knowledge of the tenets of the faith.[208] John Wycliffe reprimanded parents who neglected the task of educating their children in the spirit of Christianity and left this task to the godparents.[209] There can be no doubt that relations with godparents created new bonds and, in particular, reinforced existing ties with friends or patrons or relatives. These new ties served to compensate for the diminishing ties of consanguinity due to the Christian laws of matrimony.[210] It is more difficult to ascertain the nature of the ties between the godparents and their godson or god-daughter in the early years, and whether they were familiar figures to the small child. In Tuscany in the Late Middle Ages the contact was very limited.[211] In England ties may have been closer since the author of a manual for priests found it necessary to instruct them to caution godparents in their flock not to sleep in the same bed as their godchildren as long as the latter were at risk from suffocation under the weight of adult bodies.[212] In Spain a woman who came to visit her godson who had been born with a handicap, made a vow to the saint together with the mother to visit his shrine and bring an offering if the child were healed.[213] In all countries godparents gave gifts to their godchildren and often remembered them in their wills. According to the custom of the manor of the monastery of Weingarten in Bavaria in the eleventh century, if the child of a serf died while still in his father's care, all the gifts he had received from his parents and godparents since he was in his cradle were appropriated by the monastery. If it was deemed necessary to make special mention of the gifts of godparents, the bestowing of such gifts must have been an accepted custom.[214] In literature we sometimes read of a childless godfather who declares his godson to be his sole heir. A moral tale about the founder of the Anjou dynasty describes a widow whose late husband's relatives falsely charged her with adultery and murder. The only person willing to defend her in Trial by Battle was her godson – her spiritual relative. After he prevailed in the judicial combat, the woman retired to a convent and bequeathed all her property to him. This young sixteen-year-old knight was the founder of the dynasty.[215] In contrast, in the wills of town-dwellers and peasants, godchildren are in fact mentioned but the sums bequeathed to them are usually small – about 12 pence.[216] In one case, the god-daughter was also the niece of the testator, and inherited some 41 pounds.[217] A godson who was a servant in the home of his godfather was also bequeathed a larger sum than the other heirs.[218] A legator who had no offspring of his own bequeathed most of his property to his godson. Since the latter was still a minor, he even appointed a guardian for him.[219] Some peasants left the sum of 4 pence or one sheep or a bushel of wheat to their godchildren.[220] When children were orphaned of both parents, it was incumbent on their godparents to acknowledge their special responsibility towards them.[221] When the godparent was a man of respected status, contact with him was a means of social advancement and sometimes also a pretext for financial aid. It is not to be wondered at that parents wanted a large number of godparents for their own advantage and that of the child. However, church legislation reduced this number[222] to preclude overexpansion of the circle of marriage prohibitions based on the spiritual ties between godparent and godchild, and godparent and godparent.

With regard to wills, it should be noted that, in early fifteenth-century England, a man bequeathed one penny each to three thousand children, if such a number should attend his funeral, as against threepence and a meal for three hundred of the poor. The testator undoubtedly regarded bestowal of gifts on children (probably in return for a prayer for his soul or some task at the requiem mass) as an additional point in his favour.[223]

OBSERVATION OF SMALL CHILDREN

Just as medieval literature contains stereotypical descriptions of infants, there is a similar depiction of older children – a handsome, well-dressed child, saying what is expected of him by adults.[224] There are, however, other descriptions. To continue this chapter, I would like to cite three of these. One is taken from a book of guidance for recluse nuns from the beginning of the thirteenth century, the second from a biographical poem, and the third from a Life of Bernard of Clairvaux. In the first of these, the author compares one of God's consolations to man to a mother playing at hide-and-seek with her beloved child. She flees him and hides. The child remains alone, looks around him and calls: 'Mother, mother', and begins to cry. Then the mother emerges from her hiding-place, and runs to him with outstretched arms. She embraces him, kisses him, and wipes away his tears, and he is utterly comforted.[225] The biographical poem refers to the period in which William Marshal, later to become one of the great men in England at the end of the twelfth century, was a hostage. In 1152, King Stephen attacked the fortress of Newbury which was loyal to the rebellious marshal, John FitzGilbert, father of William, and threatened to hang the besieged inhabitants. The latter asked for a truce in order to consult with the marshal. The king agreed. When this became known to Marshal John, he asked to extend the truce in order to consult with Empress Matilda. Again the king agreed but asked for a hostage, and the marshal gave him his fourth son, William, who was then 5 or 6. Immediately afterwards, he began reinforcing the fortress and left his son to his fate. The king was enraged and threatened to execute the child. The father's reply was that he still had 'the hammer and anvil to forge one more beautiful than he'. Some historians who have studied this sentence have regarded it as proof of indifference toward children in the Middle Ages, and concluded that the father was indeed willing to sacrifice his son. Duby draws a different conclusion, which appears to me more convincing. He believes that John's statement should be seen as part of the play-acting often performed by rival feudal lords, including both words and deeds. They employed both, in addition to battle, in order to threaten, intimidate, and persuade the enemy. Duby states that, even if the events did in fact occur and were not merely part of family mythology, it was clear to both sides that the threat would not be carried out and that the little hostage would not be executed. He perceives the most interesting part of the story as the affection and understanding which the king displays toward the child, who wins his heart. One could add that, were it not for the fact that contemporaries were acquainted with five-year-old children, the author could not have described the child, or his relations with the king who had him at his mercy. The child treats the events as an exciting game. When the king's men stage preparations for his execution, he asks permission to play with the spear of the soldier who is supposed to lead him to the gallows. Later, when the soldiers pretend that they are going to catapult him to his father's fortress, he asks what kind of swing this is, and all the time he enquires what kind of game the two sides are playing. In the days which follow, he spends time with the king in his tent, and they play various games, mainly 'knights', a game in which the players compete in knocking down 'knights'; the plantains picked out from the ground in the tent serve as knights, and the king allows the child to win. As Duby points out, even if this story is in line with the aim of the poem – to describe William Marshal as having been held in childhood in the arms of a king, thus symbolizing his future power and greatness, the story would not have been recorded in writing if it had not appeared feasible.

As for the father, he did not abandon his son to his death; but, at the same time, does not appear to have been particularly attached to the child, who was not his heir. Otherwise, he would not have handed him over so lightly as a hostage. It was William's mother who sent an emissary to try and see the captive child and learn how he was faring. The child's first question was about the welfare of his mother and sisters, and not of his father.[226] We cannot deny the harshness of the act of handing over a child as hostage to the enemy, even if the father knew that his son would not be executed. (William Marshal was not the only child given as a hostage, but, in so far as we know, execution in such cases occurs only in literature.[227]) However, William's story also reflects the other face of the medieval attitude towards children: observation, understanding, and affection. In one of the biographies of Bernard of Clairvaux, the author relates a miracle which the saint wrought in his lifetime. A woman brought to him her small son, whose arm and hand were deformed from birth. The saint took pity on him, healed him, and told the mother to call the child. The mother called him 'and the child ran to her and embraced her with both arms'.[228] The author of these lines, like the author of the book of guidance for nuns, was a churchman. We simply do not know whether their descriptions were the fruit of observation of small children, an echo of a childhood memory of warmth and affection, or the expression of deprivation and yearnings for that which they had never enjoyed, but of which they were aware from observation of mothers and children.

6 Abandonment, infanticide, and accidents

It is indisputable that, in the Central and Late Middle Ages, children were sometimes abandoned, infanticide occurred, and certain customs and rituals were practised which, even if not deliberately intended to kill infants, almost always proved fatal. The birthrate was restricted to some degree, both due to the fact that not all members of society married and propagated (some of the sons and daughters of the nobility were designated for the secular church or monastic orders, and, among the urban labouring class and the peasantry, some lay men and women remained unmarried); and mainly because, in all social strata, men postponed matrimony until they were able to muster the necessary financial means to raise a family in accordance with their standing in society. The child mortality rate was high throughout society. Peasants needed progeny as a labour force, and the upper classes wanted heirs. None the less, some of the children born, both legitimately and outside wedlock, were undoubtedly unwanted. In the previous chapter we noted that prosperous families had more children than poor families in the same time and place. In Halesowen before the Black Death, for example, the average number of children per peasant family was 2·8. However, the average in prosperous families was 5·1; in middle-income families, 2·9; and in poor families, 1·8. The same correlation between the economic situation of the family and the number of offspring also characterized families in other manors in England, and the same is true of Pistoia and the rural area around it in the early fifteenth century.[1] It should be kept in mind, however, that we are dealing here with averages. The number of confinements varied from family to family. There were numerous instances of barrenness, and different families within the same social stratum were not necessarily afflicted equally by infant mortality. Even when *coitus interruptus* was practised, it was not possible to plan a family,[2] both because of the limited effectiveness of this method of birth control and, in particular, because parents had no way of knowing how many of their children would be sturdy enough to survive. Thus some poor families were childless or lost all of their children, while, for others, who had a higher-than-average number of children, the birth of another child was a heavy, sometimes intolerable, financial burden. The statement that 'there are no unwanted children, only unwanted pregnancies', which is over-optimistic, if not sanctimonious, in the context of modern society, is even more so in the medieval context. We can fathom the connection between severe deprivation and abandonment of infants from the constant references in chronicles describing famine years to the abandonment of infants in the gateways of churches and monasteries. Some parents, in their financial plight, sold their older children into slavery, and there are known cases of mothers who forced their daughters to engage in prostitution. According to Frederick II's legislation for Sicily, if it could be proved that the mother had acted thus due to poverty, the judge was permitted, at his discretion, to mete out a lenient sentence.[3] In addition to the unwanted children born in wedlock, there were bastard children whose fathers refused to accept responsibility for raising them and whose mothers were not strong enough to rear them alone.

ABANDONMENT

We learn of the abandonment of infants (known at the time as *expositio*), not only from the writings of chroniclers but also from Canon law, the resolutions of synods, and the manuals of guidance in which parish priests were instructed to excommunicate those guilty of such acts; and also from instructions to priests concerning 'conditional baptism' of an infant found abandoned, when it was not clear whether or not the child had already been baptized.[4] Also indicative is the fact that hospitals were established which initially took in the sick, the crippled, orphans, and foundlings as well, but that later special foundlings' homes were set up. Some poor parents entrusted or sold their children to noblemen or prosperous burghers whose own children had died or who were childless. The latter wanted these children either because they yearned for a child, or as a means of establishing eligibility to receive a legacy. Both ecclesiastical and secular legislation prohibited this act.[5] As for the nobility, epic literature describes cases of infants being abandoned or transferred to relatives for rearing in the event of their being born illegitimate or as one of a pair of twins. The reason for this latter case was the belief (which was rife in medieval society, as in several other societies) that a woman could conceive twice (consecutively), and that, accordingly, twins were not born of the same father. In literature a woman who feared for her good name might decide to abandon one of her twins. This is what happens in the poem known as *Galeran*, and in Marie de France's poem, *Le Fresne* (The Ash Tree). In the latter, the birth of twins is even a punishment for the mother since she once slandered a pious and chaste woman for giving birth to twins.[6] The most famous tale of abandonment, which appears in various versions in the Middle Ages, containing both an illegitimate birth and a double act of incest between brother and sister and son and mother, is the story of Gregory, who later became Pope Gregory the Great.[7] Whether, in fact, a twin was likely to be abandoned is unknown. In the poem *Milun*, also written by Marie de France, the hero, who is illegitimate, is more fortunate, since he is not abandoned but despatched far away to his mother's sister in the care of loyal emissaries and accompanied by a carefully chosen wetnurse.[8] However, the truth is that the rich also sometimes abandoned their bastard children in foundlings' homes. In Italy (where they were usually the offspring of slavewomen) their illegitimacy was the pretext which led their fathers to deposit them in foundlings' homes. On the other hand, many noblemen and prosperous burghers acknowledged their illegitimate children and undertook their upbringing, even if they were the children of slavewomen. Some masters permitted slavewomen to raise the children born to them even when they were not the fathers.[9]

From an early stage, the church made efforts to keep orphans and abandoned babies alive, and some churchmen were particularly troubled by this problem.[10] However, we know with certainty of the presence of foundlings in hospitals only from the twelfth century, a period which witnessed an increase in the overall number of hospitals and lepers' hospitals, founded initially by ecclesiastical bodies and gradually also by secular elements. The hospital of San Gallo, established in thirteenth-century Florence, took in foundlings as well as the sick and crippled; in 1316 the La Scala hospital was founded, and in 1445 the special hospital for foundlings known as the Innocenti hospital. A similar development occurred in other Euroepan towns. At the end of the twelfth century, Guy de Montpellier, founder of the Order of the Holy Spirit, one of whose missions was to care for orphans and foundlings, established in Rome the hospital of Santo Spirito. Confraternities grew up under the auspices of the Order, and the women in their ranks reared the children. The Santo Spirito closed down after some time, but was reopened in the fifteenth century, this time as a foundlings' hospital alone. According to the statutes of several hospitals in France and England, if women died there in childbirth, or even if they left their bastard newborn children behind when they left the hospital, and the father could not be located (in the event that the mother revealed the father's name and he was located, he was ordered to pay to support the child), the hospital authorities were responsible for raising the child up to the age of 7, and then for apprenticing him (or her) to an artisan so as to guarantee a future.[11] Conversely, there were hospitals, like that at Troyes in the thirteenth century, which refused to care for abandoned children. According to the compilers of the statutes, the number of foundlings was so great that the hospital's resources could not suffice to absorb them, and it was the task of the parish organization to care for them.[12] Sometimes the municipal authorities accepted responsibility for abandoned infants. The authorities of the town of Saint Cyprien, for example, undertook to farm out to wetnurses infants abandoned on the altar of the local church. The same was true in Montpellier in the Late Middle Ages.[13] Those monasteries at whose gates infants were abandoned took them in and raised them with the help of a wetnurse and later a foster family,[14] and, when the time came, they were usually among the children earmarked for the monastery as monk or servant. As noted above, childless couples, or those whose own children had died, sometimes took in the children of the poor. In these cases, it is clear that some arrangement was made with the parents in advance, and the newborn infant was handed over directly. It is possible that in some instances abandoned infants were taken in without prior arrangement with the parents. In literature, we find the recurrent motif of an infant who is abandoned, orphaned, or, due to external circumstances, separated from his parents and adopted by a couple of elevated rank.[15] But it is to be doubted whether such tales reveal anything of significance about social reality. As for the children of slavewomen, if their fathers acknowledged them, they advanced in the social scale, since they were no longer considered slaves. In a previous chapter, we mentioned the baby girl abandoned at the gate of the Bologna hospital and taken in by an elderly couple, and the mother of Gilbert of Nogent, who took an infant orphan into her home. Gilbert writes that she undertook 'to gather to her' an orphan several months old in order to raise him.[16] Gilbert apparently used the term 'to gather' and not 'to adopt' because legal adoption, which made it possible to bequeath property to the adopted child, was unknown in the Middle Ages. The type of adoption which had been customary in all the countries of the Mediterranean basin and among the Germans disappeared, at the latest, in the eighth century and was not revived until the nineteenth century.[17] Hence childless couples, or those whose children had died and who wanted a legal heir, were faced with a problem. This explains why, in legends about Christian parents who take in a foundling, they conceal the fact that the child is adopted and pretend that it is their own child, as in reality did those who purchased a child as a means of qualifying for a legacy. In one legend a great nobleman, who is closely associated with the monarch and is childless, finds an infant in a hollow tree-trunk. He and his wife conceal the infant, the wife pretends to be pregnant and later tells everyone that she has given birth to a son.[18] None the less, people sometimes adopted children and even succeeded in bequeathing all their property to them, and it was precisely this situation that the church ban on adoption was apparently aimed at preventing. At the beginning of the fourteenth century, an adopted son inherited all the property of his deceased adoptive father. A distant relative of the deceased (the grandson of his aunt) appealed to the courts, arguing that the heir was not the true son of the testator. The adopted son replied that the deceased had raised him, educated him, and recognized him as his son, and that hence he was the rightful heir, and his lawyer even cited a precedent. The wife of a certain

Henry Berkeley, he said, had never borne children, and he never had another wife, and yet, on his death, he left six sons, the oldest of which was acknowledged as his heir by the king's council. As Maitland pointed out, there were cases in which English law recognized adoption *de facto*.[19] In Late Medieval France as well, some fathers not only handed over their children to relatives to rear and educate them but did so in a form of quasi-adoption, formalized in the presence of a notary.[20] As regards childhood, in the final analysis, it was immaterial to a child if he was adopted or merely raised and educated by those who took him into their home. A child who was taken in by a family eager to rear him was certainly more fortunate than those who were raised in a foundlings' home. The latter suffered neglect and were deprived of stimuli – experiences that can retard development and instil a strong sense of insecurity for many years, if not for life (as confirmed by studies of children in modern orphanages).[21] Moreover, their very prospects for survival were slim, particularly if they were sent out to wetnurses, as was the case with most of the girl foundlings in Florence.[22]

The number of foundlings' homes increased in the sixteenth century. This almost certainly indicates growing demand, that is to say an increase in the number of abandoned children as a function of demographic and economic factors. From the mid-sixteenth century to the mid-seventeenth century, there was rapid demographic expansion, and, concomitantly, the price of food rose and the real wage dropped (whereas in the fifteenth century the price of food was relatively low and wages were high). Families from the lower strata of society had difficulty in feeding all their children, and it seems reasonable to assume that abandonment increased as a result. Medieval chroniclers, as noted before, perceived a clear connection between economic plight and the abandonment and sale of infants (and the same phenomenon is known in Third World countries today). On the other hand, it is also possible that the establishment of new foundlings' homes was the outcome not of the increased dimensions of abandonment but of greater awareness of the need to care for these children and the conviction that, by setting up more institutions able to absorb unwanted children, the incidence of infanticide would be reduced. There may also be an element of truth in what is known as the 'Protestant argument', namely that it was not demand which increased the number the of foundlings' homes but the reverse – the existence of new foundlings' homes increased demand: by providing a relatively easy opportunity for giving away a child, they increased the incidence of abandonment of children by parents who were relatively solvent.[23]

The rich deposited their bastard children in foundlings' homes, while the poor apparently brought both legitimate and bastard offspring. It will be recalled that some wetnurses handed in their own children, not always bastards. Among poor parents, some must have taken this step remorsefully and in the belief that they were doing the best they could for a child they were unable to raise. There were certainly families for whom feeding another mouth would mean that they and their other children would starve. There were, uncontestably, parents who at some stage wanted to take back their abandoned child. Otherwise the church legislator and the author of the manual for confessors would not both have asserted that a woman who abandons an infant which is subsequently taken in by the church (i.e. a monastery) and then wants it back cannot have it, having forfeited her rights by abandoning it.[24] Of the prosperous people who brought their bastard children to foundlings' homes, many promised to redeem them at some date in the future. Some even did so. Secular law did not prohibit abandoning a child, but it appears that municipal authorities none the less sometimes punished this act.[25] The church condemned parents who abandoned their offspring, and abandonment of a child carried the pain of excommunication.[26]

INFANTICIDE

In discussing child-murder, one should distinguish between the murder of older children and the murder of newborn infants. The former was indubitably very rare in all societies, except in time of famine when both infants and small children were sometimes killed. In medieval western society such acts were committed by mentally disturbed parents, sometimes with deliberate intent and sometimes as a result of violence inflicted without murderous intent. A woman was placed on trial before a secular court in England for murdering her daughter aged 2 and forcing her son aged 4 to sit on hot coals. Another woman beat her son (aged 10) to death. The court attributed her action to insanity. In one case, the mother had tried to commit suicide, but had subsequently changed her mind and killed her children. Another woman killed her children with an axe and then hanged herself.[27] It is important to emphasize that, although the courts usually attributed the murder of children over the age of 1 year to insanity (the jurors having been requested to bring evidence of the insanity of the mothers[28]), this in no way indicates that child-murder was not considered a grave crime. An attempt has been made[29] to prove that contemporary western courts tend to accept the defence argument that the murder was committed in a moment of insanity more frequently in the case of child-murder than in other cases.[30] Even if such a tendency exists (and it is disputable, since it may well be that the incidence of insanity among those who murder one of their children is, in fact, higher than in other types of murderer), it is highly doubtful if this indicates that society in general takes a more lenient view of murder of a child by a parent than of other types of murder. Perhaps the reverse is true. Perhaps it is precisely because this act is perceived as so terrible and despicable that it is hard to accept that it can be committed by a sane parent.

The murder of newborn infants, on the other hand, can be an accepted norm. We know of societies in which it occurs in order to preserve the balance between means of subsistence and demographic growth; to preserve the desired ratio between the sexes in the society, or for economic reasons (hence, more girls are killed); or in order to eliminate the problem of raising a sickly or handicapped infant whose chances of surviving to adulthood are, in any case, slim. The murder of handicapped infants might also be an expression of the desire to safeguard the purity and strength of the society. For the same reason a society could also bid a mother kill her infant born of prohibited sexual relations (and not merely castigate her).[31] In Roman society, before the spread of Christianity, it was the privilege of the paterfamilias to decide which of the children born to his wife should survive and which should be killed. Christianity, which preached the sanctity of life of all those created in the image of God, emphatically prohibited the murder of infants, including the handicapped and the illegitimate. Jean Gerson, discussing the various temptations of the Devil, writes that the Devil sometimes rouses in those to whom bastards have been born the thought that perhaps it would be better if both the child and the sin ceased to be. But the sin would be to respond to this temptation.[32] In the wake of the church's stance and ecclesiastical legislation, infanticide was prohibited in all Christian countries by secular law as well.[33] Nevertheless, some people murdered their infants immediately or shortly after birth. The scope of the phenomenon cannot be gauged, but the number of cases was certainly too great for all of them to be attributed to murderous impulses resulting from *post partum* depression or other grave mental disturbances (although these factors were certainly involved in some cases).[34]

That murder of newborn infants occurred can be learned indirectly from the censuring of this act by the authors of manuals for priests and confessors, and from sermons.[35] The reason given for the establishment of foundlings' homes was the desire to prevent infanticide. According to one author, Innocent III sponsored the establishment of the Sancti Spiritus foundlings' home, because he heard that many women threw their newborn infants into the Tiber. The same argument of 'prevention of many crimes' was also cited for the establishment of the foundlings' homes in Florence. Giovanni Boccaccio wrote in horror about mothers who murdered their infants or abandoned them in the forest as prey to beasts and birds.[36] In art, the mother who murdered her infant was depicted as doomed to eternal hell where she would suffer terrible torment.[37] Direct testimony also exists: women were placed on trial for the crime of infanticide in France, Germany, Italy, and (in isolated cases) in England as well. Brissaud examined the letters of remission of punishment given by the royal chancellery in France in the fourteenth and fifteenth centuries to women who murdered their infants immediately after birth in the rural parts of eastern France. It transpires from his study that all these women had given birth outside wedlock, and that not one of them had tried to justify her crime by citing economic reasons or apprehension at the difficulties of rearing the child, but had rather spoken of fear and a sense of shame. They included young girls, widows, and even married women, and the expression 'because of the fear and shame' recurs in all their pleas. Sometimes the murder was cruel and shocking, the outcome of temporary insanity and fear; sometimes it resulted from abandonment of the infant in an isolated spot on the ground, which rapidly caused its death. In one case, a women bore a child to the local priest, in whose house she had been living for a year and a half, and it was he who compelled her to throw the child into a ditch he dug. Married women, rightly, feared the violent reaction of a husband in the event that it proved impossible to conceal the fact that he was not the father of the child. Among young girls, there were some who were unaware that they were pregnant and due to give birth, and the delivery came as an unexpected shock. They gave birth on the bare ground and, even if the child was born alive, it died soon after. The letters of remission were granted on the basis of the following statements made under oath: that the defendant had already spent two–three years in jail, that her past was unblemished, that she had intended only to conceal the infant and not to kill it, that she was too young, that she was under pressure from someone else (as in the case of the woman who bore a child to a priest), that she had since repented through fasting and prayer, or that she would not have been reduced to committing the deed if her poor parents could have afforded to marry her off. In one case, a declaration was submitted under oath that the defendant had six young children and had already spent two years in prison, and, if she were to be executed, there would be nobody to care for her children. As for those who were not granted remission, in the thirteenth century the law still distinguished between the first offence, which could be regarded as an accident and the second, which proved that the woman was a habitual offender. This distinction was abolished in the fourteenth century, but the law continued to differentiate between sudden murder committed in rage or manslaughter as a result of neglect, and premeditated murder. For the latter the punishment was burning or burial alive, and in some cases it was carried out.[38]

Even though both the letters of remission and the court records[39] reveal that, in almost all cases, women did not murder their infants for economic reasons, it seems reasonable to assume that there were certain cases in which the cause was the poverty of the family. The authors of confessors' manuals distinguished between a woman who committed the crime because of her poverty and one who committed it in order 'to conceal her adultery', and they were lenient in imposing penance on the woman who acted 'because, due to her poverty, she could not support the child'.[40] Like abortion, infanticide was regarded as a feminine sin and crime,[41] although, in cases when it was committed for economic reasons, it seems highly unlikely that the woman acted without the consent, if not actual insistence, of the father, and consequently it was difficult to prove the murder. The historical sources are illuminating on the standpoint of legislators and judges, but do not provide information on the attitude of the community to the murder of a newborn infant. There are recorded cases in which women who committed infanticide were denounced to the authorities,[42] but we do not know if there were not cases in which the community covered up for the perpetrators. Of course it was always possible to censure and relegate to the margins a woman or couple who murdered their infant, without recourse to legal measures. In the event of the murder of a bastard, it was clear that the deed was committed by the mother, as the tragic culmination of the pregnancy she had tried to conceal as, despairing and fearful, she carried her unwanted child. Not one of the women mentioned in the letters of remission had a man at her side to help and support her. If a man was involved in the story, he brought strong pressure to bear on the woman to eliminate her newborn infant (as in the case of the priest), or treated her violently in pregnancy in order to bring on a miscarriage (as in the case of the husband who beat his wife mercilessly after she became pregnant by her master). It may be assumed that, in cases where the man supported the woman and acknowledged his paternity, she did not murder the infant even if it had been born out of wedlock.

In addition to blatant acts of murder, infants sometimes died in the beds of their parents or wetnurses, usually through stifling under the weight of an adult body, and sometimes through inadvertently being smothered by a blanket or other cover. As noted above, churchmen as well as authors of medical works cautioned against the practice of taking infants into the beds of adults, but the frequent reiteration of the warning attests to the fact that the practice was ineradicable.[43] However, secular court records before the fifteenth century list no trials for the crime of sharing a bed with an infant, thereby causing its death. The reason is that in such cases it was impossible to establish whether the death was accidental or disguised murder. Hence the deed could not be considered a crime to be tried before lay courts.[44] Abelard, who referred to a case of the smothering of an infant under the weight of its mother's body, regarded it as an inadvertent act. At the same time, he does not question the imposition of heavy penance on the mother, not because she had sinned, since she was innocent and had acted out of compassion for the infant, but as a caution to her and other women to act more carefully in the future.[45] The church legislators, like authors of confessors' manuals, were not so quick to assume that the deed was committed inadvertently. Canon law distinguishes between murder and accident under these circumstances.[46] According to authors of confessors' manuals and the resolutions of synods, the death was considered to result from negligence – this negligence being considered a grave sin – and, as in the case of premeditated murder, only the bishop was empowered to impose penance and to grant absolution. Parish priests were instructed not only to ask confessants if they had sinned by negligence but also to clarify the extent of the negligence which had caused the tragedy;[47] in other words, to try to ascertain if a covert murder had been committed and to report to the representative of the bishop whose tribunal was trying the case. In the fifteenth century, mothers and fathers as well as wetnurses and their husbands were brought to trial before the tribunals of the bishops of London and Canterbury, and, in the sixteenth century, before the court at Fiesole, for having taken an infant into their bed, and thus causing its death (this procedure was in accordance with canonic law, and contrary to the resolution of the thirteenth-century Danish synod, which attributed responsibility in such cases to the mother alone and imposed the penance on her). The bishop's representative was charged with the task of investigating whether the act had been committed deliberately or inadvertently, before deciding on the penance and granting remission. Needless to say, if the defendants claimed that the death had been caused accidentally, their version was necessarily accepted, since there was no way of refuting it. In Fiesole, the highest number of remissions was granted in the 1530s, a time of constant civil war in the region.[48] We will never know how many of the incidents were in fact cases of disguised murder, committed within the family framework and apparently for economic reasons. The testimonies presented to the tribunal of the Inquisitor Jacques Fournier include the story of a peasant woman from Montaillou, who bitterly mourned her infant, whom she found one morning dead in her bed. It is indisputable that she had not desired its death.[49] According to his biographer, Gunner, who was Bishop of Viborn in the first half of the thirteenth century, imposed rigorous penalties on those who committed murder. On the other hand, he displayed moderation and empathy towards mothers who caused their infants' death in their sleep, and treated them leniently within the framework of the law, asserting that in such cases one should act mercifully and not cause them to shed more tears than they had already shed.[50] Wetnurses (with the exception of those who received infants from foundlings' homes, which did not always pay their wages) had no reason to kill infants deliberately, since the death of their charges deprived them of income. It should also be recalled that nowadays we are aware of the existence of the phenomenon known as 'cot death', the sudden demise of an infant in the first months of life. Physicians believe that it occurs as a result of some disturbance during the transition from reflexive to cortical behaviour (namely, behaviour dictated by the cortex in the developing brain, or, in other words, learned behaviour). This phenomenon could perhaps explain some of the sudden infant deaths in the parental bed. In the Lives of the saints, which mention the numerous accidents which befell small children, reports of infant death in the beds of parents or wetnurses are very few. In the case of other accidents, parents appealed to a saint and vowed to visit his shrine and to make offerings if he would revive a child they thought to be lifeless, being unable to diagnose death accurately. If the child then rallied this was attributed to a miracle wrought by the saint. The question is why there is almost no mention of cases in which the child was 'almost smothered' (*pene oppressus*), as related in one case.[51] Was this because, in these cases, by the time the accident was discovered, the child was already lifeless, and, since appeal to the saint did not 'restore it to life', this incident was not recorded among the miracles attributed to the saint? Was it because, in relatively numerous cases, the death was a disguised murder? Or because before the fifteenth century the number of cases of smothering in the parental bed was relatively small, and this was not a common accident? There is no answer to these questions. Similarly, there is no way of knowing whether, after the Middle Ages, there was an increase or decline in the number of cases of infanticide in general and not only of infant death through smothering in bed. Felber, whose study concentrates on Germany, believes that there was a rise in the incidence of murder from the fifteenth century onward. According to Trexler, on the other hand, the gradually stricter attitude of secular law towards infanticide and the increasing number of charges brought against parents and wetnurses at bishops' tribunals because of the death of an infant in their bed (even though there was no way of distinguishing between accidents and murder) does not necessarily indicate a rise in the number either of premeditated murders or of accidental smotherings. Trexler believes it more reasonable to assume that these figures point to greater awareness of the problem, and less willingness to accept such acts.[52] Jean Flandrin and others, in addition, believe that in the sixteenth century there was an increase in the postnatal mortality rate of bastard children, because until then women and men who engaged in extramarital relations which produced bastards were not severely reprobated or punished. As a result of the Reformation and the Counter-Reformation, both censure and pressure increased, and (with the exception of monarchs and nobles) people no longer dared to rear their bastards openly. Girls who conceived outside wedlock in villages migrated to towns, since they did not dare to bear their children at home, and once in town they murdered or abandoned their infants. Those of the infants who were abandoned in foundlings' homes, which now proliferated, had poorer prospects of survival than illegitimate offspring in the Middle Ages who were raised by their parents.[53] The estimate is that in the foundlings' homes of Paris and London in the seventeenth and eighteenth centuries at best some 33 per cent and, at worst, 90 per cent of all infants died in their first year of life.[54]

Certain of the practices aimed at healing a child were, in fact, hazardous to life. Burchard of Worms, in his manual for confessors, denounces the parental custom of placing a feverish child on the roof or in the oven for the sake of its health.[55] A woman who did this was given penance for a whole year. The placing of a crying infant in a pit in the ground was apparently considered less dangerous since it was punished by only five days' penance.

As noted above, it is evident that the author of the manual did not regard these practices as disguised infanticide, and one should also differentiate between such practices and accidents of various kinds.

More complex and ambiguous are the belief in changelings and the recommendations as to measures to be adopted by parents who believed that their infant was a changeling. Belief in changelings was a popular superstition orginating in the pre-Christian era, and known to have existed among the Celts, the Germans, and the Slavs. But, like other pre-Christian customs and beliefs, it survived and adapted. The fairies which changed children were identified with demons despatched by Satan. Even some churchmen apparently adopted this belief. Jacob of Vitry, one of the greatest thirteenth-century preachers, used the changeling as an allegory in one of his sermons. Denouncing a certain type of Christian believer, he writes that he is like the child whom the French denoted *chamium*, who sucks the breast of the wetnurse until her milk dries up, but does not grow and develop; only his stomach inflates and hardens.[56] During the period of the great witch-hunt in the sixteenth–seventeenth centuries, attention shifted from changelings to the deeds of the witches who snatch children and devour them, but belief in changelings did not disappear.[57] In folklore, one finds several additional distinguishing features of changelings; the changeling is weak, sickly, and cries incessantly. For the fairies to come and take it away and return the parents' true child it was necessary to torment the changeling and make it scream and cry. This could be done through beating, scalding with boiling water, and by intimidating it by pretending to burn it. Another way was to bring it to the junction of three roads or to the estuary of three rivers and leave it there. The mother would creep away and return upon hearing its first cry in the hope that the child had been exchanged. Other methods were also proposed, and, needless to say, if adopted, they would, almost without exception, have led to the death of the child. The question is whether we are dealing with popular tales and beliefs which reflected the ambivalent attitude toward the child who was handicapped, retarded, sickly, or mewling (such being the signs of a changeling), and whom parents were forced to raise, and the defence-mechanisms they succeeded in erecting, or whether this was a genuinely accepted, if marginal, custom. From Jean-Claude Schmitt's study, it transpires that, at least in the diocese of Lyon in France, in the forest of Sandrans in Ain province, from the thirteenth century on, mothers conducted a ceremony aimed at transforming changelings (that is to say, sickly and handicapped children). The source which informs us of this custom and the details of the ceremony is a cautionary tale related by the Dominican Inquisitor, Stephen of Bourbon. The custom was born out of the legend of the greyhound of the Seigneur of Villar in the region, which became a martyr. One day the seigneur, his wife, and the wetnurse were away from home and only the greyhound remained in the castle beside the infant's cradle. When the dog saw a snake approaching the cradle, he crushed it in his jaw. When the wetnurse and parents returned and saw the upset cradle and the bloodstains around it (the greyhound had been injured in its struggle with the snake), they concluded that the dog had savaged the infant. The seigneur killed it on the spot, and only afterwards discovered the corpse of the snake and the infant safe and sound. The greyhound was given the name Guinefort, and the peasants of the neighbourhood began to regard it as a martyr and a patron saint guarding against disease, particularly childhood ailments. At the beginning of his tale, Stephen of Bourbon reproves women who believe in demons and who appeal to their aid by bringing their sick children to elder trees and ant-hills to seek a cure instead of to churches and the relics of saints. He then goes on to reproach those mothers who bring sick and handicapped children to the burial-place of Guinefort. They had learned the details of the ceremony, so he claims, from an old woman who lived in a nearby small town. They came to the wood where Guinefort was buried, and offered up salt, hung the infant's clothing on the trees, and stuck a nail in the trees. They then passed the naked infant between two tree-trunks. The mother threw the infant nine times to the old woman, who was standing at the other side, and they then adjured the fairies to come and take away the sick, weakling child and to return their own child, healthy, strong, and sturdy. Then (continues Stephen) the child-murdering mothers (*matricidi*) placed their naked infants at the foot of the tree on straw they took out of the cradle, lit two candles which they placed on the tree-trunk, and moved away so that they could no longer hear the child's cry. They then returned and picked it up. If it was still alive, they dipped it nine times in the cold river-water; if it died, this was a sign that the demons refused to bring back the human child and to take back their own. According to Stephen, after he heard all this he ordered that the greyhound's body be exhumed and the trees uprooted and burnt together with the carcass. He ordered the local lords to issue an order that any person who dared return to the spot to conduct the ceremony would have all their assets expropriated. Unlike Jacob of Vitry, Stephen of Bourbon did not believe in changelings, and was convinced that he had put an end to the practice and that his victory was complete (otherwise he would not have cited the story as an *exemplum*). However, Schmitt's historical and ethnographic study (which explains the significance of all the details of the ceremony on several planes, social, cultural, and psychological) reveals that neither belief in the curative powers of Guinefort nor the ceremony itself were thereby abolished, but continued to exist without interruption until the nineteenth century. Sick children were then still being brought to the wood, particularly those who suffered from rickets and were backward in walking. In contrast to the medieval custom, people then no longer begged the fairies to exchange children, but merely asked Guinefort for a cure. They also refrained from immersing the infants in the river.

According to Schmitt, although Stephen of Bourbon called the mothers 'child-murderers', he did not punish them severely because he regarded their actions not as ritual murder but merely as a forbidden alliance with demons and an activity which endangers the lives of the children. Even if the child escaped being burned by the flames which spread from the lighted candles, and was not torn to pieces by a wolf, it was unlikely to survive being left naked in a wood and dipped in the river. The beliefs and the ceremony are marked by profound ambivalence. They reflect concern for the salvation of the infant who had been baptized but whose baptism had not acted as protection against either disease or demons. They were a means of explaining disease and handicaps, and of overcoming reality and its difficulties, not through healing the child, since the required medical means were lacking, but through changing its identity. Since it was the child of demons, it could be banished from human society. Mothers regarded the ceremony as a means of rescue – saving the child's life and soul at the same time. It was a 'rite of passage', consisting of both separation and banishment to the margin, intended to culminate in re-acceptance into the community. In fact, however, it hastened the death of the weakest, without rousing maternal guilt. In psychoanalytical terms, one could say that this was liberation from guilt through transfer and projection. On the other hand, one of the women told Stephen of Bourbon that, after having laid her naked infant in the wood and moved away, she saw a wolf approaching it. Had it not been for her maternal love and compassion, which impelled her to return, the child would have been savaged by the wolf (writes the Inquisitor). Although the child which was about to be devoured by the wolf (or the Devil in wolf's guise), was not her own but a changeling, and its death would have served as resounding proof of this, the mother, on witnessing the approach of the wolf, was unable to act in accordance with what Schmitt calls 'the harsh and fatalistic logic' required by the ceremony. There appear to have been limits to the belief in changelings, with all its inner contradictions. According to Schmitt, it is hard to assume that the worship of Guinefort and the ceremony significantly changed the demographic curve in the regional peasant society, since the children brought to the wood were, in any case, doomed to die young.[58] In this rare case, we know details of the legend, the site of the ritual connected with it, and the ceremony itself. Did similar ceremonies exist elsewhere with the same objective? (Various versions of the Guinefort legend, like belief in changelings, were prevalent in other countries.) Were ailing infants elsewhere laid at a junction of three roads or an estuary of three rivers? Research cannot yet answer these questions. In any event no such ceremony was held at the 'fairies' tree' at Domremy, about which Joan's judges questioned her at great length. Had it existed, this would have come to light in the course of her trial.

Infanticide – as the reflection of social reality, as the expression of ambivalence towards the child or of suppressed wishes which aroused projected guilt feelings, as the reflection of fantasies of dread of a cruel father, and as conscious condemnation of the most terrible act a human being can commit – appears in folklore, in descriptions of the deeds of witches, in accusations of ritual murder against Jews, in literature, and in art. There are folktales about old women who strangle children, mothers or fathers who murder illegitimate children, and the spirits of murdered children which haunt their murderers.[59] In *Malleus Maleficarum* (The Witch Hammer), composed at the end of the fifteenth century, which established the stereotype of the witch for centuries to come, infanticide and cannibalism are attributed to the witch.[60] The fantasies of maltreatment of children characterize the charges of ritual murder levelled at Jews from the Norwich blood-libel of the mid-twelfth century onward.[61] The Jews were accused of murdering Christian children in order to use their blood for baking *matza* (unleavened bread) for the Festival of Passover. The Jews not only kill the child but abuse it as well. A woodcut in the (printed) book of the German chronicler, Hartmann Schedel, in the second half of the fifteenth century, depicts a small Christian child being tortured by nine Jews, who are letting his blood and castrating him. One may regard this description, like the descriptions of the acts attributed to witches, as projection of latent wishes which arouse guilt. Alternatively, one may accept the interpretation of Norman Cohn, that the fantastic image of the torturing and castrating father was transferred therein to the Jews.[62] On top of the column surmounting one of the fountains in Berne, known as the 'fountain of the child-devourer' (*kindlifresser*), stands the statue of a Jew preying on children. He is sadistically devouring a child and around him stand other children awaiting their turn.[63]

Children suffering from adult violence, in some cases victims of murder, figure in Chaucer's *Canterbury Tales*.[64] The most horrific story is perhaps The Prioress's Tale. She tells of a seven-year-old boy, who walked through the Jewish quarter while singing 'Alma Redemptoris', was murdered by one of the Jews, and was thrown into a privy-drain. But, even after his death, he continued to sing until the monk who brought him to burial removed the grain which the Holy Mother had placed on his tongue. Kuhn considered this little 'martyr' to be one of the earliest examples of what he calls 'the enigmatic child' in European literary tradition. The brief appearance and subsequent disappearance of the child are illogical, ominous, and loaded with significance beyond the understanding of the other characters and of the reader.[65] The story is redolent with hatred, cruelty, and violence toward the Jews and lacking in any true sympathy for the boy. Nauseating sentimentality – the other face of cruelty – prevails. The irony with which Chaucer treats the Prioress does not mitigate the impact of the tale.[66]

The children in the tale of the Count Ugolino in Dante's *Divine Comedy* are not murdered, but die of hunger because of their father's sin. In Canto 33 of the *Inferno*, Count Ugolino relates how he was cast by his enemy into a tower in Pisa, together with his four sons, and how the boys died one after another of hunger, the first on the fourth day and the others between the fifth and the sixth days. Unquestionably, the father's grief at the death of his children is the focus of the story. However, the last sentence which Dante attributes to Ugolino is 'Then fasting did what anguish could not do.' Critics differ in interpreting this line. The traditional explanation was that hunger did what grief had not succeeded in doing, that is to say Ugolino died of hunger and not of grief. However, several contemporary critics believe that the implication is that he ate the corpses of his sons, particularly since, in a previous sentence with rhetorical zeal, his sons offer themselves to him to eat:

> O Father, it will hurt much less
> If you of us eat: take what once you gave
> To clothe us this flesh of our wretchedness.[67]

Borges holds that the vagueness of this sentence is deliberate. Dante wanted us to suspect Ugolino of eating the corpses of his sons, but not to believe it. Dante himself undoubtedly sensed the falseness of the words he placed in the mouth of the sons. Moreover, the punishment inflicted on Ugolino in *Inferno* – to gnaw for ever at the skull of the enemy who incarcerated him in his tower prison – hints at the possibility that he had consumed the corpses of his sons.[68]

Antoine de La Salle's tale, *Le Reconfort de Madame du Fresne*, was written as a letter of consolation to a lady who had lost her son, and in it a thirteen-year-old boy, who was an only child, is executed. The child is handed over as a hostage, and the father's feudal code of honour obliges him not to surrender even at the price of his son's execution. The mother, aware that, whatever she does and says, she would not succeed in swaying her husband, submits to fate in great sorrow and does everything possible to pacify and fortify the father. Generally speaking, in works in which a child is murdered, we learn of the horror indirectly through the reaction of the adults. In La Salle's tale, there is a direct description of the terrible fear of the abandoned child as he is led to the gallows. The entire tragic chapter is, according to Auerbach, 'a piece of practical, graspable reality'. The harsh note is the father's statement after the execution: '... deign now to receive his soul, and forgive him that he took death unwillingly, and forgive me too that to do right I brought him to this pass'.[69]

In both the *Canterbury Tales* and the *Divine Comedy*, and in La Salle's tale, the child is an innocent victim: the victim of the wickedness and cruelty of the Jews (the Prioress's Tale); of the father's enemy and, indirectly, also of power struggles and the father's own follies (the tale of Ugolino); and again of the father's enemies, but this time directly also of the father's feudal concepts of honour (*Le Reconfort de Madame du Fresne*). Kuhn cites a long list of children in European literature who are murdered by adults or die as a result of adult action. Often death comes after the child has experienced extreme pain. He asserts that the explanation for this high rate of child mortality in literature is the perverse attraction of the destruction of innocence. It arouses sympathy, though flawed and mixed, in the heart of every reader.[70] The parents react with pain and grief to the death of their children. The mother of the little choirboy murdered by the Jews had no control over what happened. Count Ugolino was indirectly guilty for the death of his children by starvation, but he could not have prevented it. In Antoine de La Salle's tale, the father gives honour precedence over the life of his child. The mother, who is torn between her duty of obedience to her husband, who represents the world of feudal values, and her duty and love towards her child, submits to the will of the husband-father not from choice but out of awareness of her own inability to sway him. In a medieval drama on the sacrifice of Isaac, when Isaac grasps what awaits him, he expresses regret that his mother is not there. If she were present, she would kneel before his father and beg him to spare his son.[71] In La Salle's tale, the mother is present when the father takes his decision, but she does not plead for the child's life.

An echo of the murder and abandonment of illegitimate infants can be found in a dramatic episode in the works of Henry Suso. A woman who had given birth outside wedlock spread the rumour that Henry Suso was the father of her child. Then she came to him and proposed murdering the child: once it disappeared she said, the rumours of his paternity would die down and his honour would be saved. With cruel realism bordering on sadistic satisfaction, she lists the possible ways of annihilating the child: she will bury it alive, she will jab a needle into its brain, she will cut its throat and then thrust the knife into his little heart before his eyes. When Henry Suso rejects her proposals in horror, she says impatiently that, if he is not willing to allow her to kill it, he should allow her at least to place it in the early morning at the church door and then its fate will be that of all the other unfortunate foundlings. Otherwise, he will be forced to invest great effort and money in the child until its rearing and education are completed. However, Henry Suso decides to keep the child. He takes it tenderly on his knee, embraces it, and says

> Am I to murder a beautiful little child who smiles at me? I am ready to endure any suffering for his sake. Thus I will keep you 'child of my heart' from the hand of God alone. Your true father has denied you. Your murderous mother wishes to cast you out like an unwanted puppy. God wishes me to be a father to you, and thus it shall be.

The woman, shocked at what she hears, bursts into tears and takes back the child, and Suso promises her to pay all the costs of its upbringing. The description of the child is marked by tenderness and compassion (together with cruelty in the description of the proposed ways of murder), but Suso's decision is based on religious piety and not on humanitarian considerations: 'I will keep you from the hand of God alone, and since God is precious to me, you too will be my precious little child.'[72] However, piety does not always win the day in drama or in literature. A horror story about a mother who murders her infant and cooks and eats it is often reiterated in literature and in art, from Josephus' *Wars of the Jews* in the Greek original, through the fifth-century Roman Hegesippus, or through the *Josippon* in the tenth century, liturgical drama and mystery plays, a twelfth-century French narrative poem, Boccaccio's *Lives of Famous Men and Women*, and other works up to a nine-teenth-century painting by the Belgian Antoine Joseph Wiertz (1806–65). His painting known as *Hunger, Madness, and Crime* depicts a woman with bared breast and disordered hair sitting by a blazing hearth holding a blood-stained knife. On her knee is the corpse of an infant wrapped in rags, and in the cauldron suspended above the fire can be seen the leg of an infant. This deed, attributed to one Maria of Azov, who killed and ate her son during the Roman siege of Jerusalem, and related by Josephus in protest against the acts of the Zealots, was deeply entrenched in the European collective conscious-ness. It was amended and tempered in several of its literary or artistic versions but did not change significantly. What seems to underlie this story of the cannibal mother is the fear of the 'great mother', which is common to a large number of myths, of she who bestows life but also devours and destroys in her rage. In the particular context of Christian culture, Maria of Azov rep-resented the opposite pole to the Holy Mother. The cruelty of the former highlights the maternal compassion displayed by the latter. The concept of merging with the most beloved by devouring him could be accepted by Christian culture where, in the sacrament of the Eucharist, man merged with Christ through consuming his flesh and blood.[73] Religious literature and art depict not only the child Christ playing merrily with his mother or with John but also the infant Christ as the sacramental sacrifice at mass. (In the tale, mentioned above, of Thomas of Eccleston, the Franciscan friar attributes to the small hero of the tale the vision of a child being sacrificed on the altar and eaten.) Sometimes the child is revealed in the Host to a doubting Christian, who questions the real presence of God in the Host, and sometimes, conversely, the revelation is a special grace bestowed on a believer who is pure of heart. The Jew who sees the child sacrificed on the altar is convinced of the truth of Christianity. Sometimes a sinning Christian sees a vision of Christ as a small child, bleeding and torn to pieces for the sins of man. People were exhorted by preachers and didactic writers to perceive the sacrificed infant in the Host as it was raised aloft by the priest, in order to 'see with their own eyes' and reaffirm their faith. Children appear among those privileged to see the Christ-child because of their innocence and their perfect faith.[74]

Other universal themes, in addition to that of the cannibal mother, are the motif of murder of the child by its father or mother or its sacrifice for the sake of the well-being and benefit of society with the acquiescence of the parent. It reappears in religion, mythology, folklore, and literature of various and varied cultures and in different cultural contexts: from the sacrifice of Jephthah's daughter through Greek mythology and drama (Kronos who devours his sons, Medea who murders her children, Agamemnon who sacrifices his daughter, Iphigenia, the mother who tears apart her son in the *Bacchae*) to the myths and folktales of non-literate societies.[75] To cite myth of this kind as a historical source is problematic, to say the least. The archetypical and universal elements in it, by virtue of being such, are a-historical. As for the other elements, which reflect realities of life to a varying degree, it should be recalled that it is the nature of myths and folktales to linger on beyond the period whose norms they represent. Hence the appearance of infanticide in the medieval sources cannot be taken as an indication of the dimensions of the phenomenon. At most, it merely attests its existence and, even more, the dark and unconscious aspects of the human soul – its sanctimonious cruelty and its feelings of guilt.

ACCIDENTS

The authors of medical and didactic works and confessors' manuals, the preachers, and synods who warned parents and wetnurses against sharing their beds with infants also cautioned them against other accidents. It was often noted that it was not enough to lay the infant in its cradle; attention should be paid to reinforcing the cradle, lest it overturn and the infant fall on its face; care should be taken to keep the child's mouth unobstructed and it should not be left unattended by day or night and should be guarded against fire and water in particular.[76] Francesco of Barbaro directs numerous warnings at wetnurses: the child who is beginning to crawl and walk should be protected against pits, wells, rivers, fire, horses, dogs, poisonous plants, snakes, knives and other sharp instruments, small objects which can easily be put into the mouth and swallowed, and wandering beggars who steal children, disable them, and send them to beg, as well as against the evil eye (*mal ochio*) of malicious old women. The child in the cradle should be protected against birds which could peck it, and the crawling infant should be watched lest it put earth, ash, or coals in its mouth.[77] Konrad of Megenberg warns the wetnurse against drinking to excess, which could cause her to be negligent in watching the child. Many infants whose wetnurses drink are smothered under the weight of the nurse's body in bed or are savaged by household animals or fall out of the wetnurse's arms into fire or water (he writes). In discussing the importance of play for the little child, he notes that the most suitable place for playing is the house and courtyard, where it is in no danger from deep wells, animals, or the fights of older boys.[78] All the types of accidents against which writers caution, and others, befell children from all strata of society, from the nobility to the peasantry, as can be ascertained from the records of coroners who investigated whether the occurrence had been an accident or a crime, and from the miracles attributed to saints. Among the victims were infants, very many small children, and sometimes older children.

Infants in their cradles smothered under coverlets which blocked their mouths;[79] others were hurt when their cradles overturned (in one case, due to wild rocking by the wetnurse).[80] Some fell from the arms of the wetnurse or older sister on to the ground or into the fire.[81] As for toddlers aged 1 year and older, they were victims of every conceivable and inconceivable kind of accident. Some were severely scalded by boiling water (generally speaking, while their mothers were laundering); some fell into the fire while running or, as in one case, in the course of the uproar caused by a squabble among servants; and many were simply trapped in fires which broke out in the home when they were left unattended.[82] (The houses were of wood, and fires often broke out.) Many others were injured in falls: from high chairs, benches, attics, balconies, windows, stairs, and towers. One infant was injured by falling off 'a mattress (*materatium*) which the poor used as a bed'. As in the case of injury by fire, many of the falls occurred when the adults were absent (sometimes the mother's excuse for her absence was that she had gone to hear a preacher). However, many of the falls occurred when the adults (the mother, wetnurse, or servant) were not far away from the infant, but were inattentive.[83] Small children put small objects in their mouths which stuck in their throats: rings, small wooden balls connected to the mother's distaff, etc. One child almost choked on a fishbone and a five-year-old boy nearly smothered in a pile of straw which fell on him.[84] There was one who, 'while playing as children do' (*ludens pueriliter*), was injured by a sharp instrument (an axe);[85] others were bitten by dogs, rabbits, or pigs, or injured by galloping horses (in one case, the rider was drunk), or gored by oxen, or fell while trying to mount a horse and ride it. Sometimes beams or heavy objects fell on them;[86] others were lost in the forest or field to which they had gone with their mothers who wanted to gather berries or tend the flock and who only noticed their absence many hours later.[87] Some children were snatched by wolves (at least according to the writers).[88] Very many drowned in rivers and streams (having been taken to the riverbank where their mothers were laundering or because their fathers were millers), or in wells, pits, pools, ditches, barrels, and cauldrons.[89] The number of children of over 4 who were injured in accidents was smaller, and the number of those over 7 even smaller, but they too sometimes fell victim. A child sent by his father to feed the horses slipped and fell off a ladder when a pile of straw fell on him.[90] Another fell off a tower.[91] A boy fell off a horse, and a girl was injured by a galloping horse.[92] The daughter of a nobleman lost her way in a thick forest,[93] and the daughter of urban labourers was badly injured while cutting bread.[94] Children were also injured in childish fights. A boy defaced the statues in the gateway of a rich man's house; the man's son, in his rage, seized a stick, beat him, and injured his spine.[95] Another child was pushed over by a friend.[96] But the most common accident which also befell older children and adolescents was drowning: when young boys bathed in a river; when they played in winter on the river ice which cracked under their feet; and sometimes as a result of falling into the water, when proximity to a mill-wheel increased the danger.[97]

The cases mentioned in the *Acta Sanctorum* ended felicitously. Upon witnessing what had happened to the infant, toddler, small child, or boy, the parents made a vow to a saint that, if he cured the child, they would visit his shrine and give an offering to the church where it was located: they offered money, an animal, standard candles, a large candle in the shape of the affected limb, or a candle of length double or triple that of the child, and prosperous supplicants sometimes promised to bring a replica of the limb or of the entire body fashioned out of silver. In rarer cases, people appealed to the saint in his lifetime or (if the shrine was close to the site of the accident) carried the child to the shrine and prayed and made their vow there. The miracles were recorded from the oral testimony of the pilgrims by the registrars of the church where the saint was buried, and record was also made of the evidence of witnesses who appeared before the committee convened to discuss the possible canonization of the miracle-worker. Descriptions of accidents and the recovery of child victims are not typically characterized by the fantastic or supernatural. The description is usually realistic and clearly anchored in everyday life, but with a happy ending. This latter part is not the case with coroners' inquest rolls. The accidents listed in both types of sources are almost the same. In coroners' inquest rolls the great majority of the cases are drownings of toddlers and young children in ditches and pits, death by fire, and drowning of older children and adolescents in rivers and streams.[98] But these accidents were all fatal, or they would not have been brought to the attention of coroners. Mention is also made of a man who was cutting down a tree in the forest: it fell and killed a little girl. The coroners ordered his arrest since he had not summoned aid, but hid the body in the forest.[99] Another small girl was killed by a stone. The thrower was placed on trial, but witnesses attested that it had been an accident.[100] Sometimes children were killed in the course of robberies of their homes.[101] Francesco of Barbaro, it will be recalled, exhorted wetnurses to guard children against beggars who stole children. And, in fact, in England a beggarwoman stole the daughter of a shopkeeper, stripped her of her garments, and forced the child to beg with her.[102]

To return to accidents, particularly those which befell infants and small children: some of them, at least, were the consequence of what we would call today criminal negligence (as in cases where a toddler of 18 months to

2 years was allowed to wander unattended among instruments, building-materials, and barrels of water, or in a courtyard where there was an open pit; and so on). Such negligence could only end in accident. The authors who described the accidents were aware that some, at least, were the outcome of negligence and neglect. And, the views of deMause and others notwithstanding, only very rarely was the accident perceived as divine retribution for the sins of the parents.[103] Preachers sometimes explained the death of innocent children in general, and particularly in plagues, as punishment for the sins of parents who, had their children survived, would have raised them to be sinners like themselves. But these acts are presented as punishment inflicted on society as a whole and not necessarily on the greatest sinners among the parents (who, amongst their other crimes, had committed the sin of disrespect towards their own parents).[104] In referring to a specific accident which befell a certain child, the writers only rarely attribute it to divine punishment, and then only when the parents had sinned by a direct attack on a saint or on servants of God. In one instance the author perceived the accident as divine retribution since the father of the child had harassed the monks in the monastery near his manor to which the author belonged. (Needless to say, in this case, the child was not 'revived' by the saint.)[105] In another case, the son of a certain woman fell sick because she did not permit him to drink of the holy water which the saint offered him, since a sick man had drunk before him.[106] Much more frequently the authors note that the mother, wetnurse, or servantwoman acted incautiously (*minus tamen caute*)[107] or that the child was left 'without supervision' (*sine custodia*).[108] It is clear from these comments that the opinion is that these women had not acted in accordance with the proper norm. Sometimes the writers do not note specifically that this was a case of negligence, but this is clearly implicit in their description of the circumstances of the accident. Thus, in the case of a woman 'blessed with many children' who sent the infant with his older brothers who were going out to play in the orchard, the child was small, still unsteady on its feet, and fell into a well (writes the author).[109] The same approach is evident in the coroners' inquest rolls: 'A boy of three and a half fell into a ditch and drowned when his mother had gone in to the neighbours to quaff a glass of beer.' In another case, after the infant fell into the well on the common, the local residents were ordered to block the mouth of the well.[110] In York the town statutes included instructions to people leading horses to the water to keep them under proper restraint lest they injure children playing outdoors.[111] In other words, deliberate steps were sometimes taken to prevent accidents. Fathers, for their part, sometimes preferred to accuse the mother of slackness (often with justification) than to regard the accident as punishment for some sin they had committed.[112] Since, therefore, people did not attribute accidents to divine retribution (which could have dissuaded them a priori from adopting precautionary measures), but simply acted incautiously

at times, does this suggest that they were not willing to invest effort in keeping their children alive, and had no emotional investment in them? For many years historians questioned the very possibility of infanticide in the Middle Ages or, at most, were ready to admit that the phenomenon existed but claimed that it was very rare because infanticide ran counter to Christian ideals and morals.[113] When they acknowledged that the phenomenon did in fact exist and adopted Ariès's view that people took no note of small children in the Middle Ages, they began to regard accidents as the clearest manifestation of this disregard, if not as disguised murder. I regard it as highly questionable that this was indeed the case. The fact that some parents did not guard their children well does not indicate that all parents acted thus. A scholar who tried to gauge the attitude towards children in contemporary western society solely on the basis of data on accidents to children recorded in hospital emergency rooms, in police registers, or records of car accidents in which children were involved when a parent was at the wheel would be unable to gain an accurate picture not only of the attitude of society as a whole towards the child but also of the emotional investment by the parents whose children were injured or killed. There is no proof that parents who did not guard their children well did not love them. Medieval people were not, apparently, endowed with imagination about factors which might cause accidents and did not learn from experience; they were, on the one hand, governed by their instincts and were relatively fatalistic, on the other. In the *Acta Sanctorum* and the coroners' inquest rolls we find a considerable number of accidents to adults. Being caught by the spurs of the horse, tangled in the reins, wounded in knightly training, tournaments, and hunting accidents – these were some of the characteristic accidents among the nobility. In the labouring classes, both men and women were injured in various work accidents, among them falls and scalds and burns. Many were injured and killed in violent fights even when there had been no murderous intent; and many people, in all classes, drowned in rivers, lakes, and seas, and even in ponds and wells,[114] like children. It is clear that they could not swim (and knew this), but none the less they did not take care. One aspect of the fatalism was the hope that God, through his saint, would protect them and their children. A certain woman who had an infant was obliged to go to town 'and had nobody with whom to leave him to guard him apart from God and the blessed Dominic'. When she found her house on fire upon her return, she cried 'Blessed Dominic, restore my son to me.'[115] Sometimes parents were obliged to leave the house. One mother was summoned by the crier to come and fulfil her work-obligation (*bannum*) to the lord of the castle by carrying sand and stones for the building of the wall. With tears in her eyes, she told her female companion that she had nobody with whom to leave her disabled daughter. Since she was forced to go, she entrusted her to the saint.[116] Hanawalt's study of the coroners' inquest rolls shows that in rural areas the number of small children injured in accidents was greatest at the height of the agricultural season, in May–August.[117] From anthropological studies we know that, in some primitive societies, children are taught some motor-skills and cautioned against dangers most meticulously and at a very early age. (The child usually acquires these skills at the age of 3.)[118] He can then display initiative and 'explore the world' without risk to his life. This was not the case in medieval European society, where the material environment was more varied and complex (while means of preventing accidents were very limited), and, accordingly, the dangers facing the child were more numerous. It seems that children were sometimes given early liberty without sufficient inculcation of cautiousness. However, the fact that parents appealed to saints when an accident befell their child indicates that they wanted it to recover or be 'revived'. In many cases, authors depict the dread and sorrow of the father or mother whose 'entrails turned over within her from grief for her little girl whose face had been so disfigured',[119] or the lamenting and weeping mother and the father bearing the child to the shrine of the saint.[120] Coroners' inquest rolls record the accident alone, and not the reaction of the parents. In one instance, however, the tale is told of a couple who fled from a shop in which a fire had broken out, forgetting to take with them their infant which was lying in a cradle. When the mother remembered the infant, she retraced her steps to the burning shop to rescue him, was asphyxiated by the smoke, and died.[121] When an accident befell a small child, the entire neighbourhood took note of it. There are extant descriptions of neighbours assembling, helping, and proffering suggestions, including advice to make a vow to a saint, and of the general rejoicing when the child was 'revived'.[122] Some churchmen were well aware that a mother could act negligently but still mourn bitterly a child who perished in an accident. The legislation of the Archbishop of Denmark in the early thirteenth century states that, if a child dies as the result of negligence (*negligencia*) in a fire or by drowning, 'we believe' that it is enough to impose one year's penance, since 'the mother's suffering has already been greater than her guilt by force of grief'.[123]

7 Sickness, handicaps, bereavement, and orphanhood

Ariès founded his theory of indifference towards small children in the Middle Ages essentially upon what may be called 'contemporary demographic conditions', or, in other words, the high mortality rate among infants and small children. The prospects of survival of the infant and young child were so slim, he asserted, that parents developed defence-mechanisms against attachment to a tiny creature who might not be long for this world. And, since they did not become attached to their child, they generally accepted its death with equanimity.[1] In the opinion of the historical demographer, Laslett, because of the low life-expectancy and the consequent very high numbers of people who were bereaved, widowed, or orphaned, past society generally accepted death (and not necessarily only that of small children) in a different manner from our own. 'People may then have had quite a different attitude to sudden death, orphanage, widowhood and living with step-parents. The society of the pre-industrial world was inured to bereavement and shortness of life.'[2]

Before addressing ourselves to this theory, let us examine some of the responses of parents to sickness of their children, which indicate to what lengths they were willing to go in their struggle for the child's life. It is also worth examining the attitude of parents towards handicapped children, since not all parents regarded them as 'changelings' and rejected them.

SICKNESS

In previous chapters we have noted supplications to the saints in cases of barrenness, difficult deliveries, danger to the lives of mother and new-born infant, children over the age of 2 who were not yet speaking, and accidents. And, since people appealed to the saints in order to overcome misfortune and afflictions with which they could not cope alone, it is only natural that they also sought help in cases of sickness, crippling, and other handicaps. A survey by Finucane, who studied and quantified miracles attributed to some of the most popular saints of the Central Middle Ages (seven English and two

French), reveals that 90 per cent of the 3,000 attributed miracles were cures. Additional perusal of the miraculous acts of these saints and others shows that, in one-third and sometimes more of the cases in which people appealed for a cure, they were asking for the healing of infants, toddlers, or older children, both boys and girls.[3] Some saints won renown as healers of children, this being regarded as a unique gift bestowed on them by the Lord.[4] In the event of sudden sickness or accident, it was impossible to take the afflicted child on a pilgrimage to the shrine of a saint unless this was nearby. Generally speaking, the parents took a vow to make the pilgrimage after the child recovered.[5] Those fortunate enough to obtain a fragment of cloth from the garments of the saint or some other item from his holy relics placed them on the body of the sick child, in addition to taking the vow.[6] The handicapped and chronically sick, on the other hand, were taken on pilgrimages to the saint's shrine and sometimes spent days and even weeks there. Not all the illnesses specified can be identified today. Sometimes the chroniclers wrote merely that 'sickness and great pain came upon him [or her]' or 'he [she] suffered from a lengthy sickness'.[7] Many illnesses, however, can be identified from the symptoms cited and from what is known to us from other sources of the typical infant diseases of the Middle Ages and the following centuries. Among the ailments mentioned are: high fever as a result of influenza, or other types of fever; lung and bronchial diseases; whooping cough; measles; smallpox; and tuberculosis. Reference is made to breathing difficulties, attacks of shivering, and rashes or poxes which covered the body. It is often said of infants that they were almost dehydrated from fever since they refused to suckle or to take any liquid.[8] Also mentioned are: diseases of the urinary tract;[9] stomach and bowel infections and worms;[10] kidney stones;[11] rheumatism;[12] tumours;[13] swelling of the stomach or the entire body;[14] hernias;[15] ulcers, carbuncles, and sores which did not heal;[16] tuberculosis of the bone;[17] epilepsy;[18] mental illness;[19] and even toothache.[20] If the child recovered fully (and it was possible to recover from some of these ailments), or rallied temporarily (a phenomenon characteristic of chronic diseases which fluctuate in intensity, sometimes as a result of weather conditions or nutrition), this was attributed by the parents to a miracle. In many cases of prosperous parents, it is noted that, before appealing to a saint, they had summoned the aid of physicians, who had failed to effect a cure.[21] The medical writings of the period provide long lists of childhood ailments, but physicians found it difficult to diagnose diseases, and even when they did they could not usually help. It will be recalled that physicians believed it dangerous to administer medicines to infants and that bloodletting was also forbidden in these cases.[22] In cases of fractures and tumours, on the other hand, they were convinced that they could cure the patient, and often recommended an operation. Mothers, however, greatly feared surgery and preferred to appeal to saints for aid.[23]

There can be no question but that those in charge of the churches in which saints were buried did everything in their power to broadcast and laud the miracles wrought by the saint, since thereby they were advertising the church as a target for pilgrimages. They tended to inflate descriptions of the types of miracles most important to the believers. Thus if they reported the healing of children, it suggests that this kind of miracle was considered of major import- ance, enhancing the reputation of a saint. Also indicative of the importance of cures of children is the fact that Humbert de Romans, in the thirteenth century, castigated those women who had recourse to witchcraft in order, amongst other reasons, to find a cure for their children.[24]

The intense grief of parents whose child was mortally ill is sometimes explained by the fact that this was their only child;[25] or that they had already lost five children and were now witnessing the suffering of their last surviving daughter;[26] or that the child was the oldest of the family and designated heir.[27] But in many cases parental grief and pain are noted without further comment of this kind. Authors write of the love of a father or mother for a son or daughter and of their terrible sorrow in the face of the mortal illness.[28] Particularly touching is a reference to a father who was 'a renowned physician who had a little daughter whom he loved dearly' and who appealed to the saint with tears in his eyes.[29] A mother whose son suffered a fracture which confined him to a sick-bed refused adamantly to agree to surgery, saying that she preferred to nurse him all her days than to endanger his life by an operation.[30] Needless to say, not all parents displayed such devotion, and this too is reflected in the *Lives of the Saints*. A woman whose daughter had been sick for four years, vomiting almost all the food and drink administered to her, wearied of caring for her, and prayed to the saint, beseeching that the child recover or die. The child died, and this fact was registered as a miracle.[31]

Let us conclude with the telling testimony of two peasant women from Montaillou before the tribunal of Bishop Jacques Fournier. One of the women had a sick infant aged about 3 months. A peasant asked her if she wanted to introduce it into the Cathar faith (through administering the *consolamentum* on the death-bed), since this would ensure that, after its death, it would become an angel. When she asked what would be done to the infant after the ceremony, he replied that she would no longer be able to nurse it and must allow it to die. (After the administering of the *consolamentum*, the recipient, according to the practice of the Cathar Perfects, was obliged to abstain even from milk.) The woman replied that under no circumstances would she deprive her infant of her milk while he lived.[32] In the second case, a Cathar couple had a daughter aged less than 1 year, named Jacotte. The infant fell mortally sick. The parents found a Perfect who agreed to administer the *consolamentum* before death. After receiving it, the infant was prohibited from nursing. The father said that, if the child died, she would become an angel in heaven, and he then left the house together with the Perfect. The mother, who remained with the infant, could not endure the ban on nursing, which was intended to guarantee the redemption of the baby's soul, and gave her the breast. When this became known to the father and the Cathar friends of the parents, they were enraged at the woman and rebuked her harshly. The woman reported that her husband had long since ceased to love her and the baby. The infant lived another year and then expired.[33]

HANDICAPS

It was not churchmen alone who totally rejected the possibility of killing handicapped infants (despite the prevailing belief that handicapped children were born as a result of sexual intercourse on days banned by church legislation).[34] The authors of medieval medical treatises, who accepted the teachings of classical writers such as Hippocrates and Soranus of Ephesus on various issues, did not concur with the ancients on this question and never raised such a possibility in their writings.[35] We have no way of knowing whether handicapped infants were killed immediately after birth within the family framework, or whether this practice existed only in the Sandrans forest. There is, however, evidence in the literature of the rejection and neglect of handicapped offspring. In prosperous families, they were the first to be put out to nurse and then sent to monasteries. The case of Ambrose of Siena has been mentioned above. When his mother discovered that her newborn infant was handicapped, she first gave rein to feelings of self-pity mingled with acceptance of fate, and then despatched the infant to a wetnurse.[36] Another woman who had given birth to a handicapped child cried out to Heaven 'Why was he not taken from the womb straight to the grave?'[37] Gilbert of Sempringham, an ugly and misshapen child (who became a saint), was forced to eat with the servants and they too refused to sit at table with him. His father, the dauntless knight, intimidated him to such a degree that, while he lived at home, he failed to learn anything, and was considered slow-witted.[38] The parents of a future saint, a six-year-old blind girl, took her on a pilgrimage to the shrine of a saint; but, when their prayers and vows proved fruitless, they abandoned her in the monastery church.[39]

Yet there was another angle to the attitude of medieval society towards the handicapped child. As can be ascertained from the *Lives of the Saints*, very many of the congenitally handicapped (the phrase *a nativitate* appears frequently) were raised by their parents and brought by them to the shrines of the saints. In addition to the deaf and dumb, large numbers of children were blind from birth, in one eye or both, and others lost their sight as a result of illness (undoubtedly including many who suffered only from eye ailments).[40] Parents sometimes visited saints' shrines with children who suffered from uncontrollable palsy of the head or one of the limbs;[41] harelips;[42] deformities of the arms and legs which are described in cruel detail in order to emphasize the wonder of the miracle;[43] and the most difficult cases of all, the paralysed.[44] The afflicted children were brought by parents from all strata of society, from nobles to peasants. One peasant (*rusticus*) brought his dumb son aged 5, and, after the child was cured, brought a gift to the church despite his poverty.[45] In this case, the source of the affliction was apparently psychological. It is, of course, more difficult to explain the curing of physical handicaps through miracles than it is various psychosomatic ailments. In any event, people often believed that the handicap had been removed, either in full or partially, and, even when no miracle took place, they did not lose faith in the power of the saints and continued to visit their shrines.

Pilgrimages were costly and cumbersome. It was not easy to travel with a chronically sick or handicapped child under the conditions of transport of the period. We sometimes find detailed descriptions which reveal how difficult it was for a mother carrying her paralysed child to press through the throng at a shrine.[46] It was easier to make a vow and postpone the pilgrimage to a later stage, if and when the child recovered. It was essential, however, to keep the vows, and dangerous to break them, since the saints were thought to be omniscient.[47] Some handicapped children were raised by their parents and reached adulthood. They were incapable of conducting independent lives, and their parents continued to care for them and to visit the saints' shrines from time to time.[48]

In contemplating those parents who rejected handicapped children, one should recall that, in our day as well, it is not unknown for parents to refuse to accept a handicapped or retarded child and request that it be sent from the hospital direct to an institution, although such rejection is by no means accepted as a social norm. The belief in the existence of 'changelings', which could mitigate guilt-feelings by transference and which hastened the death of such children, has vanished from western society. The emotional price paid by a mother who cares devotedly for a handicapped child, despite feelings of anger, frustration, aggression, and guilt is often transference of the aggression from the child to herself or the outside world.[49]

BEREAVEMENT

The child mortality rate was very high, not only *post partum* but also in the first year of life. In the wake of studies by historical demographers, it can be crudely estimated that, in pre-industrial Europe, 200–300 out of every 1,000 infants died in their first year, and only half of the 1,000 reached the age of 5. From this age on, there was a gradual decline in the mortality rate, although it continued to be high up to the age of 10.[50] In times of epidemic the rate was, of course, even higher,[51] and it also rose during famine and war, when hunger itself claimed victims or malnutrition weakened bodily resistance to disease.[52] One can better comprehend the meaning of this mortality rate by examining the number of deaths in a particular family. The Florentine merchant, Gregorio Dati, had twenty-six legitimate children by his four wives. Of these, only eight survived. We know the age of death of some of these children: one died at birth, one at the age of 2 weeks, three at the age of a few months, one at the age of 1 year, one aged 3, one aged 4, one aged 6, one at 7 and a few months, and one at 9.[53] In the first half of the fifteenth century, a man from Limousin in France lost ten of his thirteen children. They died between the ages of a few days and 14 years. Six of them died in years of famine and plague.[54] Nor did the high child mortality rate spare royal families. Of the twelve offspring of Charles VI and Isabel of Bavaria, only eight survived to adulthood. (One was born dead; one died at 3 months; one at 2 years; and one at 9.)

It is evident that people were acquainted with death from childhood as a result of the death of relatives, siblings, and child acquaintances, or through being orphaned. And to be acquainted with death in a period when most people died in their own homes meant not only to experience the loss of a beloved person but also to see corpses. Awareness of the prevalence of death and a sense of mortal dread find expression in various sources. In a will in which a father bequeathed most of his property to his son, he adds that, if the son should die, the property is to be divided up among three other heirs.[55] An agreement drawn up between William the Marshal and Count Baldwin of Bethune for the marriage of their children, a boy of 12 and a girl of 7, stipulated that, if the boy died, the girl would be married to his brother; in the event of the death of the girl, her father's only daughter, then any future daughter born to him would be married to the marshal's son.[56] In Florence, the regulations of the special dowry funds (*monte delle dotti*) stipulate that, in the event of the death of the girl for whom the dowry was being collected (the average age of the girls when the sum was invested was 5) before payment of the capital with accrued interest fell due, the money would be handed over to the commune. Several years later, in 1433, it was decided, in order to encourage investment, that, if the girl died before the date of payment, the sum invested would be returned to her father.[57] These arrangements were made in order to safeguard interests in light of the high mortality rate.

Yet one also finds indications of awareness of the high mortality rate, which are marked by grief and dread. In Martial d'Auvergne's Death Dance of women, the small girl is dragged off to her death, and manages to say to her mother 'Take good care of my doll, my knucklebones, and my fine dress.'[58] In the description of the second coming of Christ and the resurrection of the dead, men, women, and children rise up from their graves. And there were special prayers for the resurrection of small children.[59] In an illustration from 1400 to the manuscript of the poem *Der Renner* (The Runner) by Hugh of Trimberg, who wrote of the little children at their happy play as well as of those who died in infancy, death appears in the image of a godfather, standing by the font ready to receive the child.[60] The paterfamilias in Alberti's book, who speaks of the joys and sorrows of raising children, says that what clouds joy more than anything else is fear for the lives of children, since it is well known that more children die in infancy than at any other time. 'How painful is the dread of losing such great joy,' he says.[61] The author of the tract in praise of virginity also lists among the sufferings of the mother the constant fear that her beautiful child might die.[62]

Theologians and preachers expected parents to accept the birth and the death of children with the same composure: 'The Lord giveth and the Lord taketh away.' Contraception and abortion were prohibited as was the killing of an infant, even when handicapped or illegitimate. But neither was it permitted to mourn excessively for the death of a child. Churchmen reiterated this last ban both directly and obliquely in their sermons. In the latter case, they tried to explain the death of children as an act of divine mercy. They condemned exaggerated mourning of parents more directly as the expression of lack of faith and piety. Even when the preacher condemns the sins of the current generation as the possible explanation for the death of children in a plague, he adds that, even so, the Lord is not chastising them when he frees them from imprisonment, exile, and suffering in this world and restores them to the glories of the other world. Jean Gerson was more heartless in this context. He too referred to the death of children as caused by human sin but cites as an *exemplum* the tale of a childless couple who, after years of prayer and good deeds, were blessed with a son. After the child was born, they devoted all their attention and resources to him. The Lord was angered at them for neglecting the church and the poor, and took back what he had bestowed on them.[63] Humbert de Romans writes directly of people who mourn excessively for their departed dear ones. 'They are very unhappy when their beloved ones die. This is because they do not believe they will live after this life. The faithful should not behave thus.'[64] Whereas Humbert de Romans perceives this mourning as a reflection of lack of faith in the next world, John Wyclif, in the fourteenth century, emphasizes the sinfulness of non-submission to the will of God. He castigates bereaved mothers for their tears, cries, and plaints, and says 'See now the madness of this murmuring. It is a great mercy of God to take a child out of this world'[65] (since it will reach the next world as an innocent). Wyclif's remarks were intended both to rebuke and to comfort bereaved mothers and to prepare them for the possible death of additional children. In a tract written by a 'good wyfe' of London in the fifteenth century for her daughter, she advises her to foster spiritual readiness to accept fate, which will enable her to acquiesce in the death of her children without rebelling against God.[66]

The thirteenth-century Dominican, Thomas Cantimpratanus, in a moral tract on good and bad qualities, interspersed with personal anecdotes, relates that his grandmother lost her eldest son. He was a handsome and gifted child for whom a great future was predicted. She mourned him bitterly and refused to be comforted until one day, by the wayside, she saw a vision of a group of lads marching along joyfully. At the sight, she recalled her son and tears filled her eyes. Suddenly she saw her son lagging along behind the group. She cried out bitterly 'How comes it, my son, that thou goest alone, lagging thus behind the rest?' Then he opened the side of his cloak and showed her a heavy water-pot, saying:

> Behold, dear mother, the tears which thou hast vainly shed for me, through the weight whereof I must needs linger behind the rest! Thou therefore shalt turn thy tears to God, and pour forth thy pious and devout heart in the presence of the sacrifice of Christ's body, with alms to the poor. Then only shall I be freed from the burden wherewith I am now grieved.[67]

Thomas Cantimpratanus is condemning excessive grief not only as improper conduct for a pious Christian, but also as a cause of pain to the deceased loved one. In the same spirit, in medieval folk-tales, the dead child appears to his mother in a dream and begs her to cease weeping for him so that his shroud can dry out.[68] The moralist appended to the popular tale a call for divine worship as the substitute for personal grief. In *belles-lettres* as well, the death of a child – even a tiny infant – is depicted as the source of pain and anguish for the parents and an almost insurmountable loss.[69]

We have already referred to the fatal accident which befell the son of a noble, after his father had harassed the monks in the monastery near his castle. According to the author, the innocent child went to heaven, but the father was never comforted.[70] There is no way of ascertaining whether the incident really occurred, but it undoubtedly indicates that the author considered the death of a child to be a blow from which a parent might never recover. In response to the words of the paterfamilias in Alberti's book on the constant dread entailed in childraising, his bachelor companion reiterates some banal points – the need to submit to fate, and not to mourn since God had only taken what He had given in trust and had acted mercifully towards the child in removing him from the vale of tears before he had become a sinner. But the father replies that every father is concerned for the lives of his children and lives in dread of the threat of losing those who are dearest to him. 'If you blame them for this, you condemn fatherhood itself.'[71]

Would there have been any point to the remonstrations of preachers, the literary expressions of grief at bereavement, the words of the father in Alberti's book, or the statement of the writer who considered the death of a child to be a staggering blow, if parents had in fact accepted the death of their offspring with the calm demanded of them by theologians and preachers or with the indifference attributed to them by modern historians? Moreover, in both the *Lives of the Saints* and the testimony of peasants before Jacques Fournier's tribunal, one finds the whole spectrum of responses to bereavement which is known to us today: a weeping and wailing mother, tearing her hair or beating her breast and head;[72] a mother fleeing to the forest after the death of her infant and refusing to return home;[73] a bereft mother refusing to hand over the corpse of her little son for burial;[74] a father totally paralysed with grief.[75] In one case, the mother was afflicted with such depression (*tristitia*) at the death of her son that she was unable to function as a housewife and mother. For many months she wept and groaned, refused to listen to words of comfort from those around her, and adamantly refused to attend church. Nor was she capable of looking at her living son, and everything around her aroused in her only disgust. Only when a saint prayed for her was she released from her depression 'and no bitterness remained in her'.[76] (This is described as one of the miracles wrought by the saint in his lifetime.) Sometimes parents retired to a monastery after the death of only sons or daughters.[77] Guilt-feelings, which often afflict survivors after the death of a loved one, and in particular the parent who loses a child, were not unknown at that time. Giovanni Morelli describes in his journal the death of his oldest son at the age of 10. The child was ill for two weeks, and the father apparently never moved from his bedside. After the death of the child, the father accused himself of having been harsh and demanding and never satisfied with the child's achievements. He had often berated him and whipped him, although the boy was an outstanding scholar, instead of displaying love and fatherly compassion. With merciless introspection, he writes 'you loved him but never made him happy. You never kissed him when he wanted you to ... now you have lost him and will never see him again in this world'.[78] Among the carvings on the capital of one of the pillars in the Magdalen church at Vézeley from the first half of the thirteenth century is the figure of a peasant mourning his dead infant and appealing to St Benedict to restore it to life.[79]

There were, of course, traditional mourning customs among Catholics as well as among heretics, and people came to comfort the mourners. The relatives of a Catholic woman who had lost her son tried to comfort her by telling her that he had been taken from this world in his innocence, but their words did not persuade her to cease her mourning.[80] A Cathar woman who lost her child was assured by her comforters that the soul of her dead child would enter the body of her next child, or reminded that the little girl had been privileged before her death to enter into the Cathar faith so that the redemption of her soul was guaranteed. The woman replied to these latter words of comfort that she was glad her daughter had been accepted into the Cathar faith but that she would yet weep for her more than she had already wept.[81]

Sometimes parents cited reasons and did not merely express emotions. The nobles wanted an heir to continue the lineage; the town-dwellers wanted heirs to their property or as a prop in old age (*baculum senectutis*), or for both reasons; and the peasants wanted sons as additional manpower in the family farm. (One of the peasants of Montaillou who bitterly mourned his dead son said 'With the death of my son, Raymond, I have lost all I had, there is nobody left to work for me.'[82]) The death of the last or sole offspring was particularly painful because it eradicated all hope of realizing these wishes. Yet this did not rule out sincere grief. Jean Gerson, like other preachers, upbraided parents who grieved excessively, but at the same time was aware of the anguish of loss and the particular grief of those who had no remaining children to inherit and to continue their name and lineage. It would appear that even today the pain of bereavement is particularly profound when the deceased child is the sole offspring. It is not surprising, therefore, that authors sometimes note that the deceased child or boy or girl who was believed to be in mortal danger was an only child.[83] The author of any modern biography would also have noted this fact. But, unlike medieval writers, the modern author would not specify as a particular cause of pain the fact that the dead child was the oldest son and hence the heir.

Some parents, both fathers and mothers, tried to spare themselves and, when they believed that a child was about to die, they left it in the care of a wetnurse, maidservant, or relative.[84] Although it goes without saying that this was selfish behaviour, it does also suggest that the sight of a dying child was not easy for a parent to bear. According to Herodotus, the Persians only spared fathers. As for children,

> until their fifth year they are not allowed to come into the sight of their father, but pass their lives with the women. This is done so that, if the child die young, the father may not be afflicted by its loss.[85]

Herodotus attributes psychological understanding to the Persians: one cannot mourn a person one has never known. Hence it is difficult to believe that those parents who handed their child to a wetnurse away from home immediately after birth felt a keen sense of loss when the child died or mourned him as an individual. But they failed to mourn not because they had evolved defence-mechanisms against close ties but because they had neither nurtured him nor known him, so that he never held an important place in their hearts. This is apparently also the explanation for the fact that, in all the letters of Heloïse to Abelard, their child is never mentioned. Abelard himself writes, in one brief sentence in *Historia Calamitatum* (The Story of my Misfortunes) that, after the birth of the child, it was entrusted to his sister in Brittany. Heloïse, who reiterates the tale of their love with guilt, passion, and longing, makes no reference whatsoever to the child. He is mentioned only in a letter to Peter the Venerable in which she asks for some prebend for him.[86] By then, he was a young man in his early twenties. And how could she have yearned for a child from whom she had been separated immediately after his birth and whom she scarcely knew?

It has been postulated that, since people died in their thousands in epidemics, fear of death was blunted and the grief of survivors was more diffuse and less personal in the general atmosphere of mourning.[87] One can only ask whether it is easier today for people who lose their loved ones in a war or an earthquake to bear their grief than for those who lose someone through natural causes or accidents. There is no clearcut answer. The high number of deaths in plagues could have intensified fear of death, and it is by no means clear that those who lost their children were comforted by the fact that the children of others had also died. Death was common and familiar, and, due to the high birth-rate and high infant mortality, parents could not grant each of their children the amount of attention devoted by modern western parents or mourn their children's demise for very long. But, in view of the extant evidence, it cannot be said that the death of a child was an event lacking emotional impact.

ORPHANHOOD

The psychoanalyst Krupp concurs with Laslett, who claimed that, in the society of the past, children reacted to orphanhood differently from today. Examining the socio-cultural variable in the context of orphanhood, he concluded that response to the death of a parent in pre-industrial society was much less intense than in present-day society because dependence on parents in childhood was less, and because there was greater freedom to fulfil libidinous desires after adolescence.[88] This evaluation deserves examination.

Orphans in the Middle Ages were listed among the 'miserable' (*personae miserabiles*) who were under the protection of the church, and gradually came to be considered to be entitled to the special protection of the secular rulers. It will be recalled that the church established orphanages and that clerics, who were considered the spiritual fathers of all those they had baptized, were assigned the task of teaching the basic tenets of Christian faith to children orphaned of their parents and bereaved of their godparents.[89] The king, and every feudal lord and knight, was expected to act as a protector of orphans, and the obligation to defend them was an important component of the knightly ethos. The urban authorities also recognized their special obligation towards orphans. The secular laws of inheritance of minors and guardianship, which form an important part of the various codes and writings of jurists in all regions, were aimed at safeguarding the rights of orphans and their property as well as the interests of the feudal seigneur or the lord of the manor.[90] And, just as didactic literature reflects awareness of the high rate of child mortality, so we also find indications of awareness of the possibility that children might be orphaned before attaining maturity. In this context, I shall pay attention only to the emotional significance of orphanhood and the degree of empathy felt by others with the orphan, in the course of examining several cases of an individual's response to the death of parents.

The very mention of the fact that a boy or girl was orphaned at an early age (*patre orbatus, matre orbatus*), even in those biographies in which only a few lines are devoted to the subject's childhood, shows that the author considered this event to be significant, and not only when, in consequence, the child was condemned to poverty and want (because there was now nobody to support him or because relatives or strangers seized his inheritance).

In a rare biography which contains a more detailed description of the subject's childhood, the author expresses great sympathy for the orphaned child. It will be recalled that, several days after his birth, the mother of Peter Damian began to nurse him with love and devotion. She died, however, while he was a small child, as did his father. The orphaned boy was taken to the home of one of his brothers, who ostensibly adopted him, but the brother and his wife were hostile towards him, neglected him, and beat him. Dressed in rags, barefoot, and half-starved, he was sent to herd the swine. Only at the age of 12 was he taken to the home of another brother, who was a cleric at Ravenna. This brother acted like a loving father, concerned himself with the boy's education, sent him to school and then on to higher learning. The author's attitude towards his orphanhood finds expression mainly in the tale of an event which occurred while he was still living with the first brother. One day the boy found a coin. For a moment he hesitated as to what to do with it and imagined to himself all the good things he could purchase with it. But he soon decided to give it to the priest to hold a mass for the soul of his father. It is hard to believe that the boy felt such resentment towards his mother for having neglected him in the first few days of his life that he did not request a mass for her soul and preferred his father, who is scarcely mentioned in the story of his birth. It seems that it was rather the author of the biography who could not forgive the mother. Again, it seems that he cited this story in order to illustrate the great piety of the future saint from childhood, since it was the religious duty of every person to arrange for masses and prayers for the souls of dead parents, and the objective of the author was essentially to preach through citing exemplary models. But, at the same time, it is evident that he is expressing empathy towards the orphaned child, with whose suffering the reader is expected to identify. At the age of 28, Peter Damian became a Benedictine monk.[91] External circumstances impelled him to choose the religious life. It may be assumed that he was not only grateful to his brother but also identified with him (he even adopted his surname – Damianus). His education opened up the way for a career in the church. But is it not reasonable to assume that he chose to serve God and to live the monastic life also in search of self-torment as a means of identification with his dead parents and as a way of overcoming the anxieties born out of his unhappy childhood as an orphan?

As mentioned above, it was the religious obligation of offspring to pray for the souls of their dead parents and to arrange for masses in their memory. According to the manuals for confessors, the priest was obliged to ask those who came to confess 'Hast thou honoured thy father and mother? Hast thou given them meat and raiment at their need? Hast thou had prayers said for the repose of their souls?'[92] The appearance of a dead parent in a dream or vision to a son or daughter was considered a customary occurrence.[93] Religious faith and custom helped thereby in the denial of the finality of death. In this spirit, the well-known poetess Frau Ava writes in one of her religious poems that she is the mother of two children, one living and the other dead, and that both are dear to her. The dead child exists as far as she is concerned and she asks her readers to pray for both children.[94] The future saints not only prayed for the repose of their parents' souls but, according to their biographers, also frequently saw them in dreams and were guided by them.[95] When Bernard of Clairvaux hesitated whether to hearken to the advice of his brothers and to choose an academic career, his mother appeared to him in a dream and reminded him of his true vocation.[96] When Edmund of Abingdon devoted himself to his mathematical studies, his mother appeared in a dream and ordered him to concentrate on study of the Holy Trinity.[97] The father of the mystic, Henry Suso, appeared to him in a dream, told him that he was in purgatory, and asked him to pray for the repose of his soul. His mother, to whom he was apparently particularly attached (his real name was Van Berg but he preferred to be called by his mother's family name of Suso) also appeared to him in a dream and told him of the bliss that was her lot in Heaven.[98] These and many other similar tales indicate the extent to which saints or their biographers identified with religious beliefs and customs which helped them to deny the finality of death. Yet they could also have been the reflection of the strong defence-mechanism which saints and/or their biographers constructed. Anna Freud pointed out that, even if denial is consistent with the prevailing behavioural norms of a certain culture, this does not mean that it is not pathological in nature.[99]

An unusually detailed description of the response of an adolescent to the death of his mother can be found in the biography of Anselm of Canterbury. His mother was a wise and sensitive woman, and they were very close. As a small child he longed to study and urged his parents to send him to school. He was despatched to the home of a private tutor who was also a relative. The tutor kept him indoors, did not permit him to go out to play with children his own age, and forced him to study day and night. The boy was almost driven insane and was sent back home greatly disturbed in spirit. He held aloof from other members of the household, refused to respond to his mother's questions, and would not even look her in the face. Once his mother overcame her shock at the change in her son, she decided that total permissiveness was the correct cure. The servants were ordered to leave him to his own devices, to permit him to act as he chose, and not to reprimand him. He recovered gradually and his spirits were restored. Anselm never forgot the wise and considerate conduct of his mother and it influenced his own behaviour towards young oblates when he became abbot of a monastery. At the age of 17, he asked to enter a monastery. His father was vehemently opposed, and the abbot did not dare to accept him against his father's wishes. He tried to fall ill, in the hope that if he did so he might be accepted, and did in fact sicken, but neither his father nor the abbot changed their minds. Shortly afterwards his beloved mother died, and (according to his biographer) he was distraught with grief.

> He began little by little to cool in the fervour of his desire for a religious life ... He gradually turned from study, which had formerly been his chief occupation, and to give himself up to youthful amusements. His love and reverence for his mother held him back to some extent from these paths, but she died and then the ship of his heart had, as it were, lost its anchor and drifted almost entirely among the waves of the world.

Anselm told his biographer that his father hated him and that, the more he endeavoured to act as his father wished and the greater his submissiveness, the more he aroused his hatred and anger.[100] Anselm's mother died at a time when he was apparently undergoing an identity crisis. It is immaterial whether his father did in fact hate him or whether he merely imagined this. This was the truth for him, and the relations between them were undoubtedly disrupted. His crisis was heightened by the death of his mother, and his depression and loneliness increased. Anselm's reaction – as reported by his biographer – resembled that of contemporary adolescents faced with the loss of the object of love at a time of identity crisis.

The mother of Gilbert of Nogent retired to a convent when he was 12 or 13. His ties with his mother were close and particularly complex, and his father, as noted, had died shortly after the boy's birth. None the less, his reaction to separation from his mother reveals something of the responses of children of this age to orphanhood (or separation for other reasons). Since she left him in order to take the veil he was obliged to justify her. Yet his justification reflects the significance of the act for him. He wrote that, in abandoning him, she was aware that he would become an orphan whose material needs would be supplied but would henceforth lack the love and attention so necessary for a child, which only a mother can bestow. She herself, so he claims, suffered great pain, and with good reason, since she was acting like a cruel and unnatural mother. It was love of God and concern for the redemption of her own soul which hardened her heart.[101]

An extraordinary tale of an orphan appears in the biography of Drogo, a twelfth-century Flemish saint. His father died before the child was born and his mother died in childbirth. The author conveys no details of the early childhood of the saint, and one cannot ascertain whether he suffered the loss of a maternal figure in his life. At the age of 10 he learned that his mother had died in giving birth to him, and the shock was great. He wept for days and accused himself of murder. The discovery was undoubtedly a traumatic event for the orphaned child, who was sensitive and had depressive tendencies. He apparently never recovered from the shock. He became a pilgrim and a shepherd, and, unlike other saints who became part of the church establishment and were active therein, he never again tried to cope with life.[102]

The intensity of reaction to orphanhood today varies from child to child (although the pattern of response is similar), and the same was undoubtedly true in the past. The conditions under which a child was raised after being orphaned certainly influenced his response: did the child enjoy the love of a relative or nurse who served as a mother substitute? In the case of a girl, did she have some object of identification? Did a boy have some masculine figure with whom he could identify? In such cases, the emotional damage was certainly less severe. The age of the child would also help determine the intensity of the damage. If we accept that the oedipal stage in childhood development also applies to western society of the past, then the loss of a mother or father at a tender age (between $2\frac{1}{2}$ and 3, according to Erikson) would make it difficult for the male or female child to identify with a person of their own sex and to emerge from the oedipal stage. This was compounded by the harsher impact of object-loss at an early age, which can often cause the child to grow into an adult with a propensity for anxiety and fears.[103] Giovanni Morelli describes tragic orphanhood. He lost his father when aged 3 and writes that he suffered for most of his childhood from the absence of a figure who could substitute for mother or father. For several years an adult uncle served as his father image, but the uncle died in an epidemic. He was also attached to his older sister, but she died in childbirth at the age of 22. Morelli refers to the emotional impact of his lonely orphanhood. Christiane Klapisch believes that possibly what in fact troubled him in the case of his mother was the loss of her dowry. His mother remarried but did not abandon him, and he spent a large part of his childhood and adolescence with her and his stepfather. Many other children in Tuscany who lost their fathers, on the other hand, were condemned to separation from their mothers. The strict patriarchal and patrilinear structure of society there meant that, if a woman was widowed, strong pressure was brought to bear on her by her family to return to the parental home and bring her dowry with her (and, if she was young, to remarry). If she was a 'dutiful daughter' and submitted to the demands of her father, she was forced to abandon her children to her late husband's family and was a 'cruel mother'. Morelli, in any event, never forgave his mother for her remarriage, although she did not abandon him, and he did not regard his stepfather as substitute for his father. In adulthood, he wrote:

How great is the benefit which a child receives from a living father, from his daily guidance and advice. It is the duty of every father to ensure that, if he dies, his wife will not remarry and leave their children, since there is no mother who is so bad that she is not better for her children than any strange woman.[104]

Many of the children who lost one parent lived with a stepmother or stepfather, since most widowers and widows remarried once and even twice, and not always and not everywhere were the offspring of previous marriages despatched to relatives. (In the urban inheritance laws one finds reference to the various inheritance rights of the progeny of three wives.[105]) In folk-tales as well as in the *Lives of the Saints* the character of the wicked stepmother is dominant. She favours her children over her husband's children and some-times persecutes them. According to psychoanalytical theory, stories of wicked stepmothers reflect the transference and expression of unconscious hostility towards the natural mother. When a child has a stepmother in reality, she often becomes the object of the child's unconscious hostile urges enduring from his relations with his natural mother. And, since the uncon-scious has no concept of time, the intensity of response does not necessarily wane as the child matures.[106] In the medieval folk-tale, the stepchild of the wicked stepmother is indeed sometimes in his twenties.[107] In the Icelandic saga one finds tales of hostile acts of a stepmother toward her son or daughter, and tales of the forbidden love between the stepmother and her husband's son. In one saga, the son is punished by death. In another, he does not succumb to the seductive efforts of his stepmother, and she takes cruel revenge on him.[108] But, together with these tales, there is the story of a stepmother whose stepson is killed in battle and bequeaths all his property to her. When she learns of his death and that of his brother (also her stepson), she weeps for the first time in her life. Later she urges her own sons to avenge the blood of their stepbrothers and herself heads the army which goes out to fight the killers.[109] In the *Lives of the Saints* a good stepmother who takes a vow for the sake of her stepson is also mentioned.[110]

Whereas the folk-tale and saga express profound emotional truth, the sermons describing tbe rivalries between the progeny of first and second marriages and the mutual hostility between stepmother and stepchildren[111] apparently give a clearer picture of everyday details of life. It was the custom of the young villagers in various regions to gather under the window of the widower or widow who was about to remarry and to conduct a cacophonous concert of banging percussion instruments and wailing. This ceremony, the Charivari, expressing hostility toward those who violated certain community rules, reflects not only psychological concern for the children of previous marriages but also economic anxiety.[112] It may be that it is the stepmother rather than the stepfather who is the dominant figure in folk literature because there were more cases of children raised in the paternal home by a second wife (and not by paternal or maternal relatives[113]) than of children raised by remarried mothers. Two who appear to have suffered at the hands of stepmothers were Dante and Boccaccio; but, conversely, one can find in wills examples of equal legacies to natural children and stepchildren by both mothers and fathers.[114]

8 On education in the second stage of childhood

FACTORS IN PERSONALITY FORMATION

Medieval scholars believed in the power of education. The authors of medical tracts were inspired by Aristotle, who considered the new-born babe to be a *tabula rasa* (clear slate),[1] while the didactic writers cited the image of wax. Every newborn child was burdened with the weight of Original Sin, but baptism bestowed divine mercy and forgiveness, and within the limits of the human condition it was possible to educate the child and develop in him those character traits and patterns of behaviour considered desirable. In other words, education could inculcate in him the contents of culture, guide him toward critique of the id and creation of the super-ego, in accordance with the values of the society, and raise him as an independent human being, self-supporting within the social stratum into which he had been born.

At the same time, scholars recognized the existence of heredity and of differences in temperament stemming from conditions of conception. Some theologians followed the Aristotelian physiological theories and believed that the male alone was the active factor in creating the foetus. Male semen contained the foetus *in potentia* while the female provided only the matter and the 'inner space'. According to this theory, woman's role was passive and auxiliary.[2] However, most medical authors believed that the female not only absorbed semen but also ejaculated it, and that the character of the child was determined according to the substance of both father and mother, transmitted to him through the pure blood in their semen, originating in the heart and the brain. Sometimes the blood in the father's semen was predominant, and then the foetus resembled him in character traits; and, conversely, when the mother's blood was predominant, the foetus resembled her. When it was of equal force in the semen of both parents, the child resembled father and mother to an equal degree.[3] The physical resemblance between progeny and parents was acknowledged (and satirical literature depicts the problems of a wayward woman whose newborn child resembles her lover and not her husband[4]), as was the concept of hereditary nobility.

It was widely stated that nobility was the sum total of personal traits, and that a man could foster desirable traits in himself, but also that the child born to noble parents would display noble qualities. The mother's blood was considered as important as that of the father. By means of the blood in her semen, she transmitted *nobilitas* and the accompanying genetic traits. Needless to say, this theory served to justify the tendency of the nobility to exclusivity from the twelfth century onward. This class never totally closed itself up, but the advantages and positive qualities of those who were of noble descent in both the maternal and the paternal line were manifest. Those of distinguished lineage enjoyed a particular advantage, since 'noble descent strengthens the heart against wickedness and deception'.[5] It was no accident that the biography of the ideal noble commenced with his genealogy.[6] The significant context was social, but theories regarding personality-shaping factors were also involved. In the Lives of the saints as well we find the *topos* of 'saintly root' (*sancta radix*);[7] the son of noble and pious parents is the fruit of both the proper blood-ties and the religious education bestowed by his parents. In literature and popular legend a prevalent motif is that of the son of a royal family torn from his rightful place, who is ignorant of his origins and is not raised as a prince. He gradually begins to display princely traits and comes to believe that he is a king's son before being told the truth.[8] A description of the consequence of the ideal combination of lofty origin and proper education appears in the educational utopia in *Lancelot del Lac*. The child grows up without knowing that he is the son of a king. He is given the ideal education of a knight, which bears fruit because of his origin, of which he is still ignorant.[9] At the opposite extreme to nobles whose progeny possess noble traits are the beggars who spawn bastards who will some day become beggars in their turn.[10] And the authors of scientific works caution that sin which weakens the soul also enfeebles and degenerates the body, and that this feebleness and debility is passed on from father to son.[11]

Yet it was believed that the nature of a human being was not determined solely by the substance of his parents, since his temperament was formulated by the composition of the humours in his body. The situation of the celestial bodies at the time of conception was responsible for the ratio betwen these humours. Four types of temperament were enumerated according to the fluids: sanguine – bloody fluid; melancholy – black; choleric – yellow or splenetic; phlegmatic – white.[12] The temperament, so contemporary medical writers believed, was already given expression in infancy and could not be altered either then or later, but was merely moderated by physical or spiritual counter-remedies. It was for this reason that the authors of medical books recommended rubbing melancholy or phlegmatic babies with salt, while sanguine or choleric infants who were hot and thin were to be rubbed with oil. It was also considered essential to choose a wetnurse whose temperament suited that of the infant.[13] The authors warned against administering wine to older children of sanguine or choleric temperament since this could harm their health, but advocated giving it to those with melancholy or phlegmatic temperament. They also stressed that different foods suited different children.[14] (It is interesting to note that, in the past two decades, psychologists have engaged in study of differences in temperament between infants and have studied the effect of temperament on the interaction between the infant and those around him, as well as the degree to which temperament alters with age.) According to one of the protagonists of Alberti's book, the intensity of the urges and desires implanted by nature varies in people of different temperament. The sanguine individual is more sensitive to love than the melancholic; the choleric temperament is easily angered. The phlegmatic individual is characterized by sloth and inactivity. The melancholic has a greater tendency to fear and suspicion than the others and hence develops a tendency to miserliness and greed.[15]

Medieval scholars appear to have veered between heredity and environment in their search for the factors shaping personality, and also cited celestial factors affecting temperament, and the effect of the milk imbibed. As with scholars in later periods who have debated the question of heredity versus environment, the statements of medieval thinkers echo political stands and ideologies. Yet whereas discussion of the various types of humour in theoretical works sometimes borders on determinism, suggesting that the character of a man is determined by his physiology alone, medieval didactic writers emphasize both the impact of education and the obligation to provide the child with a proper upbringing. The determinist approach is illustrated by the remarks of Hildegard of Bingen discussing the child conceived on the twentieth day after the full moon. A boy conceived on this day, she writes, is destined to become a robber and murderer who will rejoice in his actions. A girl conceived on this day will become a poisoner who destroys men at her pleasure. She will lose her mind easily and will live a long life.[16] According to Hildegard, only those of sanguine humour recall the harmonious human being of the days before the Original Sin and the Fall, while the other three types represent the loss of harmony and perfection and the frustration which is the lot of mankind in this world. Philip of Novare, on the other hand, in his didactic book, advocates faith in divine grace and human will-power: one must not say that a child is 'good' or 'evil' since God created him thus. It is true that all mercies stem from God, but God does not wish a child to grow like a chicken or a cub, without the power of speech and reason. Being endowed with both he is capable, at least from the age of 10 onward, of distinguishing between good and evil and choosing between them. The function of education is to render him capable of choosing good since 'often the child does good only out of fear and as a consequence of instruction and guidance'.[17] Giovanni Dominici discusses the claim that children are born with various natural qualities which will inevitably determine the direction of their development. Jacob and Esau were raised in the same bosom and yet one became a tent-dweller and the other a man of the field. Cain and Abel were born to the same father and the same mother; one became a miser and a murderer and the other a generous and merciful man. Dominici does not try to refute these arguments and to deny the influence of those inborn qualities but stresses the impact of education and details the proper methods of education.[18] All the didactic writers are characterized by rejection of determinism, but some, convinced of the existence of individual differences between children, favoured adapting education to the personality of the child. Since people differ in temperament by nature, each individual should be encouraged in accordance with his abilities, predilections, and existing traits. One of the speakers in Alberti's book says that it is the role of the father to select a suitable profession for his son, not only in view of the family's standing, the customs and expectations of the country, and his own circumstances and opportunities, but also on the basis of the temperament and talents of the child.[19] Bernard Gordon wrote in the early fourteenth century that, when a boy reached the age of 12, he should choose his path in life according to his wishes and predilections.[20] To sum up: if we rephrase the statements of medieval scholars in the terminology of modern educational theory, we may say that the dominant approach was a blend of cultural pedagogy (which essentially consisted of inculcation of cultural values) and utilitarian pedagogy (which can be summarized as preparation for life). Alberti (as we have seen) and others, mainly in the Late Middle Ages, also expounded the progressive pedagogic theory, based on individual self-realization. Aegidius Romanus, despite his distinction between the various stages of childhood and his remarks on the characteristics of each stage, asserted that the rate of development of children differed and that it was their personality which determined the pace. Some children were strong in body at 12 and others only at 16. The same, he claimed, was true of intellectual development. Hence he could not establish the exact age at which a child should arrive at any particular achievement. It was the task of pedagogues to determine the suitable age on the basis of the 'personality of the child'.[21]

Preachers and authors of didactic works elaborated on the evils which were the lot both of those who had not been given a proper Christian education and of those close to them, and this theme will be discussed below. Literary description of the consequence of 'antipedagogy' with regard to a young noble can be found in the medieval epic and courtly romance. In Wolfram of Eschenbach's *Parzival*, we read that, in order to protect him from danger and to keep him safe from sorrow and pain, his mother raised him in the forest far from the knightly world and without educating him. When, despite her efforts to preserve him from sorrow, the song of the birds filled his heart with melancholy, his mother ordered her men to set traps for the birds and to wring their necks. But the artificial paradise which she had created for her son was doomed to come to an end. One day the boy encountered a group of knights and left the forest in their wake. Despite his natural attributes (beauty, physical strength, courage, natural intelligence, and charm) which endear him to all those he meets, he learns all that a knight should know in the hardest way. When he leaves his mother and the forest and goes out into the world, he learns things gradually and only after a series of crude mistakes which endanger him and cause sorrow and disppointment to him and to all those with whom he comes into contact.[22] On another plane the emergence from the forest symbolizes the loss of the internal paradise – the loss of childhood and its innocence.

THE GOAL OF EDUCATION

The moral education, not only of those who dedicated themselves to a contemplative life, but also of those who pursued an active life, was based on religion. The proclaimed aim of education was to raise a Christian human being, and it was universally emphasized that Christian morals took precedence over worldly knowledge and vocational skills.[23] Certain character traits were assumed to enable the realization of Christian values and it was these traits which education was intended to foster. To be a good Christian meant to observe the rituals of worship (attendance at church, prayer, reception of the sacraments, and observance of fastdays); to fulfil the moral injunctions of the Scriptures and, above all, the Ten Commandments; to refrain from the seven deadly sins (pride, covetousness, lust, envy, gluttony, anger, and sloth); to nurture good qualities, expressed in character traits, in moods, and in basic attitudes (faith, hope, love, charity, reason, moderation, and fortitude);[24] to refrain from cursing and swearing, slander, brawls, and quarrels; to give charity to the church and to the poor, to comfort prisoners, to visit the sick, to offer hospitality to wayfarers, and to help bury the poor. All these were seen as part of the fabric constituting the expression of faith, fear of God, and love of God and the right path which one should follow in order to achieve redemption in the next world.

On another plane, the didactic writers acknowledged the secondary goals of education: to develop the ability and intellectual predilections of the individual and to prepare him to fulfil his role in society. The ideal traits which education was intended to promote were determined also by sex: modesty and chastity were to be fostered in both sexes, but were given immeasurably greater emphasis where girls were concerned. Training of girls in obedience was also considered of greater importance than the disciplining of boys, since a woman, unlike a man, was destined to be obedient all her life: in childhood, she would obey her parents and tutors, in maturity her husband; or, if she took the veil, the rule of the order to which she belonged.

Another aim of education was to teach the child to accept the social order and to respect it, since the existing order was considered both good and proper, the reflection of God's will and part of the harmonious order of things in the universe. One sometimes finds educational exhortations addressed to 'all Christian children' or 'all Christian parents', but it is clear not only that the standing of parents determined the type of education their children received, but that expectations differed for the education administered to children from different social classes. These expectations find expression in the more worldly discussions in the works of didactic writers. There are good masters and good servants, bad masters and bad servants, and different qualities are expected of the good master and the good servant.[25] The qualities required of the knight were not sought in the peasant or merchant. In the didactic literature, as in the confessors' manuals, specific sins of various classes and professions are enumerated, and these indicate what was considered the proper norm of conduct by class, occupation, and sex. In didactic literature, the general chapter devoted to children at the same stage of childhood is followed by separate chapters on the raising of those who entered the church, knights, merchants, or artisans.[26]

One of the injunctions stressed by the didactic writers, preachers, and authors of confessors' manuals in approaching the Christian flock was the biblical commandment 'Honour thy father and thy mother', which is reiterated in the New Testament ('Children, obey your parents in the Lord for this is right. Honour thy father and mother; which is the first commandment with promise. That it may be well with thee and thou mayest live long on the earth' (Eph. 6: 1–3). The scriptural commandment is clear, as is the promised reward. The authors, however, composed exegeses on the significance of the injunction, which often fitted in with their conception of the social order. Take, for example, the words of the author of *Dives et Pauper* (Rich Man and Poor Man) in the context of clarification of the practical significance of the Ten Commandments. In discussing the duty to honour parents, the author cites a series of additional verses from the Old and New Testaments and explicates them. (The texts are Lev. 20: 9; Deut. 21: 18–21; Prov. 13: 22; 28: 24; 30: 17; Matt. 15: 4–6.) Children should honour their parents because they owe them their lives. A man has two beginnings: the one from God (hence the First Commandment), and the other from his parents. To honour parents means to treat them with respect, humility, and obedience and to assist them in everything when they are in need of aid. Furthermore, honouring parents also implies moral conduct, since sinfulness and improper conduct on the part of offspring injure the parents, and injury means disrespect. Citing appropriate verses, the author notes that the obligation to honour one's father and mother does not end with maturity and that progeny must support their parents in their old age. The Scriptures state that 'the children ought not to lay up for the parents, but the parents for the children'

(2 Cor. 12: 14), but it is the duty of children to aid their parents when they are old and helpless, as their parents cared for them as children. The tree receives its fruit from its trunk, but also sometimes gives to the trunk and replenishes it. As will be recalled, the obligation to honour parents was expected to endure even after their death, since it was the duty of progeny to pray for the repose of their parents' souls. Children who honoured their parents would not only live long (as promised by the Bible) but also enjoy a good life, riches, and many children, who would honour and respect them in their turn. In this context the author cites the popular tale quoted by preachers, regarding the son who drove his old father out of his room during the cold winter and forced him to sleep in the entrance hall. The old man suffered from the cold and asked his grandson for a blanket. The father refused to give a blanket and offered him a sack. The child then said that he had better cut the sack in two – one half for the grandfather and the other for himself for when he grew old.[27] Other writers defined the role of the parents not as a 'second beginning' but rather as a partnership with God in the creation of their progeny, as a consequence of which it was the duty of the children to respect them.[28] Love for parents stemmed from the natural links between parents and children and from the benefits they received from them. Christ was perceived as the ideal example of respect for parents ('the Lord of the heavens and the earth who was modest and humble and honoured His mother and her husband Joseph all his days'[29]), and Isaac was another who was considered the archetype of the ideal son. The sermons cite *exempla* from classical literature and medieval folk-tales about ideal sons and daughters, like the daughter who came to visit her mother in prison and suckled her lest she die of hunger; or the son who hid his father in his home, since the father had grown old and was no longer able to fulfil his knightly duties and was condemned to exile in accordance with the laws of the kingdom. Also cited in illustration were examples from the animal kingdom – the storks who nurse their sick and old parents or the ravens who feed them in old age.[30] The New Testament contains a problematic verse on duties toward parents and toward Christ which can be interpreted literally as meaning that one cannot love both parents and Christ ('he that loveth father or mother more than Me is not worthy of Me; and he that loveth son or daughter more than Me is not worthy of Me' (Matt. 10: 37–38)).[31] The second half of this verse was quoted by several of the authors of the Lives of female saints as justification for their abandoning children for the sake of the religious life. Most of the authors of didactic works, however, in relating to the first half, at least, refused to interpret it literally. The author of *Dives et Pauper* put this verse in the mouth of the rich man querying the statement of the poor man on the obligation to honour parents. The poor man, in his reply (which is the author's own interpretation and solution), says that these words of Christ were uttered in the days of idol-worship and that they did not mean that a man should hate

his parents but only that he should hate their beliefs and way of life. Parents should be loved, but, even in the present day, if they should sin, their sins should be hated and their children should endeavour to bring them back to the right path.[32]

At the same time, the obligation to honour parents was not only a scriptural injunction anchored in the Christian conception of obedience and submission, but also the basis for the maintenance of the social order. Parents should be honoured also because they are the bearers of authority in the family, which is the primary and natural social partnership. Obedience toward them guarantees the perpetuation of the proper hierarchical order.[33] When a chronicler laments prevailing mores and the lapsed moral values, he lists as signs of the times disrespect towards parents, disobedience towards those in authority, and the violation of the oath of feudal fidelity of vassals towards their lords.[34] The preachers and didactic writers, almost without exception, speak in the same breath of the duty to respect parents and the obligation to display respect and obedience towards prelates and priests and all those in authority.[35] Just as the paterfamilias was expected to ensure that his children attended church on Sunday, it was his duty to see that his servants did so as well instead of spending their times in games and at taverns.[36]

It has often been pointed out that there is no scriptural injunction addressed to parents corresponding to the injunction to children. Denis Saurat, in his book, *The End of Fear* (written in the twentieth century), places the following words in the mouth of the village priest in the Pyrenees:

> The Good God was obliged to issue a commandment that children should love their parents. It is not natural for children to love their parents. But the Good God pronounced no commandment that parents should love their children; no commandment was needed. It is natural; it is an instinct. That is why parents and children can never agree.[37]

According to Richelieu, parental love is so natural that the law inscribed in the hearts of parents suffices, and there is no need of any other.[38] In the view of the medical authors of medieval Salerno, parents love their children more than the children love them because children possess something of the substance (*substantia*) of their parents, but the reverse is not so.[39] This has an additional implication in the context of Christian culture, namely, the implication of giving without expectation of reward – indeed, that of sacrifice. The association with the sacrifice of Christ in the sacrament is inevitable. Philip of Novare, who wrote of the three loves which God bestows on infants, asserted that whereas the love lavished by those who nurture them (mainly father, mother, and grandparents) increases with the years, the child's own love for these nurturers wanes with time. He concludes with a caution to offspring not to do evil to those who nurtured them in childhood.[40] Thomas Aquinas, in his commentary on 2 Cor. 12: 14 (cited above), says that parents act thus because of their natural love for their progeny.[41] And, in fact, medieval writers did not exhort parents to love their children but merely described that love in didactic works, in fables, and in popular tales. They did, however, stress constantly the parental obligation toward the pledge given into their safekeeping by God, who had charged them with the task of keeping children secure, supporting them, and giving them a Christian upbringing. We cannot discuss here the question of whether the emphasis on the duty of children to support their parents in their old age indicates that many aged parents were neglected or had their property seized, since such a discussion would touch on the second part of the third stage in human life – namely *adolescentia* – or even the fourth stage – *juventus*. It should be noted, however, that, despite the warning to parents contained in the 'King Lear' folk-tales, numerous elderly peasants in the Midlands in the thirteenth and fourteenth centuries not only handed over their property to their children in return for their keep, but did not even safeguard their rights by means of a legal contract. Such contracts between parents and children were exceptional and not usually drawn up except when the property was handed over to other relatives or when particular difficulties arose.[42] Some town-dwellers in England also handed over property and businesses to their children in their lifetime.[43]

THE INCEPTION OF EDUCATION AND THE EDUCATORS

It was universally agreed that education should begin at an early age, and this was taken to mean at the beginning of the second stage of childhood. The consensus was that the foundation of future development was laid in childhood and that what was spoiled in childhood could never be rectified.[44] To substantiate this belief, maxims were cited: a thin and flexible branch can be bended easily but, once it has thickened, it cannot be bent without breaking; fresh clay and wax can be moulded; new cloth absorbs colour well, but raw wool absorbs it better; the ox and horse can be tamed only when young; and in order to heal the patient the medicine must be administered early before the disease grows acute.[45] The authors also quoted the verse attributed to Christ ('Suffer little children and forbid them not to come to me; for of such is the kindgom of heaven' (Matt. 19: 14)), explaining that it meant 'Suffer them to be educated by me from their childhood.' Children, it was said, are as pure as angels and like them are of fiery temperament, flaring up and cooling down rapidly. The angels made their choices with fervour – some for good and others for evil – and adhered to them. Children too learn both good and evil rapidly, and one should hasten to teach them to do good. To withhold from children a Christian upbringing is like barring them from coming to Christ. The Lord summoned Samuel in childhood and bestowed His mercy on him and, likewise, He summons other children and they should be taught to respond to His call and to foster their religious piety and good qualities.[46]

In discussing the obligation to commence education at an early age, the writers place prime emphasis on the inculcation of Christian morality, but note that academic teaching and vocational training should also be started early. The sooner a child begins to study a vocation, the more skilled he will be in adulthood, and training for priesthood and knighthood in particular should commence early. But, writes Philip of Novare, every vocation should be studied well, since it is an honour to be skilled at one's craft, whatever it may be.[47] The accentuation of the importance of manual work derived from the esteem in which diligence was held, and from the conviction that the functions of the various orders of society were interdependent. Raymond Lull, who devotes a chapter of his didactic work to 'the mechanical crafts', dwells (as did many of his predecessors) on the importance of workers, without whom the social order could not exist. Without their labours the burghers, the knights, the princes, and the churchmen could not survive. Every wise man, however prosperous he is, should teach his son a trade. In this manner the child will learn diligence and, if his fortunes should be reversed some day, he will still be able to support himself.[48] (Although the social order was believed to be fixed and stable, it was accepted that the individual was exposed to the vicissitudes of fortune!)

In the second stage of childhood as well, the task of education and socialization was allotted mainly to parents, but priests and tutors were also expected to play their part. The priest was charged not only with exhorting parents to play their proper role but also with guiding the child, cautioning him discreetly, and encouraging him to confess.[49] Sometimes authors of confessors' manuals also refer to the task of the tutor. Thomas Chobham, for example, writes that the profession of teacher is among the most dangerous, since it involves heavy responsibility; he must not only teach but also inculcate Christian morality. A teacher who receives payment from parents and does not fulfil his duty is worse than a thief, since the latter steals only money, while the teacher steals knowledge and moral ways. If the pupil goes to the bad, the teacher will be responsible before God.[50] Yet it was mainly the didactic writers who concerned themselves with the child's intellectual development and education, drawing inspiration from the classical writers who dealt with the teacher's role. They often launched discussions of the education of the seven-year-old child by asserting that the time had come to entrust him to the care of a tutor. The ideal teacher should be an honest and moral person, modest despite his erudition, of clear mind, capable of explaining clearly and of reconciling apparent contradictions, not relying on books alone, able to express himself well, and enthusiastic.[51]

Parents were exhorted to teach their children love of God, discipline, and Christian morality; under no circumstances should they postpone the commencement of education and the strict insistence on proper conduct; nor should they regard the evil actions of their children as childish mischief which should be ignored; they should refrain from pampering children. There are numerous *exempla* on the bad end of those who were not properly educated by their parents. One of the commonest stories is that of the young man who became a criminal and was condemned to death by hanging. On his way to the gallows he asked to kiss his father for the last time. On approaching his father, he bit him hard on the nose (according to some versions, he bit it off), saying that his father was to blame for his death because he had not taken the trouble to educate him in childhood.[52] Just as the preachers denounced pampering (particularly on the part of mothers, who were said to be excessively indulgent toward their children, loving them 'according to the flesh alone'), they also abhorred the parental tendency to invest maximum effort in ensuring the material well-being of their children, and their desire to train them for a profession which would bring them riches, such as that of the lawyer or merchant (instead of sending them to study theology).[53] The authors also remind prosperous families that the father should select his son's tutor scrupulously and closely observe his teaching methods.

EDUCATIONAL METHODS

Education was to be achieved through the good example of both parents and teachers; through preventing the detrimental impact of a corrupt society and of literature which aroused evil instincts; and through explication, reprimand, and wielding the whip. Since children tend to imitate the acts of adults, how could they not learn evil words and deeds if their parents swore, were gluttonous, cheated, squabbled with neighbours, and did not observe other divine commandments, ask the authors.[54] Since children and young people enjoy the company of their peers (according to Aegidius Romanus they are 'over-fond of company' – a statement reminiscent of modern views on the influence of the peer-group), they must be protected against the evil influence of both their peers and corrupt adults. They should also be prevented from viewing naked men and women and lewd conduct and distanced from recitations of immoral songs and verses (such as those of Ovid). They should be required to read the appropriate literature, listen to suitable music, hear proper and moral utterances, and attend church. It will be recalled that there were special sermons composed for children.[55] In addressing noble and middle-class parents, the authors proposed that they raise their children like the Spartans, under rigorous conditions, and harden them. There was, of course, no need to cite the Spartans in order to laud the virtues of frugality and endurance. Asceticism was a central concept in the Christian outlook. Indeed, after describing Spartan education, Humbert de Romans cited one of the biographies of Bernard of Clairvaux, according to which his mother raised him as strictly as if she were preparing him for the life of a hermit in the desert.[56] According to Raymond Lull, it is nature that demands frugality in food and drink and modesty of dress, and nature knows better than mothers how children should be raised. The children of the poor are more intelligent and beautiful than the offspring of the rich because the pretentious upbringing of the latter, and parental indulgence, prevents nature from bestowing on them all that it can give.[57] If none of the specified methods achieves the desired results, it was obligatory to beat the stubborn and rebellious son. On the basis of the verse 'He who spares the rod spoils the child,' the experts, with very few exceptions, favoured 'controlled' whipping. With variations, the idea is reiterated that he who refrains from whipping when necessary can be compared to one who has seemingly refrained from an evil action, but has in fact caused a greater evil. He is also akin to a physician or surgeon who avoids operating on a patient, so as not to cause pain or give him cause for complaint, and thereby causes his death. A teacher or parent who does not chastise the child in good time causes him to choose evil ways and even to lose his life and forfeit his soul. At the same time most writers stress that a child should not be punished corporally too frequently since the punishment then loses its impact; nor did they advocate savage whipping since 'props erected incautiously around a young plant no longer support it but strangle it'; chastising in anger was also abhorred since anger was one of the deadly sins.[58] Some children were thought to be naturally better than others and not to require beating, since this would only rouse dread and despair and eventually hatred of those around them.[59] When a woman, Christine de Pisan, wrote on problems of education, she followed the same line as did male writers, asserting that beating was unavoidable, at least in the case of boys.[60] The secular legislator also acknowledged the right of a father to 'correct' his children, like his servants,[61] and guild statutes recognized the right of the master to 'correct' his apprentices.[62]

Isolated voices were raised against beating, even when 'controlled'. According to the humanists Matteo Palmieri and Maffeo Vegio, beating was contrary to nature, caused slavishness, aroused resentment and hatred against the teacher, and, finally, caused the pupil to forget his studies.[63] As early as the end of the eleventh century, Anselm of Canterbury voiced vehement opposition to the beating of children in monasteries as the main disciplinary measure. In response to the complaints of the abbot that the more he beat the children, the worse-behaved and more savage they became, Anselm called for tolerant, non-violent education, by means of personal example, compassion, love, encouragement, and correction when necessary. Like a tree requiring space for growth, the child had need of a degree of freedom; without it, both tree and child would grow bent and distorted. It was wrong to beat a child, not only because beating was ineffective, and because those who suffered violence and threats in childhood would become hate-filled, suspicious, violent, and bestial adults, but also because one should not harm a child, who is a human creature just like any adult. What an adult would not wish done to him, he should not do to a child. 'Are they not human beings? Are they not flesh and blood like you? Would you choose to be treated as you treat them?'[64] asks Anselm. Thomas Aquinas, on the other hand, describes suffering (and beating obviously causes suffering) as an integral part of the teaching of good qualities and the acquisition of knowledge. Whereas the incompleteness of childhood and the gradual process of physical and intellectual development are natural, the tears and suffering accompanying this process are the fruit of the punishment imposed on man as a consequence of Original Sin.[65]

As noted, the prevailing belief was that once a boy reached the age of 7, it was his father's task to educate him, while the mother continued the education of daughters. Some writers demanded of the mother that she also provide a Christian education for her sons even after the age of 7 (and not merely that she refrain from pampering them),[66] but her main function was always to raise her daughters – to furnish them with a religious education and to prepare them for their roles as mothers and housewives.[67]

The different assessments of the nature of boys and girls and the distribution of roles by sex, as well as the different aims set for the education of the two sexes, created the need for a separate type of education for girls. There was no demand to toughen girls, and the writers, in addressing mothers of the higher strata of society, recommended merely that they ensure that girls eat and drink sparingly and refrain from excessive preening of the body through baths, body unguents, and cosmetics.[68] Those who advocate beating do not state specifically that this disciplinary measure should be confined to boys alone, but perusal of the sections dealing with the education of girls reveals that beating was intended mainly for boys. In order to foster in girls those qualities and paths of conduct considered desirable, such as obedience, modesty, and, above all, chastity, the authors proposed mainly close supervision by parents and female tutors and the adoption of all necessary measures to repel harmful influences. They do not tire of reiterating that, due to their weakness of mind, frivolity, and propensity for sin, girls are easily seduced, and that, the less they go out and mix in company without supervision, the better. A girl may converse and even play with her brothers, but under no circumstances are they to be allowed to bring home their male friends! She is also to be taught reticence, which is both the expression of humility and discipline and an additional means of preserving her chastity. (Reticence was not stipulated as an ideal quality for boys.) The extreme misogynists, like Philip of Novare, opposed teaching girls to read and write (with the exception of those who were destined to take the veil), since such knowledge could acquaint them with sin, such as correspondence with lovers. Hence, he argued, even the daughters of noble and rich families should be instructed only in weaving and spinning as a remedy for idleness (which leads to sin) and in order to appreciate the labour of others. As for the daughters of the poor, they would be able to make a living when the time came by spinning and weaving.[69] Others approved of giving girls a basic education, at home or at school, aimed at instructing them in the basic tenets of religion and piety by teaching prayers and selected chapters in the Scriptures. Some authorities considered it sufficient to this end to teach reading without writing.[70] According to Vincent of Beauvais, who did not object to instructing girls in writing, the interest of the daughters of the nobility in reading and writing would drive out of their minds thoughts of folly and sin.[71] There were some exceptions who favoured educating the daughters of merchants, and particularly daughters of the higher nobility, arguing either that some day their education might help them to manage their landed property (or their household accounts, in the case of the merchant class), or that education elevated the mind and was a source of consolation and joy.[72] Be that as it may, in the period in which a more or less formulated curriculum was evolving for boys, through which some pupils prepared for university studies, no parallel curriculum evolved for girls. Universities were closed to them, as were the merchant-schools and the law-schools. Those girls who received schooling attended only the lowest schools.[73] The instructions about the stages in education and the desirable methods of teaching referred to boys alone. Statements about the need to develop the potential of every individual and the selection of a vocation enabling him to utilize his talents also referred exclusively to boys. One can explain the lack of emphasis on the need to beat girls as resulting from the fact that didactic writers and preachers held that girls were frailer and less rebellious than their brothers, and that strict supervision could suffice to achieve the desired results. It is also possible, however, that beating of girls is not mentioned because most writers believed that girls would not be instructed in the first place, and beatings were often administered in the course of study. In both Romanesque and Gothic art, the stick or the whip are the symbols of the teacher's occupation.[74] Mothers and nurses transmitted popular female culture to girls. Women in all regions and of all social classes played a role in popular culture, but were not permitted to take part in all its manifestations. They had their own culture (such as 'women's songs'), even though very little is known of it.[75] The fact that, in the labouring classes, girls were taught not only to be wives and mothers but also workers finds no expression in didactic literature.

The years between 7 and 14 (or 7 and 12 in the case of girls) were regarded as a single stage in human life. In exhorting parents to bestow a Christian education on their children, preachers did not usually distinguish between the various ages in the second stage of childhood. But other writings clearly reflect the awareness that it was not feasible to demand of a child of 7 what could be expected of a boy of 14, not only intellectually but also morally. Just as an infant who required milk could not be fed on bread and other solid food, no child (even if he was being trained for the monastic life), whose soul lacked experience in the service of God, could be expected to manifest all the Christian traits such as submission, avoidance of envy, and turning the other cheek.[76] Although it was generally agreed that children should not be pampered after the age of 7, and that boys should be hardened, some authors of medical and didactic works asserted that this too should be carried out in gradual fashion. Only from the age of 14 could a boy eat any coarse food, withstand arduous physical exercise, and make do with little sleep and with infrequent bathing.[77]

As noted, there was no consensus among churchmen as to whether the duty of confession should be imposed on boys and girls before the ages of 14 and 12 respectively.[78] According to those who opposed the idea, administering the sacrament to children who had not yet reached this age would be of no benefit to them and could even be considered as an act of disrespect toward the sacrament. It is also implied that the questions of the confessor might teach them about sins of which they had previously known nothing. (The same problem existed with regard to the confession of adults. Confessors were frequently cautioned against asking over-direct and detailed questions on sexual matters, lest they thereby teach their flock things of which they had hitherto been ignorant.[79]) One of the advocates of childlren's confession was Jean Gerson. He recommended that young children at confession be asked questions adapted to the psychology of the child and which did not violate the sanctity of the sacrament. He was aware that a child could not be asked the same questions posed to an adult and that this sacrament could only be administered to children if 'it is done in the correct manner'. To the question of what sins a child of 8 or 10 could commit, he replied that God does not wish evil to be done through a child or through others, but the truth is that children are taught to do evil. The questions he formulated were based on the heart and the five senses. Concerning the heart, the child should be asked if there were thoughts of hatred and revenge in his heart, whether he felt rebellious toward a sovereign, teacher, father, or mother. In respect to touch, he should be asked if he had been slothful and reluctant to rise from bed and go to school, or church or work; had he stolen anything, large or small; had he touched someone or permitted someone to touch him in an impure manner in bed or out of it for the sake of forbidden pleasure and in a manner in which he would not have dared to act before others. And so forth for sins connected to the ears, the mouth, the nose, and the eyes. The priest, he writes, should not ask the child the names of his friends or of other people with whom he had sinned, but should caution him that, if he sinned and did not confess, he could not win absolution and hence should confess even if he was ashamed.[80] Gerson's suggestions indicate psychological understanding of children. It is hard to assume that there were then (and are today) children who did not commit one or several of the specified sins. It is more difficult to gauge what they gained from confession, if they did in fact confess. Did the very act of going to confession on the instructions of the priest or parent give the child a sense of release from guilt-feelings, or was it the confession itself and the (undoubtedly mild) penance imposed which brought release?

Just as it was recognized that it was not feasible to make the same moral demands of a child as of an adult, it was widely acknowledged that the curriculum should be graded and adapted to the stages in the child's intellectual development. As noted in the previous chapter, all writers agreed that in the early years, children were capable of learning only simple things,[81] and should thus be first instructed in the vernacular and the basic injunctions and Christian ritual. They could then be taught Roman grammar and, subsequently, the two additional subjects in the *trivium* – rhetoric and dialectics, followed by the *quadrivium* (arithmetic, geometry, music, and astronomy). These subjects were taught both in the second-level schools and in the faculties of humanities at universities, and were considered preliminaries to higher studies – medicine, law, and theology. The writers reiterated that philosophy should not be taught before the age of 14 – particularly not moral philosophy, which was essential for those planning to enter politics – since only in the third stage of life does an individual arrive at 'elucidation of the intellect'.[82] Methods of study in schools will be discussed in the following chapters. For the present, I confine myself to quoting the ideal curriculum devised by Raymond Lull, according to which Blanquerna was instructed. When the child reached the age of 8, he was sent to school. First, he studied his mother tongue, the basic tenets of faith, the Ten Commandments, the significance of the sacraments, the scheme of seven sins and seven virtues. In the second stage he studied Roman grammar, dialectics, and rhetoric, and then natural philosophy and medicine to the degree required in order to preserve his health. In the final stage, he studied theology. (His father wanted to make a merchant of him, and the study of theology was something introduced by Lull for his own purposes in the plot. It was certainly not part of the curriculum for future merchants!) So much for the education of Blanquerna. As for his upbringing, despite the fact that he was the only child of prosperous parents, he was not pampered with special dishes, and his father insisted that he learn to eat anything served to him. He was taught to observe all fastdays, to pray at regular hours, and to give charity to the poor, and was also brought up to respect the customary ways of behaviour of the class to which his parents belonged. He was taught not only to find favour in the eyes of God and men but also 'not to rebel against customs fitting for a child of good parentage which good citizens and people of noble origin should ever keep in mind'.[83]

Some writers devoted attention not only to the stages in the curriculum but also to the need gradually to increase the demands made of a child – over the number of hours devoted to study and the degree of concentration and diligence which could be expected (just as some authorities believed that hardening should also be a gradual process). They claimed that a small child should not be forced to sit for long hours in the classroom against his will, nor should he be beaten, or irritated or saddened, and he should also be permitted to play. It is hard for children who still wish to play to start learning, but little by little they begin to take an interest in their studies. When they mature somewhat, they are sometimes even willing, for love of knowledge, to leave their homes and travel to far-distant centres of learning,[84] as one author writes. But, in general, whereas, with regard to the raising of small children, the dominant approach is advocacy of tenderness and avoidance of stringent demands, a stricter disciplinary approach is favoured for children from the age of 7. Without it the child can be taught nothing, and it can also help to preserve the proper hierarchical order in society. The commencement of education was thus perceived as a turning-point, marking the end of indulgence and tenderness. It is characteristic that when Giovanni Boccaccio's biographer describes his childhood, which was certainly not a happy one for the boy who probably never experienced tenderness, he writes: 'After being pampered by his parents in the first period of his childhood', he was sent to school.[85] This is said not because these were the facts, but because this was the ideal course. The biographer of Hugh of Lincoln, who dwelt on the special tenderness and affection he displayed towards infants and small children, writes that, as soon as the children reached the age of understanding, he began to keep his distance and to treat them with reservation lest they become impudent. According to Bartholomaeus Anglicus, it is those fathers who most love their children who scrupulously chastise them and rein them. Other authors write that a child should not be shown too much love nor should he be praised in his presence, lest he become proud and dare to do evil. On the other hand, Dominici, who advocated strictness with children even younger than 7 in cases of misdemeanours, cheating, or cursing, also held that, whereas the miscreant should be punished, the child who made an effort to do good should be praised. Every effort entails expectation of reward, and children, in particular, are fond of presents and appreciation. The child who endeavours to study and to do good should be rewarded with some item he needs and likes, such as new shoes or writing instruments.[86]

It is clear that parents did not always respond to the demands of the preachers and didactic writers that they raise their children strictly and teach them to observe Christian moral injunctions and obedience so as to safeguard the social order. The very fact that these writers never tire of condemning parental indulgence, demonstrations of affection, and over-permissiveness attests to this. It also sometimes appeared to parents that their children's teachers were treating them too harshly, and they then intervened on their behalf and defended them. The mother of Anselm of Canterbury was shocked at her son's emotional distress when he returned from the home of his tutor, and she reproached herself for having abandoned him to such a man.[87] The mother of Gilbert of Nogent, a dominating and ascetic woman, who, so he claimed, competed (silently) with his teacher for the child's affection and esteem, was sincerely horrified to discover blue weals on her son's hands and back. She was ready to break the vow taken by her husband while she was suffering during childbirth, and said 'If such is the case, you will no longer be a *clericus* and will not be forced to endure whippings in order to learn Latin.' She was, however, pleased when he refused to accede and to renounce a career in the church, but there can be no doubt that she truly pitied him.[88] In Bristol a father sued his son's teacher and demanded monetary compensation from him for having whipped the boy and not treated him properly, and a similar case was recorded in London.[89] The parents of boys and girls who were apprenticed to male and female artisans also sometimes took them to court for whipping the children or maltreating them.[90] Some of those charged probably exceeded normal practice, but this does also suggest that there were parents who, as may naturally be expected of a parent, had their children's welfare at heart and were not 'objective'. Be that as it may, they could not remain indifferent to maltreatment or even an unkind attitude towards their offspring.

THE BOY BISHOP

Among the popular medieval festivals and carnivals, most of which were secularly organized, was one which was held under ecclesiastical auspices, namely All Fools' Day, in December. It lasted, with intervals, for a number of weeks (in effect, until January), and included within it St Nicholas's Day (6 December), the day of the patron saint of schoolchildren, which was celebrated from the beginning of the twelfth century[91] as the Day of the Boy Bishop (*episcopus puerorum*). As was the custom at carnival time, this celebration was marked by misrule: the mighty were brought low and the lowly elevated, the forbidden was permitted and vice versa. The young clerks, some not yet even in minor orders, mocked the behaviour and speech of the priests during worship and the way in which they administered the sacraments. They danced, drank, gorged themselves, masqueraded (even as women) and wore masks, acted in unrestrained fashion, and even brought donkeys into the church. This general unruliness sometimes led to bloodshed to which the subdeacons and deacons also contributed. On the Day of the Boy Bishop one of the pupils from the church 'reading' (or 'song') school was chosen bishop. He wore bishop's apparel and carried the various symbols of office (robe, mitre, ring, etc.), and everyone bowed down to him. He offered up incense, conducted prayers, blessed the congregation, delivered a sermon, and marched in procession. He was assisted by the other schoolchildren, who sat for this day in the places of the canons (in the case of a cathedral), while the latter took the seats of the choirboys. The proper hierarchical order was also reversed in the procession. The canons took the parts of the acolytes and choirboys, carrying the books, incense, and candles. The Boy Bishop and his companions were feasted and honoured by lighted torches and dancing. After the celebration, the Boy Bishop set out on horseback accompanied by a panoply of singers and servants on a visitation to his diocese to request donations from the believers. His 'term of office' usually ended only on 28 December. These festival days were quite costly, as can be learned from the inventories of several cathedrals and of parish churches, which list all the items used by the Boy Bishop and his companions. With minor variations, the festival was celebrated in most Western European countries – England, France, Germany, and, apparently, Spain as well. From the end of the twelfth century, and mainly in the thirteenth, the church authorities became convinced that All Fools' Day in general had gone too far and that the worst excesses were connected with the conduct of the Boy Bishops. They tried to restrain the unruliness of both the clerics and the children, and of the laymen who came to watch and to take part in the celebrations.[92] Steps were also taken to stop excessive humiliation of prelates and priests. In order to guarantee some degree of supervision, it was decided in some places that the Boy Bishop would no longer be elected by the choirboys, but that the priests and teacher would propose several candidates for the task; or, alternatively, the choice fell on the longest-serving boy, who had demonstrated that he was capable of being useful, on condition that he was handsome and had a pleasant voice. The number of feast-days was also reduced, as was the area which the Boy Bishop was permitted to visit so as to solicit donations. However, it seems that the carnival (including the ritual of the Boy Bishop) was of established character, and that there was no way of restraining the conduct of the merrymakers. Although there was increasing demand for its cancellation, the festival came to an end only in the sixteenth century.[93]

Anthropologists and historians have offered several explanations for the function played by the carnivals and festivals, during which reversal of norms and unruliness were permitted. According to one opinion, they acted, in a hierarchical society, mainly as a safety-valve, diverting attention from the true social and political problems. Another theory is that such celebrations create cohesion in a society lacking contractual relationships. The ostensible disorder is, in fact, the source of order, and the reversal of norms always implies the norm which is mocked but which emerges reinforced. Stephen of Bourbon offered this explanation of the role of the carnival at the time: describing the carnival in Rome, he writes that, in its wake, 'all seven sins' were 'killed' and that immediately after it and throughout the year the good reigned and peace and tranquillity prevailed between the Pope and his Roman flock.[94] In other words, it provided an outlet which led to release, and the ritual protest involved in turning norms upside down for one day emphasized

their importance and strengthened them. In the view of the Soviet struc-
turalist, Mikhail Bakhtin, the carnival at all times and in all societies is a
source of release, destruction, and renewal, but various societies permit it
different scope for action. In a society without class and state, there was room
for both the comic and the serious; the serious and the comic aspects were
equally sacred and 'official'. In a feudal society, people were offered by the
carnival an additional plane of life, separate from the political and social
hierarchy and from high culture – a second life outside officialdom. Natalie
Zemon-Davis, who examined some of the secular festivals in fifteenth- and
sixteenth-century France, concluded that they sometimes also helped to
continue and perpetuate certain values in the community. At the same time,
criticism of the existing order was inherent in them.[95]

Originally, the feast of the Boy Bishop was simultaneously serious and
comic. When it took place on the memorial day of the Innocents, 28
December, its justification was that the Innocents were slaughtered for the
sake of the Christ-child and that consequently innocent children in their
image should be accorded status and honour by the church on this day.[96]
Emphasis gradually shifted to the comic element. But, together with the
granting of licence to reverse the proper order of things (such as ages), an
attempt was made (apparently not entirely successful) to utilize it more
directly to consolidate accepted values on the education of children and on
their place in society. This second element was expressed in the sermon which
the Boy Bishop delivered but an adult churchman composed. The existence
of books of sermons for the Boy Bishops is known, and several sermons
from late fifteenth-century England have survived.[97] These sermons contain
thoughts on the innocence of children, the tale of the slaughter of the
Innocents, an appeal to believers to be whole and innocent in their faith, like
children, remonstrations to state and church leaders, and condemnation of
the cruelty of teachers. The Boy Bishop was also expected to condemn
corruption and wild conduct among schoolchildren, both in song school and
in grammar school.

According to the author of the sermon, children behave so badly because
their parents, in their excessive affection, do not rebuke them. Fearing that
they may forfeit their children's love or cause them to lose their courage and
energy, they allow them to do as they wish. Their teachers, on the other
hand, hasten to beat them for a false note in singing, or an error in Latin or
English, but not for lying, crude behaviour, or failure to observe God's wishes.
The Boy Bishop asks the believers to pray that he will no longer suffer his
teacher's whip and expresses the wish that all his teachers will soon be
hanged from a tree. (These last words are characteristic of carnivalesque
verbal abuse.) Just as fragments of texts from secular festivals indicate their
significance for the people who planned and executed them, so we learn from
the sermon written for the Boy Bishop of its significance – not for the children

who heard it but for those who composed it (even if its impact may have been lost in the general pandemonium). The innocent child is depicted as an example for adult believers on the one hand, and yet is set in his proper place in the age-hierarchy. He is permitted to wish for the disappearance of one of his teachers who are part of the daily reality of his life, but like the parent whose duty it is to educate his children (with greater strictness than he actually employs) the teacher and his stick are part of the existing order which must continue. And the child himself attests to and reinforces the existing classification into the various age-categories, each of which has its proper place in society.

9 Education for service in the secular church and in the monastery

This chapter examines the lives of those children who were brought up for secular church service or for the monastic life. Since they spent at least a few years at school, the first part of this chapter will be devoted to schools. However, since it was not only children dedicated to the church who studied at these schools, and since the number of pupils destined to live secular lives increased gradually from the thirteenth century onwards, these schools will figure again in the following chapters without further description.

Unlike many of the progeny of people in other occupations and professions, priests, monks, and nuns did not continue the lifestyle and occupation of their parents (with the exception of the bastard sons of priests who also entered the clergy)[1]. The great majority were designated for the priesthood or the monastic life by their parents, while some chose the religious life of their own volition. In noble families, some of the younger sons who were not due to inherit and, almost without exception, all the daughters who were not destined for marriage were sent to be educated in monasteries and, in the case of boys, also for the service of the secular church. Among prosperous urban families, the girls who were not thought marriageable were sent to convents, and some of the boys were sent to be trained for ecclesiastical service. Orphan boys and girls in those classes and, on rare occasions, in lower strata as well were designated for ecclesiastical service or sent to monasteries by relatives and guardians. Sometimes this was done with good intention and in the conviction that in this way the future of the children would be guaranteed, and sometimes it was done in order to expropriate a patrimony. Juliana of Cornillon (1192–1258), for example, who was orphaned of both parents at the age of 5, was placed by her guardians in the Augustinian double monastery at Mount Cornillon near Liège, together with her sister. She was the daughter of a lower-middle-class burgher, and her guardians were convinced that by placing the little girls in a monastery they were guaranteeing their future.[2] On the other hand, Umbald, who later became Bishop of Gubbio (and died in 1160), lost his father in infancy and was sent as a small boy by his relatives to be trained for the church, apparently because of their desire to take over his inheritance.[3]

In noble families, particularly up to the twelfth century, any son who was physically frail and unsuited to knighthood was offered to the monastic life, and in the following centuries as well, when additional areas of activity were opened up for the nobility, the physically weak, handicapped, or retarded offspring were also sent to monasteries. Abbots often complained of this practice; it was denounced by the authors of didactic literature and by preachers,[4] but could not be completely stopped. In the *Lives of the Saints* mention is made of handicapped children placed in monasteries who were taken to a shrine or to a holy person in the search for a cure: they included hunchbacks, the hard-of-hearing, and cripples.[5] Orderic Vitalis tells of a frail and sickly child who was admitted to his monastery at the age of 5. (In this case, the monastic life apparently suited his constitution, since he lived to the age of 57.)[6] In one case, the parents related that their little daughter had become deaf in a monastery, which may or may not have been true. If she did in fact lose her hearing there, this could have been a case of hysterical deafness as a reaction to being placed in the nunnery, or could have resulted from some physical cause.[7]

Some illegitimate children in both noble and prosperous urban families were also earmarked for the secular church or sent to monasteries.[8] Bastards were accepted into monasteries even without special dispensation, and the monastic life was expected to cleanse them of 'the flaw of their birth'. In order to enter the service of the secular church the bastard required a dispensation. In order to join the minor orders a dispensation from the bishop sufficed, while in order to enter major orders dispensation from the Pope was needed. These dispensations were obtained without difficulty.[9] Exceptional among the monastic orders in the reservations they expressed regarding the acceptance of bastards into their ranks were the Dominicans (because of the risk of accepting people with 'a tendency to immoral conduct').[10]

In some cases, men who had lost their wives decided to retire to a monastery, sometimes with one of their sons. The father of Hugh of Lincoln, for example, retreated to a monastic house after the death of his wife, and the eight-year-old Hugh accompanied him.[11] Some women, after being widowed, retreated to convents or to a religious community. Some of them left their children with relatives while others took them with them. Elizabeth of Hungary was renowned, while her husband was still living, for her great piety, her stringent asceticism, and her charity toward the poor, which went beyond what was customary and expected of a princess. She and her husband dedicated their daughter Gertrude to the monastic life even before her birth, so that, even if her mother had not been widowed, Gertrude would have been despatched to a convent. It is unlikely, however, that she would have been sent there at the age of 2. Elizabeth's life underwent a change when her husband, the Landgraf of Thuringia, died two weeks before Gertrude's birth. She left her palace at Wartburg and wandered for a year with her children. Her wanderings came to an end on instructions from her spiritual mentor, the Inquisitor Konrad of Marburg, and in 1228 she established at Marburg a hospital for the poor, to whose treatment she devoted the rest of her life. In the same year she entrusted her two-year-old daughter to the Pre-monstratensian canonesses at Altenburg, also on the instruction of her mentor. This abandonment of her children was interpreted by her biographers as part of her total retreat from the world and absolute dedication to God and to his poor.[12] Among those she treated were children whom she even tried to divert with toys and small presents.

The last and smallest group among those offered to the secular church or to monasteries (mainly from among the upper strata of society) were those sent as the consequence of a vow taken by their parents. The most typical vow, one of the *topoi* in the *Lives of the Saints*, is that of a childless and pious couple who vow that, if a child is born to them, they will offer it to the religious life.[13] In other cases, the parents decide to dedicate the child to the religious life before it is born, as the result of a dream or vision of the mother during pregnancy in which the future greatness of the unborn son is revealed to her.[14] In describing these vows the authors tend to compare the parents to the parents of Samuel, who also dedicated their son to God: 'They accustomed him to serve God like a second Samuel from his childhood to his old age.'[15] In rare cases, vows were taken in the wake of other supplications. The parents of Ollegarius (who died in 1137), nobles from Catalonia, took a vow to dedicate him to the religious life if God would defend the kingdom against the Saracen invaders.[16] Bela, King of Hungary, and his wife, parents of St Margaret (1242–70), took the same vow in appealing for protection against the Tartars.[17] According to the biography of Thomas Cantimpratanus, his father dedicated him to priesthood in order to atone for his own sins: a hermit who lived near Antioch, and to whom the father confessed his sins, told him that he would spend a long time in purgatory unless he offered one of his sons to the priesthood.

The monasteries and the higher orders of the secular church in the Central and Late Middle Ages were, in the main, the domain of the nobility. In theory, both the secular church and the monastic orders were open to every free individual and only serfs were obliged to pay the manumission fee in order to enter them. Philip of Novare, in writing of education for clerical orders and of the importance of the role of the priest, writes that, through serving the church, a son of the poor may often become an ecclesiastical dignitary – and be father and master to him who was once his master and master of his family.[18] In practice, however, few sons of the lower strata reached the higher echelons of the secular church or the monastery, and the number of girls from the lower sections of society who became nuns in female orders (as distinct from serving women or lay sisters) was even lower. The reason was that small girls or young women were obliged to bring a dowry to the convent. This dowry was smaller than that allotted to a girl from the same class who married, but families from the labouring class were unable to supply even this small sum. Placing a boy in a monastery also usually entailed some gift to the institution, though this was not always the condition for acceptance as in the case of girls.[19] The Benedictines sometimes accepted boys from lower social strata. The Mendicant orders took in more boys and young men from the lower classes, while girls, on the other hand, who were accepted by the corresponding convents, like girls in Benedictine convents, were almost all of gentle birth.

More members of the lower classes served in the lower echelons of the church as clerks and some even became priests. We know of serfs in England in the Central Middle Ages who paid the manumission fee for their sons, sent them to school, and thus opened up the path to priesthood for them.[20] Sometimes the village priest chose one or two of the most talented and pious sons of free peasants and gave them instruction. From the thirteenth century, when the vernacular became the foundation of basic education, the priest usually taught reading and writing in the vernacular, a smattering of Latin grammar, and the liturgy and hymns in that language. In return he benefited from their services in his home and assistance in his church celebrations. In this fashion he provided them with the grounding for future studies for the priesthood. The will of the priest of Coutances in France from the beginning of the fifteenth century says

> I bequeath to G. my clerk, whom I taught for several years, food and clothing for a period of seven years and my volume of Catholicon [a very popular thirteenth-century dictionary] on condition that he continues his studies and is finally ordained.[21]

Boys from the lower urban strata had greater opportunities for studying at one of the schools which mushroomed from the twelfth century onward, and most of which, at least, took in a number of non-paying pupils, on the orders of the church authorities (amongst them the Third Lateran Council in 1179 and the Fourth in 1215). The establishment of schools and the subsidizing of poor pupils were considered acts of charity. If the children studied for only a few years, they were accepted into the minor orders. If they studied longer, they could be ordained as priests. The children of the upper strata who were dedicated to secular church service were sent, after several years of study in their home town, to schools under the supervision of a bishop uncle. (Until the rise of the universities, the cathedral schools were the highest schools in existence.) The uncle concerned himself with promoting their career and probably also served as a father figure.[22]

SCHOOLS AND TRAINING FOR SECULAR CHURCH SERVICE

Studies in the elementary school, known as 'reading school' or 'song school' (the two did not always differ), usually commenced at the age of 7, but, as already noted, some children began to study earlier and others later. The children attended this school to the age of 10 or 12. In 'song school' there was apparently more emphasis on studying religious hymns, both tune and words, and the children took part in the choir of the cathedral to which the school was attached. At 'reading school' there was more emphasis on study as such; but, despite the different names, the two categories did not always differ from one another. All pupils learned their alphabet and reading. In the twelfth century, Latin was the basis of elementary education; from the thirteenth century, reading in the vernacular was apparently taught first. (In England, French was also studied.) The schools also taught figures and a little arithmetic, a little writing, prayers and liturgical hymns, through which a smattering of spoken Latin was absorbed, and the tenets of faith. Those children who continued their studies moved up at the age of 10 or 12 to a higher school, the grammar school, which can be compared to secondary school. Sometimes they actually moved from school to school, and at times merely from stage to stage in the same school, and what mattered in the end was the number of years of schooling. Here the age-differences between the pupils were even greater than in the elementary school. Some of the pupils were over 12 when they began their studies, while sometimes adults who were already in the service of the church attended grammar school. At this stage they began to study Latin seriously. The aim was to achieve written and oral fluency in this language, and reading and comprehension of classical and Christian texts. The other subjects of the trivium (rhetoric and dialectics) were usually also taught, or were at least introduced, and sometimes some of the quadrivium subjects as well. In this fashion, a certain congruence was achieved between the curriculum of the grammar school and of the university faculties of humanities which developed from the thirteenth century. A pupil who completed his studies was expected to display (in addition to perfect knowledge of Latin) a knowledge of scriptures, of the tenets of faith, and of Christian morality, and limited knowledge of science and law, which were taught from scientific compilations and the writings of jurists. Pupils were supposed to complete grammar school studies at the age of 16, but sometimes graduated later; some, however, entered university at the age of 14. Writing was also taught at the second stage of studies. Those pupils who studied mainly writing and were intended to become scribes usually ceased all their other studies at an earlier stage than other students. Specialization in writing was not considered an integral part of contemporary Latin education, but a technical skill which required training because of the difficulties of writing with a quill on parchment. Many scholars as well as jurists often dictated instead of writing themselves.[23]

The elementary schools were day-schools, and only a few of the grammar schools were boarding-schools. Children who were sent away to distant schools naturally lived there, in the school dormitories, in colleges, in the homes of teachers, or together with their tutors, who travelled with them if they came from the upper strata of society. However, few were sent to far-off schools in the second stage of schooling, and the usual age at which they were sent to study far from home was about 16. Some of those earmarked for secular church service, particularly until the twelfth century, studied in childhood in monastery schools, though not destined for the monastic life, and lived in the cloister. In the Late Middle Ages, some rural monasteries ran almonry schools. The children who attended them were relatives of the monks or progeny of the peasants in the monastic estate. Some of them were later sent for several years of schooling to a secular school in town and eventually joined the same monastery. Some monasteries maintained song schools. However, most children apparently attended day-schools, and their parents played a role, together with teachers, in their adaptation to their new life.

Study for the priesthood began at an early age and lasted many years. At the age of 7, a child could already serve as clerk and have a tonsured head, but in order to join the minor orders several years of study were required. In most schools the children sang in the cathedral choir during their schooling, or in the choir of the parish church or the monastery, or in the chapel of the hospital (which did not always maintain a school, but boarded and supported several scholars)[24] adjacent to the school. Sometimes they recited prayers for the soul of the founder of the chantry who had funded the school attached to it, or helped the priests in their ministrations. On completing their studies they could qualify to fulfil one of the four functions of the minor orders (*ostiarius, lector, exorcisa, acolitus*). Others who studied for several years later joined the ecclesiastical bureaucracy and continued their training while working. More years of study were required in order to enter the priesthood. Although many of the parish priests, particularly in rural areas, were not highly educated (to say the least), the church authorities did their best to raise the level of education of the clergy. Examinations were conducted by one of the bishop's assistants before an ecclesiastical post in the minor orders was allotted. The candidates for parish priesthood who were responsible for 'the care of souls' (*cura animarum*), were examined by the bishop himself. Sometimes the post was awarded conditionally – in other words, the appointee was expected to appear before the examiner again after some time and to prove that he had completed his studies. The minimum age at which a man could be appointed a sub-deacon (the lowest rank among the major orders) was 18, and only when he reached this rank did a young man finally commit himself to the church. The minimum age for becoming a priest was 25 (until the Council of Vienne in 1311, it was also the minimum age for appointment as a deacon, and only then was the minimum age reduced to 20). Only from the age of 30 was a man eligible to be appointed a bishop. Those who reached the higher ecclesiastical echelons continued their studies at university, and from the faculty of humanities moved on to the faculty of theology or law. There were undoubtedly exceptions to the rule, and people under the required age who had not displayed the necessary qualifications were often appointed. However, as a rule, those who reached important positions in the service of the church usually underwent a period of study and adjustment to their new life lasting for many years, and ending only in the second stage of *adolescentia*.

Study in schools was exclusively verbal – reading and a great deal of learning by rote. Sometimes the first lessons of small children were written on a parchment sheet which was glued to a wooden board, or else they studied from a 'book' written in large letters, which was also glued to a wooden board. They went on to study reading from a Primer or a Psalter or one of the service books in the church to which the school was attached. By learning to read from these books they also gradually became acquainted with the church ritual. It is evident that for quite some time the children learned words and sentences in Latin without understanding their meaning. (On the other hand, they were acquainted with the sound of the language from listening to the church liturgy and from the prayers they had learnt at home.) It was not only the seven-year-old in the Prioress's Tale, who had learned his alphabet from the Antiphonary, who failed to understand the words of Alma Redemptoris in honour of the Holy Mother; even the boy who 'elder was than he' could say only:

> ... this song I have herd seye
> Was maked of our blisful lady free,
> Hir to salue, and eek hir for to preye
> To been our help and socour when we deye.
> I can no more expounde in this matere,
> I lerne song, I can but small grammere.[25]

In the song schools run by the monasteries, the children learned not only choir-singing but also how to read music and play the organ. Understanding of written Latin began only in the second stage of study, in grammar school. Here the scholars were given a larger selection of books at different levels (which, according to regulations, were sometimes chained to the table), from Donatus through grammar books, including exercises which dealt with everyday matters but contained quotations from the Scriptures, to textbooks on the various subjects studied, including scientific summaries and the works of law. When the pupils reached a certain level of knowledge of Latin, they also began to practise translation as a means of studying the language, to compose verses, and to write letters according to an accepted formula. The hours of study were long. They began, in accordance with the season, at 6 or 7 in the morning, and lasted until 5 or 6 in the evening, usually with two hours' intermission, one in the morning and one at lunchtime. There was generally only one class in the school, divided into groups by level. Children were often whipped, and, from the fact that the statutes of several Late Medieval schools stipulated that whipping should not be practised excessively and that other measures should be tried first, we can ascertain that teachers sometimes went too far in their use of corporal punishment. Even without whipping, it was difficult for children to sit for hours on hard wooden benches and concentrate on study-matter which, needless to say, was mostly unsuitable for their age and was transmitted by tedious methods of instruction. Many masters complained that, immediately after the lesson commenced, the children began to ask for permission to leave the room on various pretexts – to go to the lavatory, to drink water, or to go home for some reason. Others complained of the unruliness of their pupils. The schools were cramped in area and had small numbers of pupils, a fact which, in itself, could bestow a certain sense of security on a small child. However, the presence of older boys, over whom the teachers were unable to exert strict discipline, frequently in the same classroom and certainly in the same courtyard, could be somewhat intimidating. Certain writers, it will be recalled, mentioned the importance of the master's role and the responsibility it entailed, and dwelt at length on his qualifications and character traits. Yet the teaching profession, particularly in the lower school, was not considered a prestigious one, and for the more talented masters constituted an interim stage in their careers. The numerous feast-days constituted compensation of a kind for the children. On some of these days, the pupils (and masters) enjoyed only fewer hours of study than usual; on others they were given a full day's holiday, but, if they were attending boarding schools, they were obliged to remain there. On major holidays, such as Christmas and Easter, they were able to travel home. On some feast-days, debates were held between various grammar schools, resembling those held at the universities, as well as contests in knowledge of Latin grammar and Latin verse, rhetoric, and dialectics. Other amusements were also provided. In London, the pupils brought cockerels and organized cock-fights, and after the contest the dead birds were awarded to the masters. The pupils then went out into the fields to play at ball, together with the apprentices of the London guilds. Sailing and marksmanship contests were also held. Froissart described the games of the over-twelves and the younger children, including both movement and group games: hide-and-seek, riddles, 'the truth game', etc. The teaching methods in medieval schools were often criticized by scholars of the Renaissance, by the eighteenth-century Enlightenment, and by nineteenth- and twentieth-century proponents of modern educational and pedagogic theories, and it would be superfluous to repeat their assertions. It should merely be noted that the curriculum and method of studies of children earmarked for ecclesiastical service did not differ essentially from those of other children in that period, at least in the first stage. Secular administrative service also required knowledge of Latin, so that it was not only children offered to the church who studied at these schools. Those of the children destined for secular church service who continued their studies in important centres of learning benefited from the opportunity to enjoy varied experiences – travel, new places, and contact with people who were not future churchmen.[26]

MONASTERIES

In discussing boys offered to the monastic life, one should distinguish between the period up to the end of the twelfth century and that subsequent. On the other hand, the age at which girls were accepted into convents varied only slightly from period to period. Up to the twelfth century it was customary to place boys and girls dedicated to the monastic life in monasteries at the age of 5–6, and sometimes even earlier. Such a child was denoted *oblatus*, and was offered to God on the altar of the church by his parents, who vowed that, when the time came, their child would take the habit or veil. This custom of sending a boy or girl to a monastery in childhood originated in an earlier period, and is mentioned in the rule of Benedict of Nursia in the sixth century. Up to the eighth century, it was accepted that, when a boy reached 14 (or a girl, 12), he could decide for himself whether to profess and become a monk for the rest of his life. In the eighth century, children were deprived of this right, and the parental obligation became irreversible. In the Carolingian era the parental vow was apparently the sole one involved, and children did not take the vow of monasticism themselves when they reached the minimum age for vows.[27] In the twelfth century, this custom was questioned, and increasing numbers of people came to believe that to impose a lifelong obligation on a child was an unacceptable act. Many also thought that the presence of children in monasteries disrupted normal life there. These latter views prevailed and the Fourth Lateran Council (1215) proclaimed *oblatio* illegal. Henceforth, even if a small child was placed in a monastery, he was entitled by law, on reaching the appropriate age, to refuse to profess and to leave the monastery.[28] The new orders of the period, such as the Cistercians and the Carthusians, who advocated a much more stringently ascetic life than had hitherto been practised in the old Benedictine monasteries, and who regarded children as a disruptive element in monastic life, did not accept children into their monasteries. Statutes from 1134 stipulated that Cistercian monasteries would not accept as novices boys under the age of 15; in 1175 the minimum age was raised to 18.[29] The old Benedictine monasteries, on the other hand, still took in children. As Knowles has noted, the Fourth Lateran Council actually banned only the formal *oblatio*, which had deprived children in perpetuity of freedom of choice. It was still possible to place a child in a monastery for education, and this act implied a moral obligation that, when the time came, the child would make his monastic profession. However, despite this possibility, the number of boys placed in monasteries at an early age constantly decreased from the second half of the twelfth century and dropped further in the thirteenth century. At the same time, the practice did not disappear entirely. Small children were sometimes placed in monasteries, as witness Thomas Aquinas, who was born in 1225 and sent to Monte Cassino at the age of 5,[30] or a boy of less than 7 recorded at the beginning of the thirteenth century in a Benedictine priory in Normandy.[31] However, most of the young people who entered the monastery did so from the thirteenth century onward after having attended secular schools ('secular' in this context meaning a school in which the master was usually a priest and not a monk)[32] and professed, as a rule, after a period of novitiate at the age of 16–18. Some of them continued their studies as adults at a university or one of the higher institutions of the Benedictines or Cistercians on behalf of their houses.

The Mendicant orders were initially reluctant to accept children.[33] In 1260, statutes of the Franciscan order stipulated that only those over 18 could gain entry into the order. The minimum age was gradually reduced: in 1316 it was fixed at 14, and in 1341 amended to 13. In rare cases even younger children were accepted.[34] Many of the critics of the Mendicants in the thirteenth and fourteenth centuries charged them with seducing children: they claimed that, after they had lured the thirteen- or fourteen-year-old boy to join them, they no longer permitted the boy's parents to visit him lest they persuade him to retract his decision.[35] Since the Mendicants in general, and the Dominicans in particular, also maintained a wide-ranging and graded educational network, the boys who joined them could study gratis and under congenial conditions. They first pursued the curriculum of the secular grammar school and then the remaining liberal arts, natural philosophy, and theology, at one of the order's centres of study (*studium*). From there they could transfer directly to one of the higher university faculties, skipping the faculty of humanities. Some opponents of the Mendicants complained that the universities were being emptied of students because the Mendicants were enticing young men to study at their own centres instead of entering university faculties of humanities.

As noted above, the age at which girls entered convents did not vary. In the thirteenth and fourteenth centuries most of the girls offered to the monastic life were placed in convents as children, both in Benedictine convents and in those which observed the Cistercian statutes, as well as those corresponding to the Mendicant orders.[36] In the thirteenth century, Humbert de Romans addressed one of his sermons to 'little girls' (*puellae*) who are being educated by nuns in order to become nuns.[37] In the Late Middle Ages, bishops banned the observance of a festival resembling the celebration of the Boy Bishop, in which a small girl played the part of the abbess.[38] (If girls had not been present in convents, there would have been no need to impose the ban.) At the time of the formal *oblatio*, its advocates argued that education for the monastic life should commence at a very early age, before the child was exposed to evil influences in the outside world and before he was contaminated by sin. There are, indeed, examples in both convents and monasteries, of monks and nuns who entered in adulthood and found it difficult to endure the demands of the monastic rule. However, whereas in the case of boys the arguments against accepting children prevailed, the decisive factor, where girls were concerned, was fear that, if entry was postponed, some girls who had already been contaminated and corrupted by the world and its ways might reach the convent. The number of secular schools open to girls in which they could acquire any kind of education which was essential for the nun was limited. Upon entering the convent as children they learned all that they needed to know in the house itself before taking the veil. The parents, for their part, believed that in the convent their daughter would be protected against extramarital sexual relations, and considered it an advantage to place her there in childhood. After the abrogation of formal *oblatio*, girls placed in convents in childhood were entitled to refuse to take the vow at the age of 12, although this dispensation was granted in less unequivocal fashion than to boys.[39] It is, however, highly questionable whether any girls were able to take advantage of this privilege granted by canon law. They were not prepared for life outside the walls of the nunnery, and that portion of the family assets allotted to them had been invested in the convent when they entered it. If it was difficult for boys to repudiate the vow, it was impossible for girls.

Riché has noted that, since small children were placed in monasteries, the masters among the monks were obliged to tackle the problem of how to prepare a child for the monastic life. The presence of children in the monastery helped to enhance awareness that childhood was a stage in human life with its own unique characteristics. They realized that it was not possible to make the same demands of a child as of an adult monk, or even as of a young novice. Thus they evolved a curriculum for the education of the child destined to become a monk which displays psychological understanding of children.[40] Perusal of the clauses devoted to child education in the customaries of monasteries reveals a certain understanding of child psychology. However, the aim of the educators was not to develop the child's predilections and talents in accordance with his personality (and it should be recalled that the suitability of the child's personality to monastic life was not the main consideration in parental decisions to send children to monasteries) or to ensure that he enjoyed his childhood years. The aim was to raise him to be a good monk, and this aim determined educational methods. In all strata of society education aspired to develop in the child traits and patterns of conduct suited to the function and the ideals of the social stratum to which he belonged, and there was a common goal to education throughout society – to raise the child as a good Christian. It was monks, however, who adopted the most Christian way of life, entailing discipline, poverty, and abstinence, and subjugation of the material and the individual to things spiritual and to God. In no other sphere in society did education demand exertion of such great pressure on the child to suppress his drives, and no other social-professional group required such uniformity of conduct in order to survive. Even an understanding of child psychology could not justify renouncing pressure and restriction when the aim was to train the child to be a monk. It could only help to establish a certain grading in the stringency of the demands made of the child. Several clauses in the statutes of Lanfranc, Archbishop of Canterbury, composed in the second half of the eleventh century for the monastic community of his cathedral of Christ Church in Canterbury, do not give a complete picture of the life of children in the monastery; they do, however, indicate what was demanded of them and something of their way of life.

On the one hand, the children constituted a separate group in the monastery population, ruled by its owns set of statutes. They had their own masters and school and a chapter-house separate from that of the monks. On the other hand, the children were integrated in the daily routine of the monastery, which revolved around communal prayers and singing the liturgy for the salvation of the soul of the individual monk and on behalf of all the living and dead. The day was divided mainly according to the monastic offices conducted five times daily. The hours varied according to the season, but the first prayer was recited at about 2 in the morning and the last at 8 in the evening. The children took part in the liturgical duties, such as the masses conducted daily, participated in religious processions on feast-days, took part in ritual hospitality to the poor, and fulfilled various service-functions. Some of the time was devoted to reading. The child was not supposed to be left alone or exclusively in the company of other children for even one moment. Prayers and choir-singing were communal. In the common refectory, the cloister where they sat and read, and *en route* from one place to another the master was always with the children. It was he who wakened them in the morning and supervised them when they went to bed (at night, in the early morning in the season when they returned to bed after the first prayer, and during the afternoon rest). The children were forbidden to signal to one another or to speak without the permission of the master, who was expected to hear and see everything that the children said and did. They were under the supervision of the master, the chanter, the prior, and the abbot. They were expected to treat the other monks with respect, but contact with them was limited. The children were also forbidden to receive anything from or give anything to any person apart from the abbot, the prior, and their master. Nor was anyone permitted to speak to the children or to enter the school without the permission of the abbot or prior. Miscreants were whipped at the assembly where announcements were made, the statutes were read, and misdemeanours and sins were clarified. The children were also obliged to attend confession. One could describe them as a society of children, which was, however, under the maximum and constant supervision by adults and shared in their central activities without having contents of its own. The concessions granted to the children were mainly physical: they did not observe the same fasts as the adults; on days on which they too were obliged to fast, they were allowed to break their fast earlier; in the intermissions between prayers and hymns, they were permitted to lie on their seats while the monks sat upright. Understanding of what is particularly difficult for a child to endure is displayed in the ruling that a child should not take part in bathing and dressing corpses, or that a child who has been deprived of a meal as a penance should not serve during that meal at the table of the abbot.[41]

Lanfranc's statutes are the continuation of a lengthy tradition, and he consulted customaries of other monasteries in composing them. Essentially, they do not differ from those composed during the Carolingian era or those of Ulrich, Abbot of Cluny in the eleventh century, or from additional early eleventh-century usages based on the same source. In line with the rule of Benedictus of Nursia (which acknowledged the need to make life easier for the weak, including children), from the Carolingian era onward children enjoyed certain concessions about their number of hours of prayer, and the quantity and quality of food. The under-sevens enjoyed maximum concessions, but some were also granted to the under-twelves, and even those who had not yet reached 16 received some consideration. According to the rule of Hildemar in the ninth century, only from the age of 16 should complete fulfilment of obligations be expected, and from this age the young boy was no longer under the supervision of the master.[42] In Ulrich's statutes and those of the Cluniac house of Maillezais, there is more evidence than in Lanfranc's statutes of fear of sexual sinning among children and of their sexual exploitation by adults. Lanfranc too writes that children should sit in the cloister in such a fashion that they are unable to touch one another with their hands or clothing, and that they should not be awakened in the morning by the touch of a hand but a light touch with a rod. In the usages of Hildemar, Ulrich, and the Cluniac house of Maillezais, however, the number of regulations on this subject is great, including the instruction that a light is to burn all night in the dormitory. In these usages, one also finds greater encouragement of informing by children against one another. The key words in the clauses relating to children in all the usages are 'supervision' (*custodia*) and 'discipline' (*disciplina*). The compiler of the Maillezais usage boasts that even a prince in his palace does not receive such close supervision as a child in a monastery.[43] Arduous physical and emotional effort were demanded of these children in a highly disciplined way of life in which there was no room for childish diversions and innocent amusements.

Usages indicate the ideal situation. It is self-evident that rules and regulations are often more stringent than actual practice, and, moreover, effort is not always invested in enforcing them all. But, with these regulations governing the rearing of children in monasteries, it would appear that they were often enforced. From the remarks of Anselm of Canterbury to an abbot who savagely beat the children in his monastery[44] we learn that some abbots took full advantage (to say the least) of the whipping privileges granted to them. On the other hand, it is clear that in the monastery of Bec in Anselm's day, not only were children hardly ever beaten, but they enjoyed his attention, encouragement, and affection. Hugh of Lincoln, on the other hand, was apparently whipped in the monastery as a child.[45]

The abbots and abbesses were supposed to serve as father- and mother-substitutes for the boys and girls in their care, and the entire community of monks or nuns was expected to substitute for the family 'according to the flesh'. This image of the father and brothers appears frequently in monastic sources. An oblate in a Benedictine monastery made so great an effort to emulate his abbot that eventually 'the father was seen in the son and the master was recognized in the pupil'.[46] It was said of Anselm of Canterbury that he cared for the young novices in his monastery with 'paternal goodness'.[47] But could an abbot or abbess, even if relatively tender and willing, act as substitute parents for small children in the framework determined by the monastic rule? From the *Lives of the Saints* we learn that in thirteenth- and fourteenth-century convents little girls were allowed to play. According to the biographer of Margaret, daughter of the King of Hungary, who was placed in a Dominican convent in childhood, she refused to take part in the play of the other girls and prayed a great deal. From time to time she would call her companions to cease their games and come into the church to pray, saying 'This is our play.'[48] Catherine of Vadstena, daughter of St Bridget of Sweden and herself later canonized, was raised in a convent. According to her biographer, she was persuaded by her companions one day to play with dolls. She was punished that same night when demons in the shape of dolls dragged her out of her bed, kicked her, and beat her.

The story is intended to teach that 'the Lord punishes those whom he loves', but it possible that she had a nightmare and was indeed anxiety-ridden. It is further related that one night the abbess heard the child groaning, and, when she approached, found her fainting on the floor by her bed. She claimed to have been pursued by the Devil in the shape of a bull who butted her with his horns.[49] She may have been tense and anxious as a result of her separation from her parents and the cautions of the nuns about sins, the Devil, and Hell. An additional example of the inculcation of fear, this time in a young boy, can be found in the biography of the Cistercian monk, Adam of Locum. One day he began to chip at a stone which he found among the building-materials near the church, which was undergoing renovations. His master, who was a monk, told him to put it down at once, or else he would excommunicate him. The boy was so intimidated that he fell ill and feared that he was going to die.[50]

To return to the issue of play, the examples cited are from convents and from the thirteenth and fourteenth centuries. According to the customaries of Hildemar, children could be permitted to play for one hour, once a week or once a month, at the discretion of their masters. According to the customaries of other monasteries, slightly more time was allotted to play, but it was still restricted.[51] In the community of the Regular Canons, in which Hugh of Lincoln was placed (1140–1200), play was apparently forbidden. According to his biographer, Hugh told him about the games of his comrades, but he was referring to the days before he entered the monastery. He said that he had had an excellent master (who did not whip him and did not intimidate him), who

> by various devices ... overcame my inclination towards play and idle diversions, and turned it to profitable pursuits of every kind. Frequently, when my young companions were at their usual sports, he would rebuke me mildly and with parental kindness, saying 'My dear son, do not be infected by the foolish and aimless levity of your comrades.' He would add 'Little Hugh, little Hugh, I am educating you for Christ, play is not for you.'

Since, in the monastery as well, he was not allowed to play (and was beaten as well), he used to say to his close companions 'I never tasted the joys of this world. I never knew or learnt how to play.' One cannot but discern a touch of bitterness in his remarks on the circumstances under which he was placed in the monastery:

> My father, having long been at heart a canon regular, now assumed their habit [upon losing his wife], and, since he regretted that the privilege of abandoning the world had not been accorded to him at the beginning of his life, he easily persuaded me, who had no experience of it, to become his companion in the army of God.[52]

Hugh of Lincoln became an exemplary churchman who internalized completely religious values. The reason for the bitter tone was apparently not the fact that he became a monk, but the fact that his father had made the decision for him.

An example of stringent punishment for a 'sin' can be found in the life of Juliana of Cornillon. According to her biographer, since she had been influenced by what she had heard about the childhood of St Nicholas, she fasted on one of the fastdays, contrary to the instructions of the nun who was 'both nurse and teacher' to her and to her sister. As punishment for her disobedience, the nun made her sit alone in the snow. When she returned to collect the child (it is not specified how long she left her there), she took Juliana straight to the church to confess her sin. The biographer writes that the child remained in her place without moving a limb or uttering a syllable 'in the position of a penitent'. If the story is true, this suggests that the child was paralysed with fear. If it did not, in fact, take place, it still indicates what were then considered appropriate disciplinary measures in monasteries.[53] Let us follow this with an example of empathy with a small child and a more lenient approach. A small child who had been placed in a monastery not far distant from his mother's home used to run away in order to eat at home. When this was discovered, his master tried to cover for him, and, when the matter reached the ears of the abbot (who was also the child's uncle), he contented himself with rebuking him.[54]

If children in monasteries felt anger, loneliness, or anxiety, they were unable to give voice to their feelings to an adult who could justify these emotions.[55] What probably helped them was the fact that they were part of a group of children all experiencing the same way of life. Also likely to mitigate the sense of bitterness was the fact that they did not perceive the adult monks as people who enjoyed freedoms of which they themselves had been deprived, or who arbitrarily imposed on them, by force of being adults, a way of life which they themselves did not live. The monks also rose at night to pray; they too were forced to inform on one another; they too were under strict supervision and were sometimes even whipped at their chapter.

As noted above, economic and family considerations were weighty factors in the decision to dedicate a child to ecclesiastical service or the monastic life. In this fashion, parents prevented fragmentation of family assets, and their designated heirs received a larger share of the property than if it had been divided up among all the sons. In areas in which the principle of primogeniture prevailed in inheritance of fiefs, the younger sons who did not enter church service or monasteries did not receive shares of the main familial assets, but still had to receive something. The situation was easier when some of them were churchmen. The servant of the church, whether secular or regular, was unquestionably of respected standing. As for daughters, through greater investment in the dowries of some of them, and despatch of others to monasteries, it was possible to find a better match for those who were selected for matrimony. Not only was the status of the nun more respected than that of the spinster in the secular world, but in the convent a girl was also protected against the danger of extramarital sexual relations which could bring shame on the family. Since this socio-economic reality is mentioned only rarely in the Lives of the saints, it is illuminating to cite one example. St Lutgard, who lived in the first half of the thirteenth century, was the daughter of a merchant from Tongres and was destined for marriage. However, her father lost the money earmarked for her dowry in a commercial deal. Her mother then said to her 'If you wish to wed Christ, I will prepare you in fitting fashion for the convent you choose. If you wish to wed a mortal, you can only have a herdsman.' The girl was persuaded and entered a Benedictine house. She was then 12, and her conversion occurred only after she entered the convent. In contrast to the *topos*, this future saint displayed no particular signs of religious piety in childhood and loved games and pretty dresses.[56] Just as boys offered for secular church service were often sent to be raised by a bishop uncle, both boys and girls were despatched to monasteries where the abbots or abbesses were their uncles or aunts. Again, sometimes several sons or daughters were sent to the same monastery or convent. In the case of noble families, it was usually the monastery founded by one of the family's forefathers which was the focus of family piety and endowment. The burghers emulated the conduct of the nobles, and also sometimes sent more than one daughter to the convent in which they had a female relative. Economic factors and traditions determined this custom. In retrospect, however, we could guess that to enter a monastery with a brother or sister would have eased the child's parting from home.

Religious faith was, of course, also a factor in the decision to dedicate some of the progeny to the religious life, above and beyond the fact that it was considered fitting for some of one's relatives to be churchmen. Religious faith also undoubtedly sustained parents and fortified them in taking the step of sending a child to a religious house. Such encouragement was apparently necessary, particularly in the period when it was the custom to send children at an early age. (This being so, parents acted according to the practices cited by monastic leaders as right and proper.) It was no accident that they sought inspiration in the example of Samuel. Ecclesiastical service was one of the roles in medieval culture, but we cannot be sure that parents did not perceive a difference between training a child for knighthood or even for priesthood, or preparing a daughter for marriage, and educating a child for the monastic life. People sensed that to send a child to a monastery was tantamount to abandonment, even if it was done for the sake of God. 'He was abandoned by his parents of their own will and completely, and was gathered in by God,'[57] writes an author about a child sent to a monastery in childhood. Hildegard of Bingen (1098–1179), who was handed over at the age of 8 to a recluse nun to be raised, and from there was sent to a convent, dictated to her scribe the story of how her parents took a vow to offer her to the monastery, with 'a sigh' of pain (*cum suspirio*).[58] A father who placed his daughter in one of the Poor Clares' convents yearned for her after some time and 'out of love and longing for her' repented having sent her there and took her away.[59] The description of the vows of parents who dedicated an only son or daughter to the religious life is a *topos*, but only children were, in fact, sometimes dedicated to the monastic life. In these cases, parents must have felt that they were offering up a sacrifice, and they were not motivated by economic or familial considerations. Did the parents believe that the child alone would enjoy the reward for their sacrifice? Orderic Vitalis, who was sent from England at the age of 9 to the monastery of St Evroult in Normandy wrote in a supplication to God at the end of his life 'My father promised me in thy name that, if I became a monk, I should taste the joys of Paradise with the innocents after my death.'[60] However, from the tenth century onward, the centre of gravity gradually shifted from the self-consecration of the individual monk and his endeavours to save his own soul to the liturgical service of the community of monks and their prayers on behalf of all believers. The monks prayed for both their living and their deceased relatives. Hence the sacrifice could have been made on the parents' behalf as well. The dedication of a child to monastic life can also be perceived as the reflection of spiritual egotism in a centre in which, as John Boswell put it, the prevailing religion was based on sacrifice of the son by his father.[61]

Did the rearing of children in monasteries bear the anticipated fruit? Did they function properly within the social system? (And functioning within the social system is of course one of the criteria for evaluating the individual's spiritual well-being.) Did they become good monks and nuns? Knowles has pointed out that a considerable proportion of the important theologians and mystics of the eleventh and twelfth centuries were raised from childhood in monasteries. Some of them became bishops and abbots, and many were strong individuals who achieved original self-expression. They not only became integrated in the system, but also internalized its religious values. Nor can one doubt that some of them internalized these values from childhood.[62] On the other hand, it is self-evident that the sources record more of the lives of men and women, some of the extraordinary individuals, who filled important roles in the church or made a significant contribution to the high culture of their period, than about the anonymous rank-and-file. In the monasteries of St Evroult and Jumièges in the eleventh century those monks who had been placed in the monastery in childhood found their niche in the scriptorium or served as readers or chanters, or became scholars like Orderic Vitalis. None of them fulfilled administrative functions which required contact with the outside world; only one of them became an abbot, but was not a success in this position.[63] The reason is that they had experienced only one way of life – the enclosed and protected monastic life. It may well be that the inculcation of discipline and of unconditional submission to authority generated fear of new challenges and of confrontation with others. However, these were good monks. On the other side, reports of visitations of bishops or their representatives to the monasteries in their dioceses dating from thirteenth-century Normandy and Late Medieval England[64] mention deviations from the rule and trips outside the monastery on every possible occasion for innocuous or less innocuous reasons. (The records of the Late Medieval English visitations draw a graver picture than the reports from thirteenth-century Normandy.) Since these reports date from a period when boys were not longer offered to monasteries in childhood, they do not necessarily point to the failure of the contemporary methods of educating boys in cloisters. One could even deduce that it was precisely because most monks of this period had not been raised in monasteries that they did not succeed in maintaining the way of life expected of them. The truth is, however, that there were aberrations and upsets in other periods as well. The deviations from the rule and the moral decline at various stages are part and parcel of the annals of all monastic orders (which led to the reforms and the establishment of new orders). The reasons were complex: human frailty, which always creates a discrepancy between ideal and reality; political and socio-economic changes, which affected monasteries as well as everyone else; fluctuations in the emphasis placed on various components of the monastic ideal, and changes in the policies and aims of the church leaders. Yet, when we are examining a period in which the population of the monasteries consisted to a considerable extent of monks trained from childhood for the monastic life, it is reasonable to assume that this training did not always bear the hoped-for fruit and that this fact in itself was a factor in the moral decline. It seems that education was not an effective substitute for the true sense of religious vocation which impelled adults to take the habit. The reports of visitations to convents in the thirteenth century and the Late Middle Ages, when many nuns had been raised there from childhood, certainly indicate a failure of education. Among those whose education proved ineffective, the failure affected not only the convent but their own lives as well. Without a true sense of vocation, life in a monastery was merely a tedious routine. Humbert de Romans, writing in the thirteenth century about those who lacked inner satisfaction and were not resigned to their lives, described the melancholy nuns whose depression disturbed the tranquillity of their sisters, or those who were irritable, like hounds chained for too long.[65] The monastic life was inevitably self-limiting: the monks and nuns never became parents, and their own childhood experiences were not reflected in the raising of the young generation.

In addition to those destined for the monastic life by their parents, there were others who chose this life of their own free will (as well as men and women who entered monastic orders in adulthood, generally after losing a spouse). Some already requested to join monasteries in childhood. However, the typical age at which children expressed the wish to become monks or nuns or, from the thirteenth century, to join a Third Order of the Mendicants, or (rarely) to become hermits, was 12–17. This was considered the classic age of conversion in later periods as well.[66] The Mendicants were apparently aware of this fact when they fixed 13 as the minimum age at which a child could gain admission into their orders. The reasons for choosing the religious life were varied and complex. A religious vocation was undoubtedly common to all those who chose the religious life willingly. However, this sense of vocation was sometimes compounded by imponderable psychological factors. For the adolescent in a state of confusion as to his self-identity, the religious life could represent a place of his own where he could take refuge from parental values. In some cases, the religious life was more suited to the personality of the children than was the secular life in the social stratum to which they belonged. Some adolescents sought security in the monastic life as the result of bereavement or some other childhood trauma.[67] Others received particularly stringent religious upbringing in their parents' home, internalized religious values, and chose the monastery, even though they had not been dedicated to this life.[68] In Lives of the saints of the Central and Late Middle Ages, the desire to enter a monastery is usually described as the culmination of a gradual process of psychological development. Few biographies depict a sudden and dramatic conversion.[69] Authors did their best to describe the subject of the Saint's Life as having been marked by religious piety from childhood, but some of them undoubtedly had a predilection for seclusion, were highly sensitive and conscientious, found it hard to meet the demands of an upbringing in their social stratum, and identified with religious values. Hugh of Cluny was the eldest son of the Count Semur in Brionnais, and was his father's heir and designated for knighthood. However, he showed neither inclination nor talent for this life. He spent every leisure moment in a secluded place, reading, even though both his father (of whom he was in awe) and his companions in training for knighthood thought this an unfitting occupation for a knight.[70] Gerald of Wales also relates in his autobiography (though not entirely convincingly) that he had difficulties in adjusting to the way of life and training of the novice knight, and describes his inclination, from childhood, for the religious life.[71] Herman Joseph (who died in 1214) was the son of impoverished parents from Cologne. During the school vacation, while other children were playing outdoors, he would go into the church to commune with the Holy Mother and the infant Christ and John the Baptist. They, unlike the stereotypical future saint, loved to play and on one occasion invited him to join them. On another occasion when he went into the church barefoot on a cold winter's day, he heard the voice of the Holy Mother telling him that under a stone close by he would find money to buy himself shoes.[72] This 'companionship' of the poor and neglected child with Christ and St John has a clear affective aspect. The parents of St Colette (1391–1447) died when she was 17. Before his death, her father, a carpenter in a monastery, gave her into the charge of the abbot of the Corbie monastery, this also being her own wish. She was a beautiful girl but particularly short in stature and very bashful, and spent much time alone and praying. When her companions came to invite her to go out with them, she used to hide from them.[73] This suggests that, as an adolescent, she felt ill at ease in her body, and felt herself to be ugly and worthless. One could cite many other similar excerpts from Lives. It should also be recalled that in every upper-class family there were adult uncles and brothers, aunts and sisters who were bishops, priests, abbots and abbesses, monks and nuns. Children and adolescents could choose them as role-models. Among the nobility, some children were influenced by the churchmen who served in the family chapel. In the home of Peter of Luxemburg, the son of a great noble family, there were three clerks. When he was orphaned of his parents and moved to the home of his aunt, they went with him. He received his early education from the chaplain in his aunt's house. When he was sent at a particularly early age, 8 or 10, to study in Paris, the clerks accompanied him.[74]

How did parents react when their son, destined for a military, legal, or political career, or to be a merchant or financier, or their daughter, expected to marry, chose the religious life? Parental response apparently varied greatly. Some parents respected the wishes of a son (even when he was the prospective heir) or daughter and gave their blessing.[75] Some wielded emotional black-mail, reminded the son of all they had done for him since childhood, and reproached him for abandoning them in their old age. If he joined one of the less established and less respected monastic orders, they expressed regret at this fact as well. John Tossignano, who had studied to be a lawyer, excelled at his studies at Bologna University, and became a doctor at a very early age, was reproached by his parents for joining the 'miserable order' of the Gesuati.[76] Other parents from the nobility or the prosperous urban class, whose offspring joined one of the Mendicant orders in the first few decades of their existence, responded in similar fashion. The motif of the son who chose the religious life to his parents' grief also flourishes as a literary *topos*. In Raymond Lull's *Blanquerna*, when the son informs his parents of his decision to become a hermit, they remind him of all they have done for him and of his obligation toward them. He asks forgiveness for the pain he is causing them, but is determined in his mind to go out into the forest. Weeping, they give him their blessing.[77] Some parents, like Hugh of Cluny's father, expressed their disappointment and anger. Among the parents of girls who had been destined for marriage, some treated the daughter with hostility from the moment she expressed the desire to join a convent or a religious community, and tormented her in various ways in order to break down her resistance to marriage. The parents of Catherine of Siena (1335–80) constantly remonstrated with her, imposed the most arduous household tasks on her, and, since she preferred seclusion, deprived her of her small room.[78] She, it will be recalled, was a particularly well-loved child. This total change in the attitude of the parents toward their daughter as soon as she defied them and disrupted their plans for her is also found elsewhere, and was characteristic of the reaction of some other parents toward sons.[79] This indicates that there was only conditional acceptance of offspring by auth-oritative parents, and sometimes perhaps also marked the release of latent hostility, even if the parents' complete confidence in their own authority prevented them from being aware of it. Parents of both sons and daughters sometimes stopped at nothing in their efforts to prevent their children from entering monasteries, including removing them by force and incarcerating them. The similarity in the description of the reaction of several families suggests that here too a *topos* was created, particularly when the sons or daughters wanted to join the new orders of the Mendicants, affiliation to which was not anchored in the tradition of the noble families. However, some parents undoubtedly responded in this fashion even when the son or daughter had reached their majority. Daufar (1027–87), who was to become Pope Victor III, was the only son of a noble family, and entered a Benedictine monastery after the death of his father, when he was already 20 years of age. His mother came to remove him with tears in her eyes and his relatives came mounted and armed. They broke into the monastery, tore off his robe, brought him away, and locked him up. After one year of imprisonment, they agreed to allow him to go his own way.[80] Similar tales are told of Thomas Aquinas[81] (whose parents were willing for him to be the abbot of a Benedictine monastery but not a Dominican friar), Clare of Assisi and her younger sister, Agnes,[82] and Clare of Pisa. The last-named was a member of the distinguished and influential Gambacorta family. She was betrothed at the age of 7 and at 12 was sent to live in her husband's household. He died when she was 15. She adamantly refused to remarry and entered the Dominican order.[83] The story of Francis of Assisi is well known, but it should perhaps be mentioned that the amount of provocation his father had to endure was great, and in this case the transition from love to hostility appears less sharp than in other cases.[84] Francis of Assisi did not join a religious order nor did he become a hermit, but chose an entirely new path. According to canon law, if a minor entered or was placed in a monastery without the consent of his parents, he could be removed within a year and a day, as could an adult who was placed there against his will.[85] The fact that their offspring were not minors, and had not been forced into taking this step, did not prevent certain parents from trying to remove them (forcibly).

Just as there were boys and young men, or girls and young women, who chose the religious life under the influence of an older sibling, there were others who joined parents in harassing a brother or sister or bringing them home from a monastery. The biographer writes of the brother of St Francis of Assisi, 'Like his father, he persecuted him with cruel words.'[86] and Ida of Louvain was aided by Christ himself in the form of a handsome boy who appeared to her sister in a dream and beat her.[87] On one level, these are 'bad' brothers and sisters who have not undergone conversion and who lack the religious piety of their siblings. On the second level, these stories reflect sibling rivalry and resentment and the effort to please the parents. This was so regardless of the fact that, when a brother or sister chose the religious life, either the share of their siblings in the family inheritance increased or, in the case of girls, the parents were able to allot them a larger dowry. Not all young women succeeded in overcoming parental opposition. Some were forced into marriage and retreated from the secular world only after being widowed.[88] Writers note that these daughters obeyed their parents, but the descriptions clearly indicate that this submission entailed great suffering. Whatever the reason for their revulsion from contact with the opposite sex – their upbringing by their mothers, the exhortations of preachers and confessors or religious literature – it certainly existed. It was related of Frances of Rome (born 1384) that she was unable to bear the touch of a male hand, not even that of her father. She was given in marriage at the age of 13 and became severely ill after the wedding.[89]

Fromm-Reichmann claimed that, in a patriarchal society in which the father rules the household, the mother becomes the confidante and ally of the children.[90] There are, indeed, more examples of understanding and consideration on the part of the mother than of the father toward a son who frustrated his parents' plans for him by choosing to take the habit. The mothers of Hugh of Cluny and of Francis of Assisi, for example, treated their sons considerately and sympathetically. Yet this was not always so. In the struggle to bring Thomas Aquinas home, the active figure was the mother alone, and the father is scarcely mentioned.[91] It was mainly the mother of Catherine of Siena who adopted various measures in order to overcome her daughter's resistance to marriage, and her father proved more understanding and was the first to succumb and permit her to have her own way. The widowed mother of Daufar co-operated with the relatives who assaulted him in order to restore him to his home. In this case the impression is that the mother acted under pressure. There may have been other mothers who sympathized with their children but were too weak and intimidated to take a stand against their husbands and relatives and offer open support.

The obligation of respect and obedience towards parents was emphasized as one of the most important duties of the Christian. What, therefore, was the attitude of the hagiographers to those who chose a religious life in explicit opposition to the wishes of their parents? And, again, what was the stand of preachers and didactic writers and all those who attempted to present proper methods of upbringing? The authors of Central and Late Medieval Lives of the Saints obviously had their sympathies lying with the subject of the hagiography, the future saint, but they were usually restrained in their criticism of the parents who set obstacles in his path, and sometimes even tried to explain and justify their behaviour. Thomas Aquinas's mother fought like a she-lion to snatch her son from the Dominicans, but, according to one author, the Dominicans misunderstood her intentions, and in fact she only wanted to see her son and to give him her blessing. Only when this was denied her did she appeal for the aid of the Emperor.[92] Nor do the writers censure parents who forced marriage on their daughters. A young man who wanted to be a Benedictine monk, but surrendered to his father's will and chose the secular church, where he was ensured rapid advancement, was praised by a certain author 'for obedience to parents is a divine injunction'.[93] I have found only two cases of strong condemnation of parents: the fathers of Ida of Louvain and of Francis of Assisi. Both these saints greatly embarrassed their parents by their conduct, which implied total rejection of their way of life and values.

However the issue was not clearcut. In contrast to the hagiographers, some preachers and even authors of didactic works depicted separation from parents for the sake of the religious life as the fulfilment of a divine injunction and the supreme expression of love of God. In order to justify defiance of parental wishes, and in disregard of the interpretation offered by the author of *Dives et Pauper* and others, some biblical verses (Matt. 10: 37–8; Luke 14: 26) were interpreted literally.[94] Thus a thirteenth-century compilation of *exempla* for the use of preachers contains the story of a hermit who burned unread all the letters he received from his family because he had undergone a conversion and was detached from the world. In another tale, the mother of a young man who became a monk knocks on the gate of the monastery and asks the abbot to permit her to see her son. The abbot goes to summon the son, but the son paints his face black so that his mother will not recognize him. On seeing the black-faced man, she turns and leaves.[95] Extreme examples of the *topos* of abandonment appear in a letter apparently written by one of the young monks of Bernard of Clairvaux to his parents, who had opposed his entry into a monastery, as well as in the autobiography of Salimbene. After quoting the verses from Matthew, the young monk asks with rhetorical fervour 'What have we in common, what else have I received from you but sin and misery? Only the corruptible body which I bear ... Sinners, are you not satisfied that by your sin you have given birth to a sinner?'[96] Salimbene, who claimed that his father had pursued him with a group of mounted and armed soldiers, related how he quoted those same verses and adamantly withstood his father's attempts to dissuade him from becoming a Franciscan friar. Salimbene's remarks lack all tenderness. His father is depicted as a tempting demon more than as a pained and disappointed man. Nor did Salimbene try to console him by promising to pray for him.[97]

The supreme value of the religious life could provide a justification for placing small children in monasteries, for designating them for the religious life for economic and familial reasons, placing girls in convents, or for maternal neglect of children in order to retire to a nunnery. However, this same supremacy of religious values also offered young people alternative vocations. The existence of this choice was highly significant for the sons of the nobility up to the twelfth century, when new possibilities were opened up and the choice no longer lay solely between knighthood and the church.

A boy who was unwilling to become or incapable of becoming a knight, whether he was the heir or a younger son who was required to make his own way in the service of various seigneurs until he won a fief of his own, could still become a churchman. For young noblewomen the convent, which in some cases offered the possibility of gaining an education and leading an active life, was the sole alternative to marriage. The authors of didactic literature and jurists justified young men who chose the monastic life against their parents' wishes and rejected parental values. The need to grant freedom of choice to the young in accordance with their temperament, talents, and emotional needs was not always their main consideration (although some writers did stress the importance of these factors), but they could not but justify those who had chosen the religious way of life.[98] The author of *Dives et Pauper* (Rich Man and Poor Man), who did not interpret the verses from Matthew and Luke literally, emphasized that a man should refrain from becoming priest or monk only if his parents were so poor that they would literally starve if he did not provide for them. In every other case, he was permitted to do so. If his parents became impoverished after he became a priest he could assist them from his prebend; if he became a monk, he should support them from the alms which his monastery received; if he became a Mendicant friar he should collect charity for them.[99]

The ideal and the monastic life itself underwent highly significant change when, in the thirteenth century, the new orders of Mendicants were established, which were active in the secular world. From the twelfth century on, greater possibilities opened up before those nobles who were not due to inherit. It was no longer necessary to assign one of the sons of the family to a monastery in order to ensure his future livelihood without splitting up the family assets into many parts, and there was certainly a wide range of opportunities for town-dwellers. The number of secular schools increased and universities developed. Young men could train for a wider range of lay professions: becoming jurists, physicians, clerks in the new and multibranched administrative apparatuses of monarchs, feudal seigneurs, and towns. The post-Reform church also required educated and skilled manpower. Commerce and finance expanded. In the Late Middle Ages, new associations arose and new channels opened up for laymen's piety – in particular the various confraternities (which also provided different services for their members). Monasticism and priesthood were now only two out of many possibilities. However, the possibility of choosing utter dedication to the religions life continued to exist, and those who made this choice won the esteem of society. They were not relegated to being a marginal group, even if they displayed autonomy and rebellion against parental values. There is no way of ascertaining how many of the parent–child struggles described by writers did in fact take place and how many were composed according to a fixed pattern, but the very existence of the *topos*, coloured by strong sympathy for the young rebels, indicates the acknowledgement by the authors (and by society) of the right of the young to struggle to achieve their desire. For girls from the upper classes this choice remained, almost without exception, the sole way of acquiring an education, realizing organizational and educational skills, and the only refuge from undesired marriages.

10   Education in the nobility

Didactic writers asserted that the main function of mothers was to rear their sons to the age of 7. In fact, many of those designated for knighthood were separated from their mothers at the age of 7–9. In Gottfried of Strasburg's *Tristan*, the eponymous hero is raised with great love and tenderness by an adoptive mother. At the age of 7, he is forced to leave her, and, according to the author, at the peak of his joyful development, and on the threshold of the spring of his years, anxiety begins to gnaw at his heart. The blossoms of his joy wither and the most beautiful stage in his life lies behind him.[1] Contrary to the advice of authors of didactic works, when children were parted from their mothers, it was not their fathers who undertook their upbringing and vocational training. They where despatched to the courts of other nobles to be educated: to a paternal uncle, a maternal uncle (who was usually of higher social status than the father), a friend of the father or his seigneur, who were often also the child's godparents. In both literature and life, only the eldest sons of great nobles were educated at home, usually with other children and young boys, sons of the father's vassals or friends,[2] and only those who stayed at home remained in close contact with their mothers. Many noblemen acknowledged their bastard sons, reared and educated them at home or sent them, like their legitimate sons, to be raised by other nobiemen.[3]

Up to the beginning of the twelfth century, the upbringing and training of the future knight included almost no academic study. William Marshal, one of the greatest of English noblemen, who died in 1219, was illiterate. The common definition and classification into *laicus illiteratus* and *clericus literatus* essentially reflected the true situation. However, from the twelfth century onward, although there where still nobles who did not learn how to read and write, the division into distinct categories was somewhat blurred. Many of the nobles who remained in the secular world no longer confined themselves to the oral cultural traditions of their class, which were transmitted in the vernacular, but began to study Latin (though generally only a smattering). Some became fluent in this language, and thus gained access to the high culture of the period. In the thirteenth and fourteenth centuries, when the vernacular was the basis of elementary education and there was a rise in the number of works written in the vernacular and in the number of translations from Latin, a man who was ignorant of Latin could improve his education through knowledge of his own language. The changes in the education of the nobility are discussed in greater detail below. In the present context, let it merely be noted that, in the twelfth century, children learned from their mothers, nurses, or tutors (some boys being transferred at 3 or slightly more from their nurses to tutors) the three main prayers (Ave Maria, Credo, and Pater Noster), several psalms in Latin, and the basic tenets of faith. When they reached the castle where they where to be trained for knighthood, the rest of their academic and religious education was entrusted to a local clerk, chaplain, or monk.[4] It is clear, however, that study played only a marginal role in their upbringing. The objects of identification and emulation for these children were the adult knights, who inculcated in them the collective ethos and myths of knighthood, by means of which they where primed for integration in adult society. In literature, the future knight is described as imitating the actions of adults, identifying with their values, and fostering, in childhood, the qualities worthy of a knight. The feudal seigneur to whom children were entrusted for raising was the supreme arbiter of their military training, a master and father for whose love the children and young boys competed among themselves.[5]

On arriving at the court of a seigneur at the age of 7–10, the small boy became a page. He was dressed in adult male garb, which in the Late Middle Ages consisted of a shirt, a close-fitting laced or buttoned doublet, hose tied by laces to the doublet, a belt with decorated buckle slung around the hips (a distinctive sign of manhood), and over these a cloak. He became accustomed to horses at a tender age, by being seated in front of an adult equestrian, as can be learned from contemporary illuminations.[6] The distinguishing feature of a three-year-old boy in one of the *Chansons de Gestes* is the fact that he is not yet capable of 'walking the roads and riding'.[7] However, even children of 7 knew how to ride by the time they were sent to the court of the seigneur.[8] Up to the age of 12, children received only partial training, and not in all exercises, and served the knights. The castles where they were raised were familiar territory to them, reminiscent of their own homes, and the transition was certainly less drastic than in the case of children offered to monasteries.

Serious military training commenced at the age of about 12 (although Aegidius Romanus and others where of the opinion that wrestling, riding, and other knightly skills should be taught only from the age of 14).[9] Supreme responsibility rested with the feudal seigneur, but the everyday training was carried out under the guidance of the *nutricius* (tutor). It included various mounted exercises with arms, such as attacking a target, fencing, wrestling,[10] and archery. Hunting, in which the boys took part with the adult knights, and which was one of the most important occupations of the knight in peacetime, also played a part in military training, particularly in the context of horsemanship. To control a horse while out hunting called for a high degree of skill, similar to that required in battle. When Lancelot, in *Lancelot del Lac*, learns archery, he begins to hunt small birds and gradually progresses to hunting deer. Some boys also learned to tame game-birds and to use them. Military training, contests among the boys, and hunting entailed risk and were among the causes of the low life-expectancy of males in the nobility.[11] Some were injured and others lost their lives. In the second half of the eleventh century, two members of the Giroie family were killed during training. One of them was thrown on to a sharp rock while wrestling, and the other was injured during a javelin-throwing tournament. Richard, son of William the Conqueror, was apparently killed in a hunting accident before his initiation as a knight. In 1389, the seventeen-year-old Earl of Pembroke was killed while practising with a lance for a forthcoming tournament.[12]

Boys generally completed their military training at the age of 15, at the beginning of the third stage of life (*adolescentia*), which was considered the onset of adulthood, and then became squires to knights. Most of them became knights at the age of 17–19, but some were already knights at 15, immediately upon completing their military apprenticeship, and even took part in battle. Towards the end of the Middle Ages, because of changes in recruitment methods and in the structure of the army, many more young men in France, and particularly in England, postponed their taking of the order of knighthood or renounced it altogether.

Training was conducted in groups, and children constituted a single group (of mixed ages) within the population of the castle. Like children in monasteries, they too were a separate group,[13] but took part in the routine and the activities of the adults. However, whereas in the monastery, apart from those times when they participated in adult activities, they were deliberately kept apart from the monks, no attempt was made to separate future knights from adult society. They were raised in the male world of sweat, weapons, stables, horses, and hounds, with its ethos and courtly culture, as well as its lusts and unrestrained urges. A central role in the child's education was played by approval, and by the sanctions of group pride and shame. Irrespective of whether Hugh of Cluny did in fact have difficulty in performing his knightly exercises and preferred to read on every occasion, or whether it was the author who chose thus to describe the childhood of the future abbot of Cluny, the description reflects the existence of these group sanctions. The boy was obliged to confront not only his father but also his peers. The common ethos was inculcated through differentiation of the norms of conduct of the individual, as a result of cumulative interaction between children and adults and among children. Sometimes a group of young men were initiated together into knighthood on a feast-day, on some special occasion, or before a battle, by the seigneur in whose court they were raised. The training group was also a unit for various group games, and the children and boys also played various games in pairs. In a compilation of laws mention is made of a game in which the children were seated in a circle. One of the players then called to another 'Rise!' If the second player did not stand up immediately, something was thrown in his face.[14] Most popular among the boys were various ball games,[15] with or without a bat, some of which are reminiscent of tennis, golf, and croquet; bowls, games with a bat and ball of feathers, or with a small discus and a peg game. This was in addition to the game of 'knights', mentioned in a previous chapter, and other games which were also played by the nobility. The future knight also learned to play chess and tric-trac, a form of backgammon. Some of these games were also played by adult noblemen.

Among those who completed their training, some remained in the court of the seigneur who had trained them, as squires or knights under the supervision of the constable or the marshal. In peacetime, they served as the defence force of the castle and as escorts. During war, they formed the nucleus of the army.[16] Some of the eldest sons who received most of their education in their fathers' castles were sent at 15 to serve the father's seigneur, sometimes before becoming knights (so that it was he who introduced them into the alliance which confirmed their new identity), and sometimes afterwards. Others were sent on expedition with an adult knight to visit the courts of various seigneurs, and remained in their service for some time. This was also a period of participation in tournaments, the second main occupation of the knight in peacetime, after hunting. They displayed their skills and courage in these tournaments, which were also a source of monetary gain for the victor. Literature contains numerous descriptions of expeditions, journeys of intellectual and moral significance in search of knowledge and self-identity. In reality, many younger sons in noble families set out on their travels unwillingly, in search of a seigneur who would accept them into his service, and of a wife who would bring a fief as a dowry.

The childhood of those destined to become knights was brief, in the sense that their professional training began in childhood and they became involved at a very early age in the activities of the adults of their social group. However, contemporary opinion was not only aware of the 'childish' nature of children, but also distinguished between young men who had just completed their training and adult knights, and this distinction finds expression in literature. When Lancelot's tutor reproaches the boy for having given away all the booty of hunting and two horses in exchange for a greyhound, the child repeats three times, in the fashion of children, that he loves the hound more than the two horses. (The author's sympathies naturally lie with the child.)[17] In a narrative poem, a fifteen-year-old squire finds it difficult to carry the knight's heavy weapons. The knight carries them in his stead, and only before they enter the town does he give them back to avoid shaming the boy.[18] In *Raoul de Cambrai* the author sometimes refers to a young man as 'child' (*enfes*) because of his conduct, or for literary reasons. However, distinctions are also drawn between the young generation and the adults, and there is manifest tension between them. The young men are often referred to by the adults as 'children' although they have already entered the ranks of knighthood and taken part in battles.[19] The writers reflect awareness not only of the generational conflict but also of the discrepancy between the social custom according to which young boys at the beginning of *adolescentia* became warriors, and the pace of their emotional development. Be that as it may, a man could own a fief without a guardian only from the age of 21 (although 15 was considered the age of majority). And full integration in feudal society was granted only upon attainment of a fief and on marriage, irrespective of age.

Like children in all other social strata, future knights acquired their skills in what was the second stage of childhood according to the medieval classification, and the fourth according to Erikson. The latter claims that, in this stage, the child's most important goal is development of a sense of self and acquisition of skills. In addition, involvement in the society of adult knights, their tales and conversation, and the songs of the wandering minstrels who reached the castle, taught the future knights about heroism, the brotherhood of warriors, fidelity, and the honour of the family. Originally, knighthood was professional and secular. It was only in the course of the twelfth century that it became the domain of the nobility. The church added the religious element, and the courtly ideal evolved almost concomitantly. Thus the knightly ethos was composed of three elements, and, in order to realize them, the educational system was obliged to foster contradictory qualities and conduct. The ideal knight was a skilled and courageous warrior, loyal to his seigneur, generous,[20] and a man of personal honour which dictated his conduct toward both his comrades in arms and his vanquished enemy. To live up to the ecclesiastical ideal, he was supposed to be a man of justice and truth, modest (a trait irreconcilable with a sense of personal and class honour), merciful, a defender of the weak and helpless, and, in particular, a protector of the church and the Christian faith, always ready on its behalf to fight unbelievers, heretics, and any other enemy. The code of conduct towards the vanquished enemy also evolved gradually and under the influence of the church. Before the twelfth century, defeated enemies were not taken captive and released upon payment of a ransom, but were often blinded or mutilated. The tournaments which were part of the way of life of the knight were constantly denounced by churchmen as acts of slaughter and suicide which were in no way consistent with the ideal of the Christian knight, as were the private wars, which the heads of the various territorial principalities also tried to abolish.

Courtly literature, which disseminated the ideal of courtly love – namely, fidelity and service to a lady, and consequently respect for all noblewomen – led to the development of the third component of the knightly ethos, the erotic element. Since the ideal of courtly love was founded on extramarital love, it too was in conflict with ecclesiastical norms. With the emergence of the courtly ideal, which led to the partial feminization of feudal culture, the future knight was expected to learn chess (also taught to girls), to speak well, to sing and to play an instrument, to dance, and to behave courteously and respectfully in female company. In the framework of education for service of the seigneur and of the lady, it was also accepted that the future knight should wait at table, serving dishes, pouring wine, and carving meat.[21] The ecclesiastical authors of moral and didactic works sometimes denounced the feudal secular milieu in which the future knights were raised. They often exhorted parents and teachers to read to the children and instruct them in moral works instead of teaching them epic songs and courtly romances (which they called 'lascivious tales and fables of the temporal world').[22] Education gave the child the necessary knightly skills and also undoubtedly fostered certain qualities and patterns of behaviour: courage, initiative (which at least until the Late Middle Ages was the corollary of the method of combat), endurance (the didactic writers recommended that novice knights harden their bodies and accustom themselves to viewing corpses[23]), a sense of class and family pride, and certain patterns of conduct in the presence of women and girls of his class. In real life, the secular aspect of knightly training undoubtedly predominated. However, the prayer and mortification which knights sometimes undertook, like their numerous death-bed requests to gain entry into monastic orders and to die wrapped in a monk's habit, are expressions of the tension between the opposite poles of the knightly ideal (or, in sociological terminology, of role-strain). Norbert Elias has discussed the absence in the medieval nobility of childhood cultural conditioning aimed at curbing and restraining instincts, an absence deriving (so he argues) from the nature of a society in which the central authority had no monopoly over violence, in which the power to wield it was dispersed among many seigneurs, and in which the differentiation of their functions was limited. This lack of conditioning led to the development of personalities with a weak super-ego, individuals whose self-restraint was unstable and diffuse, given to emotional outbursts and veering between extremes of mood and conduct. Such fluctuations in mood and behaviour in the individual vary in different cultures. The conflicting elements of the knightly ideal created a specific form of expression of these fluctuations – unruliness and unrestrained satisfaction of appetites, as well as religious ecstasy.[24] According to a certain didactic writer, it was incumbent on the future knight not only to develop his strength and physical prowess, courage and daring, but also to learn prudence, temperance, and justice, which are part of the range of ideal qualities of a knight.[25]

The impression is, however, that moderation was not one of the qualities which was fostered in future knights.

There gradually began to appear in the 'courtly romance' the figure of the boy preparing for knighthood who not only undergoes military training and studies the rules of correct social conduct but also acquires some kind of education. In two of the versions of *Tristan*, the boy (who eventually becomes a perfect knight) learns from his master reading and writing, the seven liberal arts, several foreign languages, and the law of the land. He sets out on his travels not only in order to serve various seigneurs but also to learn foreign languages, and to be able to observe foreign countries whose language, manners, and laws differ from those of his native country.[26] In reality, in the thirteenth and fourteenth centuries, those who trained for knighthood did not study the seven liberal arts, and knowledge of Latin was usually confined to ability to read a few sentences. The didactic works which discussed the education of the future knight do not mention these subjects. The boys did, however, acquire some education. They were taught by a tutor or by the chaplain or clerk in their parents' household or in the home of the nobleman who raised them, or at private schools for the children of the nobility in castles, or at a school attached to the church near their home and run by an abbot or bishop.[27] In the second half of the thirteenth century, a textbook for study of French was written at the request of an English noblewoman. The aim was to provide the student with as large a vocabulary as possible. The words depicted familiar and common objects and scenes which were presented in suitable context and in mnemonic rhymes.[28] This book and others which followed were not intended for study at grammar school where Latin was taught, but were aimed at the children of the nobility with the goal of teaching them in a relatively easy fashion how to conduct a conversation in French. The libraries of the more educated nobles who chose a military career included books in the vernacular (or, in England, in French), such as a translation of Vegetius' treatise on the art of war (*Epitoma Rei Militaris*), epics and knightly romances, compilations of fables, religious works and missals, hagiographies, history books, and sometimes also legal works and scientific summaries from the spheres of geography, astronomy, and medicine. Their knowledge of the classical heritage was acquired from translations.[29] The little Latin they knew was learned mainly for practical purposes. Since contracts, legal rulings, and other legal documents were written in that language, any knowledge of it helped them in their legal claims and negotiations and enabled them to fulfil functions in the royal administration (such as serving as jurors in English courts of law).[30] There were exceptions to the rule who studied Latin and acquired a wider education. Abelard related in *Historia Calamitatum* (The Story of My Misfortunes) that, although he was the eldest son and was not designated for ecclesiastical service, his father, who was reasonably well-educated, ensured that each of his sons received some education before beginning his knightly training. Abelard was so drawn to study that he decided at a certain stage (as he put it) to leave the court of Mars and to bow his knee to Minerva.[31] There were other isolated similar cases particularly in the thirteenth and fourteenth centuries. Generally speaking, however, it was those young noblemen who remained in the secular world and who were not candidates for knighthood or due to inherit who attended universities. They usually studied in faculties of law, or, in England, in special schools of jurisprudence, and qualified to become jurists and administrators in the service of kings and great feudal seigneurs.

In a letter to Edmund Stonor, written in 1380, Brother Edmund reports to his patron on his son's welfare and progress. The boy studied in a private preparatory school and lived with his teacher. Brother Edmund says that the child has completely recovered from his illness (under the devoted care of the master and his wife), is healthy and joyful, and is studying Latin at a not-too-taxing pace.[32] Those boys whose tutors prepared them well for academic study skipped the faculty of humanities and went straight into the faculty or law. The lives of these young nobles (mostly younger sons, sons of minor nobles, and orphans) did not differ from those of the other strata of society who attended university, except in so far as some of them did so under more congenial conditions and were not obliged to work during their studies or to seek a patron. Unlike the young men of their class who became knights, they did not generally leave their parents' home at the age of 7–9. Often they travelled to their place of study with a tutor whose task was to supervise them, to assist them in their studies, and to share their lodgings.[33]

Contemporary sources not only mention the despatch of children of the nobility to other households for education, but also occasionally express views on the significance and consequence of this custom. According to Gottfried von Strasburg, Tristan's separation from his adoptive mother marked the end of the happiest period of his life. Whereas the author of this poem focuses on the child's pain, the subject of a popular proverb is the plight of those who raise children: 'It is bad to raise the child of another, since, when he grows up, he leaves [those who raised him] and goes his own way.'[34] According to John Bromyard, who criticized the custom of sending children away to be reared by others, children of the nobility who were sent to the royal court or to the households of great nobles grew to be ashamed of their parents and of their family name.[35] It is known that the practice of sending children to be educated away from home existed among the Vikings, the Celts, and the Anglo-Saxons. The church did not support it, considering it the duty of parents to raise and educate their own children, but neither did it fight to abolish it,[36] and only infrequently did churchmen express their disapproval. The custom has existed for generations in West Africa: children are still handed over to be raised by relatives, leaders, and English families.[37] Some historians have regarded this custom as indicative of lack of feeling for the child and of the desire to be free of its presence and of the obligation of raising it. The truth is that many of the nobles who entrusted their children to others in their turn took in and raised other people's children. Thus they were neither rid of the presence of children nor released from the obligation to raise them. It would appear that the conscious reason for this custom was the consideration that to be raised by and to serve someone of higher standing than his own parents (even if they were blood relatives) would help the child to establish the right connections in order to advance his career and guarantee his future. John Bromyard wrote that children were sent away to be educated by the great of the land 'in the hope of great advancement'.[38] Then again, the presence of the son of the vassal in the seigneur's court could not guarantee absolutely the fealty of the vassal, but certainly increased the chances that he would fulfil his obligations and remain loyal. By tacit agreement, the son acted as hostage. The exchange of sons among seigneurs of close rank also helped to strengthen ties and loyalties. Research conducted in West Africa today indicates that there, as well, this is done primarily to ensure the future of the children by providing them with a better education, adequate vocational training, and useful patronage. The fact that promotion of the son's career was in parents' interest for family and dynastic reasons did not rule out either concern for his future or affection for him. It is possible that, in regions where the eldest son alone was due to inherit the family assets, the sending away of younger sons was aimed at preventing friction with the heir, and it may well have been believed that, in the second stage of childhood, strangers would do a better job of raising the child. In any event, it is clear that once the custom became entrenched it was very difficult for a parent to avoid following it, since this would have deprived the son of various advantages. There is evidence that upper-class mothers in nineteenth-century England did not always find it easy to bear the parting from their small sons who were sent to public schools characterized by rigid discipline.[39] Yet, although they were fully aware that the child was liable to suffer there, it was clear to them that there was no alternative but to send him in order to prepare him for life in the class to which he belonged and to give him a proper start in life. One may assume, even in the absence of direct evidence, that this same conflict between social conduct and emotion sometimes existed among mothers in the medieval nobility. The child who, according to the popular proverb, abandoned those who had raised him, once he reached manhood, did not do so in order to return to his parents. In the Lives of the saints we sometimes read of a mother praying for her sons who are going out to battle (since 'she was unable to dissuade them'),[40] or a mother who tries to persuade her warrior sons to shun extreme and savage conduct.[41] However, few younger sons had real contact with their mothers after leaving home in childhood. The oldest son was usually closely attached to his mother if she had been widowed. Since the life expectancy of noblemen was low, many were fatherless at an early age, and, in most regions, the mother acted as guardian. If the son inherited a fief which entailed ruling powers, his mother wielded authority on his behalf as long as he was a minor, and often defended his rights and zealously protected his property.[42]

For many of the boys raised by a seigneur, his wife, the lady of the castle, must have appeared as a substitute mother-figure. The mother of Raoul in *Raoul de Cambrai* felt strong affection for Bernier, 'whom I had raised until he became a knight',[43] and did her best to prevent her son from going to war against his relatives, for fear that Bernier would be obliged to rally to their cause. Bernier, for his part, also felt close to Raoul's mother and was grateful to her. Consequently, he refused to fight her nephew and knew no peace until she forgave him. On the other hand, in literature, at least (Georges Duby perceives an echo of real life here), the wife of the seigneur is an object of desire for the young squires and young knights, who are unwilling bachelors and who were separated from their mothers in childhood. Tristan serves his lord-uncle, and is his wife's lover.[44] There are many fatherless heroes in literature – Raoul de Cambrai, Tristan, Parzival, and Lancelot, to name a few. On the level of social analysis this recurrent motif is an expression of the loss of the father experienced by many nobles in childhood and of the fact that in the second stage of childhood they were removed from home. On the psychological level this is a reflection of the oedipal situation: the hero 'kills' his father and finds another father, his maternal uncle, or an ideal father – King Arthur. The wives of these fathers, the objects of the desire of these young men, are not their mothers.

Sons who were raised by their fathers often suffered under the yoke of their authority. The father of Gilbert of Nogent died when his son was 8 months old. Gilbert wrote that it was better for them both that God had caused the death of his father. Had he lived, he would certainly have broken the vow he made when Gilbert's mother was suffering pangs of childbirth, that, if a son were born, he would be offered to the religious life, and would have forced his son to take up a military career.[45] This, then, was the fatherless hero's image of the authoritative noble father. According to his Life, the crippled Gilbert of Sempringham was depressed and almost totally paralysed as long as he lived in his father's house. Hugh of Cluny feared his father, peerless knight. Jean Froissart tells the story of Gaston of Foix, and his only legitimate son. The father suspected his son of trying to poison him at the behest of the King of Novare. The latter did in fact give the boy the poisoned powder, but told him that if he put it in Gaston's wine Gaston and his mother, who were separated, would be reconciled. When Gaston saw the bag of powder hanging around his son's neck, his suspicious were roused and he put some of it into his dog's bowl. The dog, a greyhound, expired at once. The father was seized with terrible rage, reminded his son of all the years he had fought in order to increase his inheritance, and sought to kill him on the spot. His companions dissuaded him by reminding him that he had no other heirs. The boy was placed in solitary confinement in a cell in the castle tower, sank into a depression 'since he was not accustomed to this', and refused to touch the food placed before him. When the father discovered that his son was dying of starvation, he interpreted his refusal to eat as rebellion, pressed a knife to his throat, and caused his death. (It is not entirely clear from the description whether he intended to kill him or only to threaten him.) The boy was the victim of the schemes of the King of Novare, but even more so of his father's unbridled rage.[46] The story is undoubtedly indicative of the image of the father in the nobility, which, though not completely accurate, was not totally detached from reality. Conversely, there were sons of the nobility who believed that, when in distress, they could count on the sympathy of their father. In the mid-fifteenth century, the earl of Rutland complained to his father that he had been beaten by his tutor for erring while reading.[47]

Jealousy and hostility among siblings have already been mentioned in the context of sons and daughters who chose the religious life against the wishes of their parents, and echoes of this jealousy can also be found in popular literature.[48] These descriptions are psychologically valid, but within the nobility where the principle of primogeniture prevailed in most regions, hostility and envy could stem not only from emotional factors but also from very concrete considerations – the rights and status of the eldest son.

We have mentioned the utopian upbringing of the future knight in *Lancelot del Lac*. The fairy who receives the infant Lancelot dives with him into the depths of the lake, which is not a real lake but represents the feudal world: a castle, forest, squires, and knights. The description of the boy's education is anchored in the actual educational methods of the day. Auerbach has already pointed out that the lifestyle is depicted realistically in the literature of the nobility. At the same time, the description is coloured not only by utopian enchantment but also by the author's attempt to amend reality on one issue decisive for emotional development. At the age of 3, Lancelot is handed over to a tutor. At about 7, he begins his training for knighthood and learns gradually how to ride, wield arms, hunt, and play chess. He is raised in the company of his peers, who are also his cousins, and older boys as well. In the evenings he spends time with his adoptive mother, the lady of the lake, serves at her table, and pours the wine. Religious education receives almost no mention, and academic study none at all. From childhood, he displays the skills and qualities required of a knight: he is an outstanding horseman, and excels in military training and hunting (which require patient and keen observation), and shows intelligence in playing chess. He is courageous, magnanimous, and protests against whatever he perceives as injustice. At the age of 10, after he gives away his game and two steeds in return for a hound, his tutor not only is angry but also beats both the boy and the hound. Lancelot rebels and flees into the forest. When he returns, his adoptive mother, who has heard the stcry from the tutor, pretends to be angry. Secretly, however, she is proud of his generosity, his keen sense of justice, and his defence of his honour. The fact that he reacted without restraint does not trouble her. She dismisses the tutor, and the boy continues his training irregularly under the guidance of different adults and through emulation of adult behaviour.[49] The author's main deviation from reality appears to be in the description of the boy's close ties with this adoptive mother up to manhood. She raises him herself to the age of 3, when he is given into the care of the tutor. From then, until her reaches 18, she is nearby, observing his upbringing and intervening in moments of crisis (as when he defies his tutor). When he turns 18, she parts from him with pain and sorrow, knowing that she must now send him to commence his knightly career at the court of King Arthur. The proximity of the adoptive mother introduces the feminine element into his upbringing. External manifestation of this is the wreath of red roses he finds every morning on his pillow, a gift he shares with his cousins. Only on Fridays and fastdays does the wreath fail to appear – one of the sole references to the obligations of the Christian ritual. The boy is raised in an atmosphere of joy and freedom. Candidates for knighthood were, in fact, trained in an atmosphere of rough freedom and the cheerful ambience is emphasized in other literary works as well. Lancelot is also reared with maternal affection, though with restraint and without pampering, in line with the recommendations of the didactic writers.

At the age of 7 approximately, the paths of the sons and daughters of the nobility diverged. Boys who were candidates for knighthood were separated not only from their mothers but also from their sisters and from the female world in which they had hitherto been reared. According to the author of the poem, William Marshal's sisters wept when he left home and set out for Normandy, where he was to be educated.[50] Girls were sometimes sent in childhood to other households to be reared, but this was not as common as among boys.[51] These were usually the daughters of princes and great feudal seigneurs, betrothed in childhood and sent to grow to womanhood in the households of their future husbands. Elizabeth of Hungary, for example, the daughter of Andrew, King of Hungary, was betrothed at the age of 4 to the Landgraf of Thuringia. In the same year she was sent to the palace of Wartburg, where she lived until her marriage at the age of 14, and henceforth until the death of her husband. Other girls were sent in early childhood to be raised in convents (often to houses founded by an ancestor), and lived there until they were given in marriage.[52] Some daughters apparently stayed at home and were instructed by a tutor (*magister*) or mistress (*magistra*), by an anchoress, or at a private school for children of the nobility (sometimes in the company of those boys who were not raised in the courts of seigneurs or who had not yet been sent away). If they were from urban noble families, they could attend elementary schools in the town. Sometimes, in addition to the tutor, the girl's nurse remained with her.[53] Some daughters of the minor nobility were instructed by the priest of a church near their home, like the two daughters of Beatrice Planissol, wife of the castellan, mentioned in the records of the Inquisition tribunal at Pamiers, who were taught by the parish priest at Dalou.[54]

Girls were educated, not in order to prepare them for an occupation or for office in the kingdom or the territorial principality, but to train them for their role as wives and to instruct them in fitting conduct and certain pastime skills. The fact that some women inherited fiefs did not lead to a redefinition of the role of women in society in general, so that only rarely was reference made to the need to educate girls to fulfil a function. One author writes that princesses and great noblewomen should be taught to read and write, so as to enable them to rule properly when the time came. This rare statement is based on true facts – women sometimes managed fiefs as heiresses, as widows by right of dowers, or as guardians of their minor sons. Christine de Pisan, aware of the tasks carried out by the wife of the noble at her husband's side or, more usually, in his absence, recommends teaching young noblewomen the proper way to conduct a budget and even instructing them in land laws. Such references, however, are not typical.[55] On another plane, the aim of education was to bring girls to observe religious injunctions and to foster in them certain traits considered ideal for a noblewoman. However, the qualities lauded as ideal in didactic literature, in family myth (as reflected in the family genealogies commissioned in order to glorify the family name), in epic poetry, and in courtly romances were not always the same. Didactic literature and family myth stressed the importance of piety, obedience, submission, devotion, and sexual chastity; the latter in particular was undoubtedly strongly valued in families. Girls were sent to convents not only in order to acquire an education but also because they were better protected there. In the castle of the earls of Guines, special place was allotted to *adolescenti* and *adolescentiae* in two separate wings on the same level. The boys slept there only when they chose to do so, and the girls regularly, because this was considered fitting.[56] The generosity cited as one of the ideal qualities of the knight was not always considered a desirable quality for a noblewoman, since she might be suspected of giving generously of her body as well.[57] Poetry also sometimes praises virtuous qualities. In Marie de France's poem, *Guigemar*, the heroine is a tender and loving figure who suffers for her love, and, through her readiness to endure tribulations and pain, redeems her beloved.[58] Fresne in *Le Fresne* (The Ash Tree) is not only the symbol of grace, sweetness, and goodness of heart, but is also marked by her forbearance and acquiescence to fate. When her lover is about to marry a noblewoman (who is her sister, though Fresne does not know this), she assists uncomplainingly in the preparations for the nuptials. In epic poetry, the woman sometimes encourages the man to continue to fight despite loss and bereavement. She instils in him the spirit to do what she knows he must do (as, later, in *Le Reconfort de Madame du Fresne*). The element of submission remains, though the tendency to moderation, often attributed to women and mothers in family myths and in the Lives of the Saints, disappears. In courtly literature, mainly Provençal lyrics, which deals with the sole component of the knightly ethos in which women were involved, it is the lady who dictates the rules of the game to the man. She tests him by means of various ordeals which are, primarily, military missions. Both obedience and self-sacrifice have vanished, as also, sometimes, has sexual chastity.

As regards the actual education which girls received (in addition to guarding their modesty): even in the twelfth and thirteenth centuries, when boys were more widely educated than in earlier periods, girls did not learn less than did candidates for knighthood. Gottfried of Strasburg, who wrote about the education of Tristan, also described how Isolde was educated. Initially, she was instructed by a tutor who was a churchman, and then by Tristan. She learnt reading and writing, poetry, foreign languages, as well as etiquette, playing an instrument, singing, and music composition. In real life, it is unlikely that girls learned languages (with the exception of England, where French was taught). They did, however, learn reading and sometimes even writing in the vernacular, a little arithmetic, excerpts from the Scriptures and from the *Lives of the Saints* as well as prayers and psalms in Latin. They were instructed in folk medicine or what we would call today 'first aid'. It was occasionally recorded that a girl studied 'liberal studies' (i.e. the seven liberal arts),[59] but this was not serious and comprehensive instruction. Girls also read narrative poetry and courtly romances, although authors of didactic works were more severely critical of the reading of such works by girls than by boys. The young noblewoman who received a good education was also expected to know how to ride, to raise and train falcons, to play chess and other social games, to tell stories, to recite, to riddle, to sing and play a string instrument, and to dance. Some of these skills were certainly acquired by most girls (singing and playing of instruments were apparently taught by professional teachers). They also occupied themselves with embroidery and fine weaving. Girls undoubtedly became skilled in the running of a household or even an estate from practical observation of the lady of the castle and through helping her. It seems that girls (like women) devoted a greater portion of their time than did future knights to reading, both of psalters and of various romances (and some of them later became patronesses of writers and poets).[60] On the other hand, there was an increasing gap in the thirteenth century between the education of girls and of those boys who were not candidates for knighthood but trained for tasks in the new administrations of kings and great feudal seigneurs. Such boys, it will be recalled, either attended grammar schools or received corresponding instruction from a private tutor, and went on to universities or to special law schools. Girls who were sent to school attended elementary schools only. Very few women, the exceptions to the rule, acquired a wider-ranging education in childhood and girlhood, among them Heloïse and Marie de France. Christine de Pisan, in contrast, gained most of her education when already a grown woman.

Girls were given the same opportunity as boys to play, and there are extant description of small or older girls playing with hoops and dolls. Just as boys are depicted in literature aping the actions of adults, little girls are sometimes described as mimicking ladies in the content and style of their talk. The authors write affectionately, further evidence of keen observation of children. So little Obilot in *Parzival* asks one of the knights to be her knight. He promises that, when the time comes, he will serve her with his sword, but adds that he must wait another five years until he can ask for her love. She wants to offer him as a token something that belongs to her, in the manner of ladies with their knights. However, a friend of her own age says to her 'Tell me what you intend to give him. We have nothing but dolls. If mine are more beautiful than yours, you can give him one of mine.' Obilot decides to ask her father's help. He lifts her on to his horse, seats her in front of him, and embraces her. He listens to her request, says that he will do his best to fulfil it, and congratulates himself on his good fortune in having a daughter like her. As he gives her a ride on his horse, she asks him about her friend, and several knights volunteer to give the friend a ride as well. Her father takes her to her mother, and he and the mother decide to give orders that a fine and costly dress is to be made for her, so that she can give one of the sleeves to the knight she has chosen.[61] The chroniclers, who wrote less of women than of men, describe the relations between a small daughter and her parents even more rarely than they do parent–son relations. Perusal of these sources gives the impression that, in the nobility, the father had almost no contact with his daughters, and intervened only toward the end of the second stage of childhood, or the beginning of the third, when it became necessary to decide on a match for her. The above anecdote and similar ones reflect another aspect of father–daughter relations.

It was less costly to educate daughters than sons, both those boys ear-marked for knighthood, who had to be provided with a horse and the accouttrements of a knight, and whose admission into the ranks of knighthood had to be financed, and boys sent to acquire a higher education. Although families tried to provide in some way for all their sons who remained in the secular world, this could not always be guaranteed in areas where primogeniture prevailed. In contrast, however, each and every daughter who married received a dowry. It was allocated to them when they were given in wedlock at an early age. One of the characteristics of what Hajnal has called 'the West European marriage pattern' – a relatively high age of matrimony for women – was non-existent in the medieval nobility.[62] Girls were sometimes married off before the age of 12 – the minimum age of matrimony according to canon law. Others married at 12 or 13, and the average marriage age for girls among the nobility in the Late Middle Ages was apparently 17.[63] Legally speaking, the marriage of a girl under 12 was considered to be a betrothal, and could be annulled if she so wished upon reaching this age. (In the twelfth century the principle that only the consent of both partners rendered matrimony valid was finally accepted.) However, girls were often pressured into consenting.[64] According to Duby, some of the non-consummations mentioned in the sources, and attributed to the evil eye and witchcraft, stemmed from the fact that girls were married too young and against their will.[65] Boys sometimes entered into matrimony at a very tender age, particularly in princely families and among the higher nobility.[66] But generally, the age of matrimony for boys (even the case of heirs, who took wives at a younger age than their brothers) was higher by several years than was the case with girls. From the twelfth century, there was an increasing age-gap between husbands and wives.[67] Whereas the transition from the first to the second stage of childhood among girls who remained at home was less sharp and significant than among boys, the transition from the second stage to the third was extremely abrupt. For most girls, *adolescentia* meant marriage, with all this implied. They bore their first child at an early age (despite the cautions of medical scholars against premature motherhood), and continued to give birth at brief intervals, often producing more than ten offspring. It is with good reason that limited space is allotted to girls in discussion of the third stage of life. The daughters of the nobility were usually given in marriage before reaching the majority at which they were entitled by law to enjoy independence in civil matters (independence of which wedlock deprived them). There was unquestionably a discrepancy between their emotional development and the social custom which burdened them with the yoke of matrimony at a tender age. A girl who married very young continued after marriage to play with glass rings 'in the manner of young girls'. This aroused the ire of her husband, who did not refrain from cursing her.[68] The chronicler who records the annals of the Guines family writes (sympathetically) about the little countess Petronella, who, at the age of 13 or 14, after her marriage, still danced with her companions, played at various girlish games with them (including dolls), and loved to bathe in the pool in the courtyard. The author explains that she did not bathe for hygienic purposes but in order to enjoy the coolness of the water and for amusement, and described her pleasure.[69] It seems that the poet, who denotes as 'infanta' the married woman who gives birth to a son when not yet 13, is aware of the existence of that gap between emotional development and social demands.[70]

11   Education in urban society

In discussing education of urban children, one should distinguish between the offspring of the urban nobility and prosperous burghers, and the progeny of the various strata of the labouring classes. This distinction is essential because of the difference in economic status, lifestyle, and political privileges between the various social strata. Each class set itself specific educational goals which, in effect, dictated its pedagogic methods. At the same time, all sections of urban society took part in popular festivals, attended theatrical performances, and listened to both the wandering minstrels and the preachers.

As noted in a previous chapter, it was not only children destined for the church who attended elementary (or 'song' schools). Most children who received any kind of education were instructed there, excluding those children of the rich who were taught by a private tutor at home, and those who were designated for monastic life and were placed in monasteries as small children. Blanquerna, who was intended to become a merchant, had a young tutor, a student, who escorted him daily both to church and to song school.[1] Gradually, first in the towns of Italy and Flanders and later in other countries as well, municipal authorities also established schools, and private schools were set up, some of them run by scribes. Giovanni Villani, describing the elementary schools in Florence in the second quarter of the fourteenth century, writes that some 8,000–10,000 children, both boys and girls, learned to read and write there.[2] Although Giovanni Dominici claimed that children who had been raised strictly by their parents were corrupted by those schools,[3] the truth is that the curriculums and methods of instruction in the various elementary schools were almost identical despite the fact that a larger proportion of the schools run by secular bodies were apparently mixed (i.e. boys and girls together), and some even had female teachers.[4] In all European towns, the great majority of the children of prosperous burghers attended elementary schools for at least a few years. Some of those who were to become merchants and bankers continued their studies at schools of commerce. They were instructed in arithmetic, book-keeping, commercial correspondence, and sometimes foreign languages and applied geography, as recommended by authors of didactic works. Most children, however, appear to have attended these schools only briefly. A member of the Valori family says that he attended a school of this kind for only eight months and was then apprenticed to a banker.[5] The man of affairs, Gregorio Dati, also attended a school of commerce for only a short period. He wrote that, at the age of 13, after having learned sufficient arithmetic, he began to work in the shop of a silk merchant.[6] Petrarch was also 'handed over to a merchant' at the age of 13 after having attended 'arithmetic school'. Their parents evidently thought it was necessary to give their children, in addition to religious education, only the basic education required for their future occupation. Among merchants and bankers, there was a tradition of apprenticeship, in the course of which most of the necessary training was given. Even those didactic writers who favoured giving professional training to future merchants stressed the importance of the period of apprenticeship with an experienced merchant. In Tuscan towns some children did not attend schools of commerce, and were apprenticed at the age of 12, becoming book-keepers at an early age.[7] In London, on the other hand, some large commercial firms refused to accept boys under 16 as apprentices.[8] One of the reasons why boys were bound apprentices at a very early age in Tuscan towns appears to have been that, although the age of majority was 25, some parents granted their sons emancipation at a very early age – about 12. Emancipation meant that the father was absolved of all legal responsibility for his son. A sum of money or piece of property was given to the son, enabling him to join one of the merchant guilds, and also serving as guarantee of his good conduct in the firm which accepted him.[9] In contrast, those who were intended to become physicians, notaries, and jurists moved on from elementary school to grammar school, where they pursued the same curriculum as pupils who were training for ecclesiastical service, and prepared themselves for university studies.[10] Notwithstanding the fact that many merchants and bankers wanted their sons to follow in their footsteps, education was held in esteem in urban society. Some towns invested resources in developing both elementary and higher schools. Members of the urban nobility and prosperous burghers funded scholarships for poor students, and the professions of notary, jurist, and physician were considered prestigious. It will be recalled that some didactic writers proposed that parents enable their sons to study a profession suited to their talents and predilections. It may be assumed that, in some cases, choice of a career was based on the boy's own preference. This was not so, however, in the case of Giovanni Boccaccio. Although he wanted to study, his studies were interrupted at an early age (according to the biographer, because of his father's greed), and he loathed working for the merchant to whom he was apprenticed for six years. Only at a later stage, after a bitter struggle and after being sent to study law because he had failed at trade, was he allowed to dedicate himself to literature.[11]

While some prosperous town-dwellers sent their bastard sons to foundlings' homes, others acknowledged them and undertook responsibility for raising and educating them. The sources also record instances of display of special affection towards them. In certain cases, when fathers died, uncles undertook to continue raising the children.[12] Leon Battista Alberti, author of *I Libri della Famiglia* (The Books of the Family), was a bastard. His father acknowledged him and his brother and raised and educated them. When a plague broke out in Genoa, which claimed their mother as victim, he sent them to Venice escorted by a master-tutor. Leon Battista studied at Padua under Gasparino Barzizza and then at the University of Bologna. As a child, he was apparently particularly attached to his father. In a letter sent from Venice to the boy's father in Genoa, the tutor described how the child wept and refused to fall asleep at night out of anxiety that his father might catch the plague. His luck changed when his father and his uncle died. His cousins took over the family business and were not particularly magnanimous toward their illegitimate cousins. Leon Battista did not attribute their conduct to his illegitimacy but to the lack of consideration of established members of the family toward younger members.[13]

The commencement of apprenticeship usually also entailed leaving home. It appears that only a proportion of those who were trained by merchants and bankers continued to live at home. Bankers and merchants kept several apprentices, and there were usually several firms in the same street which employed apprentices. These constituted (more or less) a peer-group which was also involved in adult activities. The boys also had leisure time for play and various group diversions. In Tuscany these consisted of wrestling, *palio*, fencing, and even playing instruments; in England, wrestling, sailing-contests; and in both places, card-games, dice-games, and tavern-going.

The duration of apprenticeship varied. In Florence it lasted 3–5 years; in London, sometimes even 10 years.[14] In Tuscany boys established their initial contacts in the world of commerce during apprenticeship, and, upon its completion, set out to test their mettle in that world. Giovanni Morelli, in his work of guidance, advised young men of 18 to leave their home towns and start their careers as merchants somewhere else. By so doing, they would acquire experience in trade and learn the laws and customs of other countries, which would prove of advantage to them in their careers. In literature also, the eighteen- to-nineteen-year-old was regarded as capable of conducting business affairs. When Blanquerna reached 18, his father was ready to hand over his business to him after submitting him to a kind of examination. In fact, many young men left home and started out as merchants elsewhere. Some went to towns where they had relatives, who helped them to gain acceptance as junior partners in commercial firms. Gregorio Dati (who was an orphan) served his apprenticeship for only two years and at 15 travelled to Avignon to become a merchant. He was not accepted as a partner in a commercial firm until the age of 23.[15]

As soon as children or youths became apprentices the main task of helping them adjust to their position in life was transferred from their parents to their masters. It was the latter who trained them for their future occupations, and completed the inculcation of the class ethos and values, such as economic success and fair play in financial dealings (in practice, of course, success was sometimes also achieved through deviation from the 'just price' or even through usury); family honour; loyalty to the secular corporation (namely the town), and readiness to fulfil various functions within its framework; piety, which encompassed fidelity to and veneration of the patron saints of the town and the guild; acts of charity and relief; identification with the urban culture and patronage of its creative artists: painters and poets, as well as town historians.

Those Tuscan boys who completed their apprenticeship at an early age enjoyed a large degree of liberty, particularly if they succeeded in business. If they failed, on the other hand, they often required parental assistance. Others were only emancipated at the age of 25, and then too did not always achieve economic independence. In London there were fathers who handed over their affairs to their sons in their lifetime, whereas in Genoa and Florence fathers endeavoured to conduct the family affairs to their dying day.[16] In the sixteenth and seventeenth centuries, paternal legal authority over the property and income of progeny was extended in several European countries (notably in France and England), and, in Protestant countries, even matrimony required parental consent. In the Catholic countries, marriage continued to be considered binding even without parental consent, but the secular governments exerted increasing pressure to disinherit those who got married without the approval of their parents. The impression is, however, that in the Middle Ages as well, and particularly in Italian towns, some fathers were relatively authoritarian, in line with the exhortations of didactic writers. One has only to recall how young town-dwellers who sought to take up the religious life clashed with their fathers (and sometimes their mothers as well) who opposed the scheme. A father in the Perruzi family, whose son defied him, did not refrain from cursing him and expressing the hope that, if he himself did not succeed in his lifetime in punishing his son, the Lord would do so after his death.[17] On the other hand, many young men lost their fathers at an early age and were raised by their mothers, particularly in Tuscan towns (since not all widows remarried). Herlihy believes that these boys were over-pampered (their mothers were consequently reprimanded by the preachers), and that there was often excessive mutual dependence between mother and son. The mothers tried to keep their sons at home as long as possible, this being one of the causes of postponement of marriage.[18] Generally speaking, men in the merchant class in Italian towns married late. Of those who left their home towns to seek their fortune in the world of commerce, some married only after returning home. Others postponed matrimony in their own towns until they were financially established. Since many men were in their thirties when they took wives and fathered children, they often died while at least some of their children were still small. In other European towns, men married earlier. In London, however, for example, apprenticeship in large commercial firms usually lasted from the age of 16 for ten years, and thus apprentices only married in their late twenties or early thirties.[19]

Daughters of prosperous burghers also received education, though limited. Some, as noted, attended mixed elementary schools (Froissart relates how he exchanged nuts, apples, and pears with the little girls at school).[20] As in the nobility, some girls were sent to be educated in convents, although not destined for the religious life, and others were taught by private governesses at home. The barren wife of Francesco Datini took her husband's illegitimate daughter into her home when the child was 6. She raised her with love and took pride in her, as can be ascertained from her letters. The child was given pretty clothes and toys and even had a private governess who taught her to read.[21] Girls learned to read in the vernacular and, more infrequently, to write, learned a little arithmetic and the tenets of religion, prayers, moral conduct, and etiquette. The various categories of higher schools were closed to girls.[22] At 12 or 13, at the latest, their studies ended. With the main exception of girls sent to be educated in convents, girls of this class spent their entire childhood at home, and left only upon marrying. Only rarely were girls from rich urban families sent to other households. Catherine of Bologna (born in 1413), who was the daughter of a jurist in the service of the Duke of Ferrara, was sent at the age of 11, on the request of the Duke, to be raised at his court with his daughter. She had been taught at home, and at court she learned Latin and acquired a wider education than did most girls. Her mother almost certainly came to live there with her.[23]

Little is known of the life of girls at home. It is evident that they were trained neither for a profession nor to fulfil any functions in urban society. As was the case with young noblewomen, their education was intended to foster in them piety, modesty, and obedience, and to prepare them for their roles as wives and mothers. All the discussions in various works of urban didactic literature on the fostering of ideal traits which would help to foster the class ethos relate solely to boys. Those who favoured teaching town-girls to read and write cited, in addition to the reasons mentioned in a previous chapter, the argument that this would enable them some day to correspond with their merchant husbands and sons when the latter were absent on their frequent travels. At home, the girls were instructed by their mothers, who were responsible for their education, in the art of managing a prosperous urban household, weaving, spinning, embroidering, and sewing. According to the didactic writers, at least, they were expected to learn, in addition to all these, how to clean, launder, and bake and cook, particularly as a remedy against that idleness which encourages sin. The mother of a future saint who spent much time in prayer and reading religious works cautioned her that, if she continued to neglect the needle and the loom and did not learn all that a housewife should know, it would be difficult to find her a husband!

Girls also acquired certain skills which were expected of a townsman's daughter, similar to those expected of young noblewomen, since the prosperous burgher class emulated the lifestyle of the nobility. To judge by one of the manuals of guidance, the townswoman had to be skilled in riding, dancing, parlour games, riddles, and story-telling.[24] Girls usually attended organized games and contests in the role of spectators (Froissart describes them also as spectators at private contests conducted by boys).[25] There were, however, popular games in which they took a more active part. An example of this is the game which was popular in Padua, a game of courtship and rites of spring. The young girls of the town gathered in a wood-and-cardboard fortress, and young men from various towns, dressed in the colours of their town, besieged it by throwing flowers.[26] The May Day festival was also attended by small boys and girls, youths and maidens, men and women. It was at one of these May Days that Dante first saw Beatrice.[27] There was also a separate grouping of girls. They strolled together, played various games, and in winter skated together.[28] In Italian towns, girls were apparently more restricted than in towns in north-western Europe. A girl who reached 12 and was not yet married was no longer permitted to walk out alone.[29] Mothers dressed their daughters from childhood in beautiful dresses and curled their hair. Like boys, they were apparently treated by their parents with affection, including physical contact, to judge by the disapproval of preachers. A hagiographer writes that the family of a female saint were in the habit of embracing and kissing their children. The future saint, unlike other children, shrank from contact of a male hand, even that of her father.[30]

It is again reminiscent of the nobility that the childhood of girls of the burgher class was briefer than that of their brothers. There was no intervention in their marriages similar to that of feudal seigneurs in the marriages of heiresses of fiefs, and consequently there were fewer marriages of minors in this class. Attempts (not always successful) to arrange marriages for minors were usually made only when they were orphans whose relatives or guardians were anxious to find them a match.[31] Yet most girls married at a very young age, and marital ties were established by the families out of economic and class interests, and often for political reasons, particularly in Italian towns. For young townswomen from prosperous families, as for the daughters of the nobility, the third stage of life (*adolescentia*) was synonymous with wedlock. In this class, also, marriage was sometimes forced on the young girl. Nor were parents always willing to postpone marriage.[32] In Tuscan towns in the

Late Middle Ages, 13 was considered the ideal age of matrimony for a girl; in Germany, 14. Many girls, in fact, were given in marriage at this age, and the average age of marriage for girls in European towns was 16–17.[33] Those fathers who acknowledged their bastard daughters, or the relatives who undertook to raise them, also arranged their marriages, though they usually had to compromise on the match.[34]

Like their counterparts in the nobility, the daughters of the rich burghers experienced an abrupt and difficult transition from the home of their parents to matrimony (with a considerably older husband). They conceived and gave birth at a very early age, and, although their mothers had instructed them in management of a household, this too was an arduous task for them in the early days of marriage. According to one of the interlocutors in Alberti's book, when his young wife came to his home, he began to instruct her in household management. She told him that her mother had taught her only to sew and to spin and to be chaste and obedient, telling her that she would learn all the rest from her husband. He goes on to describe her longing for her mother and home and her sadness in the first few days.[35] The Goodman of Paris, who wrote a detailed manual of guidance for his wife, who was many years his junior (as was also the custom in Tuscany, he ordered her not to leave home except with an older chaperone known for her sobriety and piety), devotes considerable space to household management.

Children earmarked as artisans or small shopkeepers also sometimes spent a year or two in elementary school. Some were sent there by their parents, regardless of whether they later learned the trade in the family workshop or were sent away to serve as apprentices. In other cases, according to a contract between the craftsman and the father, the boy was sent by his master to school for one or two years during the term of his apprenticeship. Sometimes the price of the schooling was extension of the apprenticeship.[36] However, it is clear that not all children who were designated to become craftsmen and small shopkeepers attended school, not even for one year. According to one of the didactic writers, such boys should not be expected to develop the same degree of physical strength and courage as were future warriors, but all those learning a particular occupation should become accustomed to certain things from an early age. The fisherman should become accustomed to the feel of cold water; the builder, to work in winter as well; and the merchant, to travel from place to place.[37]

Some craftsmen trained their own children. The fact that they were a significant work-force in the family workshop and greatly needed by the parents was the main reason why they were not sent to school (together with the fact that they did not particularly value learning). Examination of a number of apprenticeship contracts in a certain region in relation to the size of the population indicates that not all those designated for craftsmanship served apprenticeships with strangers.[38] The authorities of the various guilds recognized the right of an artisan to teach his occupation to his sons, daughters, wife, and even his wife's children by a previous marriage. Nor were they counted among the quota of apprentices which he was permitted to train.[39] Children who had been orphaned of their fathers and whose mother had remarried were often sent away to serve apprenticeships. Conversely, sometimes the mother's husband or she herself, in the case of a daughter, trained fatherless children. In these cases, the child's guardian signed an apprenticeship contract with the mother and her husband similar to that signed with an unrelated artisan. Occasionally an older brother trained the orphan, and in this case also a contract was signed.[40] Children who learned the trade from their fathers usually acquired it in gradual fashion. When small, they watched their father at work, and sometimes their mother as well, and became familiar with the process of production and the raw materials, and there were no abrupt changes in their process of adjustment. Psychologists hold that, in societies in which there was continuity of pursuit of the same occupation from father to son to grandson, fathers were apparently less afraid of competition on the part of their sons and felt less threatened if their sons outdid them than is the case in modern western society. As for the sons who were ready to continue the trade and way of life of their fathers, the struggle for self-identity was less acute.[41] A wood-carving from early fifteenth-century France shows Joseph teaching the boy Jesus the carpentry trade.[42]

The age at which children began to serve apprenticeships for strangers varied greatly. In some cases, training began at 7 and in others at 20.[43] However, 11–12 seems to have been the norm. The length of the apprenticeship also varied, and there are examples of a two-year term, of fourteen years, and of every duration in between. The length of service was determined by the nature of the trade, since some occupations required lengthier training than others in order to achieve expertise, both according to the policy of the guild regarding the introduction of additional craftsmen into the market, and (perhaps more important) in accordance with the sum which the parent or guardian of the boy paid to the artisan in return for the training. In Étienne Boileau's *Livre des métiers* (Book of Trades), written in Paris in the thirteenth century, for example, the number of years of apprenticeship of a cook was two years; of a silversmith, ten years; and of a maker of coral rosaries, twelve years.[44] In this case, the criterion underlying the guild regulation on the length of apprenticeship is essentially objective – the length of time estimated to be required for gaining expertise in the trade. But this text reflects the policy of the guilds on the rate of introduction of new artisans into the market, based on the demand for their products. It is unlikely, for example, that the making of 'Sarrazinois carpets' required briefer training than the production of coral rosaries. None the less, the apprenticeship for this trade was fixed at only eight years. So much for the statutes. Perusal of apprenticeship contracts reveals clearly that, the more the parents or guardian paid for the training, the shorter the term of apprenticeship. Lengthy apprenticeship placed at the disposal of the artisan the cheap labour of young men who had already attained a high professional standard. For this reason, if a young man sought to shorten the term of apprenticeship, he was obliged to compensate the artisan.[45] The guild authorities, for their part, determined the minimum period at the end of which the apprentice could be released, and prohibited him then from training his own apprentices until the end of the originally specified period of apprenticeship. Certain guilds also prohibited the master from taking on a new apprentice during this period.[46] In any event, although there are examples of very varied terms of apprenticeship, it seems that in England and France seven or eight years was the most common term, among such artisans as glovemakers, tanners, candlemakers, and sometimes also silversmiths, as well as among butchers and big merchants, such as traders in cloth, pepper, wood, and iron.[47] In Tuscan towns, on the other hand, among traders, bankers, and artisans a term of apprenticeship of only three to four years was the norm. A boy did not usually become an apprentice before the age of 11 or 12, and some children continued to live at home while apprenticed.[48] Thus there were boys who completed their apprenticeship at the beginning of the third stage of life, although most appear to have done so at a later age, in the course of the third stage. The exceptions to the rule who began their apprenticeship at the age of 17–20 naturally completed it at a more advanced age.

Apprenticeship contracts were signed between the parents or guardian and the craftsman, subject to the statutes and supervision of the guilds, and with their sanction, and were filed in the guild archives. The apprentice was bound to pay a small fee to the guild and the artisan was responsible for his payment. In some guilds, this sum was earmarked for charitable and relief purposes.[49] The guild also determined the maximum number of apprentices which any one artisan was permitted to train. In most trades this number did not exceed three, and in many guilds he was not allowed to have more than one apprentice. The most common argument cited for this restriction in the number of apprentices was their own good – guaranteeing of proper guidance and training. It is clear, however, that the restriction also stemmed from the guild policy of limiting the number of practitioners of the craft. The statutes of the various guilds also stipulated who was qualified to train an apprentice: an expert craftsman, sufficiently well-established to be able to maintain the apprentice properly, a citizen of the town known to be an honest and decent man. As for the apprentice himself, in some guilds the statutes merely declare that only the son of a freeman can be accepted.[50] They recognize the right of parents to complain about an artisan and even to sue him. Moreover, if the artisan died, it was the task of the guild authorities to transfer the apprentice to another artisan within the same guild.[51] As regards orphans, within the framework of the mutual welfare activities, it was customary in some guilds to subsidize the training of the orphans of guild-members, if they were impecunious. In other guilds, the artisans took on orphans for lower fees than customary, or gratis, and they were not included in the quota of apprentices.[52] There were towns in which the town authorities supervised the binding of orphans as apprentices.[53]

Generally speaking, a child or youth underwent his entire apprenticeship under a single artisan. The guild statutes prohibited artisans from enticing the apprentices of others into their own service, and an artisan could transfer his apprentice to another only if he himself fell severely ill, abandoned his trade, went bankrupt, or went on a pilgrimage. Despite the constantly reiterated prohibitions, however, artisans sometimes transferred or 'sold' their apprentices to others, or enticed boys apprenticed to others to come and be trained by them.[54] From apprenticeship contracts, mostly from the fourteenth and fifteenth centuries, and from the records of the guilds we learn how the craftsman was expected to treat his apprentices and what was demanded of the boys. The craftsman was supposed to be both master and father to the apprentice, to teach him his trade, and to educate him; or, in other words, to be not only a vocational mentor but also a moral authority. He was expected to provide food, lodging, and clothing, and usually also undertook to care for him if he fell sick. Some contracts, however, specified that, if the apprentice became ill, it was the duty of the parents or guardian to cover the cost of medicines, pay the physician's fee, and keep him during his illness. In some cases, the parents also guaranteed to provide his garments.[55] Apprentices usually received only pocket-money and not wages. If the artisan wanted to pay an apprentice who had been working for him for several years, he required the permission of the guild authorities; otherwise he was sued.[56] Repeatedly we find a clause in contracts stating that the artisan must maintain the apprentice in the manner of the son of a respectable man in accordance with his standing. The artisan's status as master and father also gave him the right to demand of the apprentice certain domestic services, to send him to make purchases for him, and even to 'correct' him – that is to say, to beat him if he saw fit. In one case, in which an artisan, who was a carpenter and worker in ebony, was brought to trial before the Châtelet tribunal in Paris, the judges reminded him that he alone had the right to beat his apprentice and that his wife was not authorized to do so.[57] It was with good cause that parents and guardians sometimes took care to include in contracts a clause in which the artisan guaranteed to treat the apprentice 'gently'.[58] The apprentice owed obedience and respect to his master (and to his master's wife), and devotion to the occupation for which he was being trained, as well as to all other chores imposed on him. Didactic writers who listed these duties and exhorted apprentices to observe the prayer times also described (and rebuked) the apprentice who did not hasten to rise from his bed and respond to the call of his master in the morning, lingered needlessly, complained, and gorged himself at breakfast more than he worked.[59]

What about the way of life of these boy apprentices? Since most craftsmen and shopkeepers kept only one apprentice, in contrast to the larger number kept by great merchants and bankers, apprentices did not constitute a single age-group within a workshop or shop. They lived in a family framework, with the craftsman's children, and in the same street there were other boys and youths who were also bound as apprentices. They assisted in the running of the household and were sent to purchase 'bread and wine',[60] particularly in their first years of apprenticeship. They learned their trade gradually and were even sent on business missions. The working-hours were long, (particularly in summer), but there were numerous feast-days which were also holidays from work. The sources do not indicate if children worked shorter hours than adults. The apprentices were learning their future occupation and the craftsmen, like the great merchants, were expected to inculcate in their apprentices the values of their social stratum: pride of workmanship, scrupulous observance of 'just price' and fair competition, and piety and charitable actions within the guild and fraternity. Within the context of the family workshop there was obviously also room for evaluation of character and not merely of achievement, as in the case of children put to work in later centuries in factories. An illustration from the first half of the twelfth century shows a child who is apprenticed to an illuminator, and is totally absorbed in his task – colouring a parchment scroll.[61]

Most dependent on the goodheartedness and goodwill of the craftsman and his wife were small children. They were the most in need of a father- or mother-figure and of empathy, and were the most helpless if treated harshly. This is true despite the fact that parents cannot be said to have abandoned their children to their masters and ceased to take an interest in them. It has been noted already that the guild authorities acknowledged the right of parents to submit a complaint against their child's master. If the craftsman treated a boy or girl cruelly, he was sued by the parents. If he was found guilty, the court permitted the abrogation of the contract and the transfer of the child to another craftsman. The master was sometimes even fined or imprisoned. In one case, a silversmith beat his apprentice with a bunch of keys and caused him head-injuries; a seamstress was charged with not having supplied the needs of the girl who was apprenticed to her, and of having whipped her; another was accused of having jabbed an apprentice's finger with a needle for no good cause.[62] In one instance, the intervention came too late. A small girl apprentice fell ill and died. According to witnesses, she related during her illness that she had fallen ill as a result of savage beating and kicking on the part of the craftsman.[63] This is an extreme example of violence. There is, of course, no way of knowing how many minor acts of abuse occurred which did not end tragically and never reached the knowledge of the courts. A child could be miserable in a strange house even if he were not treated cruelly. The statutes of various guilds contain clauses dealing with the flight of apprentices. The explanation given is the extreme youth and irresponsibility of the apprentices. but there is also clear indication of awareness that the negative attitude of the craftsman toward his apprentices could be a factor in the child's decision to run away. A 'recidivist' apprentice who ran away three times was no longer taken back. However, the guild authorities were charged with the task of clarifying whether his maltreatment by the craftsman had not been responsible. If there were several cases of apprentices who absconded from a single master who treated apprentices improperly, this master was severely rebuked by the guild and the apprentice was transferred to another.[64] Older apprentices were less dependent on the good will and treatment of the craftsmen and could resist them more forcefully even though they were expected to regard the employer as a father and master. A food purveyor in Paris beat his apprentice (who was obviously no longer a small child) with a stick to which keys had been attached. The apprentice was aware of his rights and submitted a complaint against his master. In the end he agreed to a notarized pardon, and the craftsman, in order to placate him, permitted him to travel to Rheims for diversion. The apprentice was not obliged to return.[65]

Needless to say, the conduct of apprentices was not always beyond reproach. Apprentices sent to sell candlesticks did as they were instructed, but then went off to drink and game and gambled away the money they had received. In order to conceal their misdeeds, they continued to sell, but used false weights in order to gain back the money they had lost, and to bring their master the entire sum.[66] Konrad of Megenberg, who, unlike Raymond Lull, does not display great sympathy for youths working in 'mechanical occupations' (*iuvenis mechanicus*), accuses them of being experts in dishonest extraction of money from people during holidays and festivals in order to finance their visits to taverns and brothels and to play dice-games.[67] In the Cook's Tale, from *The Canterbury Tales*, one of the characters is the apprentice of a food purveyor, who is handsome and dances well, 'that haunteth dys, riot or paramour'. He is castigated and punished: 'And somtyme lad in the revel to Newgate'. Eventually, his master, on discovering that he has also emptied the cash-till, casts him out with imprecations and curses.[68] Chaucer does not specify how the apprentice was punished when he reached Newgate jail. However, there is a case on record of the apprentice of a cloth merchant in one of the large commercial companies who was ceremonially flogged in the company hall by masked men for committing a lascivious act with a maidservant.[69]

Naturally, not all such cases came to court, but it is also clear that one cannot rely on court records alone in attempting to arrive at an accurate picture of the life of a child or boy apprentice in the craftsman's home. There were certainly often not only good master–apprentice relations but ties of affection and loyalty. The fact that craftsmen often remembered apprentices in their wills is proof of this. Some not only waived the years of service which the apprentice still owed (had they not done so, the apprentice would have been forced to pay monetary compensation to the craftsman's heirs) but even bequeathed to them the income from a house, money, or utensils, or a certain sum to cover the cost of their studies.[70] Some craftsmen even named apprentices among the executors of their will.[71] A former apprentice, who felt guilty for having been negligent during his apprenticeship, left his former master a sum of money in his will to compensate for his conduct.[72] Another man apparently had such good memories of his term of apprenticeship that he bequeathed a considerable sum (100 pounds) to the Carthusian Order to conduct masses for the soul of his former master.[73]

The question asked about sons of noblemen sent to be trained for knighthood in the courts of other seigneurs is also valid for children bound as apprentices to strangers. Why did their parents send them away? For the children of fathers who were not themselves established craftsmen, apprenticeship with the master of a more respectable craft than their own was not only a way of acquiring a skill but also a means of advancement. Small artisans, with limited means of production at their disposal, and with a large number of children, could not always train all of them adequately. And, here as in other social strata, it was apparently believed that strangers could better raise a child than parents, particularly during adolescence, which is a period destined to be fraught with tension and parent–child clashes. According to Paolo of Certaldo:

> If you have a son who does nothing good, so you believe, in his present place, deliver him at once into the hands of a merchant who will send him to another country. Or send him yourself to one of your close friends ... Nothing else can be done. While he remains with you, he will not mend his ways.[74]

In any event, parents who sent their children to craftsmen, like parents who sent them to great commercial companies and to banks, did so in order to guarantee their future and not merely in order for them to help support the family at that stage of their lives, and were ready to invest the necessary sum to this end. Paolo of Certaldo, at least, considers sending a child away from home as a last educational resort.

Descriptions in medieval sources of the games (both innocent and wild) of children and youths do not always make it clear if these were schoolchildren, children who worked in a family workshop, or apprentices to craftsmen. It is reasonable to assume that some refer to apprentices (with the exception of the sports mentioned above, which were mostly performed by the upper strata, who tried thereby to emulate the lifestyle of the nobility). The company of children at play described by Froissart is based both on age-group and common schooling, but also on neighbourhood. Boys often played by rivers and lakes, bathing in their waters and fishing (as can be learned from, amongst other things, the accidents which occurred on these occasions).[75] In the streets of towns, children felt completely free, or else would not have permitted themselves unbridled conduct. In 1385 the Bishop of London excommunicated boys who were 'good for nothing in their insolence and idleness, instigated by evil minds and busying themselves rather in doing harm than good', for shooting arrows and throwing stones at pigeons, ravens, and other birds nesting in the walls of St Paul's cathedral, playing ball in the gateway of the church and within its portals, and causing heavy damage to the stained glass, the pictures, and statues.[76] Nor was there a dearth of the petty torment which often characterizes boyish behaviour. A boy tied a string to the foot of a bird, freed it a little, and, as soon as the bird tried to fly, pulled on the string.[77] Anselm of Canterbury disapproved of this cruel and popular game. A future saint, who was born in Whitby and whose parents were of Scandinavian extraction, was named Tostig. The other boys often teased him and mocked him because of his foreign name.[78] His parents, who wanted to help him, changed his name to William! A group of boys tormented a poor and ugly workman, who was known for his piety but was the butt of the boys' mockery.[79] Since such actions were part of street life, depictions in art of Christ's entry into Jerusalem include children playing various tricks among themselves or tormenting the donkey he is riding.[80] The adult population of towns in general was not marked by delicate or merciful conduct. Cruel executions were carried out in public and were a source of sadistic pleasure and emotional release for the spectators who flocked to see them. It is unlikely that children were barred from these public executions. At the opposite extreme, children marched in religious processions together with the adults, and took part in the construction of a church when religious fervour gripped the population of the town and they carried out the work *en masse*.[81] Together with adults, children also watched more innocent spectacles, such as performances by jesters and bear-tamers, and came to hear the wandering minstrels who reached the town. In some of the roistering and bullying one can discern a certain hostility toward the adult world, but essentially, since they were not distanced from the adults, they never created defensive measures with any specific content.

Like the sons of the rich, the urban middle class did not marry young. Apprentices were prohibited, almost without exception, from marrying during their apprenticeship.[82] Nor could journeymen takes wives before they had established themselves financially. (In the fourteenth century it was extremely difficult for hired labourers who were not sons of guild members to gain acceptance to guilds and establish themselves.) Some, particularly the sons of the rich, probably enjoyed their protracted bachelorhood; others were bachelors by force of circumstance. Both categories belonged to the 'youth groups' of the Late Middle Ages, and it was against them that the bulk of the preachers' remonstrations were directed.

In the labouring class, not only was there greater equality between men and women (even though, in this class as well, authority was vested in the man in the family and in society), but the upbringing which girls received was closer to that of boys than in the more prosperous classes. Like their brothers, most girls were taught a trade and began to work at an early age, being considered a significant work-force. There appear to have been three main differences between the upbringing of girls and boys: a smaller proportion of girls were sent to school; a smaller proportion of girls was trained by craftsmen or craftswomen (and a larger number of girls learned their trade in the family workshops); and the variety of trades open to girls was more limited, particularly if their parents wanted them to be instructed by a craftsman or -woman.

One can find examples of daughters of craftsmen who were sent to school by their parents or guardians (like the orphan daughter of a candlemaker in London in 1390 whose guardian paid her tuition-fees at elementary school from the age of 8 to 13, or St Colette, who was the daughter of a carpenter in Corbie and attended one of the lower schools in her town).[83] In so far as we know, however, there are no examples of apprenticeship contracts in which craftsmen or -women guaranteed to provide schooling for the girl they trained, as was the case with boys. Those girls who received schooling were the daughters of established craftsmen. Some of them studied before being bound as apprentices, but most, apparently, did so before or simultaneously with their informal vocational training in the family workshop, since fewer girls than boys were bound as apprentices away from home. Michaud-Frejaville, who examined 276 apprenticeship contracts in the Orleans region between 1380 and 1450 found that 89.3 per cent of them referred to boys. It will be recalled that a craftsman was authorized to train his own sons and daughters, and most daughters who learned a trade were apparently taught in the family workshop. The lives of those girls who served apprenticeships[84] did not differ from those of boys, apart perhaps from the fact that, even if they were no longer small children but adolescent girls, it was harder for them to face a cruel master. It may be no accident that, in the case mentioned above of a cruel flogging which had fatal consequences, the victim was a girl. It was also harder for a girl to run away and hide on her own. It is clear, at the same time, that parents took an interest in daughters who served as apprentices. They sued craftsmen and women who behaved cruelly, or attempted to exploit girls for prostitution, and even in cases where inadequate training was given. (The craftswoman was accused of not having honoured her obligation and not having taught the girl either because she had no work or because of negligence.)[85] The giving in apprenticeship of orphan girls was supervised like that of orphaned boys.[86]

There was one final difference: although women played a considerable role in urban production, and were employed in a wide spectrum of occupations, including some which, today, are not considered female occupations (and a small proportion even became independent craftswomen), they were restricted by the guilds. Not all trades were open to them. They sometimes learned, in the family workshop, a craft in which female employment was limited by the guild authorities, but they could not become apprentices in that craft outside the home. The restrictions stemmed both from the protectionist policy of the guilds and from the status and image of women in medieval society in general, which enabled the guilds to limit and restrict the economic activity of women, who constituted a large marginal group within the urban labouring class.

Girls who learned their trade in the family workshop, like the daughters of the prosperous burghers, spent their childhood and girlhood at home, and were apparently given in marriage slightly later, often to someone in their father's trade, who may even have been his apprentice. It was the obligation of the guilds to collect a dowry to be given to a secular bridegroom or a convent for the orphan daughters of a guild-member or the daughter of a member who was unable to raise the money by his own efforts.[87] Collecting a dowry for a poor girl was one of the forms of charity in the Middle Ages.

Least is known about the lives of the many children in the lowest stratum or urban society – that of the skilled and, even more so, the unskilled wage-earners. When children from this class were sent to serve in strange households, then (as in the case of foundlings) this was usually done not in order to train them for a trade and educate them, but in order for them to earn their own living out of economic necessity. According to the 1427 census-book of Florence (*Catasto*), of all those reported to be servants or dependent in some other way on heads of households, 41.5 per cent of the males and 34.2 per cent of the females were children and adolescents aged 8–17. Some were orphans, some foundlings placed by foundlings' homes, and others had been placed by their parents. Among the children, there were more girls than boys (137, against 79). Some of the girls worked a number of years (varying according to the age of commencement and the wage, which was fixed on the basis of the supply and demand for workers), saved enough for a dowry, and then married.[88] Others remained in service all their lives and never married. In other European towns as well, girls who became servants went into service at an early age.[89] In fifteen out of seventeen contracts drawn up in Barcelona in the fifteenth century between the parents or guardians of girls placed as maidservants and the future employer, reference is to girls under 13. Two of them were 6 years old.[90] Some were daughters of town-dwellers, others had migrated or been sent from villages. The Goodman of Paris writes in his manual about the frivolousness and inexperience of 15-year-old servant-girls. In his words of guidance to his young wife, he instructs her in how to select a servant-girl and how to oversee her, and warns her to beware of both the impudent girl and the flatterer, but to treat the obedient and shy girl as a daughter.[91] Sibyllina of Pavia, who was eventually canonized, began to work for her living, apparently as a servant-girl, after being orphaned at the age of 10. When she was 12 she began to lose her sight and could no longer go on working. She was taken in by the women of the Dominican Third Order.[92] Zita of Lucca, a village girl, who was also to be canonized, became a servant-girl at 12 and served in the same household until her death. She became the patron saint of servant-girls.[93]

12   Education in the peasantry

As noted in a previous chapter, few peasant children received any education. Among those few who received tuition from the village priest at a school run by a monastic house, or at a secular school in the nearby town, the great majority became clerks or monks.[1] A tiny minority of peasants who remained laymen were literate, and it was from their ranks that the scribes of the manorial courts and other functionaries of manors were recruited, as well as the few who served the feudal seigneurs or the central authorities. Some members of the upper classes explicitly expressed their objections to the education of the sons of serfs.[2] Among peasant girls, to the best of our knowledge, not even a minority received any kind of instruction. In short, there were no educational institutions for the children of the peasantry. Their parents, the village community, and the village priest were responsible, both directly and obliquely, for their adaptation to a life in society. Children were involved in adult society, observed adults at work and from a very early age began to help them. They witnessed their dealings with elements outside the village community such as the representatives of the different authorities or town merchants; heard stories and folk-songs and took part in religious and popular festivals (which were often interrelated). With their parents, they listened to the wandering minstrels who sometimes visited their villages and more frequently performed in the nearby market towns, and they also attended church. The cultural traditions, moral injunctions, and rules of conduct, deviation from which was considered disgraceful by the community consensus, were transmitted to them orally. Since there were neither schools nor institutionalized apprenticeship for training these children, the village society of children existed only for purposes of communal play. But, despite the lack of institutions of education and of institutionalized training methods, childhood was unquestionably perceived by peasant society also as a distinct stage in human life. Society did not make the same demands of children as it did of adults, and the tasks and responsibility demanded of them were exacted gradually. In this context it should be recalled that a certain preacher wrote about the peasants who dressed their children 'in many-coloured shirts' in childhood, and in adulthood 'set them behind the plough'.[3] They did not usually begin to plough until the third stage of life, but (despite the preacher's words) they undoubtedly began to help adults in their work many years before they reached adulthood. The way in which children were introduced to agricultural toil illustrates the awareness of the need to impose tasks on children only gradually.

As is the case in every agricultural society, children, from a very early age, saw their parents at work at home or even in the field. At the age of about 7, they began to run errands, to bring food to the field-labourers, and to tend the geese or even the cow or a small number of pigs or sheep belonging to the family. When they were a little older, they began to feed the horses, draw water, weed, remove stones, pick vegetables, help bind the sheaves after the harvest, help in the sowing, separate wheat from chaff, help in thatching, and goad the ploughing beasts and guide them. They acquired their various skills in the course of work beside adults and under their guidance. The family hierarchy was not such that each child was dependent on an older sibling who was made responsible for him (as was the case in Samoa, according to Margaret Mead), but the task of guarding younger brothers and sisters was sometimes allotted to older children. Child-labour is mentioned in the Lives of the few saints who were of peasant extraction, and particularly in the case of miracles entailing the 'revival' of children and the healing of children injured in accidents; and also in the coroners' inquest rolls in England. The victims include both older children injured at work, and toddlers whose older siblings did not take good care of them (as mentioned in a previous chapter). Mention is sometimes made of the age of the small boy or girl who was sent out to tend the flock, to pick vegetables, or to carry out some errand: a boy of 7, a boy of 8, a girl of $12\frac{1}{2}$. Sometimes it is merely noted that they were a *puer* or *puella*.[4] In one case, the author writes that, while the child's companions were absorbed in their game, he was sent by his mother to tend several lambs.[5] According to Vasari, at least, Cimabue discovered the child Giotto while travelling from Florence to Vespignano. Giotto had gone out to the field to herd several sheep, and while they were grazing he 'was drawing one of them by scratching with a slightly pointed stone on a smooth clean piece of rock'.[6] He was then 10 years old. In another description, when the author writes of a seven-year-old girl who went out to tend the sheep on the orders of her mother, he adds that she was still fragile and weak.[7] He apparently adds this comment because of his particular sympathy for a child who was to become a saint. However, despite the fact that the tasks allotted to children were usually adapted to their age, a task was sometimes beyond their strength. A ten-year-old boy, sent by his father to bring hay for the horses, climbed a ladder in order to bring down the heavy load of hay and, staggering under the weight, fell with both ladder and load.[8] A ten-year-old girl was sent to draw water from a water-hole, and filled her utensil, but it was too heavy for her and, in trying to lift it, she fell into the hole.[9] On the other hand, there were easy and pleasant tasks. Children were sent to pick wild fruit, to gather berries, to bring peat, to gather firewood, and to fish; in rural areas close to the sea, they also collected shellfish. Some of these tasks, which helped to feed the family, were undoubtedly pleasant. Whether peasant children had toys is unknown. We know only that they played group games outdoors or played with natural materials and objects. Among other things, they chased floating feathers or scattered the geese and ducks, as can be learned from accidents which occurred in the course of these diversions. When the boys grew older, they began to practise wielding the staff in mock battles and archery.[10]

At a very early age boys and girls carried out identical tasks. Gradually, the girls began to concentrate more on female work (such as spinning, weaving, and cooking), while the older boys began to plough, to reap, and to work at building. But, since the women assisted with most of the field-work, in addition to working in the home and the household farm (by cleaning, cooking, drawing water, stoking the fire, bringing grain to be milled at the nearest mill, cheesemaking, tending the household animals, working in the vegetable garden, and in some areas even brewing ale),[11] there was no clear, unequivocal division of labour between boys and girls. Joan of Arc attested at her trial that she had worked in her parents' household, spinning and sewing in exemplary fashion, and could compete in these skills with any woman in Rouen. This was confirmed twenty years later by the men and women of her village to the inquisitors who came to re-examine her case. They added that she had sometimes also gone out with her father to plough and had taken the animals out to graze at the foot of the fortress for fear of the soldiers in the vicinity. These remarks were intended to convey the fact that Joan's tasks did not differ from those of other respectable village girls.[12] Girls usually worked more with their mothers and other women, while boys worked with their fathers and the other village males. In the course of these joint labours, and in the conversations conducted as they worked, the cultural traditions were transmitted from father to son and from mother to daughter.

Whereas the chore of 'small grazing' – of several geese, a few lambs or sheep, a cow or a horse – was allotted to both boys and girls, the 'large grazing', which entailed roaming greater distances, called for relatively pro-tracted vocational training, and was an exclusively male province. (Joan of Arc did not remain in the field with the grazing beasts, but merely took them there.) A description of the stages of training for a shepherd in the second half of the fourteenth century in France appears in Jean de Brie's Good Shepherd. At the age of 7 he was sent to tend the geese and to protect them against the magpies, the crows, and the birds of prey. At 8 he was sent to herd the swine – 'coarse and undisciplined beasts'. The year in which he was a swineherd lingered in his memory as a difficult and unhappy time. At 9 he began to help in the ploughing, and might never have returned to herding had he not been injured by a horse. When he recovered, he was given ten cows to herd. He was injured again and, upon recovery, refused to continue with this work. He was apparently afraid. This seems to be an additional example of imposition of a chore and responsibility on a child which was beyond his limited strength. At the age of 11 he was given 80 'tender and good' lambs which had never harmed any person. He loved them, guarded them, and tended them devotedly: he fed them, cropped their wool, anointed them, and let their blood when necessary, and protected them against wolves. At 12 he knew all that a shepherd should know apart from assistance at lambing. In the final stage, 120 sheep and 200 ewes were given into his care. He was then 14 and considered a complete shepherd.[13] In the Haute Ariège, children who were to become shepherds were sent to work with veteran shepherds to learn their occupation. They too were given responsibilities at the age of 12, but were not yet considered skilled shepherds who could work independently.

Additional evidence of contemporary awareness that a child could not undertake the same tasks as an adult peasant or undertake full responsibility, and required the guidance of an adult, can be found in the custody agreements drawn up in the various manorial courts in England. The lord of the manor wanted to ensure proper cultivation of the land inherited by the minor boy or girl, and fulfilment of the labour services on the demesne. For this reason he entrusted the land and the custody over the minor to an adult who could carry out these duties. Generally speaking, if the father died, the mother acted as guardian. Only in those cases in which she herself was incapable of cultivating the land or of overseeing the management of the property of her minor son or daughter and carrying out the necessary services for the lord of the manor was custody over the land and the person of the child entrusted to one of the local peasants. If the mother died, the father fulfilled this role; if the child lost both parents (as was frequently the case in the plague of 1348 and other epidemics which followed), one of the relatives acted as guardian. If the minor child had no relatives, the lord of the manor appointed a guardian or else one was selected by the rural community. The lord of the manor did not intervene in these arrangements unless the orphan boy or girl was an heir. But even children orphaned of both parents who had inherited nothing were usually taken in by relatives: older brothers and sisters, grandparents or uncles and aunts.[14] A particularly harsh fate must have awaited those who had neither relatives nor property. They were dependent on the mercies of the village community. An extreme case of neglect of two orphan girls in a village in the Abruzzi region is cited in the biography of Peter Morrone, who became Pope Celestine v. They were so badly neglected that they resembled children found after having grown up in the forest without human company.

They could neither walk nor talk. 'Good women' (*bonae mulieres*) appealed to the saint and, according to the author, because of the miracle he wrought, they began to walk and talk and eventually became 'comely and good women'. They may have been taken in by a community of religious women or a family and, since they were still small (their age is not mentioned), they began to develop as a result of proper nurturing.[15]

The inheritance rights of illegitimate offspring in peasant society varied from region to region, as was the case in other strata of society as well. Fathers invested different degrees of effort in making sure that their bastard children had a share in their property. However, if the illegitimate child of a peasant woman or girl survived, his childhood, at least, did not differ from that of the other village children. It was usually the poorest among the village girls who bore children outside wedlock. Some of them raised their children by themselves. Others married, but were forced to content themselves with a husband from among the poorest wretches of the village. Thus their children lived like other children in the poorer stratum of the community. Those whose fathers were prosperous and acknowledged them lived more like the children of the richer class.[16]

Many peasants needed their offspring as a labour-force on their farms, and, in regions where the manor had a demesne, in order to fulfil the labour services for the lord of the manor. Whether the land was an allod (which was already rare in the Central Middle Ages, and existed in only a few regions), or was leased from the lord of the manor, the augmenting of the work-force, even if the new workers were still of tender age, enabled those who had the means to purchase additional land for cultivation. In the village of Montaillou, in a poor region in the Pyrenees, even in the period preceding the plague (which left land ownerless), to have numerous progeny was considered a blessing, a source of strength and riches in the rural community.[17] But, as mentioned in a previous chapter, families could not be planned in the Middle Ages. The mortality rate was very high, but death did not take an equal toll of the various families. Parents could not predict how many of their children would remain alive. Just as sterility or the death of most of the offspring might curtail the economic potential of a peasant couple, so an excessive number of children was also a financial burden. Some families could not supply employment for all their children on the farm. Those children whose parents could not employ them on the holding became wage-earners in childhood, or servants of the lord of the manor or of prosperous peasants or of urban families, or were bound as apprentices to craftsmen in the village or in the nearest town. The same was true of orphans who did not inherit. An article in statute issued in England in 1388 states that boys or girls under the age of 12 working regularly as carters or at the plough (goading and guiding the beasts), or in any other agricultural labour, should continue this work even after reaching 12, 'and should not be put to a trade or craft'.[18] This meant that not only were they hired out as labourers before the age of 12, but that, from that age, they were included in the category of adult workers to whom the statute applied. Those who worked for peasants in their parents' village or for the lord of their parents' manor appear to have continued to live at home. Some were hired out as part-time labourers and worked part-time in the family holding.[19] Others were hired only for the height of the agricultural season.[20] In Germany, in the region between Upper Swabia and Vorarlberg, children from the age of 8 upward were sent to work in farms which suffered from a lack of manpower from the beginning of the spring season until the end of autumn. Their parents travelled with them to the Ravensburg fair and there arranged for them to hire themselves out to peasants.[21] Other children worked either as agricultural labourers or as servantmen and women outside their villages on a regular basis. In any event, peasant children were not sent away from home because it was customary to have them educated in the households of others. They were sent neither to be educated nor to acquire a profession which would advance their careers, but solely out of economic necessity – when the family had more working hands and hungry mouths than it needed or could feed.

At the beginning of the third stage of life – at 14 – peasant children completed their training. The connection between their childhood experience and their training for their adult roles was totally direct. They were trained in gradual informal fashion without acute transitions or a stage of sharp separation between the sexes, and without rites of passage. They grew up in a mixed society of men and women, boys and girls. The education of the girls and their way of life at 7–14 differed only slightly from those of boys and were closer to those of their brothers than in other social classes. Like the daughters of the urban labouring class, peasant girls were raised to be not only wives, mothers, and housewives, but also workers, who might play a role in the outside world. The function of the peasant woman in agricultural labour, first as helper to her father and then side by side with her husband, was significant and vital, and widows even managed farms. Women in peasant society were full partners in the function of their class – namely, work on the land.

Although boys were considered at 14 to be a skilled work-force, in every sense of the word, they were not recognized everywhere as adults according to customary law. In certain regions $14\frac{1}{2}$ or 15 was the age of adulthood. The orphan could then free himself of guardianship, take over the land he had inherited, and even sell it, if he so chose. In other regions, boys reached their majority at 20 or 21. The age of maturity for girls was low. In some English manors a girl was considered adult at $13\frac{1}{2}$.[22] But, as in other strata, maturity in the peasantry did not necessarily coincide with economic independence. The age at which this was achieved varied according to the structure of the peasant family, which itself varied from region to region and according to the family's financial situation (more prosperous peasants could help their sons to purchase property or could allot them part of the family plot). The demographic conditions of time and place (after the 1348 plague it was doubtless easier to acquire land), and the time of the parents' death or their willingness to hand over their property in their lifetime were also important.

As in other classes, the daughters of the peasantry married younger than the sons, irrespective of whether they were heiresses or were only allotted a dowry. According to the Halesowen rolls, in the period before the plague peasant girls married at 18–22.[23] The daughters of the rich, whose parents could supply a dowry, married earlier than the daughters of the poor. Among the very poorest stratum, the girls married late or not at all.[24] Most of the girls who migrated from their villages to work as servant-girls in towns or as hired farm-labourers or servants of prosperous peasants or of the lord of the manor came from this stratum. Some went into service or worked for wages until they had accumulated a sufficient sum for a dowry and could marry.[25] However, they were the most exposed to sexual relations outside wedlock and the most likely to give birth to bastards. After the 1348 plague there was a steep decline in the number of bastards. The population dwindled, land was left ownerless, and those who survived found it relatively easy to hand out land to a son in order to enable him to marry and set up his own family, or to provide a dowry for a daughter.[26] In Halesowen, men too married young, but were often 2–4 years older than their wives. In Montaillou at the end of the thirteenth century and the beginning of the fourteenth – that is to say, before the plague – although this was a poor mountainous area, girls still married very young. There are recorded cases of girls who married at 14, 15, 17, 18. Men took wives at about 20–25.[27] In the rural area around Pisa in the first quarter of the fifteenth century, the average age of matrimony of girls was 17.3; of men 26.3–27.1.[28] Like the members of other strata of society, peasants too were aware of the need for financial resources in order to set up a family, but many were content with little, and matrimony provided the peasant with a helpmate – a wife who added to the labour force and helped in his financial consolidation.

The fact that girls married young limited their experience of the mixed society of young, single people – *adolescenti* and *adolescentiae* – with its own special entertainments, such as dancing in the church square, dancing, singing, and games on May Day and on nocturnal festivities. On the evening of the first Sunday of Lent the Brandon dance took place in some villages in Europe. This was a nocturnal festival in which men and women, particularly the unmarried boys and girls of the villages, went out with lighted candles to the vineyards and the pastures, danced, sang liturgical songs, and recited incantations against the various pests which harmed trees. In France they also lit bonfires and, when the fire died down, young people and children would leap over the coals and embers.[29] Village girls, like girls in town, promenaded together.[30] In Domremy both small boys and girls and young men and women went out to the 'ladies' tree' or 'fairies' tree', a beech tree known for its great beauty, length of branches, and width of bough. They hung garlands of flowers on the tree and sang and danced around it. Special healing powers were attributed to the adjacent fountain, and several folk-beliefs were focused on the tree, which the villagers believed to be the dwelling-place of fairies.[31]

The religious education which peasant children received from their parents and from the village priest was limited. Joan of Arc, whose family was not among the poor families of the village and whose father held various public positions, said that she had acquired all her faith from her mother alone, who also taught her the three most important prayers.[32] A particularly pious girl of $12\frac{1}{2}$ in the village of Cubas near Madrid in the first half of the fifteenth century knew the Ave Maria, the Paternoster, and two other prayers. A father from the same village attested that his nine-year-old son knew the Ave Maria and the Paternoster and that he and the boy's mother made sure that he recited them.[33] However, as will be recalled, didactic writers believed that children should know these prayers in the first stage of childhood, while in the second stage they should expand their knowledge of the basic tenets of faith and its injunctions. According to one didactic writer, peasant children did not even have the opportunity to hear sermons frequently. In discussing the second stage of life, he recommends to peasants that they take their children with them to town on feast-days, both in order that they should not, like oxen, be totally ignorant of town customs, and so that they should hear sermons, which would enhance their religious piety.[34] Peasants were often censured for failing to rest from their labours on Sundays and for not attending church. They not only sometimes expressed derisive criticism of the clergy, and hostility towards an exploitative church which impoverished the peasants by extracting a tithe from all crops and flocks, but sometimes even pronounced heresy. Not only religious officiants but even the greatest mystery of ritual and faith – the Eucharist – was sometimes the object of mockery. A group of young men at work brandished a piece of turnip in imitation of the priest raising aloft the Host.[35] At the same time, religiosity existed among the peasants and religious problems preoccupied them, as can also be clearly seen from the testimony of the peasants of Montaillou. Religious faith could take the form of orthodoxy – but orthodoxy mingled with a lot of pre-Christian popular beliefs – or heresy. Affiliation to one of the heretic movements (and peasants did not only join the Cathars) was the expression of a search for significant religious life and satisfaction of religious emotions no less than of protest against the character and path of the Catholic clergy and the general social order of which it was part. Sometimes extreme piety already found an outlet in childhood, as in the case of the twelve-year-old girl from the village near Madrid who first went to confession at 6 and received the sacrament of the Eucharist at 9; or one of the few saints from the peasantry, Gemma Solomona. It is difficult to know if this piety was essentially the outcome of internalization of the religious education which these girls received from their parents or was inspired by some other influence, such as the ritual in church or the sermon of the priest or an itinerant preacher. In any event, Catharism usually passed down the family from fathers and mothers to sons and daughters (not only in Montaillou),[36] bearing witness to the acceptance of parental values by children. Vivid expression of the power of religious faith to motivate the children of peasants and shepherds can be found in the Children's Crusade. In 1212 two groups of children, boys and girls, set out, one from Rhineland and the other from northern France, headed by two charismatic leaders, Nicholas and Stephen, themselves still children, in order to conquer the Holy Land and redeem the Holy Sepulchre. Most of the them were the offspring of peasants and shepherds, and they were apparently joined by several children from elementary schools in towns. Impelled by the vision of redemption of the Holy Sepulchre and certainly also by psychological factors and hopes of release from their plight, they flocked after their leaders. Although various villagers and townspeople gave them food and water on their way, by the time they reached the port towns of Marseille, Pisa, and Brindisi, their ranks had dwindled. Some died *en route*, others stayed behind in the towns they passed, and a few made their way back home. The sea, which had been supposed to open up before them, did not do so, and they were unable to pass over on dry land. Shipowners offered to transport them, and those who reached the ports boarded the ships. Some of them drowned at sea, and the rest were sold into slavery in the Islamic countries. In Germany, the parents of these children accused the father of Nicholas (who did not return) of having, in his pride and craving for honour, encouraged his son in his folly. He was convicted and executed by hanging. For years before the tragic crusade of children set out on its journey, Christians had been exhorted repeatedly to redeem the Holy Sepulchre, and the children had heard the call as well. The leaders claimed to have been chosen by God to head the mission in which adults had failed and which children would carry out. The episode was born out of anarchic fervour and apocalyptic tension, and ended in catastrophe. The adult reaction to the crusade was not unanimous. Most churchmen were hostile towards it and considered it a folly from the outset. There were, however, some clergymen who gave the children their blessing. According to the chroniclers, many laypeople expressed their sympathy, extolling the power of childish innocence, as expressed in the song of the German leader of the crusade: 'Nicholas servant of Christ is going to the Holy Land, with the innocents will he enter Jerusalem.' After the débâcle, there were those who claimed that the whole event had been a devilish scheme. Others dwelt on the image of the innocent and pure child who, even if lacking in reason (and lack of reason, it will be recalled, was one of the components of the child's image), is meek in spirit and elect. The children, and in particular their leaders, apparently internalized this image fostered by adults. Upon their death, the church authorities adopted the stand that they were 'new Innocents'. On the initiative of Pope Gregory ix a 'church of the innocents' was erected in their memory on the island of San Pietro near Sardinia.[37]

The great majority of children in medieval Western Europe were born into the peasantry. However, there are no extant written descriptions of relations between a specific peasant couple and their seven- to fourteen-year-old children. In the testimony which peasants gave before the tribunal of Jacques Fournier reference is made mainly to the ailments of infants and toddlers and reactions to their death; some testimony casts light on the relations of parents and older children. The records of manorial courts in England provide details of some cases in which parents clashed with their offspring over a legacy, of other (more frequent) cases in which the asset was handed over to the heir or heiress when they reached their majority without dispute, or of cases in which parents in their lifetime transferred their holding to a son or daughter – but these also deal only with progeny over the age of 14. For our enlightenment there are few extant literary descriptions of parent–child relations in the peasantry, or surmises by authors who were not themselves of peasant birth regarding the treatment of peasant children by their parents. These few assessments and descriptions in no way suggest that the authors believed that peasants did not value their children, were not concerned for them, or did not love them. In essence, the contrary is true.

According to Étienne Fougères, who depicted children not only as a source of suffering and anxiety but also as a cause for sin, peasants cheated and evaded payment of the tithe in order to feed their children and supply all their needs.[38] William Langland writes of the efforts of poor peasants to support their children. Wolfram of Eschenbach describes an avaricious man 'of the sort that still spring from base birth, a fisherman who lacked all kindliness', and puts in his mouth the following sentence: 'I don't care about anybody but myself and after that about my children.'[39] The implication of this sentence is that even the 'base' fisherman, focused on his own ego, includes his children within it. According to the twelfth-century William Map, whereas the nobility are too arrogant or slothful to concern themselves with the education of their children, the villeins make every effort to send their progeny, 'who are degenerated and corrupt', to study the liberal arts, whose very name indicates that only free people were intended to study them. They do so, not so that through education the children 'will cast off the evil qualities but in order for them to accumulate wealth'.[40] Acquisition of education by the sons of villeins was rare. Walter Map's remarks, reflecting his revulsion from this social stratum, point to the existence of the exception to the rule – the willingness of certain parents to purchase the liberation of their children, to forgo their labour, and to enable them to attend school.

In Hartmann von Aue's poem, *Der Arme Heinrich* (Poor Henry), there appears an eight-year-old peasant girl, ready to sacrifice her life to find a cure for the lord of the manor, who is afflicted with leprosy. Her relations with her parents, at the foot of whose bed she sleeps, are described as naïve and loving. When they learn of her wish, they weep and wail, and only when they realize that her resolve is firm, and after she asks their forgiveness and expresses her love and gratitude for all they have done for her, do they agree that she may depart; but they themselves remain, seeming like those under sentence of death, wrapped in their mourning and grief, having lost the taste for life.[41] Their acquiescence is the natural outcome of the content and moral of the poem – the power of sacrifice and of the internal changes in the soul. The child's readiness to sacrifice herself transforms the leper knight and thus brings about his miraculous cure. The poem on the peasant Helmbrecht by Wernher 'the Gardener' also describes devoted and loving parents, but their son is rebellious, spurns the class into which he was born, and (despite all his parents' attempts at dissuasion) becomes a robber in the company of robber-knights. He is eventually caught, his eyes are gouged out, and one of his hands and one of his feet are lopped off on the order of the lord's bailiff. Blind and amputated, he is brought to his parents' home, where his father refuses to take him in, and cries to the boy who has led him there 'Take this horror away from me,' and to his son 'Betake yourself, you faithless boor, in greatest haste forth from my door; your suffering is nothing to me.' 'Yet the mother,' writes the author, 'who was not as hard as he, passed out – as to a child – a crust.'[42] The poem expresses the contemporary view as to the different treatment of children by father and mother in all strata of society: the mother is tender and forgiving; the father, who represents law and authority, is harsher, and it is he who must instruct his son to act according to the customary norms which are the practical translation of society's values. If the son deviates completely from these norms, he cannot forgive him. These images of the mother and father, which also reflect expectations, lingered on in western culture.

There is no room for idealization in assessing relations between parents and children in peasant society. The lives of peasants were hard, and there were wretched people among them. And the wretched are not necessarily tender and affectionate towards those close to them. Violence existed among the peasantry, as it did in other medieval social strata. The verse 'He who spares the rod spoils the child,' with all it implied, was familiar to peasants. Yet, as in every other society, parents undoubtedly differed in their treatment of their children. In general, it can be said that, taking into consideration the constraints and values of their environment, peasants made a material and emotional investment in their children.

It has been mentioned, in the context of those children taught a trade in family workshops, that some psychologists believe that the identification of son with father was easier and more natural in civilizations which changed at a gradual and slow pace and in which there was continuity of pursuit of a particular occupation and way of life from father to son and grandson than in societies marked by hectic and rapid change.[43] The slow and continual flow from generation to generation characterized peasant society even more than it did the life of urban craftsmen. The great majority of peasant children continued the way of life of their fathers, some even in the same rural community, in a society in which social mobility was restricted (if it existed at all, it was generally within the framework of the same stratum – the peasantry), in a world in which individualism had not yet become the ideal. A fourteenth-century author, John Bromyard, whose criticism of the nobility's custom of sending children to be raised by strangers was mentioned in a previous chapter, expressed a view comparable to that of the psychologists. Comparing the upbringing of the children of the nobility and those of the 'poor and simple' (i.e. mainly of the peasantry), he states that the latter, whose fathers raised and educated them, supplied them with food and clothing, and taught them to work, did not despise these fathers when the latter reached old age.[44] In reality, there were peasants who did not respect their obligations towards their aged parents and even abused them.[45] At the opposite extreme to Bromyard's description was the version of King Lear popular among the peasantry. The interesting point in Bromyard's remarks is that they constitute a positive perception of the relations of parents and their offspring in the peasantry – a stratum which was not only rarely praised or cited as an example for other classes, but was also frequently censured in a spirit of arrogance and contempt not only by town-dwellers and nobles (the pastoral genre came to the fore only at the end of the Middle Ages), but also sometimes by the minor clergy. Discussing the proper social order, churchmen emphasized the importance of the role of peasants – the feet of the social body, but conversely denounced them for ignorance, lack of religious piety, and avarice. Even the statements by Walter Map and Étienne Fougères, which reflect acknowledgement of the peasants' concern for supporting their children when young or assisting their advancement through education, appear in the context of criticism and contempt. The unique nature of Bromyard's remarks lies in their sincerity, and in the obvious sympathy for peasant ways in the upbringing of children.

Appendix

As the reader will already have noted, no attempt has been made in this book to describe medieval childhood according to the Freudian pattern of development or any other psychological theory. It was only in order to clarify the psychological significance of certain phenomena in childraising and education in the Middle Ages that I cited the interpretations of various psychologists regarding parallel phenomena in contemporary society or other societies. Hence, the following remarks belong in an appendix.

If some psychologists dispute the claim that the oedipal stage is an inevitable stage in the development of every child in contemporary western society, then it goes without saying that certain psychologists, historians, and anthropologists doubt that Freud's oedipal construction as an emotional constellation is universal, transhistorical, and transcultural.[1] There is no way of proving (even if this is a valid fact) that all people in all periods in all cultures have experienced the same interpsychic conflict – the tensions and unconscious desires which characterize the oedipal conflict.

I do not presume to attempt to refute or confirm the validity of the oedipal construction with regard to the medieval family. It is, however, interesting to point out more and less overt manifestations of oedipal tension in the literature of the nobility and in the folk-tales of the Middle Ages, and, simultaneously, to indicate expressions of the unconscious hostility of fathers towards sons – modifications of the Persian tale of Rustam and Sohrab, which also became a *topos*, in which a father slays his son on the battlefield. Sometimes this story and the story of Oedipus blend together and are two faces of the same occurrence and an expression of mutual unconscious emotions. (And here one should recall the problem of continuity which Freud noted, the fact that every father is also a son, and that his attitude toward his own son gives expression to his own childhood conflicts.) Sometimes the story is blunt and direct, and sometimes it undergoes refining and softening. The hostility of the offspring is sometimes expressed through projecting it on to the parent. We have already noted the fact that in the literature of the nobility, there are many fatherless protagonists (Raoul de Cambrai, Tristan, Parzival, Lancelot). On the psychological plane, this motif can be regarded as an expression of unconscious desire for the death of the father.

The story of Gregory, containing a double act of incest, has been mentioned in a previous chapter. There is no doubt that in the twelfth century people in general, and noblemen in particular, were highly concerned, if not obsessed, with the problem of incest. It was difficult for them, and contrary to their familial interest, to observe the church prohibition of marriage between persons related up to the seventh degree. However, the legend of Gregory, like other incest tales, might also reflect the oedipal tension. In all the legends incest is presented as a grave sin to which only atonement through extreme penance can bring pardon.[2]

Le Roman de Thèbes is a work composed by a clerk of Poitou in the twelfth century. Written in French, it is based on the *Thebaid* by the first-century Roman poet Statius. But, whereas the Roman epic is dedicated mainly to the wars of the sons of Oedipus, the medieval author elaborates on the story of Oedipus himself. To this end, he drew from the mythographers of the Middle Ages, from the volume known as *Mythographus Secundus*. In feudal garb, colour, and context, the author relates the tale of Oedipus and his sons. Laius is informed that a son will be born to him who will one day kill him. Immediately after the birth of the infant, he gives orders to have him taken to the forest and killed there despite the tears and pleas of the mother. When the weeping mother falls asleep, the slaves take the infant and bring it to the forest. Their compassion is roused and they abandon him in a tree without killing him, and he is found by King Polybus who raises him as his own son. When he reaches young manhood, his companions in the palace are envious of him and the servants remind him that he is a foundling and call him 'the son of the whore'. He asks Apollo at Delphi about his origin and is told that he will find a man whom he will kill, and thus he will come to know his father. Laius comes to visit the palace of King Polybus on a feast-day. When a dispute breaks out among the young men, which develops into a violent clash, the seigneurs intervene and Oedipus kills his father, Laius. He leaves the palace of his adoptive father, arrives at the gates of Thebes, solves the Sphinx's riddle, and enters the city. He admits to the queen that he has killed Laius, but, at the request of the barons, she weds him. Twenty years later, Oedipus discovers the truth and, as a result, puts out his eyes. His sons grind his eyes with their heels, and he curses them. The deed of the sons is a symbolic re-enactment of their father's deed – parricide. But, whereas Oedipus kills his father unknowingly, his sons commit the act deliberately. The author goes on to describe the wars of the sons, and incorporates protagonists and sub-plots which also contain parricide and murder of sons, bitter fraternal inheritance disputes (in contrast to true friendship between young men who are not brothers), where the younger brothers are motivated by jealousy of the heir and of those who have taken wives who brought them a fief. The poem is marked by fantasies of horror, and expressions of protest against the feudal world order: patrilinearity, primogeniture, and the harshness and tyranny of the father. The author's moral is that deeds which are against nature and should not be committed bring down inevitable ruin on the land, which becomes a wilderness.[3]

The ancient German ballad 'Hildebrands Lied' (The Song of Hildebrand) is reminiscent of the Persian ballad of Rustam and Sohrab, which expressed the father's unconscious hostility towards his son, his envy and fear of him. A father and son, who have not seen one another for many years, meet on the battlefield and prepare for a combat. The father recognizes that the young man he is about to fight is his son, makes himself known, and offers him his love and his money. The son refuses to believe that this man is his father – an expression of his unconscious hostility – and the father's honour obliges him to fight his son. That fragment of the poem which has survived ends with a mutual brandishing of swords and the first attack. From the way the facts are presented, it appears that the father is going to prevail, and knowingly to kill his son.[4]

Expression of unconscious hostility towards the mother, which is manifested in projection, can be found in a work by a woman – Marie de France's *Fresne* (The Ash Tree). It will be recalled that the woman gives birth to twin girls, and, in order to preserve her honour, asks that one of them be killed. It is only under the influence of the women in the birth-chamber that she agrees not to kill the infant but only to abandon her. In due course, when the daughter, Fresne, now a young girl, comes to her parents' house and her mother realizes who she is, she reveals the truth to the father, who had known nothing of her birth and abandonment, and asks his forgiveness.[5]

The motif of the meeting between father and son who do not recognize one another recurs in medieval literature, but with a significant change. In all works with the exception of *Hildebrand*, including those in which the oedipal tension is manifest, things end well, on both the physical and the psychological plane. In the ballad of *Sir Degar*, an infant, who is the fruit of rape and incest, is abandoned in the forest. He survives, however, and at the age of 10 goes out to seek his parents, equipped with his father's sword, whose point is broken, and his mother's glove. When the time comes, he identifies his father and mother by means of these items, and refrains from committing a twofold sin – killing his father and marrying his mother. In Marie de France's *Milun*, the illegitimate son is sent immediately after birth to his mother's sister. Years later, father and son meet at Mont St Michel at a tournament (and not at a battle in which each side a priori attempts to kill the other). The son wins and unhorses Milun. When he glimpses through his father's helmet his grey hair and beard, he realizes that he has vanquished an elderly man. In a chivalric gesture, he seizes the reins of his father's horse and offers it to him. This gesture reveals the ring on his finger, which was given to him by his mother when he was sent away as an infant. Father and son recognize one another. Before their encounter, the son had planned to seek out his father and to discover how he had treated his mother. In the end, the father weds the mother and the son 'gives his mother to his father' in marriage.[6] In the poem *Doon*, whose author is unknown, the father abandons the mother several days after their nuptials and he too leaves a ring to be given to the child she bears. Years later, father and son meet under the same circumstances as Milun and his son, and a similar story unfolds. The son 'led his mother to his father, whom she loved and for whom she yearned'.[7] The son extricates himself from the oedipal situation! The motif of the encounter on the battlefield between father and son who do not recognize one another also appears in the Lives of the saints. Peter Armengol, scion of the family of the counts of Urgel in Catalonia, joined a gang of robbers while a very young man. In 1285, when the King of Aragon was about to pass through the robbers' region, Peter's father was sent at the head of a troop of warriors to guard the area. Father and son were about to fight one another. At the last minute the son recognized his father, fell at his feet, offered him his sword and his body, and begged forgiveness. This encounter was the critical turning-point in his life. Shocked at the fact that he had been about to kill his own father, he undergoes a conversion and joins the Mercedian order.[8] In folk-tales as well, all ends well. A son who has reached adulthood seeks above all to kill his father, who has done him no harm. They go out together to the desert and the father proposes that the son kill him there lest their shame be revealed to all. On hearing this, the son breaks down, throws down his sword, kneels before his father, and asks his pardon.[9]

The tale of the meeting of father and son in battle or tournament appears to have been a *topos* in medieval literature. Curtius distinguished between *topoi* which are essentially literary clichés and those which are almost universal and an expression of the collective subconscious – archetypal in the Jungian sense. He also notes that a new ethos generates new *topoi*. Observation of the appearance of these in a certain culture can indicate psychological changes there.[9] The motif of Rustam and Sohrab, like the motif of Oedipus, is archetypal. The changes which occurred gradually in them in medieval literature do in fact point to changes in ethos, but it is less clear whether they indicate psychological change. It seems that the gap between the original archetype and Christian moral norms was too great and gradually led to a change of motif. Sometimes the change is so significant that we are faced not with yet another archetypal *topos* but with a mere literary cliché. This is so in those works in which the two who meet one another are no longer father and son but relatives, or friends who have been separated for many years. In other works, as we have seen, the motif, though refined and softened, still preserves its original psychological significance. Archetypal *topoi* tend to endure, but they are not eternal. The constancy of their repetition in a certain culture indicates psychological verity. Probably, both literature and folk-tales add slight weight to the view that oedipal tensions existed in medieval society.

Notes

PREFACE

1 S. Shahar, *The Fourth Estate: A History of Women in the Middle Ages* (London, 1983), pp. 98–106, 138–45, 183–9, 230–6, 50–2, 154–61, 214–16.
2 Ph. Ariès, *L'Enfant et la vie familiale sous l'ancien régime* (Paris, 1960); English edn, *Centuries of Childhood* (New York, 1962).
3 S. Shahar, op. cit., pp. 232–6, 188–9.

INTRODUCTION

1 Ph. Ariès, *L'Enfant et la vie familiale sous l'ancien régime* (Paris, 1960).
2 J. Kagan, 'Overview Perspectives on Human Infancy', in *Handbook of Infant Development*, ed. J. D. Osofsky (New York, 1985), p. 9.
3 K. Ruschky, *Schwarze Pädagogik* (Berlin, 1977). A précis of sources, with elucidation of their psychological significance for the child, is given in A. Miller, *For Your Own Good*, trans. H. and H. Hannum (London, 1983), pp. 3–4.
4 G. Barraclough, 'What is to be Done about Medieval History', *New York Review of Books*, 14/11 (June, 1970), p. 51
5 Amongst others: L. Stone, *The Family, Sex and Marriage in England, 1500–1800* (London, 1977) – Stone argues that the change for the better in attitudes to children occurred not in the seventeenth century, as Ariès claimed, but in the second half of the eighteenth century, and that there was a period of regression in the nineteenth century, although less violent methods of imposing authority and breaking the will of children and young people were employed then than prior to the eighteenth century; E. Shorter, *The Making of the Modern Family* (London, 1976) – Shorter believes that the change occurred in the sixteenth century; E. Badinter, *L'Amour en plus* (Paris, 1980) – this survey covers the seventeenth–twentieth centuries. She rejects the existence of the maternal instinct, and she claims that only at the end of the eighteenth century did maternal feeling become a supreme value, while the change for the better did not actually occur until the second half of the nineteenth century; L. deMause, 'The Evolution of Childhood', in *The History of Childhood*, ed. L. deMause (London, 1976) – deMause perceives the period from the fourth century to the thirteenth as that of the 'Abandonment Mode', and the fourteenth to seventeenth centuries as the era of the 'Ambivalent Mode'.

6 Amongst others: A. Macfarlane, *The Family Life of Ralph Josselin* (Cambridge, 1970); the book is based on the journal of a seventeenth-century clergyman. A full bibliography and critique of historical literature on the annals of childhood in western society from the fifteenth century onward can be found in L. A. Pollock, *The Forgotten Children: Parent–Child Relations from 1500–1900* (Cambridge, 1983); the book aims at refuting the theories of Ariès and his 'pessimistic' followers.

7 U. T. Holmes, 'Medieval Children', *Journal of Social History*, 2 (1968–9), pp. 164–72; M. Mclaughlin, 'Survivors and Surrogates: Children and Parents from the Ninth to the Thirteenth Centuries', in *The History of Childhood*, ed. L. deMause (London, 1976), pp. 101–82; I. H. Forsyth, 'Children in Early Medieval Art: Ninth through Twelfth Centuries', *Journal of Psychohistory*, 4 (1976–7), pp. 31–70; L. Demaitre, 'The Idea of Childhood and Childcare in Medical Writings of the Middle Ages', ibid. pp. 461–90; B. Hanawalt, 'Child Rearing among the Lower Classes of Late Medieval England', *Journal of Interdisciplinary History*, 8 (1977), pp. 1–22; ead., *The Ties that Bound: Peasant Families in Medieval England* (Oxford, 1986), pp. 156–87; E. Clark, 'The Custody of Children in English Manor Courts', *Law and History Review*, 3 (1985), pp. 1–11; S. Wilson, 'The Myth of Motherhood a Myth: The Historical View of European Child-Rearing', *Social History*, 9/2 (1984), pp. 181–98 – this illuminating article is a critique of Ariès and his school of thought as regards both the Middle Ages and later periods. I also make use of the following books and articles, amongst others: D. Alexandre-Bidon and M. Closson, *L'Enfant à l'ombre des cathédrales* (Lyons, 1985); *Annales de démographie historique* (1973); *L'Enfant au Moyen Age: Littérature et civilisation* (Senefiance, 9; Paris, 1980); N. Orme, *From Childhood to Chivalry: The Education of the English Kings and Aristocracy, 1066–1530* (London, 1984). I also consulted E. Arnold (ed. and trans.), *Kind und Gesellschaft in Mittelalter und Renaissance* (Munich, 1980), a compilation of translated sources. John Boswell's book, *The Kindness of Strangers: the Abandonment of Children in Western Europe from Late Antiquity to the Renaissance* (New York, 1988) appeared when this book was already in press. I have thus been unable to integrate its thought-provoking ideas and findings into this book

8 Pollock, op. cit., bases herself mainly on the journals of adults and children. The former write about their own childhoods and also about their children.

9 A. E. Auerbach, *Mimesis: The Representation of Reality in Western Literature* (New York, 1957), chs 5–10.

10 R. Kuhn, *Corruption in Paradise: The Child in Western Literature* (London, 1982).

11 S. Wilson, op. cit., p. 198.

1   THE ATTITUDE TO PROCREATION AND THE IMAGE OF THE CHILD IN MEDIEVAL CULTURE

1 Abelard, Sermo 33 (*De Sancto Joanne Baptista*), PL vol. 178, col. 582.

2 Bernard of Cluny, *De Contemptu Mundi*, ed. H. C. Hoskier (London, 1929), bk 2.

3 *Analecta Bollandiana*, 64 (1946), p. 15.

4 M. Bogin (ed. and trans.), *The Women Troubadours* (London, 1976), p. 144; the lack of mention of children is striking, for example, in the treatise known as *Le Ménagier de Paris*, ed. J. Pichon (Paris, 1846).

5 J. Ulrich, 'La Riote du monde', *Zeitschrift für Romanische Philologie*, 7 (1884), pp. 282–3.

6 Cited by J. Huizinga, *The Waning of the Middle Ages* (New York, 1954), p. 35.

7 Abelard, *Historia Calamitatum*, ed. J. Monfrin (Paris, 1962), p. 76; on the sufferings and tribulations of raising children, see also *Les Quinze Joyes de mariage*, ed. J. Rychner (Paris, 1963); *Proverbes français antérieurs au XVᵉ siècle*, ed. J. Morawski (Paris, 1925), p. 3; *Le Livre des proverbes français*, ed. Le Roux de Lincy (Slatkine repr.; Geneva, 1968), vol. I, p. 218.

8 Humbert de Romans, *De Eruditione Praedicatorum* (Barcelona, 1607), p. 274; quotation from Étienne Fougères, *Le Livre de manières*, in Ch. V. Langlois, *La Vie en France au Moyen Age* (Paris, 1926), vol. II, pp. 23–4; Berthold of Regensburg, *Vollständige Ausgabe seinen Predigten*, ed. F. Pfeiffer (Vienna, 1862), vol. I, p. 104; *Anecdotes historique, légendes et apologues tirés du recueil inédit d'Étienne de Bourbon*, ed. A. Lecoy de la Marche (Paris, 1877), p. 349.

9 This text was originally written in French in the thirteenth century and was translated in the fifteenth and sixteenth centuries into several European languages. The English translation is *The History of Kyng Boccus and Sydracke*, by Hugo Caumpeden (London, 1530), q. 220; on additional translations, see K. Arnold, *Kind und Gesellschaft in Mittelalter und Renaissance* (Munich, 1980), pp. 127–8.

10 *Acta Sanctorum*, ed. J. Bollandus and G. Henschenius (Paris–Rome, 1863–1940), Feb. 3, pp. 307–8; see also Luke 14: 26.

11 *Analecta Bollandiana*, 64 (1946), p. 15.

12 'Infanticide', *Dictionnaire du théologie catholique*, ed. A. Vacant and E. Mangenot (Paris, 1910), vol. 8, cols 1717–26; J. T. Noonan, *The Morality of Abortion: Legal and Historical Perspectives* (Cambridge, Mass., 1971), pp. 1–42.

13 On the postponement of the outlawry of women in Icelandic law, see H. Jacobsen, 'Pregnancy and Childbirth in the Medieval North: A Topology of Sources and Preliminary Study', *Scandinavian Journal of History*, 9 (1984), p. 100 and n. 30; on postponement of the execution of pregnant women, see R. W. Bosch, 'La Femme dans les Bays-Bas septentrionaux', in *Recueils de la Société Jean Bodin*, 12/2 (Brussels, 1962), p. 343; B. A. Hanawalt, 'The Female Felon in 14th Century England', in *Women in Medieval Society*, ed. S. Mosher-Stuard (University Park, Penn., 1976), p. 136; see, for example, *Acta Sanctorum*, Apr. 1, p. 292; G. Brucker (ed. and trans.), *The Society of Renaissance Florence: A Documentary Study* (New York, 1971) p. 167.

14 'Lectus benedictio', 'Lectulus benedictio', Abbé V. Leroquais, *Les Pontificaux Manuscrits des bibliothèques publiques de France* (Paris, 1937), vol. I, p. 167; vol. II, p. 162.

15 Alvarus Pelagius, *De Planctu Ecclesiae* (Venice, 1560), bk. II, p. 84; Konrad of Megenberg, *Ökonomik*, ed. S. Krüger (Stuttgart, 1973; MGH Staatsschriften, 111/5), bk. I/2, ch. 2, pp. 67–9. See also: J. T. Noonan, *Contraception: A History of its Treatment by the Catholic Theologians and Canonists* (Cambridge, Mass., 1965), ch. 5, pp. 212–35.

16 Thomas Aquinas, *Summa Theologiae* (London, 1966–74), Prima Secundae, q. 94, art. 2 (vol. 28, pp. 80–2); and see also Secunda Secundae, q. 152, art. 2, (vol. 43, p. 74); Aegidius Romanus, *De Regimine Principum* (Venice, 1505), bk. 2, pt. 1, ch. 7.

17 *Speculum Laicorum*, ed. J. Welter (Paris, 1914), pp. 86–7.

18 Marie de France, *Lais*, ed. A. Ewert (Oxford, 1965), pp. 35–48; Geoffrey Chaucer, *The Canterbury Tales*, ed. W. W. Skeat (Oxford, 1947), The Clerk's Tale, pp. 355–6.

19 Philip of Novare, *Les Quatre Ages de l'homme*, ed. M. de Fréville (Paris, 1888), pp. 46–7.

20 *Dives et Pauper*, ed. P. H. Barnum (EETS; London, 1976), vol. I, p. 328.
21 Bartholomaeus Anglicus, *Liber de Proprietatibus Rerum* (Strasburg, 1505), bk 6, ch. 14 (= *On the Properties of Things: John Trevisa's Translation of Bartholomaeus Anglicus* (Oxford, 1975), p. 309).
22 Thomas Chobham, *Summa Confessorum*, ed. F. Broomfield (Paris–Louvain, 1963), p. 464.
23 M. Belmont, 'Levana ou comment "elever" les enfants', *Annales ESC*, 28 (1973), pp. 77–89.
24 *Acta Sanctorum*, Apr. 1, p. 483; July 1, p. 455; Apr. 2, p. 142; Mar. 2, p. 181; *Analecta Bollandiana*, 14 (1895), p. 175; *PL*, vol. 185, col. 227.
25 Thomas Aquinas, *Summa Theologiae*, Secunda Secundae, q. 189, art. 6 (vol. 47, p. 250), and see also J. Boswell, '*Expositio* and *Oblatio*: The Abandonment of Children and the Ancient and Medieval Family', *American Historical Review*, 89 (1984), p. 22, n. 29.
26 D. Herlihy, *Medieval Households* (London, 1985), pp. 117, 127–9; for an example of the husband cited as protector of his wife – the mother of his children – see Bartholomaeus Anglicus, op. cit., bk 6, ch. 15.
27 *Sancti Augustini Confessionum Libri XIII* ed. L. Verheijen (Corpus Christianorum Series Latina; Turnhout, 1981), vol. 27, p. 6; *Sancti Augustini de Civitate Dei* (Corpus Christianorum, Series Latina; Turnhout, 1955), vol. 48, bk 22, ch. 24.
28 Innocentius III, *De Contemptu Mundi*, *PL* vol. 200, cols 703–7; Bernard Gordon, the author of the medical and didactic work, *De Conservatione Vitae Humanae* (Leipzig, 1570), wrote in similar, but more moderate, vein (see pp. 7–10); see also G. R. Owst, *Literature and Pulpit in Medieval England* (Oxford, 1961), pp. 533–4.
29 Aristotle, *Nicomachean Ethics*, in *The Basic Works of Aristotle*, ed. R. McKeon (New York, 1968), bk 3, ch. 2, pp. 967–8, and ch. 11, pp. 983–4. Writing in the Aristotelian spirit in the twelfth century, William of Conches (in an essay falsely attributed to Honorius) claimed that, in the early childhood years, the human creature lacks logic and reason, which are among the best qualities of the human soul: 'Honorius Augustodunens', *De Philosophia Mundi*, *PL* vol. 172, bk 6, ch. 18, col. 91; see also Bernard Gordon, op. cit., pp. 1–3; Vincent of Beauvais, *Speculum Quadruplex: Speculum Naturale* (Douai, 1624), cols 2350–1.
30 *Acta Sanctorum*, Apr. 3, p. 870; and see also Mar. 3, p. 506; Mar. 2, pp. 36, 471; *Analecta Bollandiana*, 9 (1890), p. 283; on the childhood of St Nicholas, see *Mirk's Festial: A Collection of Homilies*, ed. T. Erbe (EETS; London, 1905), p. 12.
31 E. R. Curtius, *European Literature and the Latin Middle Ages*, trans. W. R. Trask (New York, 1952), pp. 98–105.
32 Hildegard of Bingen, *Causae et Curae*, ed. P. Kaiser (Leipzig, 1903), p. 45; Thomas Aquinas, *In Quattuor Libros Sententiarum Magistri Petri Lombardi* (Parma, 1856), vol. 2, 20, q. 2, pp. 464–5; Aegidius Romanus, *De Regimine Principum*, bk 2, pt 2, ch. 7, 14; ' cum paululum de septennio exierunt, tunc amplius se commaculant pravis operibus, quia plus noverunt cogitare de malo', *Acta Sanctorum*, June 4, p. 525.
33 On the sins of young boys, see *The Life of Ailred of Rievaulx by Walter Daniel*, ed. and trans. M. Powicke (Nelson; London, 1950), pp. 2, 17; Vincent of Beauvaus, *De Eruditione Filiorum Nobiliorum*, ed. A. Steiner (Medieval Academy of America, 32; Cambridge, Mass., 1938), pp. 6, 7, 134; *Acta Sanctorum*, May 4, p. 617; Jan. 1, p. 553; *Analecta Bollandiana*, 30 (1912), p. 55; Philip of Novare, op. cit., p. 102.
34 *De Civitate Dei*, vol. 2, bk 22, ch. 22, p. 844; *Confessiones*, pp. 8–9.
35 See also Matt. 11: 25, 'At that time Jesus answered and said, I thank thee, O Father, Lord of heaven and earth, because thou hast hid these things from the

wise and prudent and hast revealed them unto babes'; Matt. 19: 14, 'But Jesus said, Suffer little children and forbid them not to come unto me: for of such is the kingdom of heaven'; Ps. 8: 2, 'Out of the mouths of babes and sucklings hast thou ordained strength.'

36 Bartholomaeus Anglicus, *Liber de Proprietatibus Rerum*, bk 6, ch. 5 (= *John Trevisa's Translation*, pp. 300–1).

37 John Bromyard, *Summa Praedicantium* (Antwerp, 1614), p. 5.

38 'male talis innocentia perditur et ad seniorem aetatem provehitur.' *Acta Sanctorum*, Sept. 3, p. 645; see also Hildegard of Bingen, *Liber Divinorum Simplicis Hominis*, PL vol. 189, cols 836–7.

39 *Acta Sanctorum*, Mar. 3, p. 193; Feb. 1, p. 260.

40 ibid., Jan. 1, p. 639.

41 ibid., Mar. 1, pp. 553, 574; *Magna Vita Sancti Hugonis*, ed. and trans. D. Douie and Dom. H. Farmer (Nelson Series; London, 1961), vol. I, p. 129; *Mirk's Festial*, pp. 11–12.

42 Mentioned in the letter of an abbot from Normandy in the early twelfth century; and quoted in G. G. Coulton, *Life in the Middle Ages* (Cambridge, 1967), pt 2, p. 21.

43 Quoted ibid., p. 26; G. R. Owst, op. cit., p. 34.

44 Descriptions of the child as one who does not hold a grudge, is never angry for long, says what he thinks, and is free of the temptations of the flesh can be found in writings of St Columba as early as the seventh century, and elsewhere. See P. Riché, *Education et culture dans l'Occident barbare, VIᵉ, VIIIᵉ siécles* (Paris, 1962), p. 505.

45 Bernard of Clairvaux, *In Conversione S. Pauli Sermo II*, PL vol. 183, col. 365; Jean Gerson, *De Parvulis ad Christum Trahendis*, in *Œuvres complètes*, ed. Mgr P. Glorieux, vol. 9 (Paris, 1973), p. 669. See also pp. 670–1.

46 *Inter alia*: *Acta Sanctorum*, Mar. 2, p. 57; *Das Leben des Seligen Heinrich Seuse* (Düsseldorf, 1966), p. 75; *Mirk's Festial*, pp. 21–5. The vision of the Holy Mother and Child seen by the Franciscan friar, Salimba, in a dream after the rift with his father was a confirmation of his decision to enter a monastic order: Salimbene de Adam, *Chronica*, ed. G. Scalia (Bari, 1966), p. 56.

47 *Acta Sanctorum*, Apr. 2, p. 168.

48 W. A. Christian, *Apparitions in Late Medieval and Renaissance Spain* (Princeton, 1981), pp. 116–25; *Jacobi De Voragine Legenda Aurea*, ed. T. Grässe (Leipzig, 1850), ch. 131, p. 588.

49 Berthold of Regensburg, op. cit., vol. I, pp. 411–12, 480; vol. II, p. 139.

50 Aegidius Romanus, *De Regimine Principum*, bk 1, pt 4, chs 1–4.

51 See I. H. Forsyth, 'Children in Early Medieval Art: Ninth through Twelfth Centuries', *Journal of Psychohistory*, 4 (1976–7), pp. 56–7.

52 *Das Leben des Seligen Heinrich Seuse*, p. 67.

53 *Mirk's Festial*, pp. 29, 35, 36; *The Chester Plays*, ed. H. Deimling (EETS; London, 1893), pt 1, pp. 186–205; on the 'Slaughter of the Innocents' in art, see F. Bonney, 'Enfance divine et enfance humaine', in *L'Enfant au Moyen Age: Littérature et civilisation* (Senefiance, 9; Paris, 1980), pp. 9–23. For an example of a sermon on this subject, see F. Berier, 'L'Humaniste, le prêtre et l'enfant mort: Le Sermon de Sanctis Innocentibus de Nicolas de Clamanges', ibid., pp. 125–38.

54 Cited in K. Fowler, *The Hundred Years War* (London, 1971), p. 22.

55 L. Demaitre, 'The Idea of Childhood and Childcare in Medical Writings of the Middle Ages', *Journal of Psychohistory*, 4 (1977), p. 481 and nn. 114–15.

56 Aristotle, *Nicomachean Ethics*, bk 10, ch. 9, p. 1110.

57 Guillaume de Lorris et Jean de Meun, *Le Roman de la Rose*, ed. F. Lecoy (Paris, 1968), vol. I, pp. 39–40, ll. 1259–76.
58 D. Buschinger, 'L'Enfant dans les romans de Tristan en France et en Allemagne', in *L'Enfant au Moyen Age: Littérature et civilisation* (Senefiance, 9; Paris, 1980), pp. 262–5.
59 *English Gilds*, ed. T. Smith (EETS; London, 1870), p. 30; on the place of children in religious processions in fifteenth-century Spain, see W. A. Christian, op. cit., pp. 217–18.
60 'Felix etiam ignorantia parvulorum quia dum impassibilitatis moenibis circumdatur, angelica securitate laetatur', Gilbert of Nogent, *Tractatus de Incarnatione contra Judaeos*, PL vol. 156, col. 497.
61 John Bromyard, op. cit., p. 338.
62 See R. Kuhn, *Corruption in Paradise: The Child in Western Literature* (London, 1982), ch. 3.
63 Dante, *The Divine Comedy*, trans. L. Binyon (New York, 1947), Paradise, Canto 27, p. 511.
64 See on this M. Fishbein and I. Ajzen, *Belief, Attitude, Intention and Behavior* (Reading, Mass., 1975), ch. 1, pp. 1–18; ch. 7, pp. 288–330.

2   STAGES IN CHILDHOOD

1 Jean Piaget, *Six Psychological Studies* (New York, 1967), pp. 5–6.
2 E. Erikson, 'Eight Stages of Man', in *Childhood and Society* (New York, 1963).
3 The authors of manuals for preachers who devoted separate sermons to men and women and to the different classes also wrote separate sermons for boys, young men, and even for small children. Some of the remarks in these sermons are directed at parents rather than the children themselves. Humbert de Romans, for example, devotes a sermon to the second stage of childhood (*Sermo LXXXVII Ad Pueros*); a sermon to all pupils (*Sermo LXII Ad Omnes Scholares*), and separate sermons to small children in song school (*Sermo LXIV Ad Scholares de Cantu*) and older children in grammar school (*Sermo LXIII Ad Scholares in Grammatica ... Qui pro Magna Parte Sunt Pueri*); as well as to students of the various faculties (*Sermones LXV–LXX*); see *De Eruditione Praedicatorum* (Barcelona, 1607), pp. 86–7; and see also R. Fluck, 'Guillaume de Tournai et son traité *De Modo Docendi Pueros*', *Revue des sciences religieuses*, 27 (1953), particularly pp. 349–56.

Ratherius of Verona in the tenth century already devoted separate chapters to small children (*De Parvulis*), boys (*De Pueris*), and adolescents (*De Adolescentibus*); see *Praeloquiorum Libri Sex*, PL vol. 136, cols 203–10; under the influence of Greek and Roman tradition early medieval authors also distinguished these three stages in childhood, echoing Gregory the Great (540–604) and Isidore of Seville (560–636), whose writings were an authoritative source for scholars in the following centuries. See on this J. de Ghellinck, 'Juventus, gravitas, senectus', in *Studia Medievalia in Honour of R. J. Martin* (Bruges, 1948), pp. 39–59; P. Riché, L'Enfant dans le Haut Moyen Age', *Annales de démographie historique* (1973), p. 95.

There are examples from the Central Middle Ages: Aldebrandin of Siena in the thirteenth century initially distinguished four stages in human life: (1) *adolescentia* – from birth to 25 or 30, at this age a man is hot and moist; (2) *juventus* – to 40 or 45, hot and dry; (3) *senectus* – to 60, cold and dry; (4) *senium* – to death, cold and moist. But he goes on to add that it is possible to distinguish seven stages through dividing *adolescentia* into four sub-periods: (1) from birth to the appearance of teeth – approximately at the age of 2 – *infantia*; (2) from the appearance of teeth to the age of 7 – *dentium plantativa*; (3) *pueritia* – from 7 to 14; (4) *adolescentia*. See *Le Régime du corps de Maître Aldebrandin de Sienne*, ed. L. Landouzy and R. Pépin (Paris, 1911), p. 79. Aegidius Romanus devotes a chapter to the education of children from birth to 7; a second chapter to the ages 7–14, and a third chapter to ages 14 upwards. See Aegidius Romanus, *De Regimine Principum* (Venice, 1505), bk 2, pt 2, chs 15–17. Bernard Gordon also dates the ends of periods at 7 and 14 (see L. E. Demaitre, *Doctor Bernard de Gordon: Professor and Practitioner* (Toronto, 1980), p. 12 and n. 55); in another work he distinguishes sub-stages at 4 and 12 – *De Conservatione Vitae Humanae* (Leipzig, 1570), pp. 2, 29.

On the evolvement of synonyms for describing small children (male and female) and young boys and girls, and the various words for different stages of childhood in English and Romance languages, see Hilding Back, *The Synonyms for 'Child', 'Boy', 'Girl' in Old English* (Lund, 1934); I. Pauli, *'Enfant', 'garçon', 'fille' dans les langues romanes: Essai de lexicologie comparé* (Lund, 1919), pp. vii–xvi; and see also W. A. Christian, *Apparitions in Late Medieval and Renaissance Spain* (Princeton, 1981), pp. 216–17.

4 *Acta Sanctorum*, ed. J. Bollandus and G. Henschenius (Paris–Rome, 1863–1940), Mar 1, pp. 289–90; see also Apr. 2, p. 159.

5 'ad metas adolescentiae perduxisset postquam, igitur metas pueritiae excessisset', *Acta Sanctorum*, Mar. 1, p. 290; 'deinde intervallo temporis exacto, cum iam inter pueritiam adolescentiam eaque medius esset', *Acta Sanctorum*, Feb. 3, p. 109; and see also *The Life of St Anselm, Archbishop of Canterbury by Eadmer*, ed. R. Southern (Nelson Series; London, 1962), p. 39.

6 *Acta Sanctorum*, Apr. 2, p. 803; Francesco Datini mentions the proverb in his letter to his wife (see I. Origo, *The Merchant of Prato* (London, 1957), p. 163).

7 R. Trexler, *Public Life in Renaissance Florence* (New York, 1980), pp. 368–71.

8 Bartholomaeus Anglicus, *Liber de Proprietatibus Rerum* (Strasburg, 1505), bk 6, ch. 1 (= *On the Properties of Things: John Trevisa's Translation of Bartholomaeus Anglicus* (Oxford, 1975), pp. 291–2; *Sancti Isidori Liber Numerorum*, PL vol. 83, col. 188.

9 Vincent of Beauvais, *Speculum Quadruplex: Speculum Doctrinale* (Douai, 1624), cols 1031–4; Arnold of Villanova, *De Regimine Sanitatis*, in *Opera Omnia* (Basel, 1585), cols 664–9 (this work, composed in the first half of the fourteenth century, is apparently falsely attributed to Arnold of Villanova); Konrad of Megenberg, *Ökonomik*, ed. S. Krüger (Stuttgart, 1973; MGH Staatschriften, 111/5), bk 1/2, ch. 13; Aegidius Romanus, op. cit., bk 2, pt 2, ch. 15; Bernard Gordon, *De Conservatione Vitae Humanae*, pp. 17–26; and see also L. E. Demaitre, op. cit., pp. 465–6.

10 'Honorius Augustodunens', *De Philosophia Mundi*, PL vol. 172, bk 4, ch. 18, col. 91.

11 For example Thomas Chobham, *Summa Confessorum*, ed. F. Broomfield (Paris–Louvain, 1963), p. 466.

12 In accordance with the decrees of church synods in twelfth- and thirteenth-century England, priests were instructed to inform parents of their obligation to ensure that their children received this sacrament within a year and a day of birth (*Councils and Synods with Other Documents relating to the English Church*, ed. F. M. Powicke and R. Cheney (Oxford, 1964), vol. II, pt 1, pp. 71, 453); according to Bartholomew of Exeter as well, they were obliged to do so as early as possible (*Bartholomew of Exeter: Bishop and Canonist, with Text of Bartholomew's Penitential*,

ed. D. A. Morey (Cambridge, 1937), 99, p. 266); most canonists advocated bestowing it on the child only at the age of 7 (R. Metz, 'L'Enfant dans le droit canonique mediéval', in *Recueils de la Société Jean Bodin*, vol. 36/2 (Brussels, 1976), pp. 60–1).

For the remarks of Raymond Lull, see *Doctrine d'enfant*, ed. A. Llinarès (Paris, 1969), ch. 24, pp. 70–1. The text was composed in the last quarter of the thirteenth century ('Rámon Llull', *Obres* (published Palma, 1906), vol. I, pp. 1–199); and translated into French in his lifetime. All quotations are from the French translation.

On those who received the sacrament only in adulthood, see *Les Statuts synodaux français du XIIIᵉ siècle*, ed. O. Pontal (Paris, 1971), vol. I, pp. 54, 142; Gerald of Wales writes about people whose parents deferred their confirmation and who hence never received this sacrament: *Gemma Ecclesiastica*, ed. J. S. Brewer (Rolls Series; London, 1862), vol. 21/2, pp. 45–6.

13 Bartholomaeus Anglicus, *Liber de Proprietatibus Rerum*, bk 6, ch. 1 (= *John Trevisa's Translation*, pp. 291–2); Konrad of Megenberg, op. cit., bk 1/2, ch. 13, p. 88; and see also R. Metz, op. cit. p. 18.

14 S. Nagel and S. Vecchio, 'Childhood, Speech and Silence in Medieval Culture', *Quaderni Storici*, 57/a, 19/3 (1984), n. 99.

15 Bernard Gordon, op. cit., p. 2; Philip of Novare, *Les Quatres Ages de l'homme*, ed. M. de Eréville (Paris, 1888), p. 5; R. Metz, op. cit., pp. 12–27; according to the author of the text attributed to Arnold of Villanova, the stage of *pueritia* began at 6 (op cit., col. 668).

16 *Corpus Iuris Canonici*, ed. A. Friedberg (Leipzig, 1879), vol. II, bk 4, tit. 2, chs 1–14, cols 672–9; R. Helmholz, *Marriage Litigations in Medieval England* (Cambridge, 1974), p. 98.

17 Thomas Chobham, op. cit., pp. 92–5, 152–3; *Corpus Iuris Canonici*, vol. II, col. 824; *Les Statuts synodaux français*, vol. I, p. 184; *Les Statuts synodaux de Jean de Flandre évêque de Liège*, ed. E. Schoolmeesters (Liège, 1938), p. 20; and see also R. Metz, op. cit., pp. 61–7.

18 *Bracton on the Laws and Customs of England*, ed. and trans. S. Thorne (Cambridge, Mass., 1968), vol. II, p. 384 and n. 15; Philip of Beaumanoir, *Coutumes de Beauvaisis*, ed. A. Salmon (Paris, 1899–1900), vol. I, s. 560, p. 268.

19 For examples of executions of children and, conversely, leniency towards children, see E. Cohen, 'Youth and Deviance in the Middle Ages', in *History of Juvenile Delinquency*, ed. A. G. Hess and P. F. Clement (forthcoming), ch. 1, nn. 12, 20, 29; see also W. M. Bowsky, *A Medieval Italian Commune: Siena under the Nine, 1287–1355* (Berkeley, 1981), pp. 20–1.

On views similar to those of Philip of Beaumanoir among other jurists, see: J. Iver, 'La Suspension des actions en période de minorité en France et son effacement progressif, XIIIᵉ–XVIᵉ siècles', in *Recueils de la Société Jean Bodin* (Brussels, 1976), vol. 36/2, p. 188.

20 Thomas Aquinas, *Summa Theologiae* (London, 1966–74), Prima Secundae, q. 96, art. 2 (vol. 28, p. 122); Secunda Secundae, q. 88, art. 5, (vol. 49, pp. 242–4); *Corpus Iuris Canonici*, vol. II, bk 5, tit. 23, chs 1–11, cols 824–5; on imposition of lighter acts of penance on young people for 'acts of lasciviousness against nature' see Bartholomew of Exeter, op. cit., 69, pp. 235–6; for the sin of masturbation, J. Benton, 'Commentary to L. deMause's article: "The Evolution of Childhood", *History of Childhood Quarterly*, 1/4 (1974), p. 587; on invalid oaths and vows by youths under 14 see also Bartholomew of Exeter, op. cit., 78, p. 244.

21 For Bernard Gordon's remarks see L. E. Demaitre, op. cit., p. 466.

22 Bartholomaeus Anglicus, *Liber de Proprietatibus Rerum*, bk 6, ch. 5, *De Puero* (= *John Trevisa's Translation*, pp. 300–1); other writers also considered love of apples and the rapid transition from weeping to laughter as typical of this age. See, for example, *Dan Michel's Ayenbite of Inwyt or remorse of Conscience*, ed. R. Morris (EETS; London, 1886), pp. 94, 208.

23 Bartholomaeus Anglicus, *Liber de Proprietatibus Rerum*, bk 6, ch. 6, *De Puella* (= *John Trevisa's Translation*, pp. 301–2).

24 The view was that menstruation commenced in girls at 12–13, and sometimes a little earlier or later: *Medieval Woman's Guide to Health*, ed. and trans. B. Rowland (London, 1981), p. 58; *Vrouwengeneeskunde in Vlaanderen tijdens de late Midde-leeuwen*, ed. A. B. C. M. Delva (Bruges, 1983), p. 210, n. 19; see also V. Bullough and C. Campbell, 'Female Longevity and Diet in the Middle Ages', *Speculum*, 55 (1980), pp. 322–5; C. J. Diers, 'The Age of Menarche in Medieval Europe', *Human Biology*, 45 (1973), pp. 363–9; Bartholomaeus Anglicus notes the voice-change in young boys and the fact that at 14 they are capable of fathering children, *Liber de Proprietatibus Rerum*, bk 6, ch. 5 (= *John Trevisa's Translation*, pp. 300–1).

25 Aegidius Romanus, op. cit., bk 2, pt 2, ch. 14. He denotes this age-group '*iuvenes*' but is clearly referring to the period usually referred to as '*adolescentia*'.

26 E. Le Roy Ladurie, *Montaillou: Village occitan de 1294 à 1324* (Paris, 1975), p. 320.

27 In France the formal age of maturity was 15 (Philip of Beaumanoir, op. cit., vol. 1, s. 522).

28 See, on this, G. Ashby, 'Une Analyse stylistique des formules épiques contenants "enfant" ou l'un des synonymes', in *L'Enfant au Moyen Age: Littérature et civilisation* (Senefiance, 9; Paris, 1980), pp. 221–31.

29 *Raoul de Camrai*, ed. P. Meyer and A. Longnon (Paris, 1882), p. 259.

30 A. D. Gabriel, *The Educational Ideas of Vincent of Beauvaus* (Notre Dame, Ind., 1965), pp. 39, 185; R. Barton-Tobin, 'Vincent of Beauvais on the Education of Women', *Journal of the History of Ideas*, 35 (1974), p. 488; *Six Sermons inédits de Jean Gerson*, ed. L. Mourin (Paris, 1946), pp. 416–18.

31 e.g. *Acta Sanctorum*, Feb. 2, p. 203.

32 E. Le Roy Ladurie, op. cit., p. 820.

33 Bartholomaeus Anglicus, *Liber de Proprietatibus Rerum*, bk 6, ch. 1 (= *John Trevisa's Translation*, pp. 291–2); Isidore, *Liber Numerorum*, PL vol. 83, cols 186–9.

34 Vincent of Beauvais, *Speculum Quadruplex: Speculum Naturale*, col. 2349. Ibn Sina, he adds. extends it to 32. According to Aldebrandin of Siena, *adolescentia* lasts until 25 or 30 (see note 3).

35 G. Duby, 'Dans la France du Nord-Ouest au XIIᵉ siecle: Les "Jeunes" dans la société aristocratique', *Annales ESC* 19 (1964), pp. 835–46; according to Bernard Gordon *adolescentia* ends at the age of 35 or a little later, op. cit., p. 2.

36 R. Nelli, *L'Érotique des troubadours* (Paris, 1974), pp. 223–4.

37 *Le Opera di Dante, Convivio*, 4, ed. M. Barbi (Florence, 1921), pp. 299–302.

38 The canonists, for example distinguished between first adulthood at 14 (the age at which a youth could take the monastic vow in a Benedictine monastery) and second or full adulthood (*plena pubertas*) at 18 (the minimum age for taking the monastic vow in the new monastic orders of the twelfth century): see R. Metz, op. cit. In Italian cities there were posts which a man could not fill before the age of 30: see R. Trexler, op. cit., pp. 16–17.

39 *Fleta*, ed. H. G. Richardson and G. O. Sayles (Selden Society; London, 1955), vol. II, ch. 9, pp. 18–19; ch. 11, pp. 20–1. Before the age of 21 even a nobleman was not expected to fight in the Ordeal by Battle (ibid., ch. 9, pp. 18–19; ch. 11, pp.

268   *Childhood in the Middle Ages*

20–1). For more on 21 as the age at which a man could do as he chose with the fief he had inherited, see E. J. Tardif, *Coutumiers de Normandie* (Slatkine repr.; Geneva, 1977), vols I–II, pp. 79; vol. III, pp. 101–4; Philip of Beaumanoir, op. cit., vol. I, ss. 506–550, pp. 244–63. The legal age of puberty was 15 in English cities; see *Borough Customs*, ed. M. Bateson (London, 1906), vol. II, pp. 157–9. However, there were cities in which he was not permitted to sell or give away certain types of property before the age of 20 (and girls before 16): see, e.g., Godmanchester, ibid., p. 158; on the age of adulthood according to the different customs of German manors, see H. Fehr, *Die Rechtsstellung der Frau und der Kinder in den Weistümern* (Jena, 1912), pp. 92–9.

40 *Fleta*, vol. II, ch. 7, p. 16; *Bracton on the Laws and Customs of England*, vol. II, pp. 34–5; in Frederick II's legislation for Sicily, on the other hand, 18 was determined as the age of maturity (*Die Konstitutionen Friedrichs ii von Hohenstaufen für sein Königreich Sizilien*, ed. H. Conrad, T. von Lieck-Buyken, W. Wagner (Vienna, 1973), vol. II, 42, p. 234).

41 Konrad of Megenberg, *Ökonomik*, bk I/2, ch. 10, p. 84; Thomas Aquinas, *Summa Contra Gentiles*, in *Opera Omnia*, ed. R. Busa (Milan, 1980), bk 3, ch. 122, nn. 6–8 (vol. II, pp. 100–1).

42 N. Zemon-Davis, 'Youth Groups and Charivaris in 16th Century France', *Past and Present*, 50 (1971), pp. 41–75.

43 See J. D. Osofsky, 'Historical Perspectives and Future Directions in Infant Development', in *Handbook of Infant Development*, ed. J. D. Osofsky (New York, 1985), pp. 897–917.

44 See the description of Aldebrandin of Siena in note 3.

3 A CHILD IS BORN

1 *Mirk's Festial: A Collection of Homilies*, ed. T. Erbe (EETS; London, 1905), p. 193; *Dives et Pauper*, ed. P. H. Barnum (EETS; London, 1976), vol. I, p. 306.

2 *Hali Meidenhad*, ed. F. Furnivall (EETS; London, 1922), p. 471.

3 Burchard of Worms, *Decretorum Libri Viginti*, PL vol. 140, col. 762; *Councils and Synods with Other Documents relating to the English Church*, ed. F. M. Powicke and C. R. Cheney (Oxford, 1964), vol. II, pt I, p. 590; pt. II, p. 988; Myrc, *Instructions for Parish Priests*, ed. E. Peacock (EETS; London, 1868), p. 3.

4 'Benedictio pro muliere gravida', 'De benedictione fetus in utero matris sue', Abbé V. Leroquais, *Les Pontificaux Manuscrits des bibliothèques publiques de France* (Paris, 1937), vol. I, pp. 5, 53, 184.

5 Wolfram of Eschenbach, *Parzival und Titurel*, ed. E. Martin (Halle, 1900), bk 2, 105–13, pp. 37–9; bk 9, 477, p. 168.

6 G. Jacobsen, 'Pregnancy and Childbirth in the Medieval North: A Topology of Sources and Preliminary Study', *Scandinavian Journal of History*, 9/2 (1984), p. 97. The birth of the child is also a turning-point in the two poems of Marie de France (*Milun* and *Le Fresne*) in *Lais*, ed. A. E. E. Ewert (Oxford, 1965).

7 D. Herlihy and Ch. Klapisch, *Les Toscans et leur familles: Une étude du Catasto florentin de 1427* (Paris, 1978), pp. 533–4.

8 See, on this, P. Biller, 'Childbirth in the Middle Ages', *History Today*, 36 (1986), p. 46.

9 *Medieval Woman's Guide to Health*, ed. and trans. B. Rowland (London, 1981), pp. 1–48, 75, 125–35; a similar work is the Flemish Trotula from the beginning of the fifteenth century, apparently written by a midwife *Vrouwengeneeskunde in Vlaanderen tijdens de late Middeleeuwen*, ed. A. B. C. M. Delva (Bruges, 1983). See,

on the small amount of space allotted to birth itself in one of the Latin versions of Trotula, ibid., pp. 209–10; on analysis of the text of Trotula and the problem of the author or authors, see J. Benton, 'Trotula, Woman's Problems and Professionalization of Medicine in the Middle Ages', *Bulletin of the History of Medicine*, 59 (1985), pp. 30–53; *Councils and Synods*, vol. II, pt. 1, pp. 70, 183, 234, 435; Myrc, op. cit., p. 4; *Les Statuts synodaux français du XIIIe siècle*, ed. O. Pontal (Paris, 1971), s. 58, p. 72.

Bartholomaeus Anglicus's detailed encyclopedia contains no instructions for midwives. On the number of manuscripts of this encyclopedia and its translation into various European languages, see *Bartholomaeus Anglicus on the Properties of Soul and Body*, ed. R. Long (Toronto, 1979), pp. 1–2.

10 The correspondence of the Datini family contains a detailed description of the confinement of one of the serving-women; nothing could be done to ease her suffering: I. Origo, *The Merchant of Prato* (London, 1957), p. 238.

11 T. H. Hollingworth, 'A Demographic Study of the British Ducal Families', *Population Studies*, 11 (1957), pp. 4–26. See also R. A. Houlbrooke, *The English Family, 1450–1700* (London, 1984), p. 129; and the journals of the two Florentines, Luca di Matteo di Panzano and Gregorio Dati, who write of the death of their wives in childbirth (G. Brucker (ed. and trans.) *The Society of Renaissance Florence: A Documentary Study* (New York, 1971), p. 45; id., *Two Memoirs of Renaissance Florence: The Diaries of Buonaccorso Pitti and Gregorio Dati* (New York, 1967), p. 132).

12 E. A. Wrigley and R. Schofield, *The Population History of England, 1541–1871* (London, 1981), pp. 248–9; D. McLaren, 'Fertility, Infant Mortality and Breast Feeding in the Seventeenth Century', *Medical History*, 22 (1978), pp. 380–1; Z. Razi, *Life, Marriage and Death in a Medieval Parish* (Cambridge, 1980), pp. 129, 151. On the high mortality rate among women who underwent Caesarean operations in the seventeenth–nineteenth centuries, see *Obstetrics and Gynecology*, ed. D. N. Danforth (Philadelphia, 1982), pp. 11–13.

13 *The Miracles of Simon de Montfort*, ed. J. D. Halliwell (Camden Society; London, 1849), p. 48; *Acta Sanctorum*, ed. J. Bollandus and G. Henschenius (Paris–Rome, 1863–1940), Apr. 3, p. 649; see also R. C. Finucane, *Miracles and Pilgrims: Popular Beliefs in Medieval England* (London, 1977), pp. 105–6; G. Jacobsen, op. cit., p. 102 and nn. 39, 40. On anointing 'services' supplied by the Corpus Christi guild to pregnant village women who came to town see H. F. Westlake, *The Parish Guilds of Mediaeval England* (London, 1919), p. 152.

14 *Medieval Women's Guide to Health*, p. 31; and see also C. F. Bühler, 'Prayer and Charms in certain English Scrolls', *Speculum*, 39 (1964), pp. 270–8.

15 *Acta Sanctorum*, Apr. 3, pp. 642, 656.

16 *Medieval Woman's Guide to Health*, pp. 33–4; Eliezer Ben Yehuda, *Milon ha-Ivrit ha-Yeshana veha-Hadasha* (Dictionary of Old and New Hebrew) (Jerusalem, New York, 1959) – see under *tequma*. On this custom among the Moslems see H. Nunemaker, 'Obstetrical and Genito-Urinary Remedies of 13th Century Spain', *Bulletin of the History of Medicine*, 15 (1944), p. 163; on birth girdles in seventeenth- and eighteenth-century Spain see W. A. Christian, *Apparitions in Late Medieval and Renaissance Spain* (Princeton, 1981), p. 54; in the Middle Ages: D. Alexandre-Bodon and M. Closson, *L'Enfant à l'ombre des cathédrales* (Lyons, 1985), pp. 39–45; *Medieval Woman's Guide to Health*, pp. 32–3.

17 On the development of midwifery as one of the branches of medicine, see *Obstetrics and Gynecology*, pp. 2–4.

18 See, for example, *Acta Sanctorum*, Apr. 1, p. 512.

19 *Malleus Maleficarum* (Frankfurt, 1582), pt I, q. 12, ch. II; pt II, q. 1, ch. 13. See also R. Kieckhefer, *European Witch Trials* (California, 1974), p. 56.

20 T. H. Hollingworth, op. cit.; R. C. Finucane, op. cit., p. 106; D. McLaren, op. cit., p. 383; *Medieval Woman's Guide to Health*, p. 58.

21 *Acta Sanctorum*, Mar 1, p. 591, June 7, p. 211; Jan. 1, p. 403, May 2, p. 538; Apr. 1, p. 211; Jan. 1, p. 403; May 2, p. 338; Apr. 1, p. 507; July 1, p. 516; Mar. 3, p. 197; *Analecta Bollandiana*, 64 (1946), pp. 44–5; *Acta et Processus Canonizacionis Beate Brigitte*, ed. I. Collijn (Uppsala, 1931), p. 348. On prayers and masses for barren women, see 'Oratio pro sterilitate mulieris', 'Missa pro sterilitate', *Les Pontificaux Manuscrits des bibliothèques publiques de France*, vol. I, p. 168; vol. II, p. 143.

22 For an example of the advice of a medical sage, see Arnold of Villanova, *De Regimine Sanitatis*, in *Opera Omnia* (Basel, 1585), col. 684; on the wishes of the Montaillou peasants and the amulets they used, see E. Le Roy Ladurie, *Montaillou: Village occitan de 1294 à 1324* (Paris, 1975), 309–10; on condemnation of the practice of stealing the Host, see P. Browe, 'Die Eucharistie als Zaubermittel im Mittelalter', *Archiv für Kulturgeschichte*, 20 (1930), p. 137; on the marital problems which the childlessness of Margaret Datini caused see I. Origo, op. cit., pt II, ch. 1; on the married couple's yearning for a child in literature see Ryamond Lull, *Blanquerna* (Madrid, 1924; = *Blanquerna: A 13th Century Romance*, trans. E. Alison Peers (London, 1925), ch. 1.

23 On male sterility see Aegidius Romanus, *De Regimine Principum* (Venice, 1505), bk 2, pt 1, ch. 6: L. E. Demaitre, *Doctor Bernard Gordon: Professor and Practitioner* (Toronto, 1980), pp. 85–9, 130; *Medieval Woman's Guide to Health*, p. 35; for Thomas Aquinas's remarks see *Summa Theologiae* (London, 1966–74), Secunda Secundae, q. 164, art. 2 (vol. 44, p. 178).

24 *Registrum Iohanniss de Pontissara*, ed. C. Deeds (Canterbury and York Society, 30; 1924), p. 20; *Medieval Woman's Guide to Health*, p. 7; L. Le Grand (ed.), *Statuts d'Hôtels Dieu et de Léproseries* (Paris, 1901), s. 86, 88, p. 115. In Troyes in 1270 a special wing was established in the Hôtel Dieu for confinements and for sick women. Before this, pregnant women were only accepted if they were in mortal danger during the delivery because of their cries. However, women were taken in after confinement for a convalescence period of several weeks. See also *Statuts d'Hôtels Dieu*, s. 13, p. 162; $. 31–2, pp. 124, 139; *Acta Sanctorum*, May 5, p. 103; R. Favreau, 'Pauvreté en Poitou et en Anjou à la fin du Moyen Age', in *Ètude sur l'histoire de la pauvreté (Moyen Age – XVIe Siècle)*, ed. M. Mollat (Paris, 1974), vol. II, pp. 596–7; J. Imbert, *Les Hôpitaux en droit canonique* (Paris, 1947), p. 125, nn. 3–4; M. Carlin, 'The Medieval Hospital of St Thomas the Martyr in Southwark', *Bulletin of the Society for Social History of Medicine*, 37 (1985), p. 20; M. Rubin, *Charity and Community in Medieval Cambridge* (Cambridge, 1987), pp. 157–8.

25 *Acta Sanctorum*, July 1, p. 464; Mar. 2, p. 97; May 7, p. 458; R. Favreau, op. cit., p. 601 and n. 75.

26 *Acta Sanctorum*, Mar. 3, p. 53.

27 ibid., Aug. 1, p. 652; Mar. 2, p. 465; *Thesaurus Novus Anecdotorum*, ed. E. Martène and U. Durand (Paris, 1717), vol. III, col. 1776; *Analecta Bollandiana*, 14 (1895), p. 193.

Apparently Jews also sometimes called on the services of Christian midwives, as can be learned from the decrees of the church synods which prohibited this practice. According to a decree of the 1213 church synod in Paris ' et ne Christianae obstetrices intersint puerperio Judaeorum' (S. Grazel (ed.), *The Church and the Jews in the 13th Century* (New York, 1966), p. 306). And, conversely, in northern Spain Chrisitan women sometimes summoned the aid of Jewish midwives (E. Lourie, 'A Plot which Failed? The Case of the Corpse found in the Jewish *Call* in Barcelona, 1301', *Mediterranean Historical Review*, 1/2 (86), app., p. 218).

28 *Hali Maidenhad*, p. 50.

29 *Analecta Bollandiana*, 30 (1912), p. 73; 14 (1895), p. 192; *Acta Sanctorum*, Apr. 1, pp. 308–511.

30 C. Jacobsen, op. cit., p. 107 and n. 64; D. Alexandre-Bidon and M. Closson, op. cit., p. 56.

31 *Medieval Woman's Guide to Health*, pp. 41–2; A. Delva (ed.), op. cit., p. 83, pl. 20 – see also additional illustrations depicting a herbal bath and steaming (by placing a pot of boiling water with curative herbs over coals); through pipes the steam was supposed to reach the womb of the woman in labour who was seated on a stool with an opening beneath (pp. 29, 173, 177).

32 *Acta et Processus Canonizacionis Beate Brigitte*, pp. 110, 153.

33 *Analecta Bollandiana*, 64 (1946), pp. 35, 39, 40, 43; *Acta et Processus Canonizacionis Beate Brigitte*, p. 160; *Acta Sanctorum*, May 2, p. 338; Mar. 2, p. 99; Aug. 1, p. 647; July 1, pp. 508, 509; May 2, p. 338.

34 'in partu iuvenculae magis dolent et periclitantur plures', Aegidius Romanus, op. cit., bk 2, pt 1, ch. 16; Hildegard of Bingen, *Causae et Curae*, ed. P. Kaiser (Leipzig, 1903), p. 18. According to the text attributed to Arnold of Villanova (col. 684), the ideal age for procreation for men was 25–33; according to Aldebrandin of Siena it was 20–25 (*Le Régime du corps de Maître Aldebrandin de Sienne*, ed. L. Laindouy and R. Pépin (Paris, 1911), p. 80); according to Konrad of Megenberg, the ideal age for childbirth for women depended on the climate and the local conditions – in Germany, where the foetuses were sturdy, the suitable age was 14 or 16 (*Ökonomik*, ed. S. Krüger (Stuttgart, 1973; MGH Staatsschriften, 111/5), bk 1/2, ch. 28, pp. 115–16; according to Aegidius Romanus, a woman should not give birth before the age of 18 (op. cit., bk 2, pt 1, ch. 16).

35 *Acta Sanctorum*, Mar. 2, p. 88; see also May 5, p. 103; Mar. 3, p. 197; Apr. 1, p. 308.

36 'artis chirurgicae magister', ibid., Mar. 1, p. 589; 'et magister cum ferreis instrumentis ad extrahendum foetum advenerat ...'; ibid', May 1, p. 349. See also *Analecta Bollandiana*, 9 (1890), p. 347. People feared other operations as well and tried to postpone them in so far as possible: see, *inter alia*, *Miracles of Simon de Montfort*, p. 96.

37 *Acta Sanctorum*, May 6, p. 455; Apr. 2, p. 439.

38 *Miracles of Simon de Montfort*, p. 73; *Acta Sanctorum*, Mar. 2, p. 88. Academic physicians were present at all the confinements of Blanca, wife of Jaime ii of Aragon–Catalonia: see M. McVaugh, 'The Births of the Children of Jaime ii', *Medievalia*, 6 (1986), pp. 7–16.

39 On miscarriage as the result of carrying a heavy load, see *Acta Sanctorum*, Mar. 2, p. 205. The first wife of the Florentine merchant, Gregorio Dati, died after a protracted illness resulting from a miscarriage in the fifth month of pregnancy. His fourth wife miscarried in the fourth month, but survived and bore another six children: *Two Memoirs of Renaissance Florence*, ed. G. Brucker, pp. 112, 137, 138. On the views of the authors of confessors' manuals, see Thomas Chobham, p. 464; Peter Pictavensis, *Summa de Confessione*, ed. J. Longère (Turnhout, 1980), p. 17; *Les Statuts synodaux français du XIIIᵉ siècle*, ed. O. Pontal (Paris, 1971),

vol. 1, s. 98, p. 206. If a man confessed to having had sexual intercourse with a pregnant woman, and the woman miscarried for no other known reason, the priest could not grant the man absolution, and he was sent to the bishop; for other counsel to pregnant women given by a medical sage and by the author of a didactic work, see *Le Régime du corps de Maître Aldebrandin de Sienne*, pp. 71–2; Konrad of Megenberg, op. cit., bk 1/2, ch. 7, pp. 76–8. For references to the strenuous work done by poor women during pregnancy, see Konrad of Megenberg, op. cit., bk 1/2, ch. 9, p. 82. For the statements of the peasant women, see E. Le Roy Ladurie, op. cit., pp. 309–10.

40 *Acta Sanctorum*, Jan. 1, pp. 630–1.

41 ibid., Mar. 1, p. 599.

42 Arnold of Villanova, op. cit., col. 665.

43 'Nam temperatem calidus pannus esse debet similis matrici, quantum possibile est, quia omnia subita mutatio nocet nocumento mango', ibid.

44 ibid., col. 664; 'Honorius Augustodunens', *De Philosophia Mundi*, *PL* vol. 172, col. 91.

45 This resemblance was noted by L. Demaitre, op. cit., pp. 39–42. For more remarks on the need for gradual transition, see Aegidius Romanus, op. cit., bk 2, pt 2, ch. 15.

46 F. Leboyer, *Birth without Violence* (London, 1975).

47 D. Alexandre-Bidon and M. Closson, op. cit., p. 64.

48 Bartholomaeus Anglicus, *Liber de Proprietatibus Rerum* (Strasburg, 1905), bk 6, ch. 4 (= *On the Properties of Things: John Trevisa's Translation of Bartholomaeus Anglicus* (Oxford, 1975), p. 298); Arnold of Villanova, op. cit., cols. 664–5; *Le Régime du corps de Maître Aldebrandin de Sienne*, pp. 74–5; Bernard Gordon, *De Conservatione Vitae Humanae* (Leipzig, 1570), pp. 11–12.

49 'tempore hyemis posuerunt puerum in aquam frigidissimam et nulla signa vitae perceperunt in eo', *Acta Sanctorum*, Feb. 2, p. 731; 'projiciebant aquam et vinum in faciem, volentes scire utrum esset mortuus ut videbatur', ibid., Mar. 3, p. 205.

50 *Analecta Bollandiana*, 14 (1895), p. 175; Gilbert of Nogent, *Autobiographie*, ed. E. R. Labande (Paris, 1981), bk 1, ch. 3, pp. 18–21; on the practice of darkening the delivery room in seventeenth-century England, see A. Wilson, 'Participant or Patient? Seventeenth Century Childbirth from the Mother's Point of View', in *Patients and Practitioners: Lay Perceptions of Medicine in Pre-Industrial Society*, ed. R. Porter (Cambridge, 1985), p. 134.

51 In the period preceding the Gregorian Reform, many priests were married. In time, Peter Damian became one of the adamant opponents of violation of the vow of celibacy by the priesthood.

52 *Acta Sanctorum*, Feb. 3, p. 416; on depression *post partum*, see T. Benedek, 'The Psychology of Pregnancy', in *Parenthood, its Psychology and Psychopathology*, ed. E. J. Anthony and T. Benedek (Boston, 1970), pp. 370ff; Anthony and Kreitman, 'Murderous Obsessions in Mothers towards Their Children', ibid., pp. 479–98.

53 *Analecta Bollandiana*, 33 (1914), p. 170.

54 E. Bonney, 'Enfance divine et enfance humaine', in *L'Enfant au Moyen Age: Littérature et civilisation* (Senefiance, 9; Paris, 1980), pp. 14–15; A. Delva (ed.), op. cit., p. 96; D. Alexandre-Bidon and M. Closson, op. cit., p. 83. Amongst the house utensils which a woman had the right to dispose of in her will according to the custom of one German manor, was a 'small pot in which a child can be washed': see H. Fehr, *Die Rechtsstellung der Frau und der Kinder in den Weistümern* (Jena, 1912), p. 73.

55 *Le Livre du Chevalier de La Tour Landry*, ed. M. Anatole de Montaiglon (Paris, 1854), p. 109.

56 e.g. Hildegarde of Bingen, op. cit., pp. 17, 18, 77, 78; and see also P. Dronke, *Women Writers in the Middle Ages* (Cambridge, 1984), pp. 177–8.

57 Bartholomaeus Anglicus, op. cit., bk 6, chs. 3, 4, 7 (= *John Trevisa's Translation*, pp. 294, 296, 298, 303); *Tractatus Henrici de Saxonia, Alberti Magni Discipuli de Secretis Mulierum* (Frankfurt, 1615), pp. 95–6; Aegidius Romanus, op. cit., bk 2, pt 1, ch. 17; see also D. Herlihy and Ch. Klapisch, op. cit., p. 554.

58 *Medieval Woman's Guide to Health*, pp. 35, 169.

59 G. G. Coulton, *Life in the Middle Ages* (Cambridge, 1967), pt 1, p. 224; Herlihy and Klapisch, op. cit., p. 554.

60 Leon Battista Alberti, *I Libri della Famiglia (The Family in Renaissance Florence)*, trans. R. N. Watkins (Columbia, 1969), bk 2, p. 212.

61 J. B. Ross, 'The Middle Class Child in Urban Italy: 14th to Early 16th Century', in *The History of Childhood*, ed. L. deMause (New York, 1974), p. 206.

62 A. Lecoy de la March, *L'Esprit de nos aieux: Anecdotes et bons mots* (Paris, 1892), p. 8; G. Duby, *Medieval Marriages: Two Models from 12th Century France* (London, 1978), ch. 2.

63 Wolfram of Eschenbach, *Parzival*, bk 2, 112; p. 39. This description has a strongly sexual flavour. The queen, embracing her infant, feels that her husband is restored to her.

64 *Acta Santorum*, Apr. 3, p. 91.

65 ibid., Aug. 1, p. 652.

66 *Acta et Processus Canonizacionis Beate Brigitte*, p. 282.

67 *Acta Sanctorum*, July 1, p. 509.

68 ibid., Mar. 1, p. 586.

69 Alberti, op. cit., p. 123; for more on the disappointed reaction to the birth of a daughter in Late Medieval Tuscany and on a case of joyous response, see J. B. Ross, op. cit., p. 206.

70 The New Testament verses which were cited in support of the belief in the need to baptize infants are by no means straightforward: see Matt. 19:14; Mark 10:13–17; Acts 16: 33; 1 Tim. 1: 2,4.

71 e.g. St Augustine, *De Peccatorum Meritis et Remissione*, bk 3, PL vol. 44, cols 177, 189; *De Anima et Ejus Origine*, ibid., col. 481. Augustine's stand became increasingly rigid; in *De Libero Arbitrio* he still expressed his discontent at the fate of those morally neutral infants who had not been baptised, and believed that God would compensate them in some way (bk 3, 68, in *Sancti Aureli Augustini Opera* (Corpus Christianorum; Turnhout, 1970), pt 2, p. 315).

72 He was referring to his own father's illegitimate son, who died unbaptised (*Autobiographie*, bk 1, ch. 18, pp. 149–53).

73 Dante, *The Divine Comedy*, trans. L. Binyon (New York, 1947), Inferno, Canto 4, p. 20. See also Thomas Aquinas, *Summa Theologiae*, Prima Tertiae, q. 68, art. 3 (p. 88, note a).

74 On the statements of the heretics of Arras in 1025, see *Gerardi I Cameracensis Episcopi Acta Synodi*, PL vol. 142, cols 1273–4; on the view that baptism did not atone for the infant's sin because it was without sin, see *Registre de l'inquisition de Jacques Fournier, 1318–1325*, ed. J. Duvernoy (Toulouse, 1965), vol. II, p. 245; and R. I. Moore, *The Origins of European Dissent* (New York, 1977), pp. 100–1.

75 On the stand of Catholic theologians, see Thomas Aquinas, *Summa Theologiae*, Prima Tertiae, q. 68, art. 9, pp. 106–10; *Councils and Synods*, vol. II, pt 1, p. 68; *Corpus Iuris Canonici*, ed. A. Friedberg (Leipzig, 1879), vol. II, Decretal Gregor. IX, bk 3, tit. 42, chs 1–6, cols 644–7.

76 e.g. Thomas Chobham, *Summa Confessorum*, p. 93; *Les Statuts synodaux français*, vol. 1, s. 4, p. 140; n. 7, p. 141; s. 7, p. 54; n. 5, p. 55; *Councils and Synods*, vol. II, pt 1, p. 452.

77 D. Alexandre-Bidon and M. Closson, op. cit., p. 75; J. D. Mansi, *Sacrorum Conciliorum Nova et Amplissima Collectio* (repr. Graz, 1960), vol. XXXIII, cols 419–20.

78 J. Duvernoy, *Le Catharisme: La Religion des Cathares* (Toulouse, 1976), p. 145, n. 11.

79 *Inter alia: Councils and Synods*, vol. II, pt 1, p. 68. *Les Statuts synodaux français* vol. 1, s. 8, p. 56.

80 Thomas Chobham, op. cit., pp. 397, 527.

81 *Acta Sanctorum*, Mar. 2, pp. 466, 479.

82 J. B. Ross, op. cit., p. 189; I. Origo, op. cit., p. 228.

83 E. Le Roy Ladurie, op. cit., pp. 501–2.

84 On changelings, see J. C. Schmitt, *Le Saint Lévrier: Guinefort, guérriseur d'enfants* (Paris, 1979), pp. 110–18; they were known in French as *changelins* and in German as *Wechselbalg*. On amulets for children in art, see E. Bonney, op. cit., p. 14.

85 *Corpus Iuris Canonici*, vol. II, Decretal Gregor. ix, bk 3, tit. 42, ch. 2, col. 664; *Councils and Synods*, vol. II, pt 1, pp. 31, 70, 234, 453; Thomas Chobham, op. cit., p. 97.

86 R. Trexler, 'Infanticide in Florence: New Sources and First Results', *History of Childhood Quarterly*, 1/1 (1973), pp. 98–116.

87 *Galeran*, in Ch. V. Langlois, *La Vie en France au Moyen Age* (Paris, 1926), vol. 1, p. 9.

88 *Councils and Synods*, vol. II, pt 1, p. 70, pt 2, p. 988.

89 *Raoul de Cambrai*, P. Meyer and A. Longnon (Paris, 1882), pp. 2–4, 10, 272, 276–7.

90 According to Ch. Klapisch-Zuber, in Late Medieval Tuscany the urban noble merchant families generally named the eldest son after his paternal grandfather. Girls were more often called after the maternal grandmother. In the lower classes, children were rarely named after relatives, and were usually called after popular saints ('L'Attribution d'un prénom à l'enfant en Toscane à la fin du Moyen Age', in *L'Enfant au Moyen Age: Littérature et civilisation* (Senefiance, 9; Paris, 1980), pp. 75–85). In Halesowen it was customary to name boys after their fathers (Z. Razi, op. cit., p. 15).

91 'secundo propter periculum mortis, quia non potest eis alio remedio subveniri, nisi per sacramentum baptismi'. *Summa Theologiae*, Tertia pars, q. 68, art. 3 (vol. 57, pp. 88–90).

92 Burchard of Worms, op. cit., col. 733; *Councils and Synods*, vol. II, pt 1, pp. 31, 452, pt 2, p. 988; *Les Statuts synodaux français*, vol. I, s. 4, pp. 141–3; s. 7, p. 54.

93 Thomas Aquinas, *Summa Theologiae*, Tertia pars, q. 68, art. 11 (vol. 57, pp. 114–17); 'Baptême', in *Dictionnaire de théologie catholique*, ed. A. Vacant and E. Mangenot (Paris, 1910), vol. II, cols 283–4.

94 Mansi, op. cit., vol. XXII, cols 981–2; *Councils and Synods*, vol. II, pt 1, p. 233; R. Trexler, *Synodal Law in Florence and Fiesole, 1306–1518* (Vatican City, 1971), p. 67; Thomas Chobham, op. cit., pp. 96–7.

95   For to undo hyre wyth a knyf
       And for to saue the chyldes lyf
       And hye that hyt crystened be,
       For that ys a dede of charyte.

Myrc, op. cit., p. 4, and see also pp. 5, 17, 18. At the same time, Thomas Aquinas emphasized that the mother should not be killed in order to baptize the child: 'Et ideo non debet homo occidere matrem ut baptizet puerum' (*Summa Theologiae*, Prima Tertiae, q. 68, art. 11 (vol. 57, p. 116).

96 *Acta Sanctorum*, July 1, p. 515.
97 ibid., p. 501.
98 ibid., Mar. 1, pp. 290, 581; Mar. 2, p. 97; *Analecta Bollandiana*, 9 (1890), p. 336; *Acta et Processus Canonizacionis Beate Brigitte*, p. 157.
99 An incident of this kind is described by the Florentine, Lucca di Matteo, in his diary (G. Brucker (ed.), *The Society of Renaissance Florence*, p. 45).
100 Dante, *The Divine Comedy*, Paradiso, Canto 32, p. 535.
101 *Select English Works of John Wycliffe*, ed. T. Arnold (Oxford, 1871), vol. III, p. 200.
102 R. Kuhn, *Corruption in Paradise: The Child in Western Literature* (London, 1982), pp. 109–11.
103 Y. B. Brissaud, 'L'Infanticide à la fin du Moyen Age: Ses motivations psychologique et sa répression', *Revue historique de droit français et étranger*, 50 (1972), pp. 229–56. In one case a woman was charged with the murder of her infant. She was not tried by the bishop's tribunal but apparently by a lay court, but the Bishop of Lincoln charged her with not having baptized the infant before killing it. See R. M. Wunderli, *London Church Courts and Society on the Eve of the Reformation* (Cambridge, Mass., 1981), p. 128, n. 76.
104 *Mirk's Festial*, p. 298.
105 On the uncleanliness of the woman until one hundred days after her confinement in China, see M. Topley, 'Cosmic Antagonism: A Mother–Child Syndrome', in *Religion and Ritual in Chinese Society*, ed. A. P. Wolf (Stanford, 1974), pp. 234, 237–8.
106 A. J. Schulte, 'Churching of Women', *The Catholic Encyclopedia* (New York, 1908), vol. III, p. 761. According to K. Thomas, it was the laypeople who regarded the ceremony as a ritual of purification while, according to church teachings, it was only a thanksgiving ceremony. The ceremony was the outcome of popular belief in impurity rather than the source of the belief. See K. Thomas, *Religion and the Decline of Magic* (Harmondsworth, 1973), pp. 42–3. I believe that in the Middle Ages, at least, most churchmen considered the ceremony to be also an act of purification. See the remarks of Innocent III on the uncleanliness of women in pregnancy and childbirth (*De Contemptu Mundi*, PL vol. 200, cols 703–7, summarized in the text to ch. 1, n. 28); according to these the menstrual blood of a woman, which does not flow during pregnancy, is so vile and impure that its touch can cause a tree to wither, grass to shrivel, and the loss of fruit. Dogs which licked it would suffer from rabies and a child conceived as a result of relations with a menstruating woman would be born a leper. Because of the contamination of the menstrual blood, the woman was obliged to purify herself after the confinement.

It is true that Bede writes that, according to Gregory the Great (in a letter to St Augustine of Canterbury), it was permissible for a woman to enter church to give thanks even immediately after giving birth without this being considered a sin, because the ban in the Book of Deuteronomy (12: 2–5) should be understood as an allegory (*Bede's Ecclesiastical History*, ed. B. Colgrave and R. Mynors (Oxford, 1969), p. 90). However, in the *responsa* of the medical sages of Salerno, it was stated that the infant was incapable of standing, sitting, walking, and talking immediately after birth because, unlike the animals, it was nurtured in its mother's womb on menstrual blood from which it was not easily cleansed, while animals were nurtured in the womb on purer food (*The Prose Salernitan Questions*, ed. B. Lawn (Oxford, 1979), q. 228, p. 115; see also Bartholomaeus Anglicus, op. cit., bk 6, ch. 4 and Summa de Magister Rufianus, ed. H. Singer (Aalen 1963), p. 16. Among Anglicans in the second half of the sixteenth century and in the seventeenth, it was said of a woman who was charged with not having been churched after giving birth that she had failed 'to give God thanks for her deliverance in childbirth'. In the fifteenth century it was said that she had not been purified ('non erat purificata'): see *A Series of Precedents and Proceedings*, ed. W. H. Hale (London, 1847), nos. 514, 696, 738, 812, 41, 57. On the ceremony in the book of liturgy 'Ordo intrandi mulieres in ecclesiam post partum', see Abbé V. Leroquais, op. cit., vol. I, p. 89.

The lay belief that a woman after delivery must purify herself is reflected in the words of a chronicler who wrote that a certain noblewoman slept apart from her husband after the confinement, since 'her time of purification had not yet arrived' ('que intus parturierat, nec tempus purificationis ejus instabat'). *Chroniques des Comtes d'Anjou et des Seigneurs d'Amboise*, ed. L. Halphen and R. Pourpardin (Paris, 1913), p. 99.

107   J. D. Mansi, op. cit., vol. XX, col. 399.

108   Burchard of Worms, op. cit., cols 974–5.

109   On the special practices for burial of unbaptized infants in north-eastern Scotland as late as the nineteenth century, see W. Gregor, *The Folklore of the North East of Scotland* (London, 1881), pp. 214–15; on customs of burial of infants which died immediately after birth and hence did not belong in the community of the living, and had no standing in the community of the dead, see J. Pentikäinen, *The Nordic Dead Child Tradition* (FF Communications, 202; Helsinki, 1968), pp. 61–2, 354 – the peculiar form of burial was intended to prevent the return of the dead infant to harm the living. On the custom of bringing dead infants to the shrines of saints with the plea that they revive them for a moment to permit them to be baptized and thus ensure the salvation of their soul, and on the belief (up to the nineteenth century in France) that an unbaptized dead infant was a curse, see J. Gélis, 'La Mort du nouveau-né et l'amour des parents: Quelques réflexions à propos des pratiques de répit', *Annales de démographie historique* (1983), pp. 23–31.

4   NURSING

1   *Obstetrics and Gynecology*, ed. D. N. Danforth (Philadelphia, 1982), p. 791; on the other hand, psychoanalysts, like M. Klein and D. W. Winnicott, regard maternal breast-feeding as a vitally important condition for the future psychological well-being of the child.

2   'quod gentiles lacte ferarum filios suos fecerunt nutriri ut ex inde feritates contraherent', Thomas Chobham, *Summa Confessorum*, ed. F. Broomfield (Paris–Louvain, 1963), p. 465; on the views of the philosophers of the classical world, see R. Étienne, 'La Conscience médicale antique et la vie des enfants', *Annales de démographie historique* (1973), pp. 35–9.

3   J. B. Ross, 'The Middle Class Child in Urban Italy: 14th to Early 16th Century', in *The History of Childhood*, ed. L. deMause (New York, 1974), pp. 186–7; D. Herlihy and Ch. Klapisch, *Les Toscans et leur familles: Une étude du Catasto Florentin de 1427* (Paris, 1978), p. 555. Francesco of Barbaro, who wrote a manual for

women at the beginning of the fourteenth century, addresses his cautions mainly at wetnurses who took infants into their homes. He writes that ewe's milk is less harmful than the milk of she-goats, bitches, or sows (*Reggimento e costume di Donne*, ed. G. E. Sansone (Turin, 1957), ch. 13, p. 195).

4 On the high mortality rate among infants fed on animal milk in the nineteenth century, before pasteurization, see G. Sussman, 'Wet Nursing in 19th Century France', *French Historical Studies*, 9 (1975), pp. 304–28, n. 18.

5 S. Grazel (ed.), *The Church and the Jews in the 13th Century* (New York, 1966), p. 73 and n. 141.

6 F. Piponnier, 'Les Objets de l'enfance', *Annales de démographie historique* (1973), p. 70.

7 *Le Livre de Saint Gilbert*, ed. R. Foreville (Paris, 1943), p. 81.

8 J. B. Ross, op. cit., p. 187.

9 J. Knodel and E. van de Walle, 'Breast Feeding, Fertility and Infant Mortality: An Analysis of some Early German Data', *Population Studies*, 22 (1967), p. 119.

10 M. McLaughlin, 'Survivors and Surrogates: Children and Parents from the Ninth to the Thirteenth Centuries', in L. deMause (ed.), op. cit., n. 75; D. Alexandre-Bidon and M. Closson, *L'Enfant à l'ombre des cathédrales* (Lyons, 1985), p. 145; a 1510 statue by Daniel Mauche already shows a bottle with teat with which Miriam Cleopas is feeding her infant milk (or water) – see M. Baxandall, *The Limewood Sculptors of Renaissance Germany* (London, 1981), pl. 82.

11 M. Plouzeau, 'Vingt regards sur l'enfaçonnet ou Fragments du corps puéril dans l'ancienne littérature française', in *L'Enfant au Moyen Age: Littérature et civilisation* (Senefiance, 9; Paris, 1980), pp. 203–17.

12 *Origines Islandicae*, ed. and trans. G. Vigfusson and F. Y. Powell (Oxford, 1905), vol. II, p. 649.

13 Bartholomaeus Anglicus, *Liber de Proprietatibus Rerum* (Strasburg, 1505), bk 5, ch. 34 – De Mamilla; bk 6, ch. 3 – De Creatione Infantis; ch. 7 – De Matre (= *On the Properties of Things: John Trevisa's Translation of Bartholomaeus Anglicus* (Oxford, 1975), pp. 294–8, 302–3); Arnold of Villanova, *De Regimine Sanitatis*, in *Opera Omnia* (Basel, 1585), col. 666; Hildegard of Bingen, *Causae et Curae*, ed. P. Kaiser (Leipzig, 1903), pp. 67, 111; Albertus Magnus, *Quaestiones de Animalibus*, in *Opera Omnia*, vol. XII (Münster, 1955), bk 18, q. 8, p. 301.

14 Thomas Chobham, op. cit., p. 465.

15 M. Lindemann, 'Love for Hire': The Regulation of Wet-nursing Business in 18th Century Hamburg', *Journal of Family History*, 6 (1981), p. 385; for Paris, see E. Badinter, *L'Amour en plus* (Paris, 1980), p. 57; for Lyon, see M. Garden, *Lyon et les lyonnais au XVIIIᵉ siècle* (Paris, 1970); for examples of despatch of infants to wetnurses in the country, from a small town, see A. Bideau, 'L'Envoie des jeunes enfants en nourrice: L'Example d'une petite ville: Thoissey-en-Dombes 1740–1840', in *Hommage à Marcel Reinhard: Sur la population française au XVIIIᵉ et au XIXᵉ siècles* (Paris, 1970), pp. 49–58.

16 Since the Latin word *nutrix* served in the Middle Ages to denote both a wetnurse and a nurse or female relative who nurtured the infant or child, I have refrained from citing those sources in which it is not clear that the reference is to a wetnurse. Likewise, the verb *nutrire* is used to denote breast-feeding, feeding, and rearing, as is the verb *educare*. The following are examples of use of the word *nutrix* which clearly do not refer to a wetnurse: when Bernardino of Siena lost his mother at the age of 3, he was handed into the care of his aunt and it is stated that he was 'nutriciis disciplinae obsequens', *Acta Sanctorum*, ed. J. Bollandus and G. Henschenius (Paris–Rome, 1863–1940), Apr. 1, p. 93; and, when Juliana of

Cornillon was ophaned of both parents at the age of 5, she and her sister were sent to a convent. The author writes of the nun who cared for them there 'Ipsa namque pascebat corpora sicut nutrix refeciebat, et mentes ut magistra', ibid., p. 443.

In didactic works which state that the *nutrix*, like the teacher (*magister*) and parents, should raise the child in the Christian spirit, the reference is to a nurse and not a wetnurse: see, for example, J. Bromyard, *Summa Praedicantium* (Antwerp, 1614), ch. 3, pp. 4–5. Use of the word *nutrire* alternately for suckling and educating appears in the description of how Bernard of Clairvaux's mother raised her children: 'alienis uberibus nutriendos committere illustris femina refugiebat. Cum autem crevissent, quam diu sub manu eius erant, eremo magis quam curiae nutriebat', *PL* vol. 185, col. 227. For use of the verb *educare* to mean wetnursing, see *Acta Sanctorum*, Mar. 11, p. 181; Mar. 3, p. 522; Thomas Chobham, op. cit., p. 465.

17 'Lac autem infantibus convenientius est lac matris propriae', Arnold of Villanova, op. cit., col. 666; on additional works advocating maternal breast-feeding, see L. E. Demaitre, 'The Idea of Childhood and Childcare in Medical Writings of the Middle Ages', *Journal of Psychohistory*, 4 (1967–7).

18 Bartholomaeus Anglicus, op. cit., bk 6, ch. 7 – De Matre (= *John Trevisa's Translation*, p. 303).

19 *Speculum Quadruplex: Speculum Doctrinale* (Douai, 1624), col. 1091; on the proper nutrition for wetnurses and the dangers of sexual intercourse during nursing, see also Konrad of Megenberg, *Ökonomik*, ed. S. Krüger (Stuttgart, 1973; MGH Staatsschriften, 111/5), bk 1/2, ch. 9, p. 81.

20 Hildegard of Bingen, op. cit., p. 160; Arnold of Villanova, op. cit., col. 666; Francesco of Barbaro, op. cit., ch. 13; Aegidius Romanus, *De Regimine Principum* (Venice, 1505), bk 2, pt 2, ch. 15; *Le Régime du corps de Maître Aldebrandin de Sienne*, ed. L. Landouzy and R. Pépin (Paris, 1911), pp. 76–7; Bernard Gordon, *De Conservatione Vitae Humanae* (Leipzig, 1570), pp. 12–16.

21 Konrad of Megenberg, op. cit., bk I/2, ch. 9, pp. 78–9.

22 Thomas Chobham, op. cit., pp. 464–5. It is clear from his remarks that in this context he is referring not to abandonment but merely to refusal to give suck.

23 Wolfram of Eschenbach, *Parzival und Titurel*, ed. E. Martin (Halle, 1900), bk 2, 110–11, p. 38; 113, p. 391 (English translation: *Parzival*, trans. H. M. Mustard and C. E. Passage (New York, 1961), pp. 62–3).

24 *Sancti Bernardi Opera Omnia*, ed. J. Mabillon (Paris, 1690), vol. I, ep. 322, col. 299; *Abbot Suger on the Abbey Church of St. Denis*, ed. and trans. E. Panofsky (Princeton, 1946), pp. 30–1; it was said of Hugh of Lincoln 'the more he tasted the sweet draughts of heavenly doctrine, the more he greedily sucked at the breasts of Mother Church' (*Magna Vita Sancti Hugonis*, ed. and trans. D. Douie and Dom. H. Farmer (Nelson Series; London, 1962), vol. I, p. 8); see also C. W. Bynum, *Jesus as Mother: Studies in Spirituality of the High Middle Ages* (Berkeley, 1982), ch. 4.

25 *Legends of the Holy Rood*, ed. R. Morris (EETS; London, 1871), pp. 172–3; in art, see also *A Catalogue of Misericords in Great Britain*, ed. G. L. Remnant (Oxford, 1969), pl. 12*b*, *c*, *d*; 27*b*.

26 *Blanquerna: A 13th Century Romance*, trans. E. Alison Peers (London, 1925), ch. 2, p. 38.

27 Marie de France, *Lais*, ed. A. E. E. Ewert (Oxford, 1965), *Milun*, pp. 110–13.

28 *The Vulgate Version of the Arthurian Romances*, ed. H. O. Sommer (Washington, DC, 1910), vol. III, *Le Livre de Lancelot del Lac*, p. 22.

29 *Les Lamentations de Mathieu*, in Ch. V. Langlois, *La Vie en France au Moyen Age* (Paris, 1926), vol. II, pp. 254–5; *Les Quinze Joyes de mariage*, ed. J. R. Rychner (Paris, 1963), p. 67.

30 Henry iv, in 1090, in the privilege to the Jews of Worms, granted them the right to employ Christian wetnurses. See *Regesten zur Geschichte der Juden in Frankischen und Deutschen Reiche*, ed. J. Aronius (Berlin, 1902), p. 75. The following are examples of bans on Jewish employment of Christian wetnurses: S. Grazel, op. cit., pp. 106, 198, 204, 252, 296, 306, 320–2, 332; J. D. Mansi, *Sacrorum Consiliorum Nova et Amplissima Collectio* (repr. Graz, 1960), vol. XX, col. 399; in an edict of Innocent iii, the Jews are accused of having, for three days after the wetnurses received the Host, forbidden them to nurse and forced them to pour away their milk in the latrine (S. Grazel, op. cit., p. 114).

31 *Ordonnances des Roys de France*, ed. M. de Laurière (Paris, 1729), vol. II, p. 370.

32 *Registre de l'inquisition de Jacques Fournier, 1318–1325*, ed. J. Duvernoy, (Toulouse, 1965), vol. I, 77a, pp. 382; vol. III, 257c, p. 162; vol. II, 203d–204a, p. 415; vol. I, 74b, p. 370; 18a, p. 125. See also B. A. Hanawalt, *The Ties that Bound: Peasant Families in Medieval England* (Oxford, 1986), pp. 161–2. For an example from Tuscany of a maidservant who conceived by her master and whose child was handed over to a wetnurse, see I. Origo, *The Merchant of Prato* (London, 1957), p. 167. Her master married her off, but, since the child was born six months after the wedding, it was put out to nurse and died in the care of the third wetnurse. When a child was born to her in wedlock, she nursed it herself.

33 *Saxonis Gesta Danorum*, vol. I, ed. J. Olrik and H. Raeder (Copenhagen, 1931), bk 6, p. 164.

34 Quoted in G. R. Quaife, *Wanton Wenches and Wayward Wives: Peasants and Illicit Sex in Early Seventeenth Century England* (London, 1979), p. 219; see also D. McLaren, 'Fertility, Infant Mortality and Breast Feeding in the Seventeenth Century', *Medical History*, 22 (1978), p. 387.

35 A fourteenth-century manuscript of 'The History Book from the Creation of the World', Bib. Nat., Paris. See R. Fossier, *Le Moyen Age* (Paris, 1983), p. 45.

36 G. Jacobsen, 'Economic Progress and the Sexual Division of Labour: The Role of Guilds in the Late Medieval Danish City', in *Alltag und Fortschrit im Mittelalter* (Veröffentlichungen des Instituts für Mittelalterliche Realienkunde Österreichs, 8; Vienna, 1986), p. 227, n. 10.

37 *Acta Sanctorum*, Apr. 3, p. 869.

38 ibid., July 1, p. 499; *Acta et Processus Canonizacionis Beate Brigitte*, ed. I. Collijn (Uppsala, 1931), p. 400; *The Vita Wulfstani of William of Malmesbury*, ed. R. R. Darlington (London, 1928), p. 178.

39 Ch. Klapisch-Zuber, 'Blood Parents and Milk Parents: Wet-nursing in Florence, 1300–1530', in *Women, Family and Ritual in Renaissance Florence* (Chicago, 1985), pp. 132–63.

40 *Acts Sanctorum*, Feb. 3, pp. 620–1.

41 ibid., May 1, p. 354; Apr. 1, pp. 515, 311, 708, 501; Apr. 3, pp. 258, 244; May 5, p. 193; Feb. 3, p. 357; Aug. 1, p. 649; *Analecta Bollandiana*, 9 (1890), pp. 337, 344; *Acta et Processus Canonizacionis Beate Brigitte*, p. 148.

42 *Acta Sanctorum*, May 7, p. 471; May 4, p. 621.

43 PL vol. 185, col. 227; *Analecta Bollandiana*, 14 (1895), p. 175; *Acta Sanctorum*, Apr. 1, p. 483; July 1, p. 455; Apr. 2, p. 142; Mar. 2, p. 181.

44 *Inter alia*: ibid., Mar. 1, p. 659; May 7, p. 188; Mar. 3, p. 504; Apr. 3, p. 248; *Analecta Bollandiana*, 33 (1914), p. 174; G. Brucker (ed.), *Two Memoirs of*

Renaissance Florence: The Diaries of Buonaccorso Pitti and Gregorio Dati (New York, 1967), p. 87; *The Miracles of Simon de Montfort*, ed. J. O. Halliwell (Camden Society; London, 1849), pp. 85, 107; Gilbert of Nogent mentions wetnurses who came to live in his mother's house to nurse the orphan she had taken in, and his own wetnurses (*Autobiographie*, ed. E. R. Labande (Paris, 1981), bk 1, ch. 18, p. 156; ch. 12, p. 84. The custom was adopted in the Scandinavian countries under the influence of Christian Europe: see D. J. Benedictow, 'The Milky Way in History: Feeding, Antagonism between the Sexes and Infant Mortality in Medieval Norway', *Scandinavian Journal of History*, 10 (1985), p. 39 and n. 76.

45　'Cujus mater fovit Ricardum ex mamilla dextra, sed Alexandrum fovit ex mamilla sinistra', Alexander Neckham, *De Naturis Rerum Libri Duo*, ed. T. Wright (Rolls Series; London, 1863), p. ix. On the wetnurses of the sons of the king of France, Jean the Good, see Ph. Contamine, *La Vie quotidienne pendant la Guerre de Cent Ans: France et Angleterre* (Paris, 1967), p. 165; on a wetnurse who was permitted to bring her own son to the court of the king of Aragon to which she was summoned in order to nurse the king's son, see *Archivo de la Corona de Aragón*, Canciller A. Reg. 1134, fo. 198ᵛ (this item was called to my attention by Prof. Elena Lourie); on women who were not from the minor nobility who suckled princes in England, see N. Orme, *From Childhood to Chivalry: The Education of the English Kings and Aristocracy, 1066–1530* (London, 1984), p. 12; for examples from literature see L. Gautier, *Chivalry*, trans. D. C. Dunning (London, 1965), p. 39.

46　'deceptam ut dicunt, obstetricis consilio quae pro affluentis lactis copia, puerperae mammas stricta praeceperat illigari fascia', William of Malmesbury, *De Gestis Regum Anglorum*, ed. W. Stubbs (Rolls Series; London, 1889), p. 461. Thomas Chobham notes only that they ruin the milk 'given to them by God' (op. cit., p. 465).

47　*Obstetrics and Gynecology*, p. 790.

48　*Acta Sanctorum*, Mar. 1, p. 738; a tale recorded in several biographies of Thomas Becket mentions a *nutrix*. This was apparently a wetnurse and not a nurse, though this is not certain. See William Fitz Stephen, *Vita Thomae* in *Vita Sancti Thomae Cantuariensis Archiepiscopi et Martyris*, ed. I. A. Giles (Oxford, 1845), vol. I, p. 182; and also two additional and similar versions of the same tale in two other biographies: ibid., pp. 5, 94.

49　J. Ross, op. cit., p. 189 and n. 39; Ch. Klapisch-Zuber, op. cit., pp. 140–1; J. Heers, *Esclaves et domestiques au Moyen Age dans le monde méditerranéen* (Paris, 1981), pp. 200–2.

50　J. Ross, op. cit., pp. 187–91. On children entrusted to wetnurses in the biographies of saints, see *Acta Sanctorum*, Mar. 3, p. 207; Apr. 1, p. 513; Mar. 3, pp. 330, 199, 182.

51　Marie de France, *Lais*, p. 40.

52　Leon Battista Alberti, *I Libri della Famiglia (The Family in Renaissance Florence)*, trans. R. N. Watkins (Columbia, 1969), pp. 51–4; on the great demand for wetnurses in north and central Italy, see also J. Ross, op. cit., p. 189 and n. 38; R. Trexler, 'Infanticide in Florence: New Sources and First Results', *History of Childhood Quarterly*, 1 (1973), p. 100.

53　M. Laigle, *Le Livre des trois vertus de Christine de Pisan et son milieu historique* (Paris, 1912), p. 156. Christine de Pisan was born in Venice in 1364, and before she reached the age of 7 her father went to Paris to serve as physican and astrologer in the court of Charles v, while Christine and her mother moved to the family residence near Bologna.

54 e.g. *The Miracles of Simon de Montfort*, pp. 85, 107.

55 *The Book of Margery Kempe, 1436*, ed. W. Butler-Bowdon (London, 1936), pp. 27–9; see also n. 48 above on the wetnurse of Thomas Becket.

56 Gerald of Wales, *Gemma Ecclesiastica*, ed. J. S. Brewer (Rolls Series; London, 1862), vol. 2, 1/2, p. 277.

57 *Leges Henrici Primi*, ed. L. J. Downer (Oxford, 1972), p. 270.

58 *Councils and Synods with Other Documents relating to the English Church*, ed. F. M. Powicke and C. R. Cheney (Oxford, 1964), vol. II, pt 1, p. 204; and see also pp. 274, 351, 410, 432, 457, 520, 648.

59 M. K. McIntosh, *Autonomy and Community: The Royal Manor of Havering, 1200–1500* (Cambridge, 1986), pp. 174–5 and n. 124; D. McLaren, op. cit., dealing with the seventeenth century, cites an example of the putting of an infant out to a wetnurse at the end of the fifteenth century (n. 42).

60 *Ordonnances des Roys de France*, vol. II, p. 370.

61 B. Delmaire, 'Le Livre de famille de Borgnes (Arras, 1347–1538): Contribution a la démographie historique médiévale', *Revue du Nord*, 65 (1983), pp. 305–6; Konrad of Megenberg, op. cit., bk 1/2, ch. 9, pp. 81–2.

62 *Hali Meidenhad*, ed. F. Furnivall (EETS; London, 1922), p. 51.

63 'potest esse quod complexio nutricis complexioni parvuli sit contraria', Thomas Chobham, op. cit., p. 465.

64 *Acta Sanctorum*, Mar. 3, p. 504; see also, for example, the story of the infancy of Robert de Chaise-Dieu (*PL* vol. 171, col. 1507).

65 See L. Demaitre, op. cit., p. 473 and n. 62.

66 *Acta Sanctorum*, Apr. 3, p. 248; *Analecta Bollandiana*, 33 (1914), p. 174.

67 *Acta Sanctorum*, Mar. 1, p. 659; Gervase of Tilbury, *Otia Imperialia*, MGHS vol. 22, p. 390.

68 *The Miracles of Simon de Montfort*, p. 107.

69 *Acta Sanctorum*, July 1, p. 514; Sept. 5, p. 699; Sept. 7, p. 540.

70 For an example of a woman who served as wetnurse and later as nurse to an orphan, see *Registre de l'inquisition de Jacques Fournier*, vol. 1, 18a, p. 215; E. Le Roy Ladurie, *Montaillou: village occitan de 1294 à 1324* (Paris, 1975), p. 305 and n. 3; in the family of the Earls of Leicester in the thirteenth century, as well, the same woman apparently served as wetnurse and nurse and remained with the daughter until she matured (see M. Labarge, *A Baronial Household of the Thirteenth Century* (New York, 1966), p. 45.

71 M. Mead, *Growing up in New Guinea* (New York, 1953), ch. 4; Mead, *Coming of Age in Samoa* (London, 1929), pp. 21–2; on this custom in an Indian tribe, see E. Erikson, 'Hunters across the Prairie', in E. Erikson, *Childhood and Society* (New York, 1963), p. 120.

72 Musa Alami's biographer quotes his subject as telling him that in early twentieth-century Jersualem it was customary for the midwife to bring together two mothers who had given birth at the same time, even if they were of different religion and social class, to nurse one another's infant. This was supposed to establish friendship between the families. When the children grew up, they regarded one another as adopted brothers. Musa Alami's adopted brother was the son of the Jewish grocer in his street. See Sir Geoffrey Furlonge, *Musa Alami: Palestine is my Country*, (New York, 1969), p. 6; on the custom of an infant being nursed by its father's other wives, as an expression of equality among the wives, in the Tallensi tribe in northern Ghana, see J. Goody, *The Development of the Family and Marriage in Europe* (Cambridge, 1983), p. 70.

73 Vincent of Beauvais, op. cit., col. 1091; L. B. Alberti, op. cit., p. 54; D. Herlihy and Ch. Klapisch, op. cit., p. 559.

74 *Acta Sanctorum*, Mar. 3, p. 330; J. Ross, op. cit., p. 190.

75 D. Herlihy and Ch. Klapisch, op. cit., p. 561.

76 J. Ross, op. cit., pp. 188, 191–2; and see also Ch. Klapisch-Zuber, op. cit., pp. 145–6.

77 It is interesting to note that Maimonides pointed out the harm which could be caused to a child by changing the wetnurse he could already recognize. A divorced woman should also be obliged to continue nursing her infant:

> A woman who is divorced should not be forced to nurse unless he gives her her wage and she nurses the child. If she is unwilling, she gives him her son and he cares for it. This applies only in a case where she did not nurse the child until it could recognize her. But if it recognizes her even if it is blind, it must not be taken from its mother because of the danger. But she must be forced to nurse the child for pay untill the age of twenty-four months.(*Mishneh Torah le-Rambam* (Book of Women), Hilkhot Ishut (Matrimonial laws), p. 127)

It will be recalled that, according to Erikson, to instil basic trust is the prime aim in the first fifteen months of life.

78 *Acta Sanctorum*, Mar. 3, p. 182.

79 J. Ross, op. cit., p. 191.

80 J. Bowlby, *Attachment and Loss* (New York, 1973), vol. II, ch. 2, 4.

81 B. Tizard and J. Rees, 'The Effects of Early Institutional Rearing on the Behaviour Problems and Affectional Relationship of Four-year-old Children', *Journal of Child Psychology and Psychiatry*, 16 (1975), pp. 61–73; L. J. Yarrow 'Historical Perpsectives and Future Directions in Infant Development', in *Handbook of Infant Development*, ed. J. D. Osofsky (New York, 1985), pp. 900–5.

82 M. Garden, op. cit., pp. 134–40.

83 E. Badinter, op. cit., pp. 113–16, 130–1; on the high mortality rate among wetnursed infants in seventeenth-century England, see R. H. Houlbrooke, *The English Family, 1450–1700* (London, 1984), p. 133 and n. 24.

84 In foundlings' homes in Lyon in the eighteenth century as well, the mortality rate was very high. Sometimes some 75 per cent of the children who were handed over to wetnurses died in their care (M. Garden, op. cit., p. 134).

85 On the wages of wetnurses: J. Ross, op. cit., p. 141; G. Brucker (ed.), *The Society of Renaissance Florence: A Documentary Study* (New York, 1971), p. 2; Ch. Klapisch-Zuber, op. cit., pp. 136–7. On supervision: ibid., pp. 144–5.

86 *Acta Sanctorum*, Mar. 3, p. 207.

87 ibid., Apr. 1, p. 513.

88 ibid., Mar. 3, p. 199.

89 Konrad of Megenberg, op. cit., bk 1/2, ch. 9, pp. 81–2.

90 I. Origo, op. cit., p. 200.

91 E. Badinter, op. cit., pp. 83–4.

92 M. Bogin (ed. and trans.), *The Women Troubadours* (London, 1976), p. 144.

93 Bernard Gordon, op. cit., p. 12; Vincent of Beauvais, op. cit., col. 1091; Thomas Chobham, op. cit., p. 465.

94 *Acta Sanctorum*, Mar. 2, p. 99; June 4, p. 380; July 1, p. 507; *Le Livre de Saint Gilbert*, p. 55; *Medieval Woman's Guide to Health*, p. 160.

95 G. Brucker, *The Society of Renaissance Florence*, p. 19.

96 See on this J. Knodel, 'Breast Feeding and Population Growth', in *Population Studies Center: University of Michigan* (typescript, 1977); C. A. Corsini, 'Is the Fertility Effect of Lactation Really Substantial?', *University of Florence* (typescript, 1977); D. McLaren, op. cit.

97 It is known that, in the Central and Late Middle Ages as well, when diet was richer in iron and protein than in the High Middle Ages (because of the addition of meat, vegetables, and beans), women still suffered from anaemia because of lack of protein and iron (V. Bullough and C. Campbell, 'Female Longevity and Diet in the Middle Ages', *Speculum*, 55 (1980), pp. 317–25).

98 See, for example M. Labarge, op. cit., pp. 45, 47.

99 'Narrabat siquidem quod propter frequentes conceptiones nullum ex filiis potuerat proprio lacte nutrire; hanc autem ideo usque ad finem nutrivit quia quousque tempus nutrimenti ejus completum est, non est conceptio subsecuta' (*Acta Sanctorum*, Apr. 3, pp. 569, 868).

100 J. B. Ross, op. cit., p. 187.

101 *Acta Sanctorum*, Mar. 3, p. 522; and see also ibid., Apr. 3, p. 248.

102 D. Herlihy and Ch. Klapisch, op. cit., pp. 556–7; G. Brucker, *The Society of Renaissance Florence*, p. 19.

103 See S. Shahar, *The Fourth Estate: A History of Women in the Middle Ages* (London, 1983), pp. 70–2.

104 The Indians of Nambikwara in Central Brazil, who were studied by Claude Lévi-Strauss, for example, abstained from sexual intercourse throughout the three-year nursing period. The same was once true of the Sioux Indians in Dakota, in the United States (C. Lévi-Strauss, *Tristes Tropiques: An Anthropological Study of Primitive Societies in Brazil*, trans. J. Russel (New York, 1969), p. 273; E. Erikson, op. cit., p. 19).

105 J. Noonan, *Contraception: A History of Its Treatment by the Catholic Theologians and Canonists* (Cambridge, Mass., 1965), ch. 5 and pp. 212–35.

106 Thomas Chobham, op. cit., pp. 464–5; on the ambivalent stance of churchmen in the centuries which followed, and their final decision in favour of fulfilling marital duties, see J. L. Flandrin, *Families in Past Times* (Cambridge, 1979), ch. 4 and pp. 203–31; id., 'L'Attitude à l'égard de l'enfant et les conduites sexuelles dans la civilisation occidentale: Structures anciennes et évolution', *Annales de démographie historique* (1973), pp. 143–205.

107 *The Talmud*, ed. I. Epstein, trans. I. W. Slotki (London, 1948), pp. 311, 215, and see also p. 62. It should be noted that this licence is mentioned neither in Maimonides's *Mishneh Torah* nor in Yaakov Ben Asher's *Arba'ah Turim*, written in the first half of the fourteenth century, even though sexual intercourse was permitted in the nursing period. See *Arba'ah Turim: Even ha-Ezer* (repr., Jerusalem, 1963), Hilkhot Priah u-revia, 47 $_1$; Hilkhot seder ha-onah, 25 $_2$.

108 The pronouncement of Gregory the Great is a response to the question posed by St Augustine, first Archbishop of Canterbury. The questions and answers, known as *Libellus Responsionum*, appear in Bede's *Ecclesiastical History of the English People*, ed. R. Colgrave and R. Mynors (Oxford, 1969), p. 92. Some authorities, doubt that the questions were in fact composed by Augustine and the responses by Gregory. In any event, the answer (attributed to Gregory) is that a husband should not approach his wife until the child is weaned. The author denounces the custom of handing over children to wetnurses and attributes it to unwillingness to practice sexual abstinence during nursing, but at the same time he notes that women who give their infants to wetnurses should abstain from intercourse until they purify themselves. In other words, he too acknowledges that the handing of an infant over to a wetnurse enables resumption of marital relations several weeks after the birth.

109 Ivo of Chartres, *Epistola* 155, *PL* vol. 162, col. 158.

110 J. L. Flandrin, *Families in Past Time* (Cambridge, 1979).

111 See n. 19. Francesco of Barbaro writes that, if the wetnurse wishes 'to be with her husband', she should inform the mother of this and help her to find another wetnurse (op. cit., ch. 13, p. 182).

112 See, on this, J. Goody, op. cit., pp. 37, 68–70. On the classical authors of medical works who did not object to a free woman abstaining from nursing her own child, see R. Etienne, op. cit.

113 Konrad of Megenberg, op. cit., bk I/2, ch. 8, p. 78. On the employment of wetnurses by Jews in the Middle Ages, see n. 30 and *Arba'ah Turim: Even ha-Ezer*, Hilkhot Priah u-revia, 2₁, *Mishneh Torah la-Rambam*, Sefer Nashim, Hilkhot Ishut, 821, pp. 125–7.

114 A comprehensive explanation for the above-mentioned modifications in matrimonial law and in norms which the church introduced not only for ethical and doctrinarian reasons but also as a strategical ploy which enhanced the prospects of inheritance and accumulation of property by the church, see J. Goody, op. cit.

115 On the church's struggle with the nobility to enforce the bans on incest, bigamy, and divorce, see G. Duby, *Medieval Marriage* (Baltimore–London, 1978); id., *Le Chevalier, la femme et le prêtre* (Paris, 1981); between 1065 and 1215 marriage was prohibited between blood-relatives to the seventh degree; there was a ban on marriage between relatives of the deceased (and thus, in contrast to the biblical levirate marriage law, a man was forbidden under any circumstances to marry his brother's widow). Marriage was also banned between those spiritually related, such as godparents and godchildren. At the Fourth Lateran Council in 1215 the ban on incest was relaxed and marriage between kin was prohibited definitively only to the fourth degree.

116 Stimulation of the nipple by the infant's sucking causes production of the hormone prolactin which prevents ovulation. In eighteenth- and nineteenth-century Frisia, where mothers nursed for long period, the average interval between pregnancies was 30 months. In Bavaria, where infants were weaned early and fed on pap of flour diluted with milk or water, the average interval between pregnancies was 21–22 months. See R. A. Houlbrooke, op. cit., p. 128; G. Sussmann, op. cit.; on wetnurses in France as late as the nineteenth century see F. Fay-Sallois, *Les Nourrices à Paris au XIXᵉ siècle* (Paris, 1980).

117 D. Herlihy and Ch. Klapisch, op. cit., p. 588.

118 Philp of Novare, *Les Quatres Ages de l'homme*, ed. M. de Bréville (Paris, 1888), ss. 2–3, pp. 2–3; the same idea that it is impossible not to love the children one raises is also reflected in a compilation of laws in the context of the treatment of orphans by those who raise them ('domini autem non possunt odio habere quos nutrierunt, immo eos diligent per sincere dilectionis nutrituram', cited in E. J. Tardif, *Coutumiers de Normandie* (Slatkine repr.; Geneva, 1977), vols. I–II, p. 12.

5   THE FIRST STAGE OF CHILDHOOD

1 L. Demaitre, 'The Idea of Childhood and Childcare in Medical Writings of the Middle Ages', *Journal of Psychohistory*, 4 (1976–7), pp. 463–5.

2 Arnold of Villanova, *De Regimine Sanitatis*, in *Opera Omnia* (Basel, 1585), col. 667; Francesco of Barbaro, *Reggimento e costume di Donne*, ed. G. E. Sansone (Turin, 1957), ch. 13; *Le Régime du corps de maître Aldebrandin de Sienne*, ed. L. Landouzy and R. Pépin (Paris, 1911), p. 76.

3 e.g. Hildegard of Bingen, *Causae et Curae*, p. 67.

4 Bartholomaeus Anglicus, *Liber de Proprietatibus Rerum* (Strasburg, 1505), bk 4,

ch. 4 (= *John Trevisa's Translation of Bartholomaeus Anglicus* (Oxford, 1975), pp. 298–300; and see also L. Demaitre, op. cit., pp. 476–7.

5 'et quia parvulus erat, medici medicinam dare timebant', *Acta Sanctorum*, ed. J. Bollandus and G. Henschenius (Paris–Rome, 1863–1940), Apr. 3, p. 248.

6 Arnold of Villanova, op. cit., col. 667; Bartholomaeus Anglicus, op. cit., bk 6, ch. 9; and see also L. Demaitre, op. cit. pp. 470–1.

7 Marie de France, *Lais*, ed. A. E. E. Ewert (Oxford, 1965), p. 104.

8 *Acta Sanctorum*, Feb. 3, p. 357.

9 See R. Schaffer, *Mothering* (London, 1977), ch. 5; D. Stern, *The First Relationship* (Glasgow, 1977), esp. pp. 130–42.

10 *Raoul de Cambrai*, ed. P. Meyer and A. Longnon (Paris, 1882); see also U. T. Holmes, 'Medieval Children', *Journal of Social History*, 2 (1968–9), p. 165 and n. 7.

11 Arnold of Villanova, op. cit., col. 668; *Le Régime du corps de Maître Aldebrandin de Sienne*, p. 78; Vincent of Beauvais, *Speculum Quadruplex: Speculum Doctrinale*, (Douai, 1624), cols 1091–2.

12 Konrad of Megenberg, *Ökonomik*, ed. S. Krüger (Stuttgart, 1973; MGH Staatsschriften, 111/5), bk I/2, ch. 10, p. 83.

13 J. B. Ross, 'The Middle Class Child in Urban Italy: 14th to Early 16th Century', in L. deMause (ed.), *The History of Childhood* (New York, 1974), p. 105.

14 L. L. Otis, 'Municipal Wetnurses in Medieval Montpellier', in *Women and Work in Pre-industrial Europe*, ed. B. A. Hanawalt (Bloomington, Ind., 1986), p. 88.

15 e.g. *The Miracles of Simon de Montfort*, ed. J. O. Halliwell (Camden Society; London, 1849), p. 86; *Acta Sanctorum*, May 5, p. 93; *Analecta Bollandiana*, 14 (1895), pp. 175, 193.

16 *Registre de l'inquisition de Jacques Fournier, 1318–1325*, ed. J. Duvernoy (Toulouse, 1965), vol. I, 105*a*, *b*, p. 499; *Acta Sanctorum*, Mar. 3, p. 207; *Analecta Bollandiana*, 14 (1895), p. 175; D. McLaren, 'Fertility, Infant Mortality and Breast Feeding in the Seventeenth Century', *Medical History*, 22 (1978), p. 387.

17 Aegidius Romanus, *De Regimine Principum* (Venice, 1505), bk 2, pt 2, ch. 15; Raymond Lull, *Doctrine d'enfant*, ed. A. Llinarès (Paris, 1967), ch. 91, p. 205.

18 *Acta Sanctorum*, Apr. 1, p. 515; Apr. 3, p. 248; *Analecta Bollandiana*, 14 (1895), p. 193; Vincent of Beauvais, op. cit., col. 1092; Arnold of Villanova, op. cit., col. 667; Bartholomaeus Anglicus, op. cit., bk 6, ch. 9; Bernard Gordon, *De Conservatione Vitae Humanae* (Leipzig, 1570), pp. 25–6.

19 Raymond Lull, op. cit., ch. 91, p. 205.

20 Arnold of Villanova, op. cit., col. 668; *Le Régime du corps de maître Aldebrandin de Sienne*, p. 78; Francesco of Barbaro, op. cit., ch. 13.

21 D. Alexandre-Bidon and M. Closson, *L'enfant à l'ombre des cathédrales* (Lyons, 1985), p. 117.

22 G. R. Owst, *Preaching in Medieval England* (Cambridge, 1926), p. 334; Berthold of Regensburg, *Vollständige Ausgabe seiner Predigten*, ed. F. Pfeiffer (Vienna, 1862), vol. I, p. 433; vol. II, p. 205.

23 *Robert Brunne's 'Handlyng Synne'*, ed. F. J. Furnivall (EETS; London, 1901), p. 231.

24 Raymond Lull, op. cit., ch. 91, p. 205.

25 Konrad of Megenberg, op. cit., bk 1/2, ch. 12, p. 86; and see also Bellino, Bissolo who wrote in the middle of the thirteenth century *De Regimine Sanitatis*, cited in K. Arnold (ed. and trans.), *Kind und Gesellschaft in Mittelalter und Renaissance* (Munich, 1980), pp. 122–3; Bartholomaeus Anglicus also writes (uncritically) about the wetnurse feeding the child with her fingers against his will (op. cit.,

bk 6, ch. 9; = *John Trevisa's Translation*, p. 304).

26 Francesco of Barbarino is cited in D. Herlihy and Ch. Klapisch, *Les Toscans et leur familles: Une étude du Catasto florentin de 1427* (Paris, 1978), pp. 555–6.

27 *Das Leben des Seligen Heinrich Seuse* (Düsseldorf, 1966), p. 67.

28 e.g. *Acta Sanctorum*, Feb. 3, p. 152.

29 Arnold of Villanova, op. cit., cols 663, 668; on the female who is moister and colder than the male, see also *The Prose Salernitan Questions*, ed. B. Lawn (Oxford, 1979), q. 21, p. 12; Bartholomaeus Anglicus, op. cit., bk 6, ch. 13 (= *John Trevisa's Translation*, p. 297).

30 Konrad of Megenberg, op. cit., bk 1/2, ch. 25, p. 110. For Paolo of Certaldo see D. Herlihy and Ch. Klapisch, op. cit., p. 561.

31 Bernard Gordon, op. cit., p. 16.

32 D. Herlihy and Ch. Klapisch, op. cit., p. 30; for another example of negligence in registering girls, see M. Parisse, *La Noblesse lorraine, XIe–XIIIe siècles* (Lille–Paris, 1976), vol. I, p. 306.

33 J. B. Ross, op. cit., p. 192; Ch. Klapisch-Zuber, 'Blood Parents and Milk Parents: Wet-Nursing in Florence, 1033–1530', in *Women, Family and Ritual in Renaissance Florence* (Chicago, 1985), pp. 138–9.

34 D. Herlihy and Ch. Klapisch, op. cit., pp. 338–40; R. Trexler, 'Infanticide in Florence: New Sources and First Results', *History of Childhood Quarterly*, I (1973), pp. 98–116; id., 'The Foundling of Florence, 1395–1455', *Journal of Psychohistory*, 1 (1974), pp. 284–95.

35 *Acta Sanctorum*, Mar. 1, p. 659; Apr. 1, p. 483; July 1, p. 455; Salimbene de Adam, *Chronica*, ed. G. Scalia (Bari, 1966), p. 48.

36 *Le Régime du corps de Maître Aldebrandin de Sienne*, p. 79; Bartholomaeus Anglicus, op. cit., bk 6, ch. 9 (= *John Trevisa's Translation*, p. 304); Arnold of Villanova, op. cit., col. 667; Hildegarde of Bingen, *Liber Divinorum Simplicus Hominis*, PL vol. 197, col. 837.

37 Bartholomaeus Anglicus, op. cit., bk 6, ch. 4, 10 (= *John Trevisa's Translation*, p. 294, 305); Arnold of Villanova, op. cit., col. 666; Francesco of Barbaro, op. cit., ch. 13, pp. 193–4; *Le Régime du corps de Maître Aldebrandin de Sienne*, p. 75.

38 Aegidius Romanus, op. cit., bk 2, pt 2, ch. 15; on physicians in eighteenth-century France who advocated bathing in cold water, see J. Gelis, M. Laget, and M. F. Morel, *Entrer dans la vie: Naissance et enfances dans la France traditionelle* (Paris, 1978), pp. 120–1.

39 Marie de France, *Lais*, pp. 104, 40.

40 *Acta Sanctorum*, Mar. 1, pp. 659–60; among the accidents, the drowning of a small child in the bathhouse is mentioned (ibid., Apr. 2, p. 803).

41 Bartholomaeus Anglicus, op. cit., bk 6, ch. 9; Arnold of Villanova, op. cit., col. 666; and see also J. B. Ross, op. cit., p. 191.

42 I. H. Forsyth, 'Children in Early Medieval Art: Ninth through Twelfth Centuries', *Journal of Psychohistory*, 4 (1976–7), pp. 39–44; for a description of an infant in *fasciae* see *Acta Sanctorum*, Feb. 3, p. 357.

43 Arnold of Villanova, op. cit., cols 665–6; Francesco of Barberino, op. cit., ch. 13, pp. 183–4.

44 The song of the wetnurses: J. B. Ross, op. cit., p. 194; D. Alexandre-Bidon and M. Closson, op. cit., pp. 92–102.

45 *Analecta Bollandiana*, 9 (1890), p. 327.

46 *Acta Sanctorum*, Mar. 7, p. 463.

47 E. Lourie, 'A Plot which Failed? The Case of the Corpse Found in the Jewish *Call* in Barcelona in 1301', *Mediterranean Historical Review*, I/2 (1986), app., p. 218.

48 Konrad of Megenberg, op. cit., bk I/2, ch. 9, p. 82; Bernard Gordon, op. cit., p. 12.

49 *Acta Sanctorum*, Mar. 1, p. 513.

50 F. Loux, *Le Jeune Enfant et son corps dans la medecine traditionelle* (Paris, 1978), pp. 201–3; J. Gelis, M. Laget and M. F. Morel, op. cit., pp. 119–21, 201–5.

51 'ita fasciis involutum ut infantes recenter nati solent' (*Acta Sanctorum*, Mar. 2, p. 57).

52 The biography of Hugh of Lincoln mentions a six-month-old infant whose torso and arms at least were free (*Magna Vita Sancti Hugonis*, ed. and trans. D. Douie and Dom. H. Farmer (Nelson Series; London, 1961), vol. I, pp. 128–30: L. Demaitre, op. cit., p. 473).

53 *Acta Sanctorum*, Mar. 3, p. 182.

54 R. H. Houlbrooke, *The English Family, 1450–1700* (London, 1984), p. 132 and n. 21.

55 See, particularly, L. deMause, 'The Evolution of Childhood', *History of Childhood Quarterly*, 1 (1974), p. 539.

56 Bartholomaeus Anglicus, op. cit., bk 6, ch. 4, 9; see also L. Demaitre, op. cit., pp. 471–2; on the tenderness of infant limbs, see Hildegard of Bingen, *Causae et Curae*, pp. 109–10.

57 Roger of Pontigny, *Vita*, in *Vita Sancti Thomae Cantuariensis Archiepiscopi et Martyris*, ed. I. A. Giles (Oxford, 1845), p. 94. On the infant's need for warmth, see Aegidius Romanus, op. cit., bk 2, pt 2, ch. 15; Konrad of Megenberg, op. cit., bk 1/2, ch. 14, p. 90.

58 J. B. Ross, op. cit., p. 194.

59 Lambert of Ardres, *Historia Comitum Ghisnensium*, MGHS vol. 24, p. 624. It is known that among the rich, the blankets and dresses of small children were sometimes lined with fur (Francesco of Barberino, op. cit., ch. 13, p. 183).

60 On accidents, see ch. 6.

61 *The Vulgate Version of the Arthurian Romance*, ed. H. O. Sommer (Washington, DC, 1910), vol. III, *Le Livre de Lancelot del Lac*, pp. 14–15.

62 G. R. Owst, *Literature and Pulpit in Medieval England* (Oxford, 1961), p. 35.

63 L. White, *Medieval Religion and Technology: Collected Essays* (Berkeley, 1978), pp. 273–4.

64 See R. Schaffer, op. cit., p. 55.

65 Thus in the rhyming text (from the thirteenth century) of Walter of Bibbesworth, *A Volume of Vocabularies*, ed. T. Wright (privately printed, 1857), vol. I, p. 143.

66 Leon Battista Alberti, *I Libri della Famiglia* (*The Family in Renaissance Florence*), trans. R. N. Watkins (Columbia, 1969), p. 50.

67 Arnold of Villanova, op. cit., col. 666.

68 Bartholomaeus Anglicus, op. cit., bk 6, ch. 9; Francesco of Barbaro, op. cit., ch. 13, pp. 185–6; *Le Régime du corps de Maître Aldebrandin de Sienne*, p. 75.

69 See I. H. Forsyth, op. cit., p. 46.

70 *Acta Sanctorum*, Apr. 2, p. 142; May 3, p. 628; June 2, p. 371; *Le Livre de Lancelot del Lac*, p. 7; a twelfth-century medical work of unknown authorship is known as 'Practica Puerorum in Cunabulis' (L. Demaitre, op. cit., p. 465).

71 J. B. Ross, op. cit., pp. 192, 196.

72 *Acta Sanctorum*, May 4, p. 622.

73 R. Étienne, 'La Conscience médicale antique et la vie des enfants', *Annales de démographie historique* (1973), pp. 34–5; Raymond Lull was the only one of the medieval authors, to the best of my knowledge, who believed that rocking of the cradle was not natural to the body, and that consequently some children cried

precisely when the cradle was rocked (*Doctrine d'enfant*, ch. 91, p. 206).

74 *The Early English Version of the Gesta Romanorum*, ed. S. J. H. Herrtage (London, 1879), p. 98; D. Alexandre-Bidon and M. Closson, op. cit., pp. 153, 154, 156, 158.

75 P. Piponnier, 'Les Objects de l'enfance', *Annales de démographie historique* (1973), pp. 69–70.

76 L. deMause, 'The Evolution of Childhood', *History of Childhood Quarterly*, 1 (1973), p. 523.

77 *Peter Abelard's Ethics*, ed. and trans. D. Luscombe (Oxford, 1971), pp. 38–9.

78 Bernard Gordon, op. cit., pp. 14–15.

79 On accidents resulting from children sleeping in their parents' bed, see next chapter.

80 Bartholomaeus Anglicus, op. cit., ch. 4, 9; Aegidius Romanus, op. cit., bk 2, pt 2, ch. 15; and see also L. Demaitre, op. cit., pp. 470–2.

81 Arnold of Villanova, op. cit., col. 666; and see also *Le Régime du corps de Maître Aldebrandin de Sienne*, p. 77.

82 Bernard Gordon, op. cit., p. 15; *Acta Sanctorum*, Apr. 1, p. 500.

83 Francesco of Barbaro, op. cit., ch. 13.

84 J. B. Ross, op. cit., p. 191.

85 *Acta Sanctorum*, Mar. 1, p. 720.

86 J. Ulrich, *La Riote du monde*, *Zeitschrift für Romanische Philologie*, 7 (1884), p. 286; *Hali Meidenhad*, ed. F. Furnivall (EETS; London, 1922), p. 51.

87 Thus, for example, in the biography of Vincent Ferrer, who was a saint (*Acta Sanctorum*, Apr. 1, p. 483).

88 In the *Acta Sanctorum* these sleeping potions are referred to as *medicinae*. It was after they proved ineffective that the mother went on a pilgrimage to the shrine of a saint (ibid., Mar. 1, p. 684). For amulets and oaths, see Alfonso x, *Lapidario*, ed. Sagrario Rodriguez M. Montalvo (Madrid, 1981), p. 34; *Sefer Shimush Tehillim*, a sixteenth-century manuscript of ancient origin (Wellcome Institute, *Ms. Heb* A. 34, fo. 48; an Arabic manuscript (Biblioteca nacional, Madrid, Caja 18, 586–7, IV/5, fo. 3^r); these references to amulets used to pacify crying children were given to me by Dr Ron Barkai; in modern Switzerland parents have been known to administer alcoholic liquor to infants and small children in order to put them to sleep (see A. Miller, *For Your Own Good*, trans. H. and H. Hannum (London, 1983), p. 239).

89 *Acta Sanctorum*, Mar. 1, p. 684.

90 Burchard of Worms, *Decretorum Libri Viginti*, PL vol. 140, col. 974.

91 Gilbert of Nogent, *Autobiographie*, ed. E. R. Labande (Paris, 1981), bk 1, ch. 18, p. 156.

92 See ch. 3, n. 72.

93 *Acta Sanctorum*, July 6, p. 482; *Acta et Processus Canonizacionis Beate Brigitte*, ed. I. Collijn (Uppsala, 1931), p. 176.

94 *Acta Sanctorum*, Aug. 1, p. 649.

95 According to theologians, there were no demon children, and the children held by the demons were born of human semen. However, people did not draw these fine distinctions. On changelings, see ch. 6, nn. 56–8.

96 According to Hildegard of Bingen, for example, the rate of development depended on the quality of the blood. A child born with the right blood – namely, red and thick – would gain weight quickly, crawl early, and then walk, would not tire easily, and would be cautious and intelligent. Those whose blood was bad from birth – that is to say, thin and pale – would be less intelligent, would tire easily,

tend to anger, have difficulty in making effort, and walk and talk late (*Causae et Curae*, pp. 242–3); on the fact that children should be permitted to carry out these activities at their own pace, see Arnold of Villanova, op. cit., col. 667.

97 *The Fifty Earliest English Wills in the Court Probate, London*, ed. F. J. Furnivall (EETS; London, 1882), p. 102.

98 *I Libri* (= *The Family in Renaissance Florence*), p. 63.

99 Quoted in L. Demaitre, op. cit., p. 475; see also *Le Régime du corps de Maître Aldebrandin de Sienne*, p. 78; Arnold of Villanova, op. cit., col. 667; Bernard Gordon, op. cit., p. 126.

100 D. Alexandre-Bidon and M. Closson, op. cit., pp. 110–12.

101 Konrad of Megenberg, op. cit., bk 1/2, ch. 12, p. 88.

102 Francesco of Barbarino, op. cit. ch. 13; *Le Régime du corps de Maître Aldebrandin de Sienne*, p. 78; and see also L. Demaitre, op. cit., pp. 466–7.

103 Salimbene de Adam, op. cit., p. 510. A different version of this story appears already in the works of Herodotus.

104 *Registre de l'inquisition de Jacques Fournier*, vol. I, 38a, p. 221; it is possible that, although the word used is 'servantwoman', the reference is to a wetnurse (see E. Le Roy Ladurie, *Montaillou: village occitan de 1294 à 1324* (Paris, 1975), p. 305. n. 1).

105 *De Eodum et Diverso*, ed. H. Willner, *Beiträge zur Geschichte des Mittelalters*, 4 (1906), pp. 25–6; for more on the importance of lullabies, see Bartholomaeus Anglicus, op. cit., bk 6, ch. 4 (= *John Trevisa's Translation*, p. 299).

106 *I Libri* (= *The Family in Renaissance Florence*), p. 61.

107 ibid., p. 50.

108 'Ibi parvulum jam triennem saepius attentaverant erudire ad loquendum parentes, nec persuadere poterant ut responderet aliquando verbum unum' (*Acta Sanctorum*, May 2, p. 334).

109 Some of these children were undoubtedly dumb or both deaf and dumb from birth because of physical problems (ibid., May 2, p. 329; Apr. 2, p. 44; *The Vita Wulfstani of William of Malmesbury*, ed. R. R. Darlington (London, 1928), p. 130); in other cases it is noted only that the child was dumb (*Analecta Bollandiana*, 9 (1890), p. 187; *Acta Sanctorum*, July 1, pp. 502–3; June 1, p. 150; *The Miracles of Simon de Montfort*, p. 71; *Acta et Processus Canonizacionis Beate Brigitte*, p. 131); it is sometimes said that the child had lost the power of speech because of a sudden fright (*Acta Sanctorum*, Aug. 1, p. 648; *The Vita Wulfstani*, pp. 131, 146).

110 J. B. Ross, op. cit., p. 202 and n. 125.

111 I. H. Forsyth, op. cit., p. 60, fig. 22; U. T. Holmes, op. cit., p. 167 and nn. 16, 17; D. Alexandre-Bidon and M. Closson, op. cit., pp. 83, 86, 90, 143, 153, 170, 178, 191, 198.

112 *Le Livre de Lancelot del Lac*, p. 18.

113 For example, *Raoul de Cambrai*, p. 5.

114 See M. Plouzeau, 'Vingt regards sur l'enfaçonnet ou fragments du corps puéril dans l'ancienne littérature française', in *L'Enfant au Moyen Age: Littérature et civilisation* (Senefiance, 9; Paris, 1980), pp. 203–7.

115 *Acta Sanctorum*, Apr. 2, p. 177; for Henry Suso's description, see n. 27.

116 *Magna Vita Sancti Hugonis*, vol. I, pp. 128–30.

117 Ph. Contamine, *La Vie quotienne pendant la Guerre de Cent Ans: France et Angleterre* (Paris, 1967), p. 47.

118 E. Le Roy Ladurie, op. cit., p. 317.

119 Ph. Cunnington and A. Buck, *Children's Costume in England from the 14th to the*

End of the 19th Century (London, 1965), p. 13; D. Alexandre-Bidon and M. Closson, op. cit., pp. 153, 155–6, 188–9.

120 *Sancti Bernardi Vita Prima, PL*, vol. 185, col. 257.

121 Arnold of Villanova, op. cit., col. 668; Aegidius Romanus, op. cit., bk 2, pt 2, ch. 15; Francesco of Barbaro, op. cit., ch. 13, pp. 193–4.

122 Arnold of Villanova, op. cit., col. 668; Bernard Gordon, op. cit., p. 27; Vincent of Beauvais, op. cit., col. 1092.

123 Francesco of Barbaro, op. cit., ch. 13.

124 Konrad of Megenberg, op. cit., bk I/2, ch. 10, p. 83.

125 *Blanquerna: A 13th Century Romance*, trans. E. Alison Peers (London, 1925), ch. 2, pp. 38–9; see also U. T. Holmes, op. cit., pp. 165–8.

126 Konrad of Megenberg, op. cit., bk 1/2, ch. 14, pp. 89–90.

127 Philip of Novare, *Les Quatre Ages de l'homme*, ed. M. de Eréville (Paris, 1888), s. 20, pp. 13–14.

128 Aegidius Romanus, op. cit., bk 2, pt 2, ch. 15; *Le Régime du corps de Maître Aldebrandin de Sienne*, pp. 79–80.

129 *I Libri* (= *The Family in Renaissance Florence*), p. 51.

130 Philip of Novare, op. cit., ss. 12–13, p. 9.

131 Konrad of Megenberg, op. cit., bk I/2, ch. 13, p. 88; 'quasi omnino caret rationis usu' 'Primo ergo septennio post receptionem baptismatis et sacramentorum ecclesiae intendendum est principaliter quasi circa unum; ut circa bonam dispositionem corporis' (Aegidius Romanus, op. cit. bk 2, pt 2, ch. 17); R. Levine, 'Child Rearing as a Cultural Adoption', in P. H. Tulkin and S. R. Rosenfeld (eds), *Culture and Infancy Variations in the Human Experience* (London, 1977), pp. 15–27, 38–9, 43, 51, 137, 219, 235.

132 *The Life of St. Anselm Archbishop of Canterbury by Eadmer*, ed. and trans. R. Southern (Nelson Series; London, 1962), pp. 20–1.

133 Myrc, *Instructions for Parish Priests*, ed. E. Peacock (EETS; London, 1868), pp. 5, 7.

134 *Kardinal Johannes Dominicis Erziehungslehre*, trans. A. Rosler (Freiburg, 1894), pp. 28, 34.

135 *Six sermons inédits de Jean Gerson*, ed. L. Mourin (Paris, 1946), p. 234.

136 Konrad of Megenberg, op. cit., bk 1/2, ch. 13, p. 89.

137 G. Duby, *Guillaume de Maréchal ou Le Meilleur Chevalier du monde* (Paris, 1984), pp. 49, 82.

138 Ph. Cunnington and A. Buck, op. cit., ch. 1.

139 *Analecta Bollandiana*, 9 (1890), p. 344; on an uncle who slept in the same bed with his three-year-old nephew, see *Acta Sanctorum*, Mar. 3, p. 193.

140 *Anecdotes historiques: Légendes et apologues tirés du recueil inédit d'Étienne de Bourbon*, ed. A. Lecoy de la Marche (Paris, 1877), p. 62; J. L. Flandrin, *Families in Former Times*, trans. R. Southern (Cambridge, 1979), p. 101.

141 Berthold of Regensburg, op. cit., vol. I, p. 33.

142 G. Ruggiero, *Violence in Early Renaissance Venice* (New Brunswick, NJ, 1980), pp. 158–9, 165, 167, 170; Bartholomew of Exeter, *Bartholomew of Exeter: Bishop and Canonist, with Text of Bartholomew's Penitential*, ed. D. A. Morey (Cambridge, 1937), 69, p. 236; Berthold of Regensburg, op. cit., vol. I, p. 189; and see also the infliction of the full penalty – namely, burning at the stake – for the rape of a ten-year-old boy (G. Brucker (ed.), *The Society of Renaissance Florence: A Documentary Study* (New York, 1971), pp. 205–6).

143 *Acta Sanctorum*, Apr. 1, pp. 513, 514.

144 e.g. *Analecta Bollandiana*, 56 (1938), p. 343; 64 (1946), p. 14; *Acta Sanctorum*,

May 2, p. 322; June 5, p. 500; Mar. 2, p. 94; and many more.

145 e.g. *Acta Sanctorum*, May 5, p. 103.

146 Jean Froissart, *L'Espinette amoureuse*, ed. J. Fourrier (Paris, 1963), ll. 148–286, pp. 51–5; see also A. Planche, 'Culture et contre culture dans l'Espinette amoureuse de Jean Froissart', in *L'Enfant au Moyen Age: Littérature et civilisation* (Senefiance, 9; Paris, 1980), pp. 391–403.

147 G. R. Owst, *Literature and Pulpit in Medieval England*, p. 34.

148 On the future saint playing with damp sand, see *Acta Sanctorum*, Mar. 1, p. 289–90; Mar. 3, p. 182; they were anticipated by Gerald of Wales who relates that he behaved in this fashion in childhood, in contrast to his brothers (*De rebus a se Gestis*, ed. J. S. Brewer (Rolls Series: London, 1861), vol. 21/1, p. 21. For the child who acted out the mass, see *Acta Sanctorum*, May 7, p. 453.

149 *Kardinal Johannes Dominicis Erziehungslehre*, p. 37; R. Trexler, 'Ritual in Florence: Adolescence and Salvation in the Renaissance', in *The Pursuit of Holiness in Late Medieval and Renaissance Religion*, eds Ch. Trinkhaus and H. Oberman (Leiden, 1974), pp. 200–4; id., *Public Life in Renaissance Florence* (New York, 1980), pp. 383–5.

150 *The Miracles of Simon de Montfort*, p. 74.

151 'omnia quae in ludibus infantilibus acquirebat et quae aliter habere poterat, Christi pauperibus erogabat', *Acta Sanctorum*, Sept. 7, p. 540.

152 Wolfram of Eschenbach, *Parzival und Titurel*, ed. E. Martin (Halle, 1900), bk 4, 181, p. 61; on little girls bowling hoops see, ibid, bk 7, 368, p. 129; playing with dolls, ibid., 372, p. 190; A. Planche, op. cit.; I. H. Forsyth, op. cit., pp. 50–1; K. Arnold, op. cit., p. 204; D. Kraus, *The Hidden World of Misericords* (New York, 1975), pl. 161; D. Alexandre-Bidon and M. Closson, op. cit., pp. 178, 182.

153 G. R. Owst, *Literature and Pulpit in Medieval England*, p. 27.

154 Quoted in M. McLaughlin, 'Survivors and Surrogates: Children and Parents from the Ninth to the Thirteenth Century', in *The History of Childhood*, ed. L. deMause (New York, 1974), p. 118 and n. 84.

155 N. Elias, *The History of Manners: The Civilizing Process*, vol. I, trans. E. Jephcott (New York, 1978), mainly pp. 60–70.

156 The following is said of one of the children: 'a patre imbuendus litteris traditus', (*MGHS*, vol. 30/2, col. 1323).

157 Arnold of Villanova, op. cit., col. 668; Peter Damian, *Opusculum*, 45, *PL* vol. 145, col. 698; J. B. Ross, op. cit., p. 211.

158 Gilbert of Nogent, op. cit., bk I, ch. 5, pp. 30–43.

159 *The Ecclesiastical History of Orderic Vitalis*, ed. and trans. M. Chibnall (Oxford, 1968), vol. II, p. xiii; J. B. Ross, op. cit., pp. 212–14; see also J. H. Moran, *The Growth of English Schooling, 1340–1548* (Princeton, 1985), p. 64.

160 *Acta Sanctorum*, Feb. 3, p. 152.

161 See J. P. Cuvillier, 'L'Enfant dans la tradition féodale germanique', in *L'Enfant au Moyen Age: Littérature et civilisation* (Senefiance, 9: Paris, 1980), p. 53; U. T. Holmes, op. cit., p. 165 and n. 6.

162 *Acta Sanctorum*, Apr. 3, p. 869.

163 Thomas of Eccleston, *De Adventu Fratrum Minorum in Angliam*, in *Monumenta Franciscana*, vol. I, ed. J. S. Brewer (Rolls Series; London, 1858), pp. 67–8.

164 *The Life of St. Anselm Archbishop of Canterbury by Eadmer*, pp. 4–5.

165 Wolfram of Eschenbach, *Parzival*, bk 3, 118, pp. 42–3.

166 C. Dyer, 'English Diet in the Later Middle Ages', in *Social Relations and Idea: Essays in Honour of R. Hilton*, ed. T. H. Aston, P. R. Cross, C. Dyer, and J. Thirsk (Cambridge, 1983), pp. 197–214. In the second half of the fourteenth century

and in the fifteenth century, there was a significant improvement in peasant diet in England, Germany, Sicily, and Languedoc.

167 For references and data on this, see ch. 6, n. 1.

168 From a Latin manuscript published by B. Hauréau, and quoted in Ch. V. Langlois, *La Vie en France au Moyen Age* (Paris, 1926), vol. II, p. 213, n. 2.

169 H. Kraus, *The Living Theatre of Medieval Art* (Bloomington, Ind., 1967), p. 57, pl. 34.

170 *Reliquiae Antiquae*, ed. T. Wright and J. O. Halliwell (London, 1843), vol. II, pp. 196–9.

171 See, on this, K. Thomas, *Religion and the Decline of Magic* (Harmondsworth, 1973), p. 42.

172 *The Life of St. Anselm Archbishop of Canterbury by Eadmer*, p. 102.

173 *Magna Vita Sancti Hugonis*, vol. I, pp. 127–8.

174 *Select Cases from the Coroner Rolls, 1265–1413*, ed. Ch. Gross (Selden Society; London, 1896), p. 82.

175 *Acta Sanctorum*, Feb. 3, p. 356.

176 For psychological explanations of and data from various countries on abuse and beating of children in modern times, see B. F. Steele, 'Parental Abuse of Infants and Small Children', in *Parenthood: Its Psychology and Psychopathology*, ed. E. J. Anthony and T. Benedek (Boston, 1970), pp. 447–77; S. Brody, 'A Mother is Being Beaten: An Institutional Derivative and Infant Care', ibid., pp. 427–47; the number of cases recorded in 1981 is taken from *Time*, Sept. 1983; on mistreatment in Switzerland of older children, who were able to give evidence, see A. Miller, op. cit., pp. 234–9.

177 J. B. Given, *Society and Homicide in 13th Century England* (Stanford, 1977), p. 115.

178 On warnings against excessive drinking as a result of which drunken fathers caused fires in the home or acted violently towards their children, see *Councils and Synods with Other Documents relating to the English Church*, ed. F. M. Powicke and C. R. Cheney (Oxford, 1964), vol. II, pt 1, pp. 214, 220; G. R. Owst, *Literature and Pulpit in Medieval England*, pp. 464–8, 428–9, 460.

179 A. E. Bernstein, 'Theology between Heresy and Folklore: William of Auvergne on Punishment after Death', *Studies in Medieval and Renaissance History*, 5 (1982), p. 29 and n. 80.

180 Wolfram of Eschenbach, *Parzival*, bk 16, 805–6, p. 286.

181 *I Libri* (= *The Family in Renaissance Florence*), p. 62.

182 See the words of Gilles Li Muisis, in Ch. V. Langlois, op. cit., vol. II, p. 355.

183 G. R. Owst, *Preaching in Medieval England*, p. 219; *Les Statuts synodaux français du XIIIᵉ siècle*, ed. O. Pontal (Paris, 1971), vol. I, s. 91, p. 86; s. 15, p. 150.

184 For children in processions in art, see F. Bonney, 'Enfance divine et enfance humaine', in *L'Enfant du Moyen Age: Littérature et civilisation* (Serefiance, 9; Paris, 1980), p. 9.

185 Bartholomaeus Anglicus, op. cit., bk 6, ch. 14 (= *John Trevisa's Translation*, p. 310); for more on the father as bread-winner, see Aegidius Romanus, op. cit., bk 2, pt 2, ch. 1.

186 *The Early English Version of the Gesta Romanorum*, pp. 435–6.

187 Thomas Aquinas, *Super Epistolas Pauli Lectura*, ed. R. Raphaelis (Rome, 1953), vol. I, 'Super primam epistolam ad Corinthios lectura 37', p. 296; id., *Summa Theologiae* (London, 1966–74), Secunda Secundae, q. 154, art. 2. (vol. 43, p. 212).

188 For example, *Registrum Hamonis Hethe: Diocese of Rochester*, ed. C. Johnson

(Oxford, 1948), p. 455; and see also R. H. Helmholz, *Marriage Litigations in Medieval England* (Cambridge, 1974), pp. 108–9 and n. 124; A. Lefebvre-Teillard, 'L'Enfant natural dans l'ancien droit français', in *Recueils de la Société Jean Bodin*, vol. 36/2 (Brussels, 1976), pp. 251–69; H. Fehr, *Die Rechtsstellung der Frau und der Kinder in dem Weistümern* (Jena, 1912), pp. 50, 271; the problem of bastardy arose, almost without exception, only when the child was born to an unmarried woman. The bastard child of a married woman was usually accepted by the family and considered legitimate. Neither the husband nor the judge wanted to delve into the matter, the former out of shame and the latter because it was highly difficult to prove bastardy in this case. The church distinguished between a bastard born to an unmarried couple (*ex soluto et soluta*) and one born of adultery or incest or an unknown father (*Fleta*, ed. H. G. Richardson and G. O. Sayers) (Selden Society; London, 1955), vol. II, ch. 5, p. 14; *Bracton on the Laws and Customs of England*, ed. and trans. S. Thorne (Cambridge, Mass., 1968), vol. II, p. 31; *St. Raymundi de Peniafort Summa de Poenitentia et Matrimonio* (Farnborough, 1967), pp. 579–81).

189 Raymond Lull, *Doctrine d'enfant*, ch. 91, p. 207; Vincent of Beauvais, *De Eruditione Filiorum Nobiliorum*, ed. A. Steiner (Cambridge, Mass., 1938), pp. 200–1; see also *Acta Sanctorum*, June 4, p. 525.

190 *I Libri* (= *The Family in Renaissance Florence*), pp. 49–50.

191 A. Lefebvre-Teillard, op. cit., pp. 264–5.

192 In literature, see, for example, Arnault Vidal de Castelnaudary, *Guillaume de la Barre*, ed. P. Meyer (Paris, 1895), pp. 81, 87, 90–7, 100–4.

193 *Acta Sanctorum*, Apr. 1, p. 671.

194 ibid., Mar. 3, p. 182.

195 D. Alexandre-Bidon and M. Closson, op. cit., p. 210; *A Catalogue of Misericords in Great Britain*, ed. G. L. Remnant (Oxford, 1969), p. 7.

196 See ch. 5, n. 169; ch. 7, nn. 98, 99; ch. 8, n. 66.

197 Bartholomaeus Anglicus, op. cit., bk 6, ch. 7, 14.

198 Thomas Aquinas, *Summa Theologiae*, Prima Pars, q. 92, art. 1 (vol. 13, pp. 34–6); *Summa Contra Gentiles*, in *Opera Omnia* (Milan, 1980), bk 3, ch. 122, nn. 6–8 (pp. 100–1).

199 Burchard of Worms, *Decretorum Libri Viginti*, PL vol. 140, col. 974; Bartholomew of Exeter, op. cit., 9, p. 224; Ivo of Chartre, *Decretum*, PL vol. 161, col. 893.

200 *Diplomatarium Danicum*, ed. N. Skyum-Nielsen (Copenhagen, 1958), vol. I, p. 144.

201 Burchard of Worms, op. cit., cols 835, 974.

202 *Acta Sanctorum*, May 5, p. 214; Feb. 1, p. 261; Apr. 2, p. 460.

203 R. C. Finucane, *Miracles and Pilgrims: Popular Beliefs in Medieval England* (London, 1977), p. 148; A. Sen, *Poverty and Famines: An Essay on Entitlement and Deprivation* (Oxford, 1981), pp. 98–110.

204 See, on this, B. H. E. Niestroj, 'Modern Individuality and the Social Isolation of Mother and Child', *Comparative Civilizations Review*, 15/1 (1987), pp. 23–40 (the quotation from Erasmus is ibid., p. 36 and n. 51); *Kardinal Johannes Dominicis Erziehungslehre*, p. 26.

205 Marie de France, *Lais*, Le Fresne, p. 35.

206 J. B. Ross, op. cit., p. 190.

207 Myrc, op. cit., pp. 5, 36.

208 Gerald of Wales, *Gemma Ecclesiastica*, ed. J. Brewer (Rolls Series; London, 1862), vol. 21/2, p. 45; *Old English Homilies of the Twelfth Century*, ed. R. Morris (EETS; London, 1873), p. 17; see also R. Fluck, 'Guillaume de Tournai et son traité *De*

Modo Docendi Pueros', *Revue des sciences religieuses*, 27 (1953), pp. 342–3.

209 *Select English Works of John Wycliffe*, ed. T. Arnold (Oxford, 1871), vol. III, p. 196.

210 See, on this, J. Goody, *The Development of the Family and Marriage in Europe* (Cambridge, 1983), ch. 9.

211 Ch. Klapisch-Zuber, 'L'Attribution d'un prénom à l'enfant en Toscane à la fin du Moyen Age', in *L'Enfant au Moyen Age: Littérature et civilisation* (Senefiance, 9; Paris, 1980), pp. 75–8.

212 Myrc, op. cit., p. 5; in a fourteenth-century English text, godparents are cautioned against sexual exploitation of their godchildren. This suggests that the author believed that some contact was maintained, since he would not have seen fit to issue a warning otherwise (*Robert of Brunnes' 'Handling Synne'*, p. 303).

213 *Acta Sanctorum*, Aug. 1, p. 645; one small girl was fortunate enough to have a future saint as her godmother. The latter's prayers effected her cure (ibid., Apr. 2, p. 191).

214 J. P. Cuvillier, op. cit., pp. 51–2.

215 The *exemplum* is cited in G. Duby, *Le Chevalier, la femme et le prêtre* (Paris, 1981), pp. 254–7.

216 *The Fifty Earliest English Wills in the Court of Probate London*, pp. 39, 80.

217 ibid., p. 50.

218 ibid., p. 95.

219 ibid., pp. 101–1.

220 B. A. Hanawalt, *The Ties that Bound: Peasant Families in Medieval England* (Oxford, 1986), pp. 246–7.

221 Thomas Chobham, *Summa Confessorum*, ed. F. Broomfield (Paris–Louvain, 1963), p. 96.

222 For example, *Councils and Synods*, vol. II, pt 1, p. 183. It was eventually determined that a boy would have no more than two godfathers and one godmother; and a girl no more than two godmothers and one godfather; see also Gerald of Wales, *Gemma Ecclesiastica*, p. 46.

223 *The Fifty Earliest English Wills in the Court Probate London*, p. 27.

224 See, e.g., *Raoul de Cambrai*, p. 10.

225 *The Latin Text of the Ancrene Riwle*, ed. Ch. D. Evelyn (EETS; London, 1944), p. 84.

226 M. Bloch believed that the father was ready for his son to be executed (*La Société féodale* (Paris, 1939), vol. I, p. 210); *L'Histoire de Guillaume le Maréchal*, ed. P. Meyer (Paris, 1891), ll. 513–634, pp. 19–24; G. Duby, *Guillaume le Maréchal ou Le Meilleur Chevalier du monde*, pp. 79–81).

227 On the execution of child-hostages in literature, see ch. 6, n. 69. There are other examples of children handed over as hostages: Louis of Toulouse was handed over as a hostage at the age of 14, together with his two younger brothers (*Analecta Bollandiana*, vol. 9 (1980), p. 284); the Irishman Laurence O'Toole was handed over as a hostage at 10 years old (*Analecta Bollandiana*, 33 (1914), pp. 129–30); as was Pierre of Luxemburg while about the same age (R. Kieckhefer, *Unquiet Souls: Fourteenth Century Saints and their Religious Milieu* (Chicago, 1984), pp. 33–4).

228 *Sancti Bernardi Vita Prima*, P.L., vol. 185, col. 253.

6 ABANDONMENT, INFANTICIDE, AND ACCIDENTS

1 Z. Razi, *Life, Marriage and Death in a Medieval Parish* (Cambridge, 1980), pp. 83–5; in the manors of Rickinghall, Redgrave, ibid., p. 86 and note 178 to p. 164; the number of progeny in villages was higher than in towns in corresponding social classes. According to records from 1427, the average number of offspring in prosperous urban families was 2.26; in prosperous rural families, 3.21; in poor urban families, 0.86; in poor rural families, 1.47. D. Herlihy, *Medieval and Renaissance Pistoia* (New Haven, 1967), pp. 117–18.

2 On the use of contraception in the Middle Ages, see J. Noonan, *Contraception: A History of Its Treatment by the Catholic Theologians and Canonists* (Cambridge, Mass., 1965), ch. 6 and pp. 212–35; P. Biller, 'Birth Control in the West in the 13th and 14th Centuries', *Past and Present*, 94 (1982), pp. 5–26. According to Biller, the scope of practice of *coitus interruptus* in the Middle Ages was of demographic significance.

3 J. M. Bienvenu, 'Pauvreté, misères et charité en Anjou aux XIᵉ et XIIᵉ siècles', *Moyen Age*, 72 (1966), pp. 399, 408–9; *Magna Vita Sancti Hugonis*, ed. and trans. D. Douie and Dom. H. Farmer (Nelson Series; London, 1961), vol. I, p. 132; *Corpus Iuris Canonici*, ed. A. Friedberg (Leipzig, 1879), vol. II, Decretal Gregor. ix, bk 5, tit. 11, ch. 1, col. 793; and see also J. Boswell, *Expositio* and *Oblatio*: The Abandonment of Children and the Ancient and Medieval Family', *American Historical Review*, 89 (1984), p. 17 and n. 14; *Die Konstitutionen Friedrichs* ii *von Hohenstaufen für sein Königreich Sizilien*, ed. H. Conrad, T. von Lieck-Buyken, W. Wagner (Vienna, 1973), vol. II, 80, p. 338; on a charge of having forced a child to engage in prostitution, see G. Ruggiero, *Violence in Early Renaissance Florence* (New Brunswick, NJ, 1980), p. 70.

4 See ch. 3, nn. 85–7, and also *Corpus Iuris Canonici*, vol. II, bk 3, tit. 42, ch. 11, col. 644; Myrc, *Instructions for Parish Priests*, ed. E. Peacock (EETS; London, 1868), pp. 19, 23.

5 *Councils and Synods with Other Documents relating to the English Church*, ed. F. M. Powicke and C. R. Cheney (Oxford, 1964), vol. II, pt I, pp. 357, 455, 632; vol. II, pt II, p. 1073; *Fleta*, ed. H. G. Richardson and G. O. Sayles (Selden Society; London, 1955), vol. II, ch. 15, pp. 31–4; *Bracton on the Laws and Customs of England*, ed. and trans. S. Thorne (Cambridge, Mass., 1968), vol. II, pp. 201–4; *Magna Vita Sancti Hugonis*, vol. II. pp. 20–7; and see also M. McLaughlin, 'Survivors and Surrogates: Children and Parents from the Ninth to the Thirteenth Century', in *The History of Childhood*, ed. L. deMause (New York, 1974), n. 126.

6 *Galeran*, in Ch. V. Langlois, *La Vie en France au Moyen Age* (Paris, 1926), vol. I, p. 75; Marie de France, *Lais*, ed. A. E. E. Ewert (Oxford, 1965), pp. 35–48; this belief that twins are born of different fathers also prevailed in Africa, South America, and the Scandinavian countries in the pre-Christian era. See *The Nordic Dead Child Tradition* (FF Communications, 22; Helsinki, 1968), pp. 60, 68.

7 Hartmann of Aue, *Gregorius*, ed. F. Maurer (Berlin, 1968); and see also P. F. Baum, 'The Medieval legend of Judas Iscariot', *Publications of the Modern Language Association of America*, 31 (1916) pp. 481–632.

8 Marie de France. *Lais*, pp. 107–15.

9 D. Herlihy and Ch. Klapisch, *Les Toscans et leur familles: une étude du Catasto florentin de 1427* (Paris, 1978), p. 339; Ch. Klapisch-Zuber, 'Women Servants in Florence during the 14th and 15th Centuries', in *Women and Work in Preindustrial Europe*, ed. B. A. Hanawalt (Bloomington, Ind., 1986), p. 70.

10 e.g. *Vita Beati Bernardi Auctore Gaufrido Grosso*, PL vol. 172, col. 1441.

11 L. Le Grand (ed.), *Statuts d'hôtels dieu et de léproseries* (Paris, 1901), pp. 124, 139, 162; and see also J. Imbert, *Les Hôpitaux en droit canonique* (Paris, 1947), p. 125 and n. 6; *Medieval Woman's Guide to Health*, ed. and trans. B. Rowland (London, 1981), p. 7.

12 L. Le Grand, op. cit., s. 99, p. 115.

13 In the hospital of Auffredi at La Rochelle in 1471–2, there were 33 orphans and abandoned children (14 boys and 19 girls) who were sent out to wetnurses: see B. Loriaud, 'Les Pauvres Malades et le personnel de l'aumonerie Auffredi à La Rochelle vers 1470', *Revue de la Société d'archéologie et d'histoire de la Charente maritime*, 25 (1973–4), p. 141; on the farming-out of infants to wetnurses by the Florence foundlings' home, see R. Trexler, 'Infanticide in Florence: New Sources and First Results', *History of Childhood Quarterly*, 1/1 (1973), pp. 98–116; for farming-out to wetnurses by the town authorities of Saint Cyprien, see R. Favreau, 'Pauvreté en Poitou et en Anjou à la fin du Moyen Age', in *Études sur l'histoire de la pauvreté (Moyen Age XVIᵉ Siècle)*, ed. M. Mollat (Paris, 1974), pp. 597, 602; for Montpellier, see L. L. Otis, 'Municipal Wetnurses in Medieval Montpellier', in B. A. Hanawalt (ed.), *Women and Work in Pre-industrial Europe* (Bloomingdale, Ind., 1986), pp. 83–93.

14 In the Lives of the saints a future saint, who was blind, was abandoned by her parents at the age of 6 in the church of a convent after they had taken her to the shrine of a saint and no miracle had occurred. The nuns found a family willing to take her in. This was St Margaret of Città-di-Castello: *Acta Sanctorum*, ed. J. Bollandus and G. Henschenius (Paris–Rome, 1863–1940), Apr. 2, p. 190; other examples: *Analecta Bollandiana*, 19 (1900), p. 24; *Magna Vita Sancti Hugonis*, vol. I, pp. 131–3; see also C. Billot, 'Les Enfants abandonés à Chartres à la fin du Moyen Age', *Annales de démographie historique* (1973), pp. 167–86.

15 In the poem *Guilllaume de la Barre*, the little boy is adopted by the King of Armenia (Arnault Vidal de Castelnaudary, *Guillaume de la Barre*, ed. P. Meyer (Paris, 1895), pp. 97–8). Conversely, the infant Julien, whose father has been taken prisoner, is adopted by a Saracen who is a simple warrior) *Raoul de Cambrai*, ed. P. Meyer and A. Longnon (Paris, 1882), p. 272).

16 'paucorum admodum mensium infantulum, parentibus orbatum, ad se contrahens nutrire delegit' (Gilbert of Nogent, *Autobiographie*, ed. E. R. Labande (Paris, 1981), bk 1, ch. 18, p. 156; on the children of slaves whose fathers acknowledged them, see J. Heers, *Esclaves et domestiques au Moyen Age dans le monde méditerranéen* (Paris, 1981), pp. 230–2.

17 J. Goody, *The Development of the Family and Marriage in Europe* (Cambridge, 1983), pp. 39–45, 71–5.

18 'Polfinus a wise Emperoure', in *The Early English Version of the Gesta Romanorum*, ed. S. J. H. Herrtage (London, 1879), pp. 206–19.

19 *Year Books of Edward* ii, vol. I, ed. F. W. Maitland (Selden Society; London, 1904), pp. 186–7.

20 A. Lefebvre-Teillard, 'L'Enfant naturel dans l'ancien droit français', in *Recueils de la Société Jean Bodin*, vol. 36/2 (Brussels, 1976), p. 265, n. 25.

21 See, on this, W. Denis, *Children of the Creche* (New York, 1973).

22 See R. Trexler, op. cit.

23 According to Herlihy and Klapisch (op. cit., pp. 338–40), many children were abandoned in Tuscany as early as the beginning of the fifteenth century mainly in years of famine, plague, and war. But, with the establishment of the Innocenti foundlings' home, the number apparently increased.

24 *Corpus Iuris Canonici*, vol. II, bk 5, tit. II, ch. 1, vol. 793; Thomas Chobham,

Summa Confessorum, ed. F. Broomfield (Paris–Louvain, 1963), p. 218.

25 In the recorded rulings of the *échevins* of Ypres in Flanders from the beginning of the fourteenth century, there appear one case of a man and one of a woman who left behind them a child younger than 7. They were sentenced to five years' exile, with a sanction for the man of perpetual exile and for the woman of execution by being buried alive. It is not specified whether these were their own children, but, since in cases of the luring and stealing of children it is noted that reference is to the children of others or, at least, this is implied by the phrasing, it is reasonable to assume that, in these two cases, it was their own children they abandoned:

> Pierre de Grise est banis V ans hors le pays de Flandre, sous se teste, pour ce qu'il laissa un petit enfant desous sept ans derrière luy, et luy est jugiet d'ammenner le dit enfant aveuc luy, sous estre banit à tous jours hors le pays de Flandre.
>
> Grielle Paets est banie choine ans hors le pays de Flandres, sour le fosse, pour ce qu'elle laissa un petit enfant dessous vij ans derrière elle, et lui est jugiet de ammener le dit enfant aveuc luy.
>
> (*Registres sur sentences des échevins d'Ypres*, in *Coutumes de Pays et Comté de Flandre: Quartier d'Ypres*, ed. Prosper de Pelsmaeker (Brussels, 1914), 751, p. 297).

On trials for luring and stealing children in order to force them to engage in prostitution or to beg, see ibid. pp. 405, 258, 460, 263, 855, 316.

26 *Council and Synods*, vol. II, pt 1, p. 137; Myrc, op. cit, p. 23.

27 B. A. Hanawalt, 'The Female Felon in 14th Century England', in *Women in Medieval Society*, ed. S. Mosher-Stuard (University Park, Penn., 1976), p. 130–1; N. Hurnard, *The King's Pardon for Homicide before 1307 A.D.* (Oxford, 1969), pp. 161–3; B. A. Kellum, 'Infanticide in England in the Later Middle Ages', *History of Childhood Quarterly*, 1 (1974), p. 373 and n. 42.

28 On the fact that jurors were asked to bring evidence of the insanity of women on trial, see B. A. Hanawalt, *The Ties that Bound: Peasant Families in Medieval England* (Oxford, 1986), p. 183 and n. 42, p. 184 and n. 46.

29 See, e.g., B. A. Kellum, op. cit., p. 382.

30 C. Damme, 'Infanticide: The Worth of an Infant under Law', *Medical History*, 22 (1978), pp. 1–24.

31 J. Pentikäinen, op. cit., pp. 63–8.

32 Jean Gerson, *Traité des diverses tentations de l'ennemi*, in *Œuvres complètes*, ed. Mgr P. Glorieux, vol. II (Tournai, 1960), pp. 355–6.

33 In the secular legislation of the Central Middle Ages, there is no prohibition on the murder of a new-born infant since law did not differentiate between infanticide and homicide. There is a separate discussion only of abortion and injury to a pregnant women (which causes her to miscarry); *Fleta*, ch. 23, pp. 60–1; *Bracton*, vol. II, p. 341–2; according to Norman law, if a father murdered his son intentionally (*inique*) he was sentenced to be burned at the stake. If he killed him unintentionally (this is apparently the meaning, since it is otherwise difficult to reconcile the contradiction between the two statements), he is merely banished: E. J. Tardif (ed.), *Coutumiers de Normandie* (Slatkine repr.; Geneva, 1977), vol. I–II, s. 35, p. 29; *Corpus Iuris Canonici*, vol. II, bk 5, tit. 10, ch. I–II, col. 792.

34 Most acts of infanticide today are committed by psychopathic mothers. See E. J. Anthony and N. Kreitman, 'Murderous Obsessions in Mothers towards Their Children', in *Parenthood: Its Psychology and Psychopathology*, ed. E. J. Anthony

and T. Benedek (Boston, 1970), pp. 479–98.

35 Burchard of Worms, *Decretorum Libri Viginti*, PL vol. 140, cols. 972–3. Myrc, op. cit., p. 23; Thomas Chobham, *Summa Confessorum*, ed. F. Broomfield (Paris–Louvain, 1963), pp. 463–5. John Wyclif refers to this in the context of the sins of the clergy. Sometimes the licentious relationships entered into by priests lead to the murder of the infant born of them (*The English Works of Wyclif Hitherto Unpublished*, ed. F. D. Matthew (EETS; London, 1880), p. 100.

36 R. Trexler, op. cit., pp. 99–100 and n. 14.

37 Herrad of Lansberg, *Hortus Deliciarum*, ed. J. Walter (Strasburg, 1952), pl. 44 and p. 101. The punishment of the murderess is to gnaw at the corpse of her infant for ever.

38 Y. Brissaud, 'L'Infanticide à la fin du Moyen Age: Ses motivations psychologiques et sa répression', *Revue historique de droit français et étranger*, 50 (1972), pp. 229–56.

39 On cases of trial for the murder of new-born infants in Italy and England, see R. Trexler, op. cit., n. 49; G. Brucker (ed.), *The Society of Renaissance Florence: A Documentary Study* (New York, 1971), pp. 146–7; N. D. Hurnard, op. cit., p. 169; B. A. Hanawalt, 'The Female Felon in 14th Century England', p. 130; G. Ruggiero, *Violence in Early Renaissance Florence*, p. 178. On the basis of the population records of Florence in 1427, it appears that the lower classes did not register illegitimate offspring. This may have stemmed from the fact that, in these classes, bastard children were absorbed into families more easily than among the rich. It may also be, however, that some of them were murdered immediately after birth (D. Herlihy and Ch. Klapisch, op. cit., p. 339).

40 Burchard of Worms, op. cit., cols 972–3; *Un manuel de confession archaique dans le manuscrit Avranche 136*, ed. P. Michaud-Quantin (Paris, 1962), p. 38.

41 See, e.g., Philip of Beaumanoir, *Coutumes de Beauvaisis*, ed. A. Salmon (Paris, 1899–1900), vol. II, s. 1813, pp. 417–18; Burchard of Worms, op. cit., col. 972; *Corpus Iuris Canonici*, vol. II, Decretal Gregor. IX, bk 5, tit. 10, ch. I–II, col. 792.

42 See, e.g., R. M. Wunderli, *London Church Courts and Society on the Eve of the Reformation* (Cambridge, Mass., 1981), p. 128.

43 For cautions to parents see (e.g.) Thomas Chobham, op. cit., p. 215; *Councils and Synods*, vol. II, pt 1, pp. 32, 70, 183, 214, 235, 590; cautions to wetnurses, ibid., pp. 204, 274, 351, 410, 432, 457, 520, 648; Francesco of Barbaro, *Reggimento e costume di Donne*, ed. G. E. Sansone (Turin, 1957), p. 195; and see also: L. E. Boyle, 'The "Oculus sacerdotis" and some other works of William of Pagula', *Transactions of the Royal Historical Society*, 5 (1955), p. 89; cautions to godparents: Myrc, op. cit., p. 5.

44 See, on this, R. Trexler, op. cit., p. 108; B. Hanawalt, 'Child Rearing among the Lower Classes of Late Medieval England', *Journal of Interdisciplinary History*, 8 (1977), pp. 20–2.

45 *Peter Abelard's Ethics*, ed. and trans. D. Luscombe (Oxford, 1971), pp. 38–9.

46 *Corpus Iuris Canonici*, vol. II, Decretal Gregor IX, bk 5, tit. 10, ch. II, col. 793.

47 *Councils and Synods*, vol. II, pt 1, p. 441; pt 2, p. 1073; Thomas Chobham, op. cit., pp. 215, 466; Myrc, op. cit., p. 45.

48 *A Series of Precedents and Proceedings*, ed. W. H. Hale (London, 1847), 89, p. 21; 150, p. 41; 185, p. 52; R. M. Wunderli, op. cit., pp. 128–30; R. Trexler, op. cit., pp. 103–9; id., *Synodal Law in Florence and Fiesole, 1306–1518* (Vatican City, 1971), pp. 64, 126–7; R. H. Helmholz, 'Infanticide in the Province of Canterbury during the 15th Century', *Journal of Psychohistory*, 2 (1975), pp. 379–90;

according to the rulings of the Danish synod, the mother was assigned three years of penance (*Diplomatarium Danicum*, ed. N. Skyum-Nielsen (Copenhagen, 1958), vol. I, pp. 143–4); as also according to Bartholomew of Exeter in his confessors' manual (*Bartholomew of Exeter: Bishop and Canonist, with Text of Bartholomew's Penitential*, ed. D. A. Morey (Cambridge, 1937), 9, p. 224).

49 *Registre de l'inquisition de Jacques Fournier 1318–1325*, ed. J. Duvernoy (Toulouse, 1965), vol. I, 33 c, d, p. 202.

50 *Scriptores Minores Historiae Danicae Medii Aevi*, ed. M. G. L. Gertz (Copenhagen, 1970), p. 275.

51 *Acta Sanctorum*, Mar. 2, p. 103; *Analecta Bollandiana*, 9 (1890), pp. 344–5; R. C. Finucane, *Miracles and Pilgrims: Popular Beliefs in Medieval England* (London, 1977), p. 109; again, in the list of miracles attributed to Edmond of Abingdon, we find *inter alia* the revival of infants who had died of suffocation in the parental bed. This is not personal testimony (*Thesaurus Novus Anecdotorum*, ed. E. Martene and U. Durand (Paris, 1717), vol. III, col. 1821).

52 A. Felber, *Unzucht und Kindsmord in der Rechtsprechung der freien Reichstadt Nordlingen von 15 bis 19 Jahrhundert* (Bonn, 1961), p. 95; quoted in R. Trexler, 'Infanticide in Florence', p. 103 n. 39.

53 J. Flandrin, *Families in Past Times*, pp. 180–4; J. Pentikäinen, op. cit., pp. 96–9; Flandrin estimates that there was an increase not only in the number of illegitimate children abandoned, but also in the number of births outside wedlock in general. See J. Flandrin, 'Repression and Change in the Sexual Life of Young People in Medieval and Early Modern Times', *Journal of Family History*, 2 (1977), pp. 203 ff.

54 E. A. Wrigley, *Population and History* (London, 1969), pp. 125–6.

55 'pro sanitate febrium', Burchard of Worms, op. cit., col. 835.

56 G. G. Coulton, *Life in the Middle Ages* (Cambridge, 1967), pt II, p. 38.

57 On belief in changelings in the Middle Ages and later centuries, see J. Pentikäinen, op. cit., p. 59; W. Gregor, *The Folklore of the North East of Scotland* (London, 1881), pp. 5, 9, 11–12, 61–2; M. A. Courtney, 'Cornish Folk-Lore', *Folk-Lore Journal*, 5 (1887), pp. 183–4.

58 J. C. Schmitt, *Le Saint Lévrier: Guinefort guérisseur d'enfants depuis le XIIIe siècle* (Paris, 1979); for the report of Stephen of Bourbon, see ibid., pp. 13–15.

59 F. C. Tubach, *Index Exemplorum* (FF Communications, 204; Helsinki, 1969), 5138, p. 388; *The Early English Version of the Gesta Romanorum*, p. 235; *The English and Scottish Popular Ballads*, ed. F. J. Child (New York, 1965), vol. I, pp. 218–27.

60 *Malleus Maleficarum* (Frankfurt, 1582), pt 2, q. 1, ch. 13; *The Malleus Maleficarum of Heinrich Kramer and James Sprenger*, trans. M. Summers (New York, 1971), pp. 140–4.

61 A recent study of this first blood-libel, which cites previous studies, is G. I. Langmuir's 'Thomas of Monmouth: Detector of Ritual Murder', *Speculum*, 61 (1984), pp. 820–46.

62 See N. Cohn, *The Pursuit of the Millenium* (New York, 1961), pl. 4 and pp. 72–3.

63 See P. S. Schenk, *Berner Brunnen Chronik* (Berne, 1969), pp. 26–8.

64 See on this F. Xavier Baron, 'Children and Violence in Chaucer's Canterbury Tales', *Journal of Psychohistory*, 7/1 (1979), pp. 77–104.

65 R. Kuhn, *Corruption in Paradise: The Child in Western Literature* (London, 1982), p. 31.

66 Geoffrey Chaucer, *The Canterbury Tales*, ed. W. W. Skeat (Oxford, 1947), The Prioress's Tale, pp. 161–7.

67 Dante, *The Divine Comedy*, trans. L. Binyon (New York, 1947), Inferno, Canto 33, pp. 176–9.

68 J. L. Borges, *Nueve Ensayos Dantescos*: a selection of excerpts from this essay. including the section on Ugolino, appeared in translation in *FMR* 3 (1984), pp. 76–80.

69 E. Auerbach, *Mimesis: The Representation of Reality in Western Literature*, trans. W. Trask (New York, 1957), pp. 203–29 (including excerpts in the original French). There is an even earlier medieval version of this story. In Jourdain de Blaivies, the vassal sacrifices his own son in order to rescue the son of the seigneur from captivity. The mother accepts this, since this is the father's wish: he feels that the feudal code of honour and loyalty requires him to sacrifice his son. See L. Gautier, *Chivalry*, trans. D. C. Dunning (London, 1965), p. 41. And see also D. Poirion, 'Edyppus et l'énigme du roman médiéval', in *L'Enfant au Moyen Age: Littérature et civilisation* (Senefiance, 9; Paris, 1980), p. 292.

70 R. Kuhn, op. cit., ch. 4.

71 *The Chester Plays*, ed. H. Deimling (EETS; London, 1893), pt 1, p. 76.

72 *Das Leben des Seligen Heinrich Seuse* (Düsseldorf, 1966), pp. 153 ff.

73 Flavius Josephus, *The Wars of the Jews*, trans. H. St. J. Thackeray (Loeb Classical Library; Cambridge, Mass., 1961), bk 6, ch. 3, pp. 434–7; *The Josippon (Josephus Gorionidis)*, ed. D. Flusser (Jerusalem, 1978; in Hebrew), vol. I, pp. 40, 407; on this tale in medieval literature and later, and its analysis, see N. Deutsch, 'The Myth of Maria of Azov', *Zmanim*, 17 (1984), pp. 20–8 (in Hebrew); in an amended version, the story also appears among the miracles attributed to St Vincent Ferrer. According to one version, he restored to life an infant whose mother had dismembered it, cooked it, and was about to offer it as food to the father and to the saint, who had returned from preaching a sermon. The author attributes her deed to an attack of insanity, such as afflicted her from time to time. According to the second version, this was the act of a pregnant woman who longed to eat meat, and therefore murdered her two-year-old son. The father brought the hacked-up corpse to the shrine of the saint, who moulded the pieces together and restored the child to life (*Acta Sanctorum*, Apr. 1, pp. 500–1).

74 The following are a few limited sources which describe the revelation of the Christ-child (sometimes bleeding and torn) in the sacrament of the Eucharist: *Magna Vita Sancti Hugonis*, vol. II, p. 86; *Robert of Brunne's 'Handlyng Synne'*, ed. F. J. Furnivall (EETS; London, 1901), pt. 1, pp. 25–9, 312–17; in the life of Edward the Confessor it is related how he saw an infant in the sacrament, when the mass was conducted at Westminster. The illustration of the incident dates from the thirteenth century (Cambridge University Library, Ee.3.59, p. 212); Humbert de Romans, *Sermones* (Venice, 1603), 49, p. 59; and see also ch. 5, n. 163; for reference to additional relevant sources and analysis of them, see L. Sinanoglou, 'The Christ Child as Sacrifice: A Medieval Tradition and the Corpus Christi Plays', *Speculum*, 48 (1973), pp. 491–509; for the various versions in Greek, Latin, and the vernaculars of the tale of the Jewish child who seeks to convert to Christianity after the Christ-child is revealed to him in the host and on the miracle which befalls him (his father puts him in a blazing oven and Mary rescues him), see E. Wolter, *Der Jüdenknabe* (Halle, 1879).

75 E. S. Stern, 'The Medea Complex: The Mother's Homicidal Wishes to Her Child', *Journal of Mental Science*, 94 (1948), pp. 321–31; J. Pentikäinen, op. cit., pp. 353–560.

76 Thomas Chobham, op. cit., p. 215; *Councils and Synods*, vol. II, pt 1, pp. 70, 183, 214.

77 Francesco of Barbaro, op. cit., ch. 13.

78 Konrad of Megenberg, *Ökonomik*, ed. S. Krüger (Stuttgart, 1973; MGH Staatschriften, 111/5), bk 1/2 ch. 9, p. 81; ch. 14, p. 90.

79 *Acta et Processus Canonizacionis Beate Brigitte*, ed. I. Collijn (Uppsala, 1931), p. 143; *Acta Sanctorum*, Mar. 3, p. 213. In the sixteenth century in Italy, protective devices were added to the cradle: a small arch (*arcuccio*) to prevent the bedcovers from falling on the infant and to prevent him from falling out in the event that he was rocked too vigorously; in the cradle itself, a hole was drilled in the side to enable the wetnurse to suckle the infant in the cradle and to keep the cradle in her bed (see R. Trexler, 'Infanticide in Florence', p. 108); in earlier times the infant was sometimes tied to the cradle by a band (see ch. 5, n. 74).

80 *Acta Sanctorum*, May 4, p. 622.

81 ibid., May 1, p. 378; June 2, pp. 374, 375, 377, 380; *Analecta Bollandiana*, 4 (1890), p. 325.

82 *Acta Sanctorum*, Feb. 1, p. 261; Mar. 1, p. 737; Apr. 3, pp. 93, 681; Aug. 1, p. 649; *Acta et Processus Canonizacionis Beate Brigitte*, p. 130.

83 *Acta Sanctorum*, Mar. 1, pp. 332, 496, 736; Mar. 3, pp. 57, 199, 207, 237, 238, 524; Apr. 1, pp. 513, 514, 515; Apr. 2, pp. 193, 460, 461; Apr. 3, p. 958; May 1, p. 352; Aug. 1, p. 586; St Bonaventure, *Legenda Sancti Francisci*, in *Opera Omnia* (Karachi, 1898), p. 552; *Analecta Bollandiana*, 19 (1900), p. 32.

84 *Acta Sanctorum*, Mar. 3, p. 329; Aug. 1, pp. 644, 645, 651; Aug. 3, p. 687; *Acta et Processus Canonizacionis Beate Brigitte*, p. 120.

85 *Acta Sanctorum*, Mar. 1, p. 597.

86 ibid., Jan. 2, p. 70; Apr. 1, p. 311; May 7, p. 472; Aug. 1, p. 607.

87 ibid., Apr. 1, p. 514.

88 ibid., Mar. 3, p. 528; *Analecta Bollandiana*, 64 (1946), p. 44.

89 *Acta Sanctorum*, Mar. 2, pp. 496, 497, 661.

90 ibid., Mar. 1, p. 297; Mar. 3, pp. 199, 524; Apr. 1, p. 512; Apr. 2, p. 193; May 4, p. 621; May 5, p. 103; May 7, p. 464; July 1, pp. 500, 501; Aug. 1, p. 653; *The Miracles of Simon de Montfort*, ed. J. O. Halliwell (Camden Society; London, 1849), pp. 74, 77, 87, 101; *The Vita Wulfstani of William of Malmesbury*, ed. R. R. Darlington (London, 1928), p. 160; *Acta et Processus Canonizacionis Beate Brigitte*, p. 140; *Analecta Bollandiana*, 33 (1914), pp. 160, 170, 171; 64 (1946), p. 44; and many more.

91 *Acta Sanctorum*, Mar. 3, p. 525; another fall from a ladder, ibid., Mar. 3, p. 723.

92 ibid., Mar. 1, p. 597.

93 ibid., Apr. 1, p. 709; *Analecta Bollandiana*, 9 (1890), p. 345.

94 *Acta et Processus Canonizacionis Beate Brigitte*, p. 139.

95 *Acta Sanctorum*, Mar. 3, p. 524.

96 *The Vita Wulfstani*, p. 176.

97 *Acta Sanctorum*, Apr. 1, p. 709; Mar. 3, p. 516; May 5, p. 103; *Acta et Processus Canonizationis Beate Brigitte*, pp. 125, 131, 158, 159, and more.

98 *Select Cases from the Coroners' Rolls, 1265–1413*, ed. Ch. Gross (Selden Society; London, 1896). For cases of drowning of small children, pp. 5, 7, 8, 11, 13, 41, 42, 50, 81; children burnt to death when left alone in a house, p. 6; scalding with boiling water, pp. 39, 40; a boy drowned while bathing in a river, p. 12; death as a result of a landslide or of the collapse of a wall, pp. 50, 81. See also B. A. Hanawalt, 'Child Rearing among the Lower Classes of Late Medieval England', pp. 15–21. Reference is made in the life of the English saint, Richard

of Wyche, of the coroners coming to investigate the case of a child injured by a galloping horse ridden by a drunk (*Acta Sanctorum*, Apr. 1, p. 311).

99 *Select Cases from the Coroner's Rolls*, p. 38.

100 *Select Pleas of the Crown*, ed. F. W. Maitland (Selden Society; London, 1888), vol. 1, p. 67.

101 *Select Cases from the Coroners' Rolls*, pp. 4, 6, 14.

102 *Calendar of Letter Books: Letter Book G: 1352–1374*, ed. R. R. Sharpe (London, 1905), p. 306; William Langland, in *Piers Plowman*, expresses disapproval of the beggars who beget children in order to use them to collect alms. These parents distort and break the children's limbs in order to rouse pity (William Langland, *Piers Plowman*, an edn. of the C text, ed. D. Pearsall (London, 1978), passus 9, ll. 61–281; on other cases of child-stealing, see E. Cohen, 'Youth and Deviance in the Middle Ages', in *History of Juvenile Delinquency*, ed. A. G. Hess and P. F. Clement (forthcoming), n. 68.

103 L. deMause, 'The Evolution of Childhood', *History of Childhood Quarterly*, 1/4 (1974), pp. 511–12.

104 For example: *Six sermons français inédits de Jean Gerson*, ed. L. Mourin (Paris, 1946), pp. 80, 297; G. R. Owst, *Literature and Pulpit in Medieval England* (Oxford, 1961), pp. 207, 464; however, the biographer of the Bishop of Soissons (who became a saint) attributes the death of all the children of a sinning nobleman to divine retribution. According to the author, the noble's wife thought the same (*Ex Vita Arnulfi Episcopi Suessionensis Auctore Hariulfo*, in *MGHS* vol. 15/2, pp. 883–4.

105 *Acta Sanctorum*, Mar. 1, p. 332.

106 ibid., June 4, p. 369.

107 ibid., May 7, p. 464; *Acta et Processus Canonizacionis Beate Brigitte*, pp. 140, 143; 'minus tamen caute', *Acta Sanctorum*, Apr. 1, p. 311.

108 *The Miracles of Simon de Montfort*, p. 86.

109 *The Vita Wulfstani*, p. 160.

110 *Select Cases from the Coroners' Rolls*, pp. 8, 42.

111 M. Sellers (ed.), *York Memorandum Book* (Surtees Society; London, 1912), vol. I, p. lxx.

112 *Acta Sanctorum*, Feb. 1, p. 261; Apr. 2, p. 460.

113 See R. Trexler, 'Infanticide in Florence', n. 7.

114 For injury or death as a result of fights without homicidal intent, see *Select Cases from the Coroners' Rolls*, pp. 3, 8, 10, 12, 17, 44, 54, 60, 62, 69, 83, 89, 91, 93, 95; during the game known as 'stone-throwing', a stone hit the head of one of the players, killing him (p. 60); a glowing coal fell on the straw in a man's bed, and he died of his burns (p. 52); a man died of burns received during a fire in the home (p. 107); knights were killed when their horses stumbled and fell (pp. 68, 125); women fell into boiling water and were scalded to death (pp. 6, 15, 91); a man fell on to a wheelshaft which pierced his innards (p. 7); a man was killed when the load of a cart fell on him (p. 54); for other work accidents and falls, see pp. 94, 95, 96, 98, 99, 105, 117, 121, 122, 126; death as a result of the collapse of a wall, or falling into a ditch, or falling from the parapet of a bell-tower (while hunting pigeons), pp. 77, 82, 94; cases of drowning, pp. 5, 10, 12, 16, 49, 51, 59, 61, 105, 109, 121, 122, 124, 126, 127. See also R. C. Finucane, op. cit., pp. 147–51; B. A. Hanawalt. 'Seeking the Flesh and Blood of Manorial Families', *Journal of Medieval History*, 14 (1988), pp. 37–40.

115 *Acta Sanctorum*, Aug. 1, p. 649.

116 ibid., May 3, p. 633.

117 B. A. Hanawalt, *The Ties that Bound: Peasant Families in Medieval England*, pp. 175–82.

118 M. Mead, *Growing up in Guinea* (New York, 1953), ch. 3.

119 'maternis viceribus super prole sic deformata commotis, irremediabiliter doleret', *Acta Sanctorum*, Mar. 1, p. 738.

120 ibid., Mar. 1, p. 597, Apr. 1, p. 709; July 1, p. 500; Aug. 3, p. 687; *Acta et Processus Canonizacionis Beate Brigitte*, p. 140; *Analecta Bollandiana*, 9 (1890), p. 325.

121 B. A. Hanawalt, 'The Female Felon in 14th Century England', pp. 20–1.

122 e.g. *Acta Sanctorum*, Feb. 1, p. 260.

123 *Diplomatarium Danicum*, vol. 1, p. 144 ('cum magis notari possit in matre pena ex doloris vehemencia quam culpa').

7   SICKNESS, HANDICAPS, BEREAVEMENT, AND ORPHANHOOD

1 Ph. Ariès, *L'Enfant et la vie familiale sous l'ancien régime* (Paris, 1960), p. 30.

2 P. Laslett, *The World we have Lost* (New York, 1965), pp. 95–6.

3 R. Finucane, *Miracles and Pilgrims: Popular Beliefs in Medieval England* (London, 1977); in the church of St Remi de Reims in 1145, miraculous cures accounted for 98% of the miracles (49% of these were cures of children). In the compilation of miracles of St Foy, miraculous cures of children account for 32%; among the miracles of St Wulfran in the eleventh century, 40%. See P. A. Sigal, 'Maladie, pélérinage et guérison au XIIᵉ siècle: Les Miracles de Saint Gibrien', *Annales ESC* 24 (1969), pp. 1526, 1535–8. In the register of the miracles of St Catherine-de-Fierbois, in contrast, the percentage was lower – only 19%. However, the percentage of miraculous cures was generally low in this period of the fifteenth century, and miraculous rescues from the gallows and from imprisonment or finding of lost animals (etc.) were much more common (Y. Chauvin, 'Le Livre des miracles de Sainte Catherine-de-Fierbois', *Bulletin de la Société des antiquiaires de l'ouest*, 13 (1975), pp. 281–307).

4 e.g. *Acta Sanctorum*, ed. J. Bollandus and G. Henschenius (Paris–Rome, 1863–1940), Jan. 1, p. 343.

5 e.g. ibid., Jan. 2, p. 905. In one case a father vowed that, if his son recovered, he would help to build the Dominican church in the town (he had appealed to St Dominic): ibid., Aug. 1, p. 616.

6 e.g. ibid., Apr. 1, p. 475.

7 ibid., Mar. 1, p. 718; Apr. 1, p. 475.

8 ibid., Mar. 1, p. 722; Mar. 2, p. 497; Apr. 3, pp. 91, 94; Aug. 1, p. 555; Sept. 7, p. 548; *Analecta Bollandiana*, 33 (1914), p. 173.

9 *Acta Sanctorum*, Jan. 1, p. 345; May 5, p. 214; Aug. 3, p. 687.

10 ibid., Jan. 2, p. 70; Apr. 1, p. 709; July 1, p. 514; *Analecta Bollandiana*, 33 (1914), p. 171. In France in the seventeenth century and the first half of the eighteenth, and in the Late Middle Ages, the infant mortality rate was particularly high in the months of September and October due to stomach and bowel infections. At the end of the winter, many died of lung and bronchial diseases due to the cold and damp. One of the sons of Gregorio Dati died at the age of 3 months in the month of October from dysentery. See also A. Armengaud, *La Famille et l'enfant en France et en Angleterre du XVIᵉ au XVIIIᵉ siècle: Aspects démographiques* (Paris, 1975), p. 74; D. Herlihy and Ch. Klapisch, *Les Toscans et leur familles: Une étude du Catasto florentin de 1427* (Paris, 1978), p. 467; G. Brucker (ed.), *Two Memoirs*

of Renaissance Florence: The Diaries of Buonaccorso Pitti and Gregorio Dati (New York, 1967), p. 127.

11 *Analecta Bollandiana*, 9 (1890), p. 196.

12 *Acta Sanctorum*, Jan. 2, p. 906; Apr. 1, p. 301; Apr. 3, p. 13.

13 ibid., Jan. 1, p. 345; Apr. 1, 312.

14 ibid., Jan. 2, p. 906; Apr. 3, p. 928.

15 ibid., Apr. 3, p. 91; July 1, p. 507; Aug. 1, p. 554.

16 ibid., Apr. 3, p. 93; May 5, p. 98; July 1, p. 508; *Analecta Bollandiana*, 9 (1890), p. 199.

17 Acta Sanctorum, Apr. 3, p. 91.

18 ibid., Jan. 1, p. 346; *Acta et Processus Canonizacionis Beate Brigitte*, ed. I. Collijn (Uppsala, 1931), p. 149.

19 *Acta Sanctorum*, Jan. 2, p. 905; May 2, p. 338; July 1, p. 506; *The Miracles of Simon de Montfort*, ed. J. O. Halliwell (London, 1849), p. 86.

20 *Acta Sanctorum*, Apr. 1, p. 708; *Analecta Bollandiana*, 14 (1895), p. 192.

21 *Acta Sanctorum*, Mar. 2, pp. 86, 241; Apr. 2, p. 113; Apr. 3, pp. 475, 957; July 1, p. 518; Aug. 1, p. 554; *Analecta Bollandiana*, 9 (1890), p. 196.

22 See L. Demaitre, 'The Idea of Childhood and Childcare in Medical Writings of the Middle Ages', *Journal of Psychohistory*, 4 (1976–7), pp. 476–7; the father in Alberti's book also lists several childhood diseases – chicken-pox, measles, etc. (*I Libri della Famiglia* = *The Family in Renaissance Florence*, trans. R. N. Watkins (Columbia, 1969), p. 52). For an example of a work dealing with childhood diseases and medicines, see *Practica Puerorum*, ed. K. Sudhoff (Munich, 1925).

23 *Acta Sanctorum*, Mar. 1, p. 720; Aug. 1, p. 615; *Analecta Bollandiana*, 33 (1914), p. 174.

24 Humbert de Romans, *Sermones* (Venice, 1603), 99, p. 98.

25 *Acta Sanctorum*, Mar. 2, p. 496; Mar. 3, p. 526; Apr. 1, p. 512; thus also in the case of a child who disappeared: Mar. 1, p. 735.

26 ibid., Mar. 1, p. 722; Apr. 1, p. 514.

27 *Analecta Bollandiana*, 33 (1914), p. 174.

28 *The Miracles of Simon de Montfort*, p. 82; *Acta Sanctorum*, Mar. 2, p. 497; *Analecta Bollandiana*, 9 (1890), pp. 196, 199; St Bonaventure, *Legenda Sancti Francisci*, in *Opera Omnia* (Karachi, 1898), p. 552.

29 'Sofredus, arte medicinae peritus Medicus, filiam habebat parvulam quam tenere diligebat ... cum lacrymis dixit', *Acta Sanctorum*, June 4, p. 37.

30 *Analecta Bollandiana*, 33 (1914), p. 174.

31 *Acta Sanctorum*, Apr. 3, p. 247; Jan. 2, p. 906.

32 *Registre de l'inquisition de Jacques Fournier, 1318–1325*, ed. J. Duvernoy (Toulouse, 1965), vol. 1, 105 *a*, *b*, p. 499.

33 ibid., vol. II, 203 *c*, *d*, pp. 414–15. These testimonies are cited by E. Le Roy Ladurie, *Montaillou: Village occitan de 1294 à 1324* (Paris, 1975), but I believe that they deserve to be repeated.

34 Berthold of Regensburg, *Vollständige Ausgabe seiner Predigten*, ed. Franz Pfeiffer (Vienna, 1862), vol. I, pp. 323–8. He believes that it was mainly the peasants who were guilty of this sin, because of their ignorance. See also Ivo of Chartres, *Decretum*, PL vol. 161, cols. 893–4; and Peter Pictavensis, *Summa de Confessione*, ed. J. Longère (Turnhout, 1980), p. 17. For some time, the church in Norway permitted the abandonment of handicapped infants (after baptism) because it had difficulty in enforcing the prohibition on abandonment, which was prevalent for economic reasons (J. Pentikäinen, *The Nordic Dead Child Tradition* (FF Communications, 22; Helsinki, 1968), pp. 78–81, 93.

35 R. Étienne, 'La Conscience médicale antique et la vie des enfants', *Annales de démographie historique* (1973), p. 15.
36 *Acta Sanctorum*, Mar. 3, p. 182.
37 Cited by R. Finucane, op. cit., p. 106.
38 *Acta Sanctorum*, Feb. 1, p. 572.
39 ibid., Apr. 2, p. 190; *Analecta Bollandiana*, 19 (1900), p. 24.
40 For blindness, see *Acta Sanctorum*, Jan. 1, p. 345; Jan. 2, p. 905; Mar. 1, p. 586; Mar. 2, p. 241; Apr. 1, p. 709; July 1, p. 518; *The Miracles of Simon de Montfort*, p. 88; *The Vita Wulfstani of William of Malmesbury*, ed. R. R. Darlington (London, 1928), pp. 128, 119, 161, etc.; deafness, *Acta Sanctorum,*, Apr. 1, p. 710; July 1, p. 504; Aug. 1, p. 607; *Le Livre de Saint Gilbert*, ed. R. Foreville (Paris, 1843), p. 69 etc.; dumbness, see ch. 5, nn. 108, 109.
41 *Acta Sanctorum*, Jan. 1, p. 630; Apr. 3, p. 91.
42 ibid., Mar. 1, p. 738.
43 ibid., Jan. 1, p. 346; May 1, p. 329; June 4, p. 782; *Acta et Processus Canonizacionis Beate Brigitte*, p. 131; *Analecta Bollandiana*, 9 (1890), pp. 327–8; *Legenda Sancti Francisci*, p. 563; *Sancti Bernardi Vita Prima*, PL vol. 185, col. 253.
44 For those paralysed in the loweer limbs or entire body, see *Acta Sanctorum*, Mar. 1, p. 723; Mar 1, p. 318; Aug. 1, p. 649; *Le Livre de Saint Gilbert*, p. 69; *Acta et Processus Canonizacionis Beate Brigitte*, p. 133; *Analecta Bollandiana*, 9 (1890), p. 187.
45 *Analecta Bollandiana*, 9 (1890), p. 187.
46 *Acta Sanctorum*, Jan. 1, p. 635; and see also Jan. 2, p. 905 (in this case it was the father who carried the child to the saint's shrine).
47 e.g. ibid., Aug. 1, p. 650.
48 ibid., May 7, p. 458.
49 See, on this, C. Haffter, 'The Changeling: History and Psychodynamics of Attitude to Handicapped Children in European Folklore', *Journal of the History of Behavioral Sciences*, 4 (1968), p. 55 and nn. 2, 7, 22.
50 E. A. Wrigley and R. Schofield, 'Infant and Child Mortality in England in the Late Tudor and Early Stuart Period', in *Health, Medicine and Mortality in the 16th Century*, ed. C. Webster (Cambridge, 1979), p. 65; T. H. Hollingworth, 'A Demographic Study of the British Ducal Families', *Population Studies*, 11 (1957), table 5; on F. Lebrun's research, see E. Badinter, *L'Amour en plus* (Paris, 1980), p. 129.
   On the lower mortality rate in the parish of Colyton, see E. Wrigley, 'Mortality in Pre-Industrial England: The Example of Colyton, Devon, over Three Centuries', *Daedalus*, 97 (1968), pp. 546–80.
   According to A. Armengaud, it is possible that the number of infant deaths in Colyton was actually higher (that is, more than 108 out of 1,000 in the first year of life) but that some had not yet been baptized so that the death was not recorded in the parish register (op. cit., pp. 175–7).
   In mid-fifteenth century Florence, the mortality rate among girls up to the age of 5 was twice as high as among the ten- to fourteen-year-olds; see J. Kirshner and A. Molho, 'The Dowry Funds and the Marriage Market in Early Quattrocento Florence', *Journal of Modern History*, 50 (1978), p. 421; see also ch. 3, nn. 10, 11.
51 According to a study by Zvi Razi, the victims of a plague in 1360–5 were mainly children (*Life, Marriage and Death in a Medieval Parish* (Cambridge, 1980), pp. 129, 151). According to Herlihy and Klapisch (op. cit., pp. 466–7), the percentage of children among the dead was very high. Out of 874 victims of the 1427 plague,

604 were children (69.1%), whereas in 1385–1436 children constituted only 40–50% of the dead. The rise in the mortality rate of infants and old people in the plague was lower, since among both categories many also died of other diseases. Of 41 infants who died in 1427, only 10 died of plague.

52 This was so, for example, in 1290–1340 in Picardy in France and in Winchester in England: R. Fossier, *Le Moyen Age* (Paris, 1983), p. 45.

53 *Two Memoirs of Renaissance Florence*, pp. 134–6.

54 Cited by Ph. Contamine, *La Vie quotienne pendant la Guerre de Cent Ans: France et Angleterre* (Paris, 1967), p. 43.

55 *The Fifty Earliest English Wills in the Court Probate, London*, ed. F. J. Furnivall (EETS; London, 1882), p. 13.

56 G. Duby, *Guillaume le Maréchal, ou Le Meilleur Chevalier du monde* (Paris, 1984), pp. 165–6; Francesco Datini insisted that the marriage contract with the bridegroom of his fifteen-year-old daughter stipulate that, if the girl died of plague within two years, the entire dowry or any part of it he claimed would be returned to him (I. Origo, *The Merchant of Prato* (London, 1957), p. 189).

57 J. Kirschner and A. Molho, op. cit., pp. 406–25.

58 Cited in J. Huizinga, *The Waning of the Middle Ages* (New York, 1954), p. 150.

59 *Mirk's Festial: A Collection of Homilies*, ed. T. Erbe (EETS; London, 1905), p. 3; *Medieval Manuscripts in British Libraries*, ed. N. Ker (Oxford, 1983), no. 10, p. 255.

60 Hugo of Trimberg, *Der Renner* (The Runner), in K. Arnold (ed. and trans.), *Kind und Gesellschaft in Mittelalter und Renaissance* (Munich, 1980), p. 132. For the illustration, see Leiden University Library, Ms Voss GG F4, fo. 247^v (Photograph in K. Arnold, op. cit., p. 28).

61 *I Libri* (= *The Family in Renaissance Florence*), p. 52.

62 *Hali Meidenhad*, ed. F. Furnivall (EETS; London, 1922), p. 50.

63 G. R. Owst, *Preaching in Medieval England* (Cambridge, 1926), p. 207; J. Gerson, *Œuvres complètes*, ed. Mgr P. Glorieux, vol. VII (Paris, 1966), p. 322.

64 'notandum est quod infideles solent contristari multum de morte carorum suorum et hoc quia non credunt eos vivere post hanc vitam. Set hoc non debent facere fideles': cited by A. Murray, 'Religion among the Poor in Thirteenth Century France: The Testimony of Humbert de Romans', *Traditio*, 30 (1974), p. 323 and n. 219.

65 *Select English Works of John Wycliffe*, ed. T. Arnold (Oxford, 1871), vol. III, pp. 199–200.

66 Cited in S. Thrupp, *The Merchant Class of Medieval London* (Ann Arbor, 1976), p. 172.

67 Thomas Cantimpratanus, *Bonum Universale de Apibus* (Douai, 1607), bk 3, ch. 153, 17, p. 501. English translation G. G. Coulton (ed. and trans.), *Life in the Middle Ages* (Cambridge, 1967), vol. I, pp. 118–19.

68 J. Pentikäinen, op. cit., p. 57; J. Huizinga, op. cit., p. 150.

69 Beatrice and Bernier in *Raoul de Cambrai* do not forget their son, Julien, lost to them as an infant, even after the birth of another son: see *Raoul de Cambrai*, ed. P. Meyer and A. Longnon (Paris, 1882), pp. 258–9. The mother of Lancelot in Lancelot del Lac never ceases mourning the baby son she lost: *Le Livre de Lancelot del Lac* (*The Vulgate Version of the Arthurian Romance*, ed. H. O. Sommer (Washington, DC, 1910), vol. III), pp. 14–16, 18, 41.

70 *Acta Sanctorum*, Mar. 1, p. 332.

71 *I Libri* (= *The Family in Renaissance Florence*), p. 55.

72 *The Vita Wulfstani*, 139; *Acta Sanctorum*, Apr. 3, pp. 245, 357.

73 R. C. Finucane, op. cit., p. 109.

74 ibid., p. 109; *Acta Sanctorum*, Apr. 1, p. 513.

75 'pater ipsius qui rigescentibus membris, se movere non poterat prae dolore' St Bonaventure, op. cit., p. 554; see also *Acta Sanctorum*, Mar. 3, p. 526.

76 'totaliter a corde ejus abrasa tristitia, ut in ipsa nulle amaritudinis reliquiae remanerent', *Acta Sanctorum*, May 7, pp. 466–7.

77 ibid., Mar. 3, p. 361; July 3, p. 770.

78 Cited by D. Herlihy and Ch. Klapisch, op. cit., p. 561.

79 J. Le Goff, *La Civilisation de l'occident médiéval* (Paris, 1964), ill. 143.

80 *The Vita Wulfstani*, p. 139.

81 *Registre de l'inquisition de Jacques Fournier*, vol. I, 61*a*, *b*, p. 320; 33 *c*, *d*, p. 202.

82 On the testimony of the peasant from Montaillou, see E. Le Roy Ladurie, op. cit., p. 313.

83 Jean Gerson, *Œuvres complètes*, vol. VII, p. 322; for examples of references to the fact that children were sole offspring or heirs, see *Acta Sanctorum*, Mar. 1, p. 514; Mar. 3, p. 528; *The Vita Wulfstani*, p. 124.

84 'Accersivit mater ancillam suam nolens infantem in manibus suis mori', *The Vita Wulfstani*, p. 178; 'Unde pater pueri, filii sui orbitatem praesentialiter ferre non sustinens, relictis ibidem qui funeri necessaria providerent, a praedicto castro recessit', *Acta Sanctorum*, Apr. 1, p. 308.

85 Herodotus, *The Persian Wars*, trans. G. Rawlinson, bk 1, 136, in *The Greek Historians*, ed. F. R. B. Godolphin (New York, 1942), vol. I, p. 60.

86 Heloïse, *Epistola XXI, PL* vol. 189, col. 428.

87 Ph. Contamine, op. cit., p. 43.

88 G. Krupp, 'The Bereavement Reaction: A Special Case of Separation Anxiety', in *The Psychoanalytic Study of Society* (New York, 1962), pp. 64–5; cited in W. Saffady, 'The Effects of Bereavement and Parental Remarriage in 16th Century England: The Case of Thomas More', *History of Childhood Quarterly*, 1 (1973), p. 311.

89 Thomas Chobham, *Summa Confessorum*, ed. F. Broomfield (Paris–Louvain, 1963), p. 96.

90 e.g. *Borough Customs*, ed. M. Bateson (Selden Society; London, 1906), vol. II, p. 16; *Die Konstitutionen Friedrichs* II *von Hohenstaufen für sein Konigreich Sizilien*, ed. H. Conrad, T. von Lieck-Buyken, W. Wagner (Vienna, 1973), vol. II, 152, p. 234; see also J. Yver, 'La Suspension des actions en période de minorité et son effacement progressif (XIIIe–XVIe siècles)', in *Recueils de la Société Jean Bodin*, vol. 36/2 (Brussels, 1976), pp. 184–249; F. Pollock and F. Maitland, *A History of English Law* (Cambridge, 1898), vol. II, pp, 390, 443–5.

In England, when a minor (male or female) whose father had died inherited an estate, the seigneur (or some person appointed by him), and not the mother, acted as guardian. He was also responsible for arranging the minor's marriage. See S. Sheridan-Walker, 'Widow and Ward: The Feudal Law of Child Custody in Medieval Society', in *Women in Medieval Society*, ed. S. Mosher-Stuard (University Park, Penn., 1976), pp. 159–72. For examples of minors being married off by the seigneur who was their guardian, see *Rotuli de Dominabus et Pueris et Puellis de XII Comitatibus*, ed. J. H. Round (London, 1913); in towns, if both parents died without appointing a guardian, the town authorities made the appointment. The guardian was supposed to be a relative who was not in line for inheritance of the assets bequeathed to the minor by his parents (see, for example, *Borough Customs*, vol. II, p. 147; *Year Books of Edward* II, vol. I, ed. F. W. Maitland (Selden Society; London, 1904), pp. 158, 108). Guardianship required approval by the town authorities and the guardian required official authorization for any expenditure from the minor's legacy and for any marriage arranged: see *Calendar of Letter Books: Letter Book E: 1314–1337*, ed. R. R. Sharpe (London, 1903), pp. 267, 242; *Calendar of Letter Books: Letter Book I: 1400–1422*, ed. R. R. Sharpe (London, 1909), pp. 55, 141–2.

Pressure was often exerted on orphans to marry while they were still minors, occasionally by the mother who had remarried and acted as guardian. The courts sometimes then transferred guardianship to some other person. For example: *Letter Book E*, pp. 47–8.

91 *Acta Sanctorum*, Feb. 3, p. 417. See also M. M. McLaughlin, 'Survivors and Surrogates: Children and Parents from the Ninth to the Thirteenth Century', in *The History of Childhood*, ed. L. deMause (New York, 1974).

92 Myrc, *Instructions for Parish Priests*, ed. E. Peacock (EETS; London, 1868), p. 31.

93 e.g. *Die Exempla des Jacob von Vitry*, ed. G. Frenken, in *Quellen und Untersuchungen zur lateinischen Philologie des Mittelalters*, 5/1 (1914), p. 114; *The Early English Version of the Gesta Romanorum*, ed. S. J. H. Herrtage (London, 1879), pp. 401–2; F. C. Tubach, *Index Exemplorum* (FF Communications, 204; Helsinki, 1969), 4716, p. 357; 4363, p. 334; 1441, p. 115.

94 M. McLaughlin, op. cit., p. 110 and n. 30.

95 e.g. *Acta Sanctorum*, Feb. 2, p. 345; May 5, p. 77; *Analecta Bollandiana*, 57 (1939), p. 381.

96 *Sancti Bernardi Vita Prima*, cols 231–2.

97 *Thesaurus Novus Anecdotorum*, ed. E. Martène and U. Durand (Paris, 1717), vol. III, col. 1780.

98 *Das Leben des Seligen Heinrich Seuse*, (Düsseldorf, 1966), pp. 73–4.

99 Anna Freud, *The Ego and the Mechanism of Defence* (London, 1961).

100 *The Life of St. Anselm Archbishop of Canterbury by Eadmer*, ed. and trans. R. W. Southern (Nelson Series; London, 1962), pp. 5–7, 172–3.

On depression and identity crisis during adolescence, see E. J. Anthony, 'Two Contrasting Types of Adolescent Depression and their Treatment', in *The Psychology of Adolescence*, ed. A. H. Esman (New York, 1975), pp. 285–300; E. Erikson, 'The Problem of Ego Identity', ibid., pp. 318–46 (according to Erikson, the decisive task in the fifth stage – the stage of youth – is to complete the sense of self-identity. This process is often connected with a period of depression).

101 Gilbert of Nogent, *Autobiographie*, ed. E. R. Labande (Paris, 1981), bk 1, ch. 14, p. 102.

102 *Acta Sanctorum*, Apr. 2, p. 439.

103 See, on this, J. Bowlby, *Attachment and Loss* (New York, 1973), vol. II, pp. 5–6.

104 Ch. Klapisch-Zuber, 'La Mère cruelle: Maternité, veuvage et vot dans la Florence des XIVᵉ–XVᵉ siècles', *Annales ESC* 38 (1983), pp. 1097–109.

105 Thus in Gayton's laws: 'et fiet divisio inter coheredes post mortem duarum matrum suarum vel trium quot sint et erit divisio firma' (*Borough Customs*, p. 135).

106 Helen Deutsch, *The Psychology of Women: A Psychoanalytic Interpretation* (London, 1947), vol. II, pp. 383–401.

107 The wicked stepmother: *The Early English Version of the Gesta Romanorum*, pp. 237–8; *Acta Sanctorum*, Jan. 2, p. 249; *The Vita Wulfstani*, p. 124; the wicked stepmother of a twenty-year-old youth: *The Early English Version of the Gesta Romanorum*, pp. 233–4.

108 *The Saga of the Volsungs*, trans. M. Schlauch (New York, 1930), p. 177; *Eirik the Red and other Icelandic Sagas*, trans. G. Jones (Oxford, 1980), pp. 247, 262–8. In

folk-tales there are more examples of the stepmother mistreating boys than of them mistreating girls (F. C. Tubach, op. cit., 4618, 4620–2, p. 350).

109 *The Saga of Ragnar Lolbrok*, in *The Saga of the Volsungs*, pp. 218–26.
110 *Acta Sanctorum*, July 1, p. 499.
111 Ch. V. Langlois, *La Vie en France en Moyen Age* (Paris, 1926), vol. II, p. 272; on Bernardino of Sienna see J. B. Ross, 'The Middle Class Child in Urban Italy: 14th to Early 16th Century', in *The History of Childhood*, ed. L. deMause (New York, 1974), p. 197 and n. 81.
112 See C. Gauvard and A. Gokalp, 'Les Conduites de Bruit et leurs significations à la fin du Moyen Age: Le Charivari', *Annales ESC* 29 (1974), pp. 693–704; N. Zemon Davis, 'Youth Groups and Charivaris in 16th Century France', *Past and Present*, 50 (1971), p. 53.
113 For examples of the raising of children orphaned of their mothers by female relatives, mainly maternal aunts, see *Acta Sanctorum*, Sept. 7, p. 544; July 1, pp. 455–6; May 5, p. 23; *Vita Sancti Brigitte*, in *Scriptores Rerum Svecicarum Medii Aevi*, ed. C. Annerstedt (Uppsala, 1871), vol. III, pp. 190, 166.

The mother of Jacob the Venetian (the child who liked to play at mass) retired to a convent after being widowed and left the child with his paternal grandmother (*Acta Sanctorum*, May 7, p. 453). Sometimes children who lost their fathers, and whose mothers had remarried, were apprenticed at an early age: see, on this, F. Michaud-Frejaville, 'Contrats d'apprentissage en Orléanais: Les Enfants au travail (1380–1540), in *L'Enfant au Moyen Age: Littérature et civilisation* (Senefiance, 9; Paris, 1980), pp. 63–71. Some children were given into the care of foster families. Francesco Datini, who lost both parents in the 1348 Black Death at the age of 13, was handed over by his guardian, together with his brother, to a woman who may have been a relative. He spent only one year and several months in her home, but remained grateful to her all his life (see I. Origo, op. cit., pp. 30–1). For further references to orphaned boys and girls, see chs 9–12.
114 B. A. Hanawalt, *The Ties that Bound: Peasant Families in Medieval England* (Oxford, 1986), p. 250.

8 ON EDUCATION IN THE SECOND STAGE OF CHILDHOOD

1 See, on this, L. Demaitre, 'The Idea of Childhood and Child Care in Medical Writings of the Middle Ages', *Journal of Psychohistory*, 4 (1976–7), p. 481.
2 Aristotle, *De Generatione Animalium*, 729[b], 730[a], in *The Basic Works of Aristotle*, ed. R. McKeon (New York, 1968), pp. 676–8; on the development of this concept in the context of the inherited Original Sin passed on to each child, see K. E. Børresen, *Subordination and Equivalence: The Nature and Role of Woman in Augustine and Thomas Aquinas*, trans. C. H. Talbot (Washington, DC, 1981), pp. 219–21.
3 Bartholomaeus Anglicus, *Liber de Proprietatibus Rerum* (Strasburg, 1505), bk 6, ch. 3 (= *On the Properties of Things: John Trevisa's Translation of Bartholomaeus Anglicus* (Oxford, 1975), p. 295); *The Prose Salernitan Questions*, ed. B. Lawn (Oxford, 1979), q. 101, p. 47; L. Demaitre, *Doctor Bernard de Gordon: Professor and Practitioner* (Toronto, 1980), p. 80 and n. 39. On the two opposing concepts, see also C. Thomasset, 'Quelques Principes de l'embryologie médiévale (de Salerne à la fin du XIIIe siècle)', in *L'Enfant au Moyen Age: Littérature et civilisation* (Senefiance, 9; Paris, 1980), pp. 109–21.
4 According to the medical writers of Salerno, the child of an errant wife would resemble her lover more than it did her: *The Prose Salernitan Questions*, q. 46, pp.

22–3; see also F. C. Tubach, *Index Exemplorum* (FF Communications, 204; Helsinki, 1969), 5288, p. 400.

5 Raymond Lull, *Blanquerna* (Madrid, 1924; = *Blanquerna: A 13th Century Romance*, trans. E. Alison Peers (London, 1925)), ch. 1, p. 32).

6 See, for example, G. Duby, *Guillaume le Maréchal ou Le Meilleur Chevalier du monde* (Paris, 1984), p. 73.

   A detailed discussion of the question of hereditary nobility can be found in a political-didactic treatise from the second half of the fourteenth century, *Le Songe du Vergier*, repr. of Brunet, 1731 (Strasburg, 1957), pp. 183–92; on the *belles-lettres* of the period dealing with this subject, see E. R. Curtius, *European Literature and the Latin Middle Ages*, trans. W. R. Trask (New York, 1953), pp. 179–80.

7 *Acta Sanctorum*, ed J. Bollandus and G. Henschenius (Paris–Rome, 1863–1940), Apr. 3, p. 83; Apr. 1, p. 671; July 1, pp. 464–5; *Analecta Bollandiana*, 56 (1938), p. 343.

8 For example, in the Icelandic saga: *The Tale of Geinmund Heljarskin*, in *Sturlunga Saga*, in *Shorter Sagas of the Icelanders*, trans. J. H. McGrew and R. G. Thomas (New York, 1974), vol. II, pp. 17–19.

9 *Lancelot del Lac* in *The Vulgate Version of the Arthurian Romances*, ed. H. O. Somner, vol. III (Washington, DC, 1910), and see also Jean Frappier, *Amour courtois et table ronde* (Geneva, 1973), ch. 10.

10 William Langland, *Piers Plowman*, an edn of the C text, ed. D. Pearsall (London, 1978), passus 9, p. 168.

11 *The Opus Majus of Roger Bacon*, ed. J. H. Bridges (Oxford, 1897), vol. II, pt 6, p. 205.

12 *The Prose Salernitan Questions*, q. 113, p. 194.

13 See ch. 3, n. 48; ch. 4, n. 21.

14 Arnold of Villanova, *De Regimine Sanitatis*, in *Opera Omnia* (Basel, 1585), col. 668; and ch. 5, n. 25.

15 Leon Battista Alberti, *I Libri della Famiglia* (*The Family in Renaissance Florence*), trans. R. N. Watkins (Columbia, 1969), pp. 75–6. On research on infant temperament, see L. J. Yarrow, 'Historical Perspectives and Future Directions in Infant Development', in *Handbook of Infant Development*, ed. J. D. Osofsky (New York, 1985), p. 898.

16 P. Dronke, *Women Writers of the Middle Ages* (Cambridge, 1984), pp. 171–83, 245–50; for more on the superiority of the sanguine temperament, see Konrad of Megenberg, *Ökonimik*, ed. S. Krüger (Stuttgart, 1973; MGH Staatsschriften, 111/5), bk 1/2, ch. 8, p. 79

17 Philip of Novare, *Les Quatre Ages de l'homme*, ed. M. de Éreville (Paris, 1888), s. 6, pp. 4–5; caution against determinism in medical works: L. Demaitre, *Doctor Bernard de Gordon: Professor and Practitioner*, p. 147.

18 *Kardinal Johannes Dominicis Erziehungslehre*, trans. A. Rosler (Freiburg, 1894), pp. 37–8.

19 *I Libri* (= *The Family in Renaissance Florence*), pp. 76, 56, 36, 66.

20 'debet eligere viam quam intendit et ad quam magis inclinatur', Bernard Gordon, *De Conservatione Vitae Humanae* (Leipzig, 1570), pp. 29–30.

21 'secundum diversitatem personarum', Aegidius Romanus, *De Regimine Principum* (Venice, 1505), bk 2, pt 2, ch. 16.

22 Wolfram of Eschenbach, *Parzival und Titurel*, ed. E. Martin (Halle, 1900), bk 2, 112, p. 39; bk 3, 119–21, pp. 42 ff.; bk 3, 154–9, pp. 53–5.

   On the same motif in other works, see M. Combarieu, 'Enfance et démesure dans l'épopée médiévale', in *L'Enfant au Moyen Age; Littérature et civilisation* (Senefiance, 9; Paris, 1980), pp. 418 ff.

23 For example, 'Litterae sine bona vita non salvant', Humbert de Romans, *Sermones* (Venice, 1603), Sermo 63, p. 62.

24 *Anecdotes historiques, légendes et apologues tirés du recueil inédit d'Étienne de Bourbon,* ed. A. Lecoy de la Marche (Paris, 1877), pp. 221 ff. R. Bultot, 'La Doctrine du mépris du monde chez Bernard le clunisien', *Moyen Age,* 70 (1964), p. 191. From the age of 12, boys and girls were obliged to observe fast-days: *Dictionnaire de théologie catholique,* vol. 8, 'Jeûne', pp. 1415 ff.

25 Bartholomaeus Anglicus, op. cit., bk 6, chs 16–19.

26 Konrad of Megenberg, op. cit., bk 1/2, chs 15 ff.

27 *Dives et Pauper,* ed. P. H. Barnum (EETS; London. 1976), pp. 305–30. *Robert of Brunne's 'Handlyng Synne',* ed. F. J. Furnivall (EETS; London, 1901), pt 1, pp. 41–2; on the concept that every sin is an insult to parents, see also Vincent of Beauvais, *De Eruditione Filiorum Nobiliorum,* ed. A. Steiner (Medieval Academy of America, 32; Cambridge, Mass., 1938), p. 112; on the rewards for those who treat their parents with respect, see *Speculum Laicorum,* ed. J. Welter (Paris, 1914), pp. 86–7.

28 R. J. Iannuci, *The Treatment of the Capital Sins and the Decalogue in German Sermons* (New York, 1942), p. 81.

29 Philip of Novare, op. cit., s. 5, pp. 3–4; Humbert de Romans, *Sermones,* Sermo 63, p. 63.

30 *The Sermons of Thomas Brinton, Bishop of Rochester, 1373–1389,* ed. M. Aquinas Delvin (London, 1954), p. 20; *The Early English Version of the Gesta Romanorum,* ed. S. J. H. Herrtage (London, 1879), pp. 45–8, 153–5.

According to Bartholomaeus Anglicus, *pater* comes from *pascendo* because at first he feeds his children, and, in his old age, they feed him like ravens (op. cit., bk 6, ch. 14, *de patre;* = *John Trevisa's Translation,* p. 310).

Among the stories about ingrate children, one of the most prevalent is the tale of 'King Lear' in various versions, which was also included in sermons: *Historia Regum Britanniae,* ed. A. Griscon and R. E. Jones (New York, 1929), pp. 262 ff; *The Sermons of Thomas Brinton,* p. 297; *The Early English Version of the Gesta Romanorum,* pp. 48 ff; *Liber Exemplorum,* ed. A. G. Little (Aberdeen, 1908), pp. 80–7.

The satirical literature also records tales of cruel treatment of an old, dying father by his children. They do not nurse him properly, urge him to change his will, and spread the rumour that he has lost his faculties. The worst offenders are the oldest son and the wife, who collaborates with her sons against her husband (see *Les Quinze Joyes de mariage,* ed. J. Rychner (Paris, 1963), pp. 73–6).

31 And see also Luke, 14: 26.

32 *Dives et Pauper,* p. 313.

33 ibid., pp. 227–8; Aegidius Romanus, op. cit., bk 2, pt 1, ch. 3.

34 e.g. *Ottonis et Rahewini Gesta Frederici I Imperatoris,* ed. G. Waiz (Hanover, 1884), bk 1, p. 19.

35 *Sermons of Thomas Brinton,* p. 20; Aegidius Romanus, op. cit., bk 2, pt 2, ch. 17.

36 John Bromyard, *Summa Praedicantium* (Antwerp, 1614), p. 6; G. R. Owst, *Literature and Pulpit in Medieval England* (Oxford, 1961), p. 468, n. 5.

37 Denis Saurat, *The End of Fear* (London, 1938), p. 29.

38 Cited in J. Flandrin, *Families in Past Times* (Cambridge, 1979), p. 138.

39 *The Prose Salernitan Questions,* q. 101, p. 47.

40 Philip of Novare, op. cit., ss. 2–3, pp. 2–3.

41 'ideo naturaliter amor parentum est ad hoc, ut congregent filiis', Thomas Aquinas, *Super Epistolas Pauli Lectura,* ed. R. Raphaelis (Rome, 1953), vol. I, 317, p. 296.

312   *Childhood in the Middle Ages*

42 Z. Razi, 'Family, Land and Village Community in Later Medieval England', *Past and Present*, 93 (1981), pp. 7–8; id., 'Was the English Peasant Family Small and Ego-focused?' (in publication); C. Dyer, 'English Diet in the Later Middle Ages', in *Social Relations and Ideas: Essays in Honour of R. Hilton*, ed. T. H. Aston, P. R. Cross, and J. Thirsk (Cambridge, 1983), p. 198. For the story of King Lear, see n. 29 and *Robert of Brunne's 'Handlyng Synne'*, ed. F. J. Furnivall (EETS; London, 1901), pt 1, pp. 40–2.

43 *Calendar of Plea and Memoranda Rolls preserved among the Archives of the Corporation of the City of London at the Guildhall, 1364–1381*, ed. A. Thomas (Cambridge, 1929), p. 294; S. Thrupp, *The Merchant Class of Medieval London (1300–1500)* (Ann Arbor, 1976), p. 151, n. 150.

44 Philip of Novare, op. cit., ss. 10–11, pp. 7–9; John Bromyard, op. cit., p. 6; *Select English Works of John Wycliffe*, ed. T. Arnold (Oxford, 1871), vol. III, p. 195; Vincent of Beauvais, op. cit., p. 62; Bernard Gordon, op. cit., p. 28.

45 Philip of Novare, op. cit., s. 7, p. 6; John Bromyard, op. cit., pp. 5–6.

46 J. Gerson, *De Parvulis ad Christum Trahendis*, in *Œuvres complètes*, ed. Mgr P. Glorieux (Paris, 1973), vol. IX, p. 674.

47 Philip of Novare, op. cit., s. 18, p. 12; see also Humbert de Romans, *Sermones*, 62, pp. 61–2; 87, pp. 86–7.

48 Raymond Lull, *Doctrine d'enfant*, ed. A. Llinarès (Paris, 1969), ch. 91, p. 208; ch. 79, pp. 169–71.

49 Myrc, *Instructions for Parish Priests*, ed. E. Peacock (EETS: London, 1868), pp. 31, 45; J. Gerson, *Œuvres complètes*, vol. IX, pp, 669–86; *Les Statuts synodaux français du XIIIᵉ siècle*, ed. O. Pontal (Paris, 1971), vol. I, s. 45, p. 166.

50 Thomas Chobham, *Summa Confessorum*, ed. F. Broomfield (Paris–Louvain, 1963), p. 298.

51 Aegidius Romanus, op. cit., bk 2, pt 2, ch. 16; Vincent of Beauvais, op. cit., pp. 8–17; Bernard Gordon, op. cit., pp. 31–4.

52 *Anecdotes historiques, légendes et apologues tirés du recueil inédit d'Étienne de Bourbon*, s. 43, pp. 51–2; *Speculum Laicorum*, pp. 60–1; Humbert de Romans, *Sermones*, 96, p. 96; Jean Gerson, *Œuvres complètes*, vol. VII, p. 339; *Dives et Pauper*, vol. I, p. 324.

53 *Select English Works of John Wycliffe*, pp. 195–8; Raymond Lull, *Doctrine d'enfant*, pp. 158–9.

54 According to Bartholomaeus Anglicus, corruption is like leprosy (op. cit.,, bk 6, ch. 5; = *John Trevisa's Translation*, p. 301); and see also J. Gerson, *Œuvres complètes*, vol. IX, pp. 669–86; G. R. Owst, op. cit., pp. 466–7; Alberti, *I Libri* (= *The Family in Renaissance Florence*), pp. 36, 73.

55 'iuvenes sunt nimius amatores amicitiae', Aegidius Romanus, op. cit., bk 2, ch. 13; Raymonde Lull, *Doctrine d'enfant*, ch. 91, pp. 204, 207; Bernard Gordon. op. cit., p. 28; on special sermons for children, see ch. 2, n. 3.

56 Humbert de Romans, *Sermones*, 85, pp. 86–7.

57 Raymond Lull, *Doctrine d'enfant*, ch. 91, pp. 204, 206, 207. On Giovanni Dominici's advocacy of spartan education, see I. Origo, *The Merchant of Prato* (London, 1957), p. 186.

58 John Bromyard, op. cit., p. 4; Jean Gerson, *Œuvres complètes*, vol. VII, pp. 334–5; Philip of Novare, op. cit., s. 8, pp. 6–7; *Dives et Pauper*, vol. I, pp. 324 ff; *Speculum Laicorum*, p. 61; Bartholomaeus Anglicus, op. cit., bk 6, ch. 14 (= *John Trevisa's Translation*, pp. 310–11).

59 Vincent of Beauvais, op. cit., p. 62.

60 Christine wrote a book of instruction for her son, but, in effect, it is a general

manual for young men and fathers. See M. Laigle, *Le Livre des trois vertus de Christine de Pisan et son milieu historique* (Paris, 1912), pp. 157–8.

61 See, for example, E. J. Tardif, *Coutumiers de Normandie* (Slatkine repr., Geneva, 1977), vol. III, 85, p. 204.

62 T. Smith (ed.), *English Gilds* (EETS; London, 1870), p. 390.

63 See D. Herlihy, 'Medieval Children', in B. K. Lachen and K. R. Pelp, eds, *Essays on Medieval Civilization* (Austin, 1978), p. 125 and n. 62.

64 *The Life of St. Anselm, Archbishop of Canterbury by Eadmer*, ed. and trans. R. W. Southern (Nelson Series: London, 1962), pp. 37–9.

65 Thomas Aquinas, *In Quattuor Libros Sententiarum* (Parma, 1856), 2, 20, q. 11, art. 1, p. 183.

66 See ch. 5, n. 196.

67 See, for example, Lull's *Blanquerna*, ch. 1, 3, p. 32; or Bernardino of Sienna on this matter (G. G. Coulton (ed. and trans.), *Life in the Middle Ages* (Cambridge, 1967), pt 1, p. 217).

68 See A. L. Gabriel, *The Educational Ideas of Vincent of Beavais* (Notre-Dame, Ind., 1956), pp. 38–9.

69 Konrad of Megenberg, op. cit., bk 1/2, chs 25–7, pp. 109 ff; Philip of Novare, op. cit., ss. 21–31, pp. 14–21; Bernard Gordon, op. cit., pp. 38–40.

70 Humbert de Romans, *Sermones*, 97, pp. 96–7; B. Jarret, *Social Theories in the Middle Ages, 1200–1500* (Boston, 1926), p. 88; A. A. Heutsch, *La Littérature didactique du Moyen Age* (Halle, 1903), p. 151.

71 Vincent of Beauvais, op. cit., pp. 172–219; A. L. Gabriel, op. cit., p. 38; see also R. Barton-Tobin, 'Vincent of Beauvais on the Education of Women', *Journal of the History of Ideas*, 35 (1974), pp. 488 ff.

72 Konrad of Megenberg, op. cit., bk 1/2, ch. 25, pp. 110–11; A. A. Heutsch, op. cit., pp. 53–4, 101.

On Pierre Dubois's plan for educating women who were to be sent to the Holy Land within the framework of his general scheme for reoccupying the country, see *De Recuperatione Terre Sancte*, ed. C. V. Langlois (Paris, 1891), pp. 50–2, 57–71.

73 See on this chs 9 and 11.

74 See, for example, *A Catalogue of Misericords in Great Britain*, ed. G. L. Remnant (Oxford, 1969), pl. 20*b*.

75 P. Burke, *Popular Culture in Early Modern Europe* (London, 1979), pp. 49–50.

76 *The Life of St. Anselm, Archbishop of Canterbury*, pp. 20–1; and also pp. 37–9.

77 Arnold of Villanova, op. cit., col. 668; Aegidius Romanus, op. cit., pt. 2, chs 16, 17.

78 Among those who favoured confession at this age were Humbert de Romans, *Sermones*, 63, p. 63; and Myrc, *Instructions for Parish Priests*, pp. 31, 45.

79 e.g. *Les Statuts synodaux français*, vol. I, s. 26, p. 62; s. 95, p. 204.

80 J. Gerson, *De Parvulis ad Christum Trahendis*, in *Œuvres Complètes*, vol. IX, pp. 669–86; *Brève manière de confession pour les jeunes*, ibid., vol. VII, pp. 408–9; *Notes sur la confession*, ibid., pp. 355, 411–12; the confessors were not supposed to ask adults either with whom they had sinned (*Les Statuts synodaux français*, vol. I, s. 37, p. 64).

In the Spanish village of Cubas near Madrid in the mid-fifteenth century, a particularly devout girl aged $12\frac{1}{2}$ used to go to confession regularly. She first did so at the age of 6, and first received the Eucharist at 9: see W. A. Christian, *Apparitions in Late Medieval and Renaissance Spain* (Princeton, 1981), pp. 58–9.

81 The Dominican Robert Holcot is quoted in J. M. Moran, *The Growth of English*

Schools, 1340–1548 (Princeton, 1985), p. 40.

82 Aegidius Romanus, op. cit., bk 2, pt 2, ch. 17.

83 It may be added that Raymond Lull expresses his reservations with regard to *quadrivium* studies; he is against arithmetic and algebra because they tend to absorb the student entirely and to divert his attention from divine teachings; against music because it is dominated by jongleurs; and against astronomy because it is dominated by astrologers. On the other hand, a certain knowledge of medicine is needed by everyone (*Doctrine d'enfant*, ch. 78, pp. 164–9).

84 See n. 77 and Humbert de Romans, *Sermones*, 87, p. 87; *Le Régime du corps de Maître Aldebrandin de Sienne*, ed. L. Landouzy and R. Pépin (Paris, 1911), p. 80; Bernard Gordon, op. cit., p. 27.

85 'post infantiles parentum indulgentias', *Iannotii Manetti Vita Boccaccii Poetae Florentini*, in *Philippi Villani Liber de Civitatis Florentiae Famosis Civibus*, ed. G. Mazzoni (Florence, 1847), p. 89.

86 *Magna Vita Sancti Hugonis*, ed. and trans. D. Douie and Dom. H. Farmer (Nelson Series; London, 1962), vol. I, p. 132; Bartholomaeus Anglicus, op. cit., bk 6, ch. 14; Philip of Novare, op. cit., ss. 8–10, pp. 6–8; *The Book of Vices and Virtues: A Fourteenth Century English Translation of the Somme Le Roi of Lorens D'Orleans*, ed. M. Francis (EETS; London, 1942), p. 58 – originally written in French in the thirteenth century; Giovanni Dominici, in *Kardinal Johannes Dominicis Erziehungslehre*, trans. A. Rosler (Freiburg, 1894), p. 28.

87 See ch. 7, n. 100.

88 Gilbert of Nogent, *Autobiographie*, ed. E. R. Labande (Paris, 1981), bk 1, ch. 5, pp. 38–43.

89 See N. Orme, *English Schools in the Middle Ages* (London, 1973), pp. 128–9; S. Thrupp, op. cit., p. 159.

90 See ch. 11.

91 Until the beginning of the twelfth century, the children's festival was held on December 28, the day of the Holy Innocents.

92 On the participation of laymen in Bristol, for example, see T. Smith, *English Gilds*, p. 422.

93 E. K. Chambers, *The Medieval Stage* (Oxford, 1903), vol. I, pp. 276–371, vol. II, pp. 282–5, 287–9; A. Leach, *The Schools of Medieval England* (London, 1915); J. M. Fletcher, *The Boy-Bishop at Salisbury and Elsewhere* (Salisbury, 1921).

  One of those who emphatically demanded the abolition of the feast was Jean Gerson (*Contre la fête des fous*, in *Œuvres complètes*, ed. Mgr P. Glorieux (Paris, 1966), vol. VII, pp. 409–11.

94 A. Lecoy de la Marche, *Anecdotes historiques, légendes et apologues tirés du recueil inédit d'Étienne de Bourbon*, pp. 423–4.

95 M. Bakhtin, *Rabelais and His World*, trans. H. Iswolsky (Cambridge, Mass., 1968), pp. 5–12; N. Zemon Davis, 'The Reasons of Misrule: Youth Groups and Charivaris in 16th Century France', *Past and Present*, 50 (1971), pp. 41–75.

96 'et pueri in ipso festo Innocentium, quia innocentes pro Christo occisisunt', *Rationale Divinorum Officiorum Auctore Joanne Beletho*, PL vol. 202, col. 77; 'ratione innocentiae assecutae quoniam in ipso martirio assecuti sunt', *Jacobi De Voragine Legende Aurea*, ed. T. Grässe (Leipzig, 1850), ch. 10, pp. 62–6; and the fifteenth-century English translation 'Jesu Christ was slain in every each of them', *The Golden Legend or Lives of the Saints as Englished by William Caxton*, ed. F. S. Ellis (London, 1900), vol. IV, p. 153.

97 See J. M. Fletcher, op. cit., G. R. Owst, *Preaching in Medieval England* (Cambridge, 1926), p. 220, and nn. 2, 3, 4.

9 EDUCATION FOR SERVICE IN THE SECULAR CHURCH AND IN
THE MONASTERY

1 A 'dynasty' of priests figures in the Lincolnshire Assize Rolls. A nephew went to
   court to claim the legacy of his uncle, who was a bastard and a priest, and the
   son of a bastard priest (*The Early Lincolnshire Assize Rolls, 1202–12–3*, ed. D. M.
   Stenton (London, 1926), pp. 69, 105).
2 *Acta Sanctorum*, ed. J. Bollandus and G. Henschenius (Paris–Rome, 1863–1940),
   Apr. 1, p. 443.
3 ibid., May 2, p. 628. When he reached adulthood, his friends tried to persuade
   him to abandon the church, marry, and demand of his relatives that they restore
   his inheritance to him.
4 Vincent of Beauvais, *De Eruditione Filiorum Nobiliorum*, ed. A. Steiner (Medieval
   Academy of America, 32; Cambridge, Mass., 1938), p. 218; G. R. Owst, *Literature
   and Pulpit in Medieval England* (Oxford, 1961), p. 263 and n. 2; E. Power, *Medieval
   English Nunneries* (Cambridge, 1922), pp. 31–2; P. Riché, 'L'Enfant dans le Haut
   Moyen-Age', *Annales de démographie historique* (1973), pp. 90–3; R. Rapp, 'Les
   Abbeyes, hospices de la noblesse: L'Influence de l'aristocratie sur les couvents
   bénédictins dans l'empire à la fin du Moyen Age', in *La Noblesse au Moyen Age*,
   ed. Ph. Contamine (Paris, 1976), pp. 321–2.
5 e.g. *Analecta Bollandiana*, 33 (1913), p. 180; *Acta Sanctorum*, May 2, p. 338.
6 *The Ecclesiastical History of Orderic Vitalis*, ed. and trans. M. Chibnall (Oxford,
   1968), vol. II, pp. 126–8.
7 *PL* vol. 135, col. 340.
8 On the higher number of illegitimate as compared to legitimate girls offered to
   convents in Florence in the first half of the fifteenth century, see J. Kirshner and
   A. Molho, 'The Dowry Funds and the Marriage Market in Early Quattrocento
   Florence', *Journal of Modern History*, 50/3 (1978), pp. 429–30.
9 A. Lefebvre-Teillard, 'L'Enfant naturel dans l'ancien droit français', *Recueils de la
   Société Jean Bodin*, vol. 36/2 (Brussels, 1976), pp. 251–69; A. Beinard, 'Bâtard',
   Dictionnaire de droit canonique, ed. R. Naz (Paris, 1924–65), vol. II, cols 250–61.
10 W. Hinnebusch, *The History of the Dominican Order* (New York, 1965), p. 286.
11 *Magna Vita Sancti Hugonis*, ed. and trans. D. Douie and Dom. H. Farmer (Nelson
   Series; London, 1962), vol. I, pp. 6–7.
12 *Acta Sanctorum*, Aug. 3, p. 143; A Vauchez, 'Charité et pauvreté chez Saint
   Élisabeth de Thuringie d'après les actes du proces de canonisation', in *Étude sur
   l'histoire de la pauvreté (Moyen Age–XVIᵉ siècle)*, ed. M. Mollat (Paris, 1974), vol.
   I, pp. 163–73; the mother of James the Venetian (died 1231), who joined the
   Dominican Order at 17, retired to a convent when he was a small child. She left
   him in the care of his paternal grandmother (*Acta Sanctorum*, May 7, p. 453).
13 e.g. *Acta Sanctorum*, Sept. 3, pp. 644–5; *MGHS* vol. 30/2, p. 873.
14 *Acta Sanctorum*, Feb. 3, p. 152; Mar. 1, pp. 699, 508, 800; Apr. 3, p. 677, and
   elsewhere.
15 ibid., Jan. 1, p. 336. And see also ibid., Apr. 3, p. 677; June 1, p. 341, and
   elsewhere. If they did not cite the tale of Samuel, they cited the story of the
   bringing of Christ into the Temple.
16 ibid., Mar. 1, p. 481.
17 ibid., Jan. 2, p. 900.
18 Philip of Novare, *Les Quatre Ages de l'homme*, ed. M. de Éreville (Paris, 1888), s.
   15, pp. 10–11.
19 Edmund of Abingdon (1180–1240) who sought a convent which would accept

his sisters without a dowry (which he considered a simony) found this extremely difficult. In the end, they were accepted into the Catesby convent (*Thesaurus Novus Anecdoturum*, ed. E. Martène and U. Durand (Paris, 1717), vol. III, col. 1780). Among the poor, there were foundlings who found their way to monasteries (see, e.g., *Magna Vita Sancti Hugonis*, vol. I, pp. 132–3.

20 N. Orme, *English Schools in the Middle Ages* (London, 1973), pp. 16–17.

21 Cited in Ph. Contamine, *La Vie quotidienne pendant la Guerre de Cent Ans: France et Angleterre* (Paris, 1967), p. 169. See also M. T. Clanchy, *From Memory to Record: England, 1066–1307* (London, 1979), pp. 192–5.

22 The Lives of the saints frequently mention boys sent to be raised by a bishop uncle: e.g. St Theotonius (1160) *Acta Sanctorum*, Feb. 3, pp. 102, 118; St William, ibid., Jan. 1, p. 636; St Dominic (died 1221), ibid., Aug. 1, p. 524; Roger le Fort (died 1307), ibid., Mar. 1, p. 120. Gerald of Wales was also sent to be raised by his maternal uncle at St David.

23 See on this M. T. Clanchy, op. cit., pp. 181–3.

24 For examples from hospitals in York and Norwich, see M. Rubin, *Charity and Community in Medieval Cambridge* (Cambridge, 1987), p. 272. On assistance to poor pupils and students in France from the thirteenth century on, see J. M. Reitzel, 'The Medieval Houses of Bons-Enfants', *Viator*, 10 (1980), pp. 179–207.

25 Geoffrey Chaucer, *The Canterbury Tales*, ed. W. W. Skeat (Oxford, 1947), The Prioress's Tale, p. 163.

26 On schools, see A. F. Leach, *The Schools of Medieval England* (London, 1915); J. Leclerq, *The Love of Learning and the Desire for God* (New York, 1962); N. Orme, op. cit.; J. H. Moran, *The Growth of English Schooling, 1340–1548* (Princeton, 1985); H. M. Jewell, 'The Bringing up of Children in Good Learning and Manners: A Survey of Secular Educational Provisions in the North of England, 1350–1550', *Northern History*, 18 (1982), pp. 1–30.

27 The following are examples of oblates from the eleventh and twelfth centuries: Peter the Venerable (1092–1150) was handed over to one of the Cluny houses as a small child (*PL* 189, col. 17); Hugh of Lincoln, as mentioned above, was placed in a monastery at the age of 8; Suger of St Denis was placed in a monastery at nine (he came from a poor family) (*Abbot Suger of the Abbey Church of St. Denis*, ed. and trans. E. Panofsky (Princeton, 1946), pp. 30–1); Hildegard of Bingen was placed in a nunnery at the age of 8 (*Acta Sanctorum*, Sept. 5, p. 683); William Godman, Abbot of the Abbey of Gloucester (1113–30) was offered in *oblatio* at 7 (D. Knowles, *The Monastic Orders in England* (Cambridge, 1963), p. 420).

28 The Toledo Church Council of 633 stipulated that a man could become a monk 'because of the piety of his father' (*paterna devotio*), or his own profession (*professio*). Rabanus Maurus and others reiterated this in the Carolingian period: *PL* vol. 107, col. 419. For the clause on *oblatio* in the Benedictine rule, see *La Règle de Saint Benoit*, ed. J. Neufville (Paris, 1972), s. 59, p. 632; the ban on *oblatio*, *Corpus Iuris Canonici*, ed. A. Friedberg (Leipzig, 1879), vol. II, bk 3, tit. 31, chs 12, 14, cols 572–3. And see also D. Knowles, op. cit., pp. 418–22; for a description of the ceremony of offering a child in *oblatio* in the eleventh century, see *Decreta Lanfranci*, ed. D. Knowles (Nelson Series; London, 1951), pp. 110–11; on *oblati* in art see I. H. Forsyth, 'Children in Early Medieval Art: Ninth through Twelfth Centuries', *Journal of Psychohistory*, 4 (1976–7), pp. 39–41.

29 *Statuta Capitolorum Generalium Ordinis Cisterciensis*, ed. J. Canivez (Lourain, 1933), vol. I, pp. 31, 84.

30 *Acta Sanctorum*, Mar. 1, p. 659.

31 *The Register of Eudes of Rouen*, trans. S. M. Brown (New York, 1964), p. 259; on

children in Benedictine monasteries in Imperial Germany in the Late Middle Ages, see F. Rapp, op. cit., pp. 315–38; a ten-year-old orphan boy in England was placed in the priory of Lewes at his request (S. Thrupp, *The Merchant Class of Medieval London* (Ann Arbor, 1976), p. 188).

32 See N. Orme, *Education in the West of England, 1066–1548* (Exeter, 1976), p. 1.

33 On changes in conditions for acceptance into monasteries from the middle of the twelfth century, see D. Knowles, op. cit., pp. 418–22; on monks from various orders who studied at Oxford in the Middle Ages, see T. H. Aston, 'Oxford's Medieval Alumni', *Past and Present*, 74 (1968), pp. 3–35.

34 J. Moorman, *The History of the Franciscan Order* (Oxford, 1968), pp. 344–8, 352–3.

35 Among the strongest critics was John Wyclif, *The English Works of Wyclif Hitherto Unpublished*, ed. F. D. Matthew (EETS; London, 1880), pp. 9–10, 223, 269–78, 500; and see also J. Moorman, op. cit., pp. 343–4, 346.

36 Gertrude of Altenburg, daughter of Elizabeth of Hungary, was placed in a Premonstratensian nunnery in 1228, at the age of 2 (see n. 12); St Margaret, daughter of the King of Hungary, was sent to a Dominican convent in 1246 when not yet 4 years old. Her nurse went with her and became a nun 'for love of her and in order to serve God' (*Acta Sanctorum*, Jan. 2, p. 900); a seven-year-old girl was accepted into a Cistercian convent at the end of the twelfth century (ibid., June 1, p. 427); a five-year-old girl entered a double Augustinian nunnery at the end of the twelfth century (ibid., Apr. 1, p. 443); at the end of the fourteenth century, a ten-year-old girl entered a nunnery of the Poor Clares (ibid., Sept. 1, p. 697); R. Trexler estimates that the average age at which girls entered nunneries in Florence was 9 ('Le Célibat à la fin du Moyen Age: Les Religieuses de Florence', *Annales ESC* 27 (1972), pp. 1329–50); Kirshner and Molho, however, show that the average age was higher because the decision to send a daughter to a nunnery was sometimes taken only when she had already reached puberty (op. cit., pp. 424–5).

37 Humbert de Romans, *Sermones* (Venice, 1603), sermo 52, p. 53.

38 E. K. Chambers, *The Medieval Stage* (Oxford, 1903), vol. I, pp. 361–2.

39 *Corpus Iuris Canonici*, vol. II, bk 3, tit. 31, ch. 12, col. 572.

40 R. Riché, *De l'éducation antique à l'éducation chevaleresque* (Paris, 1968), p. 30; id., *Éducation et culture dans l'occident barbare VIᵉ–VIIIᵉ siècles* (Paris, 1962), p. 504.

41 *Decreta Lanfranci*, pp. 3, 5, 7, 21, 24, 28, 31, 46, 49, 74, 115–17, 124.

42 See M. de Jong, 'Growing up in a Carolingian Monastery: Magister Hildemar and his Oblates', *Journal of Medieval History*, 9 (1983), pp. 99–128.

43 On Lanfranc's citing of the customs of other monasteries, see *Decreta Lanfranci*, pp. xi–xii; for Ulrich's customs, *Uldaricus Cluniacensis Monachus Consuetudines Cluniacenses*, *PL* vol. 149, ch. 9 (de custodia juvenum), cols 741–7; for the statutes of the Maillezais monastery, see J. Becquet, 'Le Coutumier clunisien de Maillezais', *Revue Mabillon*, 55 (1965), pp. 16–18; additional expression of awareness of the possibility of sexual exploitation of children and young boys by adult churchmen can be found in a letter of Antoninus of Florence in which he writes that he always avoided having in his house not only women but also young boys; all the members of his household were men over 25; and, as in the case of women, he only spoke to boys in public (*Acta Sanctorum*, May 1, p. 322).

44 See ch. 8, n. 64.

45 *Magna Vita Sancti Hugonis*, vol. 1, p. 6.

46 *Acta Sanctorum*, Jan. 1, p. 336; Bernard of Clairvaux wrote in the same spirit in a letter to the parents of one of the novices in his monastery that he would be the

boy's father and mother, brother and sister, and that all the monks of Clairvaux would accept him as their brother (*Sancti Bernardi Opera Omnia*, ed. J. Mabillon (Paris, 1690), vol. I, ep. 110, col. 118.

47 *The Life of St. Anselm Archbishop of Canterbury by Eadmer*, ed. and trans. R. W. Southern (Nelson Series; London, 1962), p. 24.

48 *Acta Sanctorum*, Jan. 2, p. 900.

49 ibid., Mar. 3, p. 504.

50 *Caesarii Heisterbacensis Monarchi Dialogus*, ed. J. Strange (Cologne, 1851), p. 33.

51 M. de Jong, op. cit., p. 114.

52 *Magna Vita Sancti Hugonis*, vol. I, pp. 6–8.

53 *Acta Sanctorum*, Apr. 1, p. 443–4.

54 ibid., July 1, p. 482.

55 On the emotional damage to a child who was not able to express his pain, frustration, and hostility towards adults, see A. Miller, *For Your Own Good*, trans. H. and H. Hannum (London, 1983), particularly pp. 254–9. This problem and this book were brought to my attention by a psychologist, Prof. Veronica Grimm-Samuel.

56 *Acta Sanctorum*, June 4, p. 191; the parents of Mechthild von Edelstetten (died 1160) established a double monastery on their estate at Dissen in Bavaria, and she was placed there at the age of 5. When the monastery was in financial straits, she reminded her father that he had sent her there, and that if she had married a mortal man he would have had to give her a dowry. Her father agreed to extend financial assistance to the monastery (ibid., May 7, pp. 437–8, 445).

57 'a suis progenitoribus voluntaris salubriter derelictus, a Domino autem assumptus', ibid., June 1, p. 341; and see also ibid., Jan. 2, p. 1132.

58 Hildegard was apparently nursed by her mother. Jutta was a recluse who lived near the church of St Disibond not far from the home of Hildegard's parents. She was sister to Count Spondheim, the feudal seigneur of Hildegard's father (ibid., Sept. 5, p. 683).

59 This story appears in the life of St Colette (died 1447), who became an abbess. The child did not want to leave the convent and her father took her out against her will. Thanks to Colette's prayers, he was given a sign from heaven: his horse stumbled and fell several times and he took the child back (ibid., Mar. 1, p. 559).

60 *The Ecclesiastical History of Orderic Vitalis*, vol. VI, pp. 552–5.

61 J. Boswell, '*Expositio* and *Oblatio*: The Abandonment of Children and the Ancient and Medieval Family', *American History Review*, 89 (1984), pp. 10–33; I believe that the author's comparison between *expositio* and *oblatio* is valid, but he does not emphasize sufficiently the fact that, in the Central Middle Ages, the latter was essentially practised in the upper classes alone.

62 One may recall the little girl from Colette's nunnery who did not wish to leave (see n. 59). The parents of St Margaret, daughter of the King of Hungary, despite their vow, tried twice to remove her from the convent in order to give her in marriage. On the first occasion, when they wanted to marry her to the King of Poland, she was still a child, but she adamantly refused to leave the convent, and her parents were forced to concede (*Acta Sanctorum*, Jan. 2, p. 909).

63 M. Chibnall, *The World of Orderic Vitalis* (Oxford, 1984), pp. 74–6.

64 L. Delisle, 'D'après le registre d'Eudes Rigaud', *Bibliothèque de l'école de chartes*, 25 (1840), pp. 495 ff.; *The Registre of Eudes of Rouen*, trans. S. M. Brown (New York, 1904); *Visitations of Religious Houses in the Diocese of Lincoln 1420–1436*, vol. I, ed. A. H. Thompson (Horncastle, 1915). On the moral decline in the monasteries in Imperial Germany at the end of the Middle Ages, see F. Rapp, op. cit. The

reports of visitations give a picture of the deviations but are of restricted value as a source of information on their scope: on the one hand, they only refer to deviations because, where everything was in order, there was no need to mention it, and on the other hand there were things which the bishop or his representative could not discover. It should also be recalled that most of the texts are incomplete and hence that the picture is also incomplete (see, on this, C. R. Cheney, *Episcopal Visitations of Monasteries in the Thirteenth Century* (Manchester, 1931), mainly pp. 149–67).

65 Humbert de Romans, op. cit., 45, p. 47.

66 W. James, *The Varieties of Religious Experience* (The Gifford Lectures, delivered at Edinburgh, 1901–1902; London, 1960), p. 203. An example of a small girl who requested, at the age of 9, to enter a convent and whose parents consented was Agnes of Montepulciano: she became abbess of a Dominican convent at a very early age (*Acta Sanctorum*, Apr. 2, p. 791).

67 See ch. 7 for the story of Anselm of Canterbury. On the problem of loss of a sense of identity in adolescence, see E. H. Erikson, 'The Problem of Ego Identity', in *The Psychology of Adolescence*, ed. A. H. Esman (New York, 1975), pp. 318–46.

68 Bernard of Clairvaux and Edmond of Abingdon can serve as examples of these, as can Anthony of Padua (L. de Kerval, *St. Antonii de Padua Vitae Duae* (1904), pp. 26–8).

69 The conversion of Bernard of Parma and Francis Fabriano was sudden (*MGHS* vol. XXX, pp. 1323–4; *Acta Sanctorum*, Apr. 3. In the case of Francis of Assisi it was a gradual process, lasting several years.

70 *Acta Sanctorum*, Apr. 3, pp. 642–56.

71 Gerald of Wales, *De Rebus a se Gestis*, ed. J. S. Brewer (Rolls Series; London, 1861), vol. 21/1, p. 22.

72 *Acta Sanctorum*, Apr. 1, pp. 687–9. At the age of 12, he requested to be accepted by the Premonstratensians, but they refused because of his youth.

73 ibid., Mar. 1, pp. 540–1.

74 On Peter of Luxemburg, see ibid., July 1, pp. 455–6; and see also R. Kieckhefer, *Unquiet Souls: Fourteenth Century Saints and their Religious Milieu* (Chicago, 1984), pp. 33–4.

75 Such, for example, was the response of the parents of Robert of Knaresborough, who was the eldest son (*Analecta Bollandiana*, 57 (1939), pp. 378–80); of Beatrix Atestina (*Acta Sanctorum*, Jan. 1, p. 1136); and of Gemma Solomona (ibid., May 3, p. 181).

76 *Acta Sanctorum*, July 5, p. 790. And see also the reaction of the parents of Blessed Advertanus, who joined the Carmelites (ibid., Feb. 3, pp. 620–1).

77 *Blanquerna* (Madrid, 1924; = *Blanquerna: A 13th Century Romance*, trans. E. Alison Peers (London, 1925)). ch. 5. pp. 54–5; ch. 7, pp. 71–7.

78 *Acta Sanctorum*, Apr. 3, p. 874; her parents accepted the manifestations of her piety in childhood. She had her first vision at 6. The pressures to marry were exerted on her after the death of her older sister, when she was 15.

79 For the reaction of Ida of Louvain's father, see ibid., Apr. 2, pp. 159, 168; for the father of Margaret the 'Barefoot', see ibid., Aug. 2, p. 121.

80 ibid., Sept. 5, p. 403.

81 ibid., Mar. 1, pp. 661–2.

82 ibid., Aug. 3, p. 766; *The Life of St. Clare*, trans. P. Robinson (London, 1910), pp. 7–18, 40–3.

83 *Acta Sanctorum*, Apr. 2, pp. 504–5.

84 Thomas of Celano, *Legenda Prima in S. Francisci Assisiensis Vita et Miracula*, ed. P.

E. Alencon (Rome, 1906), pp. 6–17; *Legenda Secunda*, ibid., pp. 169–77; *St. Francis of Assisi: Writings and Early Biographies*, ed. and trans. M. A. Habig (Chicago, 1973), pp. 891, 898; St Bonaventure, *Legenda Sancti Francisci*, in *Opera Omnia* (Karachi, 1898), pp. 510–11.

85 *Corpus Iuris Canonici*, vol. II, bk 3, tit. 31, chs I–II, col. 569.

86 *Legenda Secunda*, p. 711.

87 See ch. 1, n. 47.

88 See, for example, *Acta Sanctorum*, May 5, pp. 207–8; Aug. 2, p. 121; Mar. 2, pp. 93–4; May 5, pp. 207–9.

89 ibid., Mar. 2, p. 93. On this phenomenon of revulsion from the opposite sex and the search for a refuge in a convent or religious community, see also W. McDonell, *The Beguines and Beghards in Medieval Culture* (New York, 1954), pp. 354–5; in the Lives of the saints I have not encountered the case of a boy who chose the religious life and did not succeed in carrying out his wishes.

90 F. Fromm-Reichmann, 'Note on the Mother Role in the Family Group', in *Psychoanalysis and Psychotherapy*, ed. R. A. Harper (Chicago, 1959), pp. 290–305.

91 The father is not mentioned at all in the Vitae but only in testimony given before the council which discussed the possibility of canonization (*Acta Sanctorum*, Mar. 1, p. 711).

92 ibid., Mar. 1, pp. 661–2.

93 Reference is to Heribert, who became Bishop of Cologne (ibid., Mar. 2, p. 463); St Alda was also praised for having obeyed her parents and agreed to marry (ibid., Apr. 3, p. 473).

94 Saint Jerome, *Lettres*, ed. J. Labourt (Paris, 1949), vol. I, Letter 14, pp. 33–45. On the commentary of the author of *Dives and Pauper*, see ch. 8, n. 32.

95 *Die Exempla des Jacob von Vitry*, ed. G. Frenken, in *Quellen und Untersuchungen zur lateinischen Philologie des Mittelalters*, 5/1 (1914), pp. 130–1.

96 St Bernard, op. cit., vol. I, ep. 113, col. 119; *The Letters of St. Bernard of Clairvaux*, ed. and trans. B. S. James (London, 1953), pp. 169–71.

97 Salimbene de Adam, *Chronica*, ed. G. Scalia (Bari, 1966), pp. 53–6; when Salimbene's father came with letters from Frederick II with the intention of removing him, he was told that his son had reached an age when he could speak for himself ('etatem habet, ipse de se loquatur', ibid., p. 55): he was then 17.

98 Vincent of Beauvais, *De Eruditione Filiorum Nobiliorum*, ed. A. Steiner (Medieval Academy of America, 32; Cambridge, Mass., 1938), p. 218; *The Letters of John of Salisbury, 1153–1161*, ed. W. J. Millors and S. J. and H. E. Butler (Nelson Series; London, 1955), p. 230.

99 *Dives and Pauper*, ed. P. H. Barnum (EETS; London, 1976), pp. 316–17; Thomas Aquinas, *Summa Theologiae*, Secunda Secundae, q. 189, art. 6 (vol. 47, p. 250).

10   EDUCATION IN THE NOBILITY

1 Gottfried of Strasburg, *Tristan* (Stuttgart, 1980), pt 1, 2070–85, p. 133.

2 On the large number of children and youths educated in the castle of the count of Guines, for example, note 'cum multi in hac domo ab infancia educati et in virilem etatem producti' (Lambert of Ardres, *Historia Comitum Ghisnensium*, MGHS vol. 24, ch. 127, p. 624; on Ailred of Rievaulx, son of a priest from Northumbria, brought up in the court of the King of Scotland together with the king's son, see *The Life of Ailred of Rievaulx by Walter Daniel*, ed. and trans. F. M. Powicke (Nelson Series; London, 1963), pp. xxxv, 2; Walter Map writes about a boy brought up in the home of relatives (*De Nugis Curialium*, ed. M. R. James (Oxford, 1983), pt

4, ch. 1, p. 278); examples from England of upbringing in the royal court in N. Orme, *From Childhood to Chivalry: The Education of the English Kings and Aristocracy, 1066–1530* (London, 1984), p. 28.

3 Baldwin II, Count of Guines, for edample, had 23 illegitimate offspring and 20 legitimate ones (G. Duby, *Medieval Marriage: Two Models from 12th Century France* (London, 1978), pp. 94–5); we learn that an affectionate paternal attitude towards bastards was considered acceptable from the fact that, because of Henry II's special attitude towards Hugh of Lincoln, it was widely thought that Hugh was his bastard son (*Magna Vita Sancti Hugones*, ed. and trans. D. Douie and Dom. H. Farmer (Nelson Series; London, 1962), vol. II, p. 69); on the legitimate son and the bastard of the Count of Foix who were brought up together, see *Œuvres de Froissart: Chroniques*, ed. K. de Lettenhove (1867–77; repr. Osnabrück, 1967), vol. XI, pp. 93–4; on the inheritance rights of bastards, see, e.g., A. Lefebvre-Teillard, 'L'Enfant naturel dans l'ancient droit français', in *Recueils de la Société Jean Bodin*, vol. 36/2 (Brussels, 1976), pp. 251–69.

4 On the education of nobles, see M. T. Clanchy, *From Memory to Written Record: England 1066–1307* (London, 1979), pp. 175–201; on the various meanings of *litteratus* and *illitteratus*, ibid.; Gilbert of Nogent relates that the clerk who was his private tutor had previously served as tutor to the children of Gilbert's relatives and lived in their home (*Autobiographie*, ed. E. R. Labarde (Paris, 1981), bk 1, ch. 4, pp. 27–30).

5 See, on this, G. Duby, *Guillaume le Maréchal ou Le Meilleur Chevalier du monde* (Paris, 1984), pp. 82–6.

6 L. Gautier, *Chivalry*, trans. D. C. Dunning (London, 1965), pp. 40–1.

7 'Que il ne peut chevalchier ne errer', *Raoul de Cambrai*, ed. P. Meyer and A. Longnon (Paris, 1882), p. 9.

8 In the literary work, *Doon*, 'when the child learned to ride' he was sent to be raised in the court of the King of France (G. Paris, 'Lais inédits', *Romania*, 8 (1897), Lay de Doon, p. 63.

9 'ut postea in XIIII anno instructi in luctativa et in equistativa et in aliis quae ad militiam requiruntur', Aegidius Romanus, *De Regimine Principum* (Venice, 1505), bk 2, pt 2, ch. 17.

10 See the description of training in Gerald of Wales, *De Rebus a se Gestis*, ed. J. S. Brewer (Rolls Series; London, 1861), vol. 21/1, p. 22.

11 On the low life-expectancy of men in the nobility, see T. H. Hollingworth, 'A Demographic Study of the British Ducal Families', *Population Studies*, 11 (1957), pp. 4–26; J. T. Rosenthal, 'Medieval Longevity and the Secular Peerage, 1350–1500', *Population Studies*, 27 (1973), pp. 287–93; G. Duby, 'Dans la France du Nord-Ouest au XIIe siècle: Les "Jeunes" dans la société aristocratique', *Annales ESC* 19 (1964), pp. 839–43.

12 See M. Chibnall, *The World of Orderic Vitalis* (Oxford, 1984), p. 132; *The Westminster Chronicle 1381–1394*, ed. and trans. L. C. Hector and B. F. Harvey (Oxford, 1982), pp. 408–10.

13 For a description of a company of children, see Wolfram of Eschenbach, *Parzival und Titurel*, ed. E. Martin (Halle, 1900), 147, p. 124; *PL* vol. 175, col. 236; *Analecta Bollandiana*, 9 (1890), p. 283.

14 E. J. Tardif (ed.), *Coutumiers de Normandie* (Slatkine repr.; Geneva, 1977), vols I–II, p. 57.

15 Froissart mentions a ball game. In one manuscript it is called 'le jeu de paume' and in another 'le jeu de cache', It was played by the legitimate and bastard sons of the Count of Foix (*Oeuvres de Froissart: Chroniques*, vol. XI, p. 94, and nn. 4, 5).

16 See F. Barlow, *William Rufus* (London, 1983), p. 13.
17 *Le Livre de Lancelot del Lac* (*The Vulgate Version of the Arthurian Romance*, ed. H. O. Sommer (Washington, DC, 1910), vol. III, p. 38.
18 The excerpt is from the *Chanson de Willalme*, cited in U. T. Holmes, 'Medieval Children', *Journal of Social History*, 2 (1968–9), p. 170 and n. 30.
19 See, on this, M. Combarieu, 'Enfance et demesure dans l'épopée mediévale française', in *L'Enfant au Moyen Age: Littérature et civilization* (Senefiance, 9; Paris, 1980), pp. 407–56.
20 Philip of Novare elaborates on the importance of generosity (*Les Quatre Ages de l'homme*, ed. M. de Eréville (Paris, 1888), s. 19, p. 13); Doon wins the hearts of all those being raised with him in the royal court because of his generosity (G. Paris, op. cit., p. 62); as kingdoms consolidated, it was the duty of the knight not only to be the protector of all the non-combatants but also to be the 'defender of the kingdom' (see, for example, Raymond Lull, *Doctrine d'enfant*, ed. A. Llinarès (Paris, 1967), ch. 80, p. 175.
21 For a description of the son of the Count of Foix serving his father at table, see *Oeuvres de Froissart: Chroniques*, vol. XI, pp. 94–5.
22 e.g. John Bromyard, *Summa Praedicantium* (Antwerp, 1614), p. 5; *Select English Works of John Wycliffe*, ed. T. Arnold (London, 1871), vol. III, p. 196.
23 Bernard Gordon, *De Conservatione Vitae Humanae* (Leipzig, 1570), p. 29.
24 N. Elias, *The Civilizing Process: State Formation and Civilization*, trans. E. Jephcott (Oxford, 1982), particularly pp. 229–333.
25 Bernard Gordon, op. cit., pp. 29–30.
26 *Le Roman de Tristan par Thomas: Poème du 12ᵉ siècle*, ed. J. Bedier (SATF; Paris, 1902), pp. 28–9; Gottfried of Strasburg, op. cit., pt 1, 2055, pp. 131 ff.; J. Frappier, *Amour courtois et table ronde* (Geneva, 1973), p. 170; D. Buschinger, 'L'Enfant dans les romans de Tristan en France et en Allemagne', in *L'Enfant au Moyen Age; Littérature et civilisation* (Senefiance, 9; Paris, 1980), pp. 255–68.
27 On these private schools, see J. M. Moran, *The Growth of English Schooling, 1340–1548* (Princeton, 1985), pp. 70, 83; N. Orme, op. cit., p. 56; on the education of the knight in didactic literature, Konrad of Megenberg, *Ökonomik*, ed. S. Krüger (Stuttgart, 1973; MGH Staatsschriften, 111/15), bk I/2, ch. 17, p. 95.
28 T. Wright, *A Volume of Vocabularies* (privately printed, 1857), vol. I, pp. 142–74.
29 N. Orme, *English Schools in the Middle Ages* (London, 1973), p. 31.
30 See M. T. Clanchy, op. cit., ch. 7.
31 Peter Abelard, *Historia Calamitatum*, ed. J. Monfrin (Paris, 1962), p. 63; on an eleventh-century nobleman trained for knighthood who was none the less educated, see Orderic Vitalis. It is not precisely clear what education he received. He eventually became a monk, although this had not been the intention of his father (*The Ecclesiastical History of Orderic Vitalis*, ed. and trans. M. Chibnall (Oxford, 1968), vol. II, p. 40).
32 *The Stonor Letters and Papers*, ed. C. L. Kingsford (Camden 3rd Series, vol. XXIX; London, 1919), vol. I, p. 21.
33 J. H. Moran, op. cit., pp. 29, 70; J. Verger, 'Noblesse et savoir: Étudiants nobles aux Universités d'Avignon, Cahors, Montpellier et Toulouse (fin du XIVᵉ siècle)', in *La Noblesse au Moyen Age*, ed. Ph. Contamine (Paris, 1976), pp. 283–313.
34 'Il fait mal nourrir autruy enfant, car il s'en va quant il est grant', *Proverbes français antérieurs au XVᵉ siècle*, ed. J. Morawski (Paris, 1925), p. 32.
35 John Bromyard, op. cit., p. 5.
36 J. Goody, *The Development of the Family and Marriage in Europe* (Cambridge, 1983), p. 68.

37 E. Goody, 'Parental Strategies, Calculation or Sentiment? Fostering Pratices among West Africans', in *Interest and Emotion: Essays on the Study of Family and Kinship*, ed. H. Medick and D. W. Sabean (Cambridge, 1984), pp. 266–77.

38 'per tale servitium spes est de magna promotione', John Bromyard, op. cit., p. 5.

39 For an authentic description of a child's life in a prep school at the turn of the century, see George Orwell, 'Such Such Were the Joys ...' in *A Collection of Essays* (New York, 1954), pp. 9–5 (he was sent to prep school at the age of 8); for a description of the anxieties of a mother whose son was about to be sent to Eton, see L. A. Pollock, *Forgotten Children: Parent–Child Relations from 1500 to 1900* (Cambridge, 1983), p. 197.

40 *Acta Sanctorum*, ed. J. Bollandus and G. Henschenius (Paris–Rome, 1863–1940), Apr. 1, p. 420.

41 ibid., Apr. 1, p. 38.

42 For examples of mothers who acted as guardians to their sons, the heirs of fiefs, see Havoise of Brittany (M. Planiol, *Histoire des institutions de la Bretagne* (Rennes, 1955), vol. III, p. 30); Blance of Navarre, widow of the Count of Champagne (J. Longnon, 'La Champagne', in F. Lot and R. Fawtier, *Histoire des institutions françaises au Moyen Age*, vol. 1, *Institutions seigneuriales* (Paris, 1957), pp. 128, 134); Ermessend, who acted as guardian in the counties of Barcelona, Gerona, and Ausone (P. Bonnassie, *La Catalogne du milieu du Xe à la fin du XIe siècle* (Toulouse, 1975), vol. I, pp. 276–7. In England heirs were not made the wards of their mothers. The seigneurs acted as guardians. If children lost their fathers it was, therefore, the eldest son who was sent to the seigneur or whoever was appointed guardian by him.

43 *Raoul de Cambrai*, p. 35.

44 G. Duby, *Le Chevalier, la femme et le prêtre* (Paris, 1981), pp. 234–7.

45 Gilbert of Nogent, *Autobiographie*, bk 1, ch. 4, pp. 24–5.

46 *Œuvres de Froissart: Chroniques*, vol. XI, pp. 90–100.

47 J. T. Rosenthal, *Nobles and the Noble Life, 1295–1500* (London, 1976), p. 91.

48 *The Early English Version of the Gesta Romanorum*, ed. S. J. H. Herrtage (London, 1879), pp. 443–4.

49 *Le Livre de Lancelot del Lac*; J. Frappier, *Amour courtois et table ronde*, ch. 10.

50 G. Duby, *Guillaume le Maréchal ou Le Meilleur Chevalier du monde*, p. 85.

51 See, for example, N. Orme, *From Childhood to Chivalry*, p. 29.

52 On the daughters of the Guines family educated in a convent see Lambert of Ardres, op. cit., ch. 122, p. 621; on thirteenth- and fourteenth-century England, N. Orme, *Education in the West of England, 1066–1548* (Exeter, 1976), pp. 54, 201, 204; on Imperial Germany in the Late Middle Ages, F. Rapp, 'Les Abbayes, hospices de la noblesse: L'Influence de l'aristocratie sur les couvents bénédictins dans l'empire à la fin du Moyen Age', in *La Noblesse au Moyen Age*, ed. Ph. Contamine (Paris, 1976), p. 320; see also N. Orme, *From Childhood to Chivalry*, p. 65.

53 For a nurse to a thirteen-year-old girl in the parents' home, see M. W. Labarge, p. 45; in *Le Fresne*, by Marie de France, Le Coudre, the sister of Fresne, lives at home when her parents are planning her marriage; two of the sisters of William Marshal were with their mother at the bedside of their dying father (G. Duby, *Guillaume le Maréchal ou Le Meilleur Chevalier du monde*, pp. 49–50); on female tutors and anchoresses who fulfilled this function, see U. T. Holmes, op. cit., p. 168 and nn. 19–21; J. H. Moran, *The Growth of English Schooling, 1340–1548*, pp. 69–70.

54 *Registre de l'inquisition de Jacques Fournier, 1318–1325*, ed. J. Duvernoy (Toulouse, 1965), vol. I, p. 252.

55 There are more examples of works written for the guidance of adult women, in which there is reference to the woman's various tasks in the household, the estate, and the fief. See, for example, the manual of guidance for the management of the estate written by Robert Grosseteste for Margaret, widow of the Earl of Lincoln: *Walter of Henley's Husbandry together with an Anonymous Husbandry, Senechaucie and Robert Grosseteste's Rules*, ed. E. Lamond (London, 1890), pp. 121–50.

56 Lambert of Ardres, op. cit., ch. 127, p. 624. Of one of the mothers of the family in the annals of the seigneurs of Amboise it was said that she was a faithful daughter, an obedient wife, a kind lady, and a good mother – 'Dionisia Pia filia, morigera conjux, domina clemens, utilis mater' (*Chroniques des Comtes d'Anjou et des Seigneurs d'Amboise*, ed. L. Halphen and R. Pourpardin (Paris, 1913), p. 98); see also G. Duby's commentary on this excerpt, 'An International Background: The Aristocratic Woman in France in the Twelfth Century', in *Danish Medieval History: New Currents*, ed. S. Skyum-Nielsen and N. Lund (Copenhagen, 1981), p. 62.

57 Philip of Novare, op. cit., ss. 21–31, pp. 14–21.

58 Marie de France, *Lais*, ed. A. E. E. Ewert (Oxford, 1965), pp. 5–6.

59 'non taman nutrienda quam moribus erudienda et liberalibus studiis imbuenda', Lambert of Ardres, op. cit., p. 621.

60 The fact that some kind of education was the condition for acceptance of adult women into convents also indicates that it was customary to give some kind of education to young noblewomen. See *Visitations of Religious Houses in the Diocese of Lincoln*, vol. I, *1420–1436*, ed. A. H. Thompson (Horncastle, 1915), p. 53; E. M. McDonell, *The Beguines and Beghards in Medieval Culture* (New York, 1969), p. 320; John of Salisbury mentions women who are better at falconry than men, 'because the inferior sex has a greater tendency to rapacity', *Policraticus*, PL vol. 199, col. 393.

61 Wolfram of Eschenbach, op. cit., bk 7, 368–75, pp. 129–31.

62 J. Hajnal, 'European Marriage in Perspective', in *Population in History*, ed. D. V. Glass and E. C. Eversley (London, 1965), pp. 101–43.

63 See, on this, e.g. T. H. Hollingworth, op. cit., pp. 4–26.

64 The church authorities acknowledged that, if such pressure and violence had been exerted as a 'constant' man or woman were unable to withstand, the marriage could be annulled. It was not easy to establish which cases were included in the definition. See R. H. Helmholz, *Marriage Litigations in Medieval England* (Cambridge, 1974), pp. 91–4.

65 G. Duby, *Le Chevalier, la femme, et le prêtre*, p. 153.

66 In southern France in the fourteenth century there was a case in which the betrothal was drawn up when the boy was 10 and the girl 12; the marriage was solemnized when the bridegroom was 13 and the bride 15 (*Acta Sanctorum*, Sept. 7, p. 540); for an example of a marriage which took place when both partners were 8 (they became parents before the age of 14), see E. Power, *Medieval Women*, ed. M. M. Postan (Cambridge, 1975), p. 39; and see also J. T. Rosenthal, *Nobles and the Noble Life, 1295–1500*, pp. 177–8; on papal dispensations regarding under-age marriages, see R. Metz, 'L'Enfant dans le droit canonique médiéval', in *Recueils de la Société Jean Bodin*, vol. 36/2 (Brussels, 1976), p. 31.

67 The average age of matrimony for younger sons in northern France in the twelfth century was the late twenties (G. Duby, 'Dans la France de Nord-Ouest au XIIe siècle: Les "Jeunes" dans la société aristocratique', pp. 835–46: for men in English ducal families in the fourteenth century, it was 22 (see n. 11); on the growing

age-gap between husbands and wives, see D. Herlihy, *Medieval Households* (London, 1985), pp. 105, 121.

68 'iuveni matrimonialiter copulata ... vitreis annulis more puellari luderet', *Acta Sanctorum*, Jan. 1, p. 345.

69 Lambert of Ardres, op. cit., ch. 134, p. 629; court rolls record the case of a girl who was playing with a stone when it fell on the head of a passer-by and injured him. When she was brought to trial, it was not claimed in her defence that she was a minor (*Select Pleas of the Crown*, ed. F. W. Maitland (Selden Society; London, 1888), vol. 1, p. 119).

70 Arnaut Vidal de Castelnaudary, *Guillaume de la Barre*, ed. P. Mayer (Paris, 1895), pp. 113–14.

11 EDUCATION IN URBAN SOCIETY

1 Raymond Lull, *Blanquerna: A 13th Century Romance*, trans. E. Alison Peers (London, 1925), p. 39.

2 *Chronica di Giovanni Villani*, ed. F. G. Dragomanni (Florence, 1845, rep. Frankfurt, 1969), vol. III, bk 11, ch. 94, p. 324; see also D. Herlihy, 'Medieval Children', in *Essays on Medieval Civilization* (Austin, 1978), pp. 122–3; on Giovanni Morelli, who was taught alternately by a private tutor and in primary school, see J. B. Ross, 'The Middle Class Child in Urban Italy: 14th to Early 16th Century', in *The History of Childhood*, ed. L. deMausé (New York, 1974), pp. 212 ff.; on the various types of schools in fourteenth- and fifteenth-century London, see S. Thrupp, *The Merchant Class of Medieval London (1300–1500)* (Ann Arbor, 1976), pp. 155–63.

3 Giovanni Dominici, in *Kardinal Johannes Dominicis Erziehungslehre*, trans. A. Rosler (Freiburg, 1894), pp. 27–8.

4 N. Orme, *English Schools in the Middle Ages* (London, 1973), pp. 54–5; in Paris, the lower mixed schools, known as *basses écoles*, were under the supervision of the Chancellor of Notre Dame. In 1357 the first ordinances on separation of boys and girls were issued, but were not immediately implemented. In 1380 there were 41 male and 22 female teachers in Paris. See M. Jourdain, *L'Éducation des Femmes au Moyen Age* (Paris, 1871); on mixed schools in Germany run by beguines, see E. M. McDonnel, *The Beguines and Beghards in Medieval Culture* (New York, 1969), pp. 272, 383, 386. In Tuscan towns boys and girls were separated in lower schools apparently in the fifteenth century; see D. Herlihy and Ch. Klapisch, *Les Toscans et leur familles: Une étude du Catasto florentin de 1427* (Paris, 1978), p. 332. Froissart describes his studies at a mixed town school in Valenciennes (Jean Froissart, *L'Espinette amoureuse*, ed. J. Fournier (Paris, 1963), ll. 35–45, p. 48; and see also A. Planche, 'Culture et contre culture dans L'Espinette amoureuse de Jean Froissart', in *L'Enfant au Moyen Age: Littérature et civilisation* (Senefiance, 9; Paris, 1980), pp. 396–7).

5 J. B. Ross, op. cit., pp. 212–13; on the curriculum for future merchants, see Raymond Lull, *Doctrine d'enfant*, ed. A. Llinarès (Paris, 1969), ch. 79; Konrad of Megenberg, *Ökonomik*, ed. S. Krüger (Stuttgart, 1973; MGH Staatsschriften, 111/5), bk 1/2, ch. 15, p. 92.

6 G. Brucker (ed.), *Two Memoirs of Renaissance Florence: The Diaries of Buonaccorso Pitti and Gregorio Dati* (New York, 1967), p. 108.

7 Konrad of Megenberg, op. cit., bk 1/2, ch. 21, p. 101; D. Herlihy and Ch. Klapisch, op. cit., p. 575.

8 S. Thrupp, op. cit., pp. 192–3.

9 D. Herlihy and Ch. Klapisch, op. cit., pp. 575–8.

10 Giovanni Villani writes of 500–600 boys attending these schools as against 1000–1200 at schools of commerce in Florence (*Chronica di Giovanni Villani*, p. 324).

11 *Iannotii Manetti Vita Ioannis Boccaccii Poetae Florentini*, in *Philippi Villani Liber de Civitatis Florentiae Famosis Civibus*, ed. G. Mazzoni (Florence, 1847), p. 89.

12 *Two Memoirs of Renaissance Florence*, pp. 112, 134; for an example of special love, see *Acta Sanctorum*, ed. J. Bollandus and G. Henschenius (Paris–Rome, 1863–1940), Apr. 1, p. 516.

13 Leon Battista Alberti, *I Libri della Famiglia* (*The Family in Renaissance Florence*), trans. R. N. Watkins (Columbia, 1969), pp. 5, 11.

14 D. Herlihy and Ch. Klapisch, op. cit., pp. 567–8; S. Thrupp, op. cit., pp. 167–9.

15 *Two Memoirs of Renaissance Florence*, p. 108.

16 W. M. Bowsky, *A Medieval Italian Commune: Siena under the Nine, 1287–1355* (Berkeley, 1981), p. 20 and n. 53; for London, see S. Thrupp, op. cit., p. 151, n. 50; Genoa, D. Owen Hughes, 'Urban Growth and Family Structure in Medieval Genova', *Past and Present*, 66 (1975), p. 18; Florence, D. Herlihy and Ch. Klapisch, op. cit., p. 608.

17 *Two Memoirs of Renaissance Florence*, p. 10 and n. 2.

18 D. Herlihy, 'Vieillir à Florence au Quattrocento', *Annales ESC* 24 (1969), pp. 1338–52.

19 S. Thrupp, op. cit., pp. 192–3, 196.

20 Jean Froissart, op. cit., ll. 35–45, p. 48.

21 I. Origo, *The Merchant of Prato* (London, 1957), pp. 162, 169, 170, 186–91.

22 Giovanni Villani, who describes schools in Florence in the second half of the fourteenth century, writes about boys and girls who attended lower schools. Grammar schools and schools of commerce were exclusively male (*Chronica di Giovanni Villani*, p. 324).

23 One of her biographies states 'imperio Ferrariam migravit cum matre' (*Acta Sanctorum*, Mar. 2, p. 47; and see also ibid., p. 36.).

24 The mother's remarks to her daughter appear in the biography of Juliana Falconieri (ibid., June 4, p. 768; *Le Ménagier de Paris*, ed. J. Pichon (Paris, 1846), vol. 1).

25 Jean Froissart, op. cit., ll. 217–18, p. 53.

26 J. Heers, *Fêtes, jeux et joutes dans la société d'occident à la fin du Moyen Age* (Paris, 1971), pp. 112–13.

27 *Iannotii Manetti Vita Dantis Poetae Florentini*, in *Philippi Villani Liber de Civitatis Florentiae Famosis Civibus*, pp. 71–2.

28 See *Acta Sanctorum*, Apr. 2, p. 273.

29 The hagiographer of Catherine of Sienna, describing her childhood, writes that this was the custom in her country (ibid., p. 273).

30 'more quo solent infantes a propinquis tangi et amplexari', ibid., Mar. 2, p. 93.

31 In one case the mother and her second husband wanted to marry her minor daughter to the second husband's minor son. The girl's relatives submitted a complaint to the town court and the child was removed from the couple's custody. The couple appealed to the royal court, but the town court refused to give way. It is not clear how the matter ended (*Calendar of Letter-Books of the City of London at the Guildhall: Letter Book E*, ed. R. R. Sharpe (London, 1902), pp. 47–8).

32 In the life of Lydwina of Schiedam it is related that, when she reached the age of 12, many suitors sought her hand. Her father urged her to marry one of the suitors, and her mother tried to dissuade him from exerting pressure on her because of her youth. At 15 she was injured in an accident and never recovered (*Acta Sanctorum*, Apr. 1, p. 272).

33 D. Herlihy, 'Vieillir à Florence au Quattrocento', p. 1346; id., *Medieval Households*, p. 104; D. Owen Hughes, 'From Bride Price to Dowry in Mediterranean Europe', *Journal of Family History*, 3 (1978), pp. 262–96; P. Desportes, 'La Population de Reims au XIVe siècle d'après un dénombrement de 1422', *Le Moyen Age*, 72 (1966), pp. 463–509; S. Thrupp, op. cit., p. 196.

34 For example, G. Brucker (ed. and trans.), *The Society of Renaissance Florence: A Documentary Study* (New York, 1971), pp. 41–2.

35 *I Libri* (= *The Family in Renaissance Florence*), pp. 208–12.

36 G. Fagniez, *Études sur l'industrie et la class industrielle à Paris aux XIIIe et XIVe siècles* (Paris, 1877), p. 66; S. Thrupp, op. cit., pp. 158–9; H. M. Jewell, 'The Bringing Up of Children in Good Learning and Manners: A Survey of Secular Educational Provisions in the North of England, 1350–1550', *Northern History*, 18 (1982), p. 3; J. H. Moran, *The Growth of English Schooling, 1340–1548* (Princeton, 1985), p. 68.

37 Bernard Gordon, *De Conservatione Vitae Humanae* (Leipzig, 1570), pp. 30–1.

38 F. Michaud-Frejaville, 'Contrats d'apprentissage en Orleanais: Les Enfants au travail (1380–1450)', in *L'Enfant au Moyen Age: Littérature et civilisation* (Senefiance, 9; Paris, 1980), pp. 63–71.

39 *Règlements sur les arts et métiers de Paris, redigés au XIIIe siècle et connus sous le nom du Livre des métiers d'Étienne Boileau*, ed. G. B. Depping (Paris, 1887), pp. 57, 64, 72, 131, 171, 184.

40 P. Viollet, 'Registre judiciaire de quelques établissements religieux du Parisis au XIIIe et au XIVe siècle', *Bibliothèque de l'École des Chartes*, 34 (1873), p. 329; *Calendar of Letter Books of the City of London: Letter Book E*, p. 19; if the mother remarried, custody was often taken away from her. See, e.g., J. Beauroy, 'Family Patterns and Relations of Bishop Lynn Will Makers in the 14th Century', in *The World We Have Gained: Essays in Honour of P. Laslett*, ed., L. Bonfield, R. Smith, and A. Wrighton (Cambridge, 1986), p. 39.

41 T. Benedek, 'Fatherhood and Providing', in *Parenthood: Its Psychology and Psychopathology*, ed. E. J. Anthony and T. Benedek (Boston, 1970), pp. 167–83.

42 D. Kraus, *The Hidden World of Misericords* (New York, 1975), pl. 135.

43 G. Fagniez (ed.), *Documents relatifs à l'histoire de l'industrie et du commerce en France* (Paris, 1900), no. 72, p. 169; no. 110, p. 209; id., *Études sur l'industrie et la classe industrielle à Paris aux XIIIe et XIVe siècles*, pp. 56, 70; L. F. Salzman, *English Industries of the Middle Ages* (Oxford, 1923), p. 339; F. Michaud-Frejaville, op. cit., p. 65.

44 *Le Livre des métiers*, pp. 38, 69, 175.

45 G. Fagniez (ed.), *Documents relatifs à l'histoire de l'industrie et du commerce en France*, no. 140, p. 241; id., *Études sur l'industrie et la classe industrielle à Paris aux XIIIe et XIVe siècles*, p. 74; one extraordinary contract stipulated that the term of apprenticeship could be shortened in return for monetary compensation (*Recueil des documents relatifs à l'histoire de l'industrie drapière en Flandre*, ed. F. Espinas and H. Pirenne (Brussels, 1906), vol. I, p. 121).

46 *Le Livre des métiers*, pp. 70, 72, 81, 115.

47 Examples of 7–8-year terms of apprenticeship: *Calendar of Letter Books of the City of London at the Guildhall: Letter Book D*, ed. R. R. Sharpe (London), pp. 141, 142, 147–50, 136, 138–40, 104, 107, 111, 113, 114, 124, 125, 131, 172, 175, 178; B. Geremek, *Le Salariat dans l'artisanat Parisien aux XIIIe–XVe siècles*, trans. A. Posner and Ch. Klapisch (Paris, 1968), pp. 30–1.

48 D. Herlihy and Ch. Klapisch, op. cit., pp. 573–4.

49 *Le Livre des métiers*, p. 57; T. Smith (ed.), *English Gilds* (EETS; London, 1870), pp.

180, 183, 315–16; examples of fines imposed on a craftsman for failing to register an apprentice in the guild: *Calendar of Letter Books of the City of London at the Guildhall: Letter Book I: 1400–1422*, ed. R. R. Sharpe (London, 1909), p. 38; *Letter Book D*, pp. 37, 66, 67, 97.

50　*Letter Book H*, p. 309.

51　*Le Livre des métiers*, pp. 65, 69, 235, 116; B. Geremek, op. cit., pp. 45–6; G. Fagniez, *Études sur l'industrie et la classe industrielle à Paris aux XIIIᵉ et XIVᵉ siècles*, pp. 62–3; L. F. Salzman, op. cit., p. 342.

52　*Le Livre des métiers*, pp. 234–5, 212, 216.

53　G. Fagniez (ed.), *Documents relatifs à l'histoire de l'industrie et du commerce en France*, no. 72, p. 169.

54　*Letter Book D*, p. 171; B. Geremek, op. cit., p. 32; G. Fagniez, *Études sur l'industrie et la classe industrielle à Paris aux XIIIᵉ et XIVᵉ siècles*, p. 66; S. Thrupp, op. cit., p. 112.

55　G. Fagniez, *Études sur l'industrie et la class industrielle à Paris aux XIIIᵉ et XIVᵉ siècles*, pp. 64–5; E. Martin Saint-Léon, *Histoire des corporations des métiers* (Paris, 1922), pp. 95–6.

56　G. Fagniez (ed.), *Documents relatifs à l'histoire de l'industrie et du commerce en France*, no. 85, p. 182; B. Geremek, op. cit., pp. 52–3.

57　T. Smith (ed.), op. cit., pp. 389–90. G. Fagniez (ed.), *Documents relatifs à l'histoire de l'industrie et du commerce en France*, no. 74, p. 170.

58　F. Michaud-Frejaville, op. cit., p. 67.

59　G. Fagniez (ed.), *Documents relatifs à l'histoire de l'industrie et du commerce en France*, no. 54, pp. 112–13; no. 91, pp. 188–9; *Reliquiae Antiquae*, ed. T. Wright and J. H. Halliwell (London, 1843), vol. II, pp. 223–4; Konrad of Megenberg, *Ökonomik*, ed. S. Krüger (Stuttgart, 1973; MGH Staatsschriften, 111/15), bk 1/2, ch. 23, p. 106.

60　B. Geremek, op. cit., p. 34.

61　I. H. Forsyth, 'Children in Early Medieval Art: Ninth through Twelfth Centuries', *Journal of Psychohistory*, 4 (1976–7), p. 53 and n. 59.

62　G. Fagniez (ed.), *Documents relatifs à l'histoire de l'industrie et du commerce en France*, no. 73, p. 170; *Calendar of Plea and Memoranda Rolls Preserved among the Archives of the Corporation of the City of London at the Guildhall, 1364–1381*, ed. A. Thomas (Cambridge, 1929), p. 107; S. Thrupp, op. cit., p. 164 and n. 21.

63　G. Fagniez, ed., *Documents relatifs à l'histoire de l'industrie et du commerce en France*, no. 101, p. 198; other examples of flogging: id., *Études sur l'industrie et la classe industrielle à Paris aux XIIIᵉ et XIVᵉ siècles*, pp. 68, 73.

64　*Le Livre des métiers*, pp. 49, 67; E. Martin Saint-Léon, op. cit., pp. 97–8.

65　G. Fagniez, *Études sur l'industrie et la classe industrielle à Paris aux XIIIᵉ et XIVᵉ siècles*, p. 67 and n. 4.

66　ibid.

67　Konrad of Megenberg, op. cit., bk 1/2, ch. 23, pp. 106–7.

68　G. Chaucer, *The Canterbury Tales*, ed. W. W. Skeat (Oxford, 1947), The Cook's Tale. pp. 114–15.

69　S. Thrupp, op. cit., p. 170.

70　*The Fifty Earliest English Wills in the Court Probate, London*, ed. F. J. Furnivall (EETS; London, 1882), pp. 22, 78–9; S. Thrupp, op. cit., pp. 170, 158.

71　J. Beauroy, op. cit., p. 30.

72　*The Fifty Earliest English Wills*, p. 12.

73　Quoted in Ph. Contamine, *La Vie quotidienne pendant la Guerre de Cent Ans: France et Angleterre* (Paris, 1967), p. 175.

74 Cited in D. Herlihy and Ch. Klapisch, op. cit., p. 574.

75 e.g. *Analecta Bollandiana*, 1 (1882), p. 360; 14 (1895), p. 192; *Acta Sanctorum*, Apr. 1, p. 510. *Acta et Processus Canonizacionis Beate Brigitte*, ed. I Collijn (Uppsala, 1931), p. 131.

76 W. O. Hassall, *How They Lived: An Anthology of Original Accounts Wirtten before 1485* (Oxford, 1965), p. 106.

77 *The Life of St. Anselm Archbishop of Canterbury by Eadmer*, ed. R. Southern (Nelson Series; London, 1962), p. 90.

78 *Acta Sanctorum*, June 5, p. 714.

79 ibid., June 2, p. 366.

80 I. H. Forsyth, op. cit., pp. 50–1.

81 e.g. L. Delisle, 'Lettre de l'abbé Haimon sur la construction de l'église de Saint-Pierre-Sur-Dives en 1145', *Bibliothèque de l'école des Chartes*, s. 21 (1860), pp. 113–39.

82 For an example of a ban on marriage during apprenticeship, see *York Memoranda Book*, ed. M. Sellers (Surtees Society; London, 1912), vol. I, p. 54.

83 S. Thrupp. op. cit., p. 171; *Acta Sanctorum*, Mar. 1, p. 551; and see also J. H. Moran, op. cit., p. 70.

84 F. Michaud-Frejaville, op. cit. For examples of apprenticeship contracts for girls (or requests submitted by guardians to the town tribunal to approve the use of the minor girl's own funds in payment for her training), see G. Fagniez, *Études sur l'industrie et la classe industrielle à Paris aux XIIIᵉ et XIVᵉ siècles*, p. 70; *Letter Book E*, p. 200; S. Thrupp, op. cit., p. 172; on compensation paid to a craftswoman when the fourteen-year-old girl she was training wanted to break the contract and take the veil, see G. Fagniez, ibid., p. 74.

85 G. Fagniez (ed.), *Documents relatifs à l'histoire de l'industrie et du commerce en France*, no. 16, pp. 201–2; no. 77, p. 172.

86 id., *Études sur l'industrie et la classe industrielle à Paris aux XIIIᵉ et XIVᵉ siècles*, pp. 61–2.

87 T. Smith (ed.), op. cit., pp. 194, 340.

88 D. Herlihy and Ch. Klapisch, op. cit., p. 331.

89 L. Lallemand, *Histoire de la charité* (Paris, 1906), pp. 135–51; M. Kowaleski, 'Women's Work in a Market Town: Exeter in the Late Fourteenth Century', in *Women and Work in Pre-industrial Europe*, ed. B. A. Hanawalt (Bloomington, Ind., 1986) – see in particular pp. 148, 153.

90 J. Heers, *Esclaves et domestiques au Moyen Age dans le monde meditérranéen* (Paris, 1981), pp. 148–54; on a five-year-old boy and an eight-year-old-boy in service in England, see B. H. Putnam, *The Enforcement of the Statute of Labourers* (New York, 1908; repr. 1970), pp. 185–6 and n. 3.

91 *Le Ménagier de Paris*, ed. J. Pichon (Paris, 1846), vol. II, pp. 53–72.

92 *Acta Sanctorum*, Mar. 3, p. 68.

93 ibid., Apr. 3, pp. 502–32.

12   EDUCATION IN THE PEASANTRY

1 See ch. 9, nn. 20–1; also J. H. Moran, *The Growth of English Schooling, 1340–1548* (Princeton, 1985), p. 67; E. Le Roy Ladurie, *Montaillou: Village occitan de 1294 á 1324* (Paris, 1975), p. 318; B. A. Hanawalt, *The Ties that Bound: Peasant Families in Medieval England* (Oxford, 1986), pp. 161–2.

2 The House of Commons, whose members were prosperous burghers and gentry, submitted a petition in Parliament in 1399 expressing opposition to the education

of the sons of serfs (N. Orme, *English Schools in the Middle Ages* (London, 1973), p. 192. In the twelfth century, Walter Map denounced the serfs who made every effort to send their children to study the liberal arts which were intended only for freemen (Walter Map, *De Nugis Curialium*, ed. and trans. M. R. James (Oxford, 1983), pt. 1, ch. 10, p. 12).

3 'Rustici filios suos quando parvuli sunt, sublimant et faciunt eis tunicas radiatas, et quando sunt adulti mittunt eos ad aratum': 'Notices et extraits de quelques manuscrits latins de la bibliothèque nationale', in Ch. V. Langlois, *La Vie en France au Moyen Age* (Paris, 1926), vol. II, p. 213, n. 2.

4 On a little girl picking vegetables, see L. de Kerval (ed.), *S. Antonii Padua Vitae Duae* (1904), p. 92; on an eight-year-old boy running an errand, see St Bonaventure, *Legenda Sancti Francisci*, in *Opera Omnia* (Karachi, 1898), p. 554; for other children injured in work accidents whose age is not specified see *The Miracles of Simon de Montfort*, ed. J. O. Halliwell (Camden Society; London, 1849), p. 87; *The Vita Wulfstani of William of Malmesbury*, ed. R. R. Darlington (London, 1928), p. 131; *Acta Sanctorum*, ed. J. Bollandus and G. Henschenius (Paris–Rome, 1863–1940), Apr. 2, p. 256; Mar. 3, p. 520; May 3, p. 181; for a seven-year-old boy sent to herd the cows, see M. Coens, 'La Vie de Christian de l'Aumône', *Analecta Bollandiana*, 52 (1934), p. 14; on a girl of $12\frac{1}{2}$ in a village south-west of Madrid at the beginning of the fifteenth century who herded the swine (her father was apparently the village swineherd), see W. A. Christian, *Apparitions in Late Medieval and Renaissance Spain* (Princeton, 1981), pp. 57–9; on eight- and nine-year-old children who herded sheep and helped in the harvesting, see ibid., pp. 116–17.

5 *Acta Sanctorum*, Mar. 1, p. 289.

6 Giorgio Vasari, *The Lives of the Artists*, trans. G. Bull (Harmondsworth, 1980), pp. 57–8.

7 *Acta Sanctorum*, Aug. 2, p. 120.

8 ibid., Mar. 3, p. 525.

9 B. Hanawalt, op. cit., p. 159 and n. 9.

10 ibid., pp. 183–4; on English royal statutes which directed the lower classes to practise archery, see N. Orme, *From Childhood to Chivalry: The Education of the English Kings and Aristocracy, 1066–1530* (London, 1984), p. 202.

11 In the thirteenth-century German-language work, *Meier Helmbrecht*, when the hero tries to dissuade his sister from marrying a peasant, he lists all the chores she will have to carry out as a peasant's wife (*Peasant Life in Old German Epics: Meier Helmbrecht and Der Arme Heinrich*, trans. C. Hayden Bell (New York, 1931), pp. 73–4); on female labour in peasant society, see J. E. T. Rogers, *Six Centuries of Work and Wages* (London, 1917), p. 235; R. Hilton, *The English Peasantry in the Later Middle Ages* (Oxford, 1975), p. 101; id., *The Economic Development of Some Leicestershire Estates in the 14th and 15th Centuries* (Oxford, 1974), pp. 145–6; E. Le Roy Ladurie, op. cit., pp. 27–30.

12 *Procès de condamnation de Jeanne d'Arc*, ed. P. Tisset (Paris, 1960–70), vol. I, p. 45, n. 2; the little girl who herded the swine also engaged in spinning at home (W. A. Christian, op. cit., pp. 57–9).

13 M. T. Kaiser-Guyot, *Le Berger en France au XIe–XVe siècles* (Paris, 1974), pp. 23–4.

14 E. Clark, 'The Custody of Children in English Manor Courts', *Law and History Review*, 3/2 (1985), pp. 1–13; for additional examples of mothers awarded custody of their small sons and daughters, see F. Maitland (ed.), *Select Pleas in Manorial and Other Seignorial Courts* (Selden Society; London, 1889), vol. I, pp. 6, 28; G. C. Homans, *English Villagers of the Thirteenth Century* (Cambridge, Mass., 1941), p.

440, n. 4; Z. Razi, *Life, Marriage and Death in a Medieval Parish* (Cambridge, 1980), pp. 61, 62, 68; on orphans taken in by relatives, ibid., p. 43, n. 53, p. 105; see also B. A. Hanawalt, *The Ties that Bound: Peasant Families in Medieval England*, pp. 249–51; an exception was the custom of transferring land to minors as practised in the royal manor of Havering. During the child's minority one of the relatives took care of him and of the land (M. K. McIntosh, *Autonomy and Community: The Royal Manor of Havering, 1200–1500* (Cambridge, 1986), p. 118); on wardship in German manors see H. Fehr, *Die Rechtsstellung der Frau und der Kinder in den Weistomern* (Jena, 1912), pp. 168–80.

15 *Analecta Bollandiana*, 9 (1890), p. 104.

16 On bastards in Montaillou, see E. Le Roy Ladurie, op. cit., pp. 60–1, 74–6, 78; in Halesowen, see Z. Razi, op. cit., pp. 70–1; see also R. Smith, 'A Note on the Net Work Analysis in Relation to Bastardy-prone Subsociety', in *Bastardy and its Comparative History*, ed. P. Laslett, K. Osterveen, and R. Smith (London, 1980), pp. 240–6.

17 E. Le Roy Ladurie, op. cit., pp. 300–4.

18 'The Statute of Cambridge', in *Statutes of the Realm*, ed. A. Luders, T. E. Tomlins, and J. Raithby (London, 1810–28), vol. II, p. 56; see also B. H. Putnam, *The Enforcement of the Statutes of Labourers* (New York, 1908; repr. 1970), p. 79, n. 4; on children's work in German manors see H. Fehr, op. cit., pp. 87–92, 235.

19 R. H. Hilton, *The English Peasantry in the Later Middle Ages*, pp. 51–2; Z. Razi, 'Was the English Peasant Family Small and Ego Focused?', (forthcoming).

20 B. A. Hanawalt, *The Ties that Bound*, pp. 162–6.

21 J. P. Cuvillier, 'L'Enfant dans la tradition féodale germanique', in *L'Enfant au Moyen Age: Littérature et civilisation* (Senefiance, 9; Paris, 1980), p. 53.

22 *Select Pleas in Manorial and Other Seignorial Courts*, vol. I, p. 121; E. Clark, op. cit.; B. Hanawalt, *The Ties that Bound*, p. 189; Z. Razi, op. cit., p. 43, n. 53.

23 Z. Razi, op. cit., p. 63.

24 Z. Razi, 'Family, Land and the Village Community in Later Medieval England', *Past and Present*, 93 (1981), p. 6.

25 See ch. 11, nn. 84–7 and also B. A. Hanawalt, 'Peasant Women's Contribution to the Home Economy in Late Medieval England', in *Women and Work in Pre-industrial Europe*, ed. B. A. Hanawalt (Bloomington, Ind., 1986), p. 18, n. 14.

26 As against the general decline in the numbers of bastards, there was a rise in the number of illegitimate offspring of widows. When there was no longer a shortage of land, the demand to marry widows decreased (Z. Razi, *Life, Marriage and Death in a Medieval Parish*, pp. 65–72, 138, 139).

27 E. Le Roy Ladurie, op. cit., pp. 274–8.

28 C. Klapisch and M. Demonet, ' "A uno pane et uno vino": La Famille toscane au début du XVᵉ siècle', *Annales ESC* 27 (1972), pp. 873–901. In Thornbury manor (near Bristol), widows who remarried, often married very young men with no inheritance; see P. Franklin, 'Peasant "Widows' Liberation" and Remarriage before the Black Death', *Economic History Review*,[2] 39 (1986), p. 200.

29 M. Sahlin, *Étude sur la Carole médiévale* (Uppsala, 1940); G. C. Homans, op. cit., ch. 23; Ph. Contamine, *La Vie quotidienne pendant la Guerre de Cents Ans: France et Angleterre* (Paris, 1967), p. 47.

30 *Procès de condamnation de Jeanne d'Arc*, vol. I, p. 63.

31 ibid., vol. I, pp. 65–7; vol. II, p. 65, n. 2, p. 66, n. 2.

32 ibid., vol. I, p. 41.

33 W. A. Christian, op. cit., pp. 57–8, 119.

34 Konrad of Megenberg, *Ökonomik*, ed. S. Krüger (Stuttgart, 1973; MGH Staatsschriften, 111/5), bk 1/2, ch. 15, p. 92.

35 *Registre de l'inquisition de Jacques Fournier, 1318–1325*, ed. J. Duvernoy (Toulouse, 1965), vol. III, p. 464.

36 ibid., pp. 53 ff.

37 A brief description of the journey occurs in S. Runciman, *A History of the Crusades*, vol. III (Cambridge, 1955), pp. 139–44; for an analysis of the works of the chroniclers describing the crusade and reference to the folklorist elements in the description, see P. Alphandery, *La Chrétienté et l'idée de Croisade* (Paris, 1959), pp. 115–48.

38 Étienne Fougères, *Le Livre de manières*, in Ch. V. Langlois, op. cit., vol. II, p. 23.

39 Wolfram of Eschenbach, *Parzival und Titurel*, ed. E. Martin (Halle, 1900), vol. I, bk 3, 142: p. 50.

40 See n. 2.

41 *Peasant Life in Old German Epics: Meier Helmbrecht and Der Arme Heinrich*, pp. 110–11.

42 ibid., p. 86.

43 See ch. 11, n. 41.

44 John Bromyard, *Summa Praedicantium* (Antwerp, 1614), p. 5.

45 Cases of fathers and mothers suing their children for violating the agreement to support them: on 7 Aug. 1341, Alice, the widow of Thomas Green, a half yardlander from Ridgacre, sued her son William for breaking his promise to maintain her (*Birmingham Reference Library*, no. 346259); Philip and his brother John de Pitway, large-holders from Cakemore, undertook to provide for their mother in her old age. However, John did not keep the agreement and therefore, on 13 Feb. 1370, Philip sued him in the manor court for not doing his share in supporting their mother (*Birmingham Reference Library*, no. 346314); on 20 Nov. 1279, Thomas, son of Thomas of Linacre, was sued by his father in the manor court for not keeping his maintenance agreement with him (J. Amphlet, in S. G. Hamilton and R. W. Wilson (eds.), *Court Rolls of the Manor of Hales, 1270–1307* (Worcestershire Historical Society; 1910–33), p. 115).
   These references were given to me by Zvi Razi.

NOTES TO APPENDIX

1 J. Laplanche and J. B. Pontalis, *The Language of Psychoanalysis*, trans. D. Nicholson-Smith (London, 1973), pp. 282–7; as regards western culture in the past, according to Lawrence Stone, one of the outcomes of the custom in sixteenth- to eighteenth-century England of sending children away at an early age to be raised and to work in strange households was the reduction of oedipal tensions and the risk of incest. According to A. Mcfarlane as well, upbringing by strangers not only absolved parents of the need to tackle the problem of imposing discipline on adolescent children, but also reduced sexual tensions in households in which people lived in crowded conditions in close proximity. M. Mitterauer and R. Siedler believed that, in addition to the fact that children spent only relatively few years in the parental household (with the exception of the oldest son), the large number of people in the household mitigated oedipal tensions. In most households, in addition to the nuclear family, there were relatives, hired labourers, and servants. The child maintained superficial and diffuse relations with a number of people and less intimate and intensive relations with his parents. See L. Stone, *The Family, Sex and Marriage in England, 1500–1800* (London, 1977), p. 108; A. Mcfarlane, *The Family Life of Ralph Josselin* (Cambridge, 1970), p. 205; M. M. Mitterauer and

R. Sieder, *The European Family: Patriarchy to Partnership from the Middle Ages to the Present*, trans. K. Oosterveen and M. Horzinger (Oxford, 1982), pp. 67, 100–1.

It is worth noting that, according to psychoanalytical theory, the oedipal situation (or oedipal conflict), with all it implies for human development, commences at 3, an age at which children were not yet sent away from home. The despatch of children could only have prevented the expression of the conflict in the everyday life of the family, and not its actual existence. As for a contemporary society, Bruno Bettelheim claims that in the Israeli kibbutz, where children do not live with their parents even in early childhood, oedipal conflicts have not disappeared but have been reduced. This, he writes, is because what creates the oedipal situation is the economic and social dependence of children on their parents, as well as mutual emotions originating in intimate life under one roof and not the biological fact of parenthood (*The Children of the Dream* (New York, 1957), pp. 183–7, 194–5).

2 See also Ch. 6, n. 7.

3 Le Roman de Thèbes, ed. G. Raynaud de Lage (Paris, 1966–7); D. Poirion, 'Edyppus et l'énigme du roman médiéval', in *L'Enfant au Moyen Age: Littérature et civilisation* (Senefiance, 9; Paris, 1980), pp. 287–97.

4 *Denkmäler deutscher Poesie und Prosa aus dem VIII–XII Jahrhundert*, ed. K. Müllenhoff and W. Scherer (Berlin, 1892), pp. 2–6; *The Hildebrandslied*, trans. F. A. Wood (Chicago, 1914), pp. 4–7.

5 Marie de France, *Lais*, ed. E. E. Ewert (Oxford, 1965), pp. 35–47.

6 ibid., pp. 102–15.

7 G. Paris, 'Lais inédits', *Romania*, 8 (1897), pp. 63–4; see also Arnault Vidal de Castelnaudry, *Guillaume de la Barre*, ed. P. Meyer (Paris, 1895).

8 *Acta Sanctorum*, ed. J. Bollandus and G. Henschenius (Paris–Rome, 1863–1940), Sept. 1, p. 318.

9 *The Early English Version of the Gesta Romanorum*, ed. S. J. H. Herrtage (London, 1879), p. 225.

10 E. R. Curtius, *European Literature and the Latin Middle Ages*, trans. W. R. Trask (New York, 1953), pp. 70–1, 82, 101.

Index

Italy: Florence   + Padua
    : Rome
    : Siena
England: London   : Cambridge
        : Canterbury   : Salisbury
        : Exeter
France: Paris

        Normandy

Spain : Verona
            Tuscany

12th – mid 15th

16th – 17th

Vilanova ?
Aragon – Catalonia

Scandinavia   seigneurs ?
Sicily   demesne ?
Germany

            # 93 p. 314
             + 94
                 180–1